XML
Problem - Design - Solution

Mitch Amiano,
Conrad D'Cruz,
Kay Ethier,
and Michael D. Thomas

Wiley Publishing, Inc.

XML Problem - Design - Solution

Published by
Wiley Publishing, Inc.
10475 Crosspoint Boulevard
Indianapolis, IN 46256
www.wiley.com

Published simultaneously in Canada

ISBN-13: 978-0-471-79119-5
ISBN-10: 0-471-79119-9

Manufactured in the United States of America

10 9 8 7 6 5 4 3 2 1

1B/SV/QV/QW/IN

Library of Congress Cataloging-in-Publication Data:

XML problem design solution / Mitch Amiano [... et al.].
p. cm.
Includes index.
ISBN-13: 978-0-471-79119-5 (paper/website)
ISBN-10: 0-471-79119-9 (paper/website)
1. XML (Document markup language) 2. Web sites-Design. I. Amiano, Mitch, 1963--
QA76.76.H94X45474 2006
006.7'4--dc22

2006009326

For general information on our other products and services please contact our Customer Care Department within the United States at (800) 762-2974, outside the United States at (317) 572-3993 or fax (317) 572-4002.

XML
Problem - Design - Solution

About the Authors

Mitch Amiano

Mitch Amiano began his career developing process automation applications for small businesses. Quietly using markup languages since 1994, and database management systems since 1989, Mitch has worked in process/quality teams and advanced tool departments at Fortune 500 companies, as well as consulting to small and medium-sized businesses. In 2003, Mitch founded Agile Markup Corporation where he provides XML and open source training and development services. In his spare time, Mitch plays with number theory and edible landscaping. He also serves on his town's Parks and Recreation Advisory Board, of which he was 2005 Chair.

Conrad D'Cruz

Conrad D'Cruz, an independent consultant with more than 14 years' experience, loves to work in the area where business meets technology. He is active in the technology and business users' groups in the Research Triangle Park area of North Carolina. He was contributing author for *Enterprise Integration Patterns: Designing, Building, and Deploying Messaging Solutions* and coauthored *Cocoon 2 Programming: Web Publishing with XML and Java*. When he is not working, he can be found at the controls of a light aircraft exercising the privileges of his private pilot's certificate or participating in search and rescue exercises with the U.S. Civil Air Patrol.

Kay Ethier

Kay Ethier is an Adobe Certified Expert in FrameMaker with long experience in structured document publishing with SGML and XML. She is also a certified trainer with WebWorks University. Kay instructs in XML and other training classes, consults, and provides hotline support for clients in a variety of industries. In 2001, Kay coauthored the book *XML Weekend Crash Course*. That same year, she was technical editor for *GoLive 6 Magic*. In 2004, Kay was a contributing author for *Advanced FrameMaker*, and sole author of *XML and FrameMaker*. Her most recent collaboration was on a Korean-English book, *Learning Korean: Martial Arts Terminology*.

Michael D. Thomas

Michael D. Thomas is a technical architect with SAS. He has authored two other books, *Java Programming for the Internet* and *Oracle XSQL*. He is a frequent conference speaker on XML, Java, and web services topics. Throughout his career, he has designed and implemented enterprise-class web-based systems. While working at IBM, he was one of the youngest people to ever receive an Outstanding Technical Achievement Award, due in part to his work with web services.

Credits

Senior Acquisitions Editor
Jim Minatel

Development Editor
Maryann Steinhart

Technical Editor
Todd Meister

Production Editor
Felicia Robinson

Copy Editor
Foxxe Editorial Services

Editorial Manager
Mary Beth Wakefield

Production Manager
Tim Tate

Vice President and Executive Group Publisher
Richard Swadley

Vice President and Executive Publisher
Joseph B. Wikert

Graphics and Production Specialists
Stephanie D. Jumper
Barbara Moore
Heather Ryan
Alicia B. South

Quality Control Technician
Jessica Kramer

Proofreading and Indexing
Techbooks

To my son Craig and wife Samantha, who put up with a lot this year, and my parents for that much appreciated break.—Mitch Amiano

To my parents, family, and friends ... and to life!! —Conrad D'Cruz

To my children, J, Ri, and Nad, for making life so wonderful—Kay Ethier

To the new ones, Alexander, Ali, and Jackson, and to darling, Aylett.—Michael D. Thomas

Acknowledgments

In business there is no shortage of people wearing poker faces, presenting an air of close-minded elitism. The XML world no doubt has its share as well. Fortunately, my experience has often been to come into contact with an apparently skewed population: most say what they mean and listen to what others have to say. Several were a source of constant encouragement whenever we happened to meet, which wasn't as often as I'd wish. Chief among these were B. Tommie Usdin, Debbie Lapeyre, Wendell Piez, Steve Newcomb, Michel Biezunski, Jonathan Robie, and G. Ken Holman.

My coauthors Kay, Conrad, and Michael should also be so counted. I have to especially thank Kay for inviting me to participate in the project, and getting access to Earl at Americana Vineyards & Winery (who I thank for examples and feedback). Kay's continued support of the Tri-XML group has brought a little of that open XML community that much closer to home and made working in this profession that much more enjoyable.

Bob Kern's encouragement and guidance has also been critical. I recall being introduced to Bob during one of the Tri-XML conferences—by both Jonathan and Kay. The timing never seemed quite right, but Bob seemed to know just what to do and when to do it to get the ball rolling. If I wore a hat, I'd take it off to you, Bob!

Finally, I have to thank again my family. To my wife Samantha and son Craig, who patiently put up with the writing and the meetings—I couldn't have done it without your support.

—Mitch Amiano

First and foremost, I would like to acknowledge my parents, the late Albert and Wilma D'Cruz, who placed great emphasis on education and hard work. May they rest in peace. To my brothers (Errol and Lester) and sisters (Vanessa, Charlene, and Denise) and their families, thank you for your love and support. To my friends and coworkers, thank you for your patience and understanding when I belabor a point of view. I would like to thank all my teachers and mentors through the years for challenging me to strive toward excellence and reach for the stars. To my colleagues in the U.S. Civil Air Patrol, I appreciate your patience and understanding during my absence to write this book.

Thank you, Bob Kern, for going above and beyond in shepherding this project, channeling our energies, and focusing four very strong and different points of view. Spring is almost here and we are done, so maybe it's time to go for another ride in the convertible with the top down.

To Jim Minatel, Maryann Steinhart, and Carrol (Griffith) Kessel at Wiley, thanks for keeping us in line with all the paperwork and deadlines.

Finally, thank you, Kay, Mitch, and Michael, for being great colleagues in Tri-XML as well as on this endeavor. One of these days, I may actually step outside the box and try some of that sushi.

—Conrad D'Cruz

In addition to thanking my children for the time they spared me to write, I have others around me whom I want to thank for helping make this book possible, as well as for keeping work and play interesting.

Acknowledgments

Personally, thank you to my parents, for their support and tolerance through these many (well, not too many) years of my life so far. Mom and Dad, thank you for caring for Ri and Nad while I was writing. Thank you to Kim, Doug, and Candace who I respect, admire, and look to for guidance. Thanks also to Gramma Ruth and PopPop, always there to listen and show interest in our happenings; and to Grampa Riley and NaNa, whom we miss much. I also would like to thank Denis, who continues to perplex me and keeps things interesting for the kids—and me. Family provides a great foundation on which many other things are possible.

Professionally, thank you to Bob Kern for again helping me to bring a project to fruition. Thank you very, very much to my coauthors, whom I've worked with for years through the Tri-XML users group. I admire all three of you gentlemen and am very pleased that you chose to write this book with me. That really means a lot.

I would also like to thank Bernard, Greg, Ken, Andrew, Ann, Bret, and other buddies who help make conferences and work enjoyable. Thank you for the great networking time . . . you know what I mean.

Thanks also to clients-become-friends like Eduardo, Leslie, Bodvar, Leatta, Pam, and Charlie.

Although low in this list, certainly foremost in my mind, thank you to long-suffering Vicky, David, and Scott. Thank you for working with me every day and putting up with my frequent bouts of playing hooky with my kids.

To my Sabom Nim for teaching me many things, including patience, the importance of basics, and positive stress release. Also thank you to the moms of the do jang (Judy, Karen, Dianne, Sue, and all) for their friendship and support through our hours together each week. There is such an importance to sharing life with friends and having happy moments—and striving for no ordinary moments.

Speaking of which, a small thank you to an unnamed friend for the worst game of pool every played in Apex, during an absolutely perfect October eve. Sometimes the simple things can become great moments.

Let me also mention my appreciation to Bob at Connolly's, who kept the iced tea coming and ignored my papers spread all over the place while I wrote parts of this book.

Last but not least, to Socrates for showing me another path, to Dan who brought Socrates to life, and Earl who led me to both. (Earl, also thank you for providing the example files from Americana Vineyards.)

How am I doing, Soc?

—Kay Ethier

Thanks to my family, especially my wife Aylett, for supporting this latest writing effort. Thanks to Bob Kern, who was invaluable in getting this project and my last writing project to fruition, and thanks to the other authors for making this an interesting and fun project to work on. Thanks to my employer, SAS, and my manager, Gary Young, for supporting my work on this book.

Thanks to my one-year-old, Alexander, for his deep interest in my writing—or at least his deep interest in my laptop—and his eagerness to help with the typing.

—Michael D. Thomas

Contents

Introduction

If you're reading this, you are likely ready to work with the Extensible Markup Language (XML) and are seeking some direction.

This book provides information about XML and the issues involved in designing XML-based solutions for business problems. It does so in a case-study format, with each chapter taking one part of the single, main project, and leading you through the design of a solution for that, so that by the end of the book, you will understand every aspect of using XML to design business solutions.

After a broad-stroke introduction to XML technologies, the book surveys solutions to typical business and technology needs that are best solved using XML. You'll tackle XML markup—more specifically, the kind of markup that you find "under the hood" of everyday applications and web services. Commonly available resources are used to show you the fundamentals of what XML markup is, how to get at valuable information through these resources, and how to begin providing valuable information to others through XML. The book thus emphasizes the fundamentals of structured markup, and uses commodity technologies such as XSLT and scripting to build working examples. Discussion of XML Schema languages is limited to comparing and contrasting the major approaches within the framework of the working example.

This book is a nuts-and-bolts guide to help you leverage XML applications, some of which you didn't even know you had. It covers XML 1.0, and related technologies such as XSLT, XQuery, and XPath. The focus of the examples is on use of XML to share information across the enterprise.

An XML primer helps novice users get off to a quick start. Readers then move into sections of increasing depth, each developing a more advanced treatment of XML than the one before. Readers who have some familiarity with the material are welcome to dive right in to a section to consider specific XML application scenarios.

Who This Book Is For

This book is intended for users new to XML who want to understand its potential uses. You may be a business manager or analyst needing to get some breadth of knowledge of XML to make informed decisions. You may be a business professional upon whom XML is encroaching and for whom XML is an unknown—a risk previously avoided and now found to be inescapable. A mitigating action is needed—you need to get a good cross section of different XML areas, but mostly you need to be conversant on the topic.

Perhaps you're an English major looking for a job, a tech writer in a department converting to structured editorial process, an out-of-the-loop programmer who missed the first waves, a software configuration manager with rusty skills, a web monkey who knows only PHP and HTML tag soup, an executive without enough understanding of where the man-hours are going, a corporate staffer in charge of training who needs training materials for your team—whoever you are, this book will help you grasp the concepts of XML markup, and lead you to problems solved in practice using XML capabilities.

How This Book Is Structured

The first three chapters present an introduction to XML concepts. Chapter 1 provides an XML primer to get you going and an overview of the problem of sharing XML data with a partner. The projects in this book all involve your new winery.

Chapter 2 is an exploration of well-formed and valid XML, with discussions of the plan for validating the winery data. By the end of this section, the information model will be refined for moving forward.

Chapter 3 covers creating and distributing the refined structure so that others—internal and external—can use the winery data.

The next four chapters provide you with a firm foundation in presenting and publishing techniques. In Chapter 4, you begin presenting XML, styling it for browser presentation. You can follow the examples to produce a display on your own computer.

Chapter 5 looks at stylesheets further and provides data on converting XML content online using the XML transformation language, XSLT.

Chapter 6 examines options for rendering XML to print. In this chapter you produce printable data sheets using the XSL-FO technology. XML-to-PDF is covered fairly extensively.

In Chapter 7, you shift to considering your audience and dealing with issues of branding and individualized publishing. You explore data manipulation, sorting, and retrieval.

Chapters 8–10 arm you with operational tactics. Chapter 8 instructs you on searching and merging XML documents, and also covers XQuery.

In Chapter 9 you examine XML integration with other business data, tackling issues of relational data and databases.

Chapter 10 looks at different strategies for transforming XML documents and provides examples for transforming common business documents

The last four chapters focus on business integration strategies, starting with Chapter 11, which takes on web services. You learn some common needs of accessing web services and incorporating RSS feeds into your web site.

Chapter 12 explains how you can provide web services to those who want to access your winery catalog.

Then, in Chapter 13, you examine strategies and data merge points for combining XML documents.

Finally, Chapter 14 shows you strategies for designing enterprise solutions using XML, workflow engines, and business process management systems.

In addition, there are three appendixes and a glossary to help you through the learning process. Appendix A describes the tools for working with XML, Appendix B provides additional readings that may interest you, and Appendix C presents XML resources and links that may be of help to you.

What You Need to Use This Book

To use the basic principles of design and work with XML, you need a text-editing tool. As you do more with your XML, you may need a database, additional editing tools, file management tools, parsers, and more. Different software tools are used throughout this book. These are described in Appendix A.

Conventions

To help you get the most from the text and keep track of what's happening, we've used a number of conventions throughout the book.

> **Boxes like this one hold important, not-to-be forgotten information that is directly relevant to the surrounding text.**

Tips, hints, tricks, and asides to the current discussion are offset and placed in italics like this.

As for styles in the text:

- We *highlight* new terms and important words when we introduce them.
- We show keyboard strokes like this: Ctrl+A.
- We show filenames, URLs, and code within the text like so: `persistence.properties`.
- We present code in two different ways:

```
In code examples, we highlight new and important code with a gray background.
```

```
The gray highlighting is not used for code that's less important in the present
context, or has been shown before.
```

Source Code

As you work through the examples in this book, you may choose either to type in all the code manually or to use the source code files that accompany the book. All of the source code used in this book is available for download at `www.wrox.com`. Once at the site, simply locate the book's title (either by using the Search box or by using one of the title lists) and click the Download Code link on the book's detail page to obtain all the source code for the book.

Because many books have similar titles, you may find it easiest to search by ISBN; this book's ISBN is 0-471-79119-9 (changing to 978-0-471-79119-5 as the new industry-wide 13-digit ISBN numbering system is phased in by January 2007).

Once you download the code, just decompress it with your favorite compression tool. Alternately, you can go to the main Wrox code download page at `www.wrox.com/dynamic/books/download.aspx` to see the code available for this book and all other Wrox books.

Errata

We make every effort to ensure that there are no errors in the text or in the code. However, no one is perfect, and mistakes do occur. If you find an error in one of our books, like a spelling mistake or faulty piece of code, we would be very grateful for your feedback. By sending in errata you may save another reader hours of frustration and at the same time you will be helping us provide even higher-quality information.

To find the errata page for this book, go to `www.wrox.com` and locate the title using the Search box or one of the title lists. Then, on the book details page, click the Book Errata link. On this page, you can view all errata that has been submitted for this book and posted by Wrox editors. A complete book list, including links to each's book's errata, is also available at `www.wrox.com/misc-pages/booklist.shtml`.

If you don't spot "your" error on the Book Errata page, go to `www.wrox.com/contact/techsupport.shtml` and complete the form there to send us the error you have found. We'll check the information and, if appropriate, post a message to the book's errata page and fix the problem in subsequent editions of the book.

p2p.wrox.com

For author and peer discussion, join the P2P forums at `p2p.wrox.com`. The forums are a Web-based system for you to post messages relating to Wrox books and related technologies and interact with other readers and technology users. The forums offer a subscription feature to e-mail you topics of interest of your choosing when new posts are made to the forums. Wrox authors, editors, other industry experts, and your fellow readers are present on these forums.

At `http://p2p.wrox.com`, you will find a number of different forums that will help you not only as you read this book, but also as you develop your own applications. To join the forums, just follow these steps:

1. Go to `p2p.wrox.com` and click the Register link.
2. Read the terms of use and click Agree.
3. Complete the required information to join as well as any optional information you wish to provide, and click Submit.
4. You will receive an e-mail with information describing how to verify your account and complete the joining process.

You can read messages in the forums without joining P2P, but in order to post your own messages, you must join.

Once you join, you can post new messages and respond to messages other users post. You can read messages at any time on the Web. If you would like to have new messages from a particular forum e-mailed to you, click the Subscribe to this Forum icon by the forum name in the forum listing.

For more information about how to use the Wrox P2P, be sure to read the P2P FAQs for answers to questions about how the forum software works as well as many common questions specific to P2P and Wrox books. To read the FAQs, click the FAQ link on any P2P page.

1

XML and the Enterprise

XML is short for Extensible Markup Language (sometimes written as eXtensible Markup Language), which enables information to be encoded with meaningful structure and in a way that both computers and humans can understand. It is excellent for information exchange, and is easily extended to include user-specified and industry-specified tags. XML's recommendation — its specifications — is set by the W3C (World Wide Web Consortium).

Because XML is formatting-free, it can be used in a variety of processes. It can replace or work with other technologies, and it can be used instead of or to supplement scripts. It also works with databases or on its own to store readable content.

In this chapter, you:

- Learn the basics of XML.
- Explore the structure of an XML document.
- Discover what you can do with XML.
- Find out what you need to get started.

You are introduced to the winery and will examine the potential for modifying its data and using XML enterprise-wide. This project is expanded upon throughout the book.

Problem

You are owner of a winery in the Finger Lakes area of New York. You've just purchased the winery and are interested in automating much of the administrative detail and marketing data for your newly hired staff to work with.

Your winery's data must be properly structured to enable internal use as well as the sharing of the wine catalog externally. Interoperability with partners, online wine distributors, and tourism agencies is of key importance.

The winery starts with some initial data on the wines that it produces, as well as data on competing wineries. This data must be carefully reviewed and augmented so that by the end of the implementation — the end of this book — the data structure is refined.

The winery has data requirements that run enterprise-wide. The winery needs to have information on its own wines primarily available as a retrievable and accurate list. The inventory control system must be capable of accessing the list and marking, via a Web form, what product is on hand each year. Marketing must pull data from this same set of information to create handouts on the available wines. Up-to-date information on all the winery products and order data should be accessible.

Design

As a text-based format, XML can stand in for text or scripts within programming and scripting files. It also can be used as an authoring markup for producing content. In the case of the winery, there is the potential for using XML information throughout, from storing winery data in a database to drawing XML from the database to use on marketing sheets to outputting sortable information on customer shipments. Before you begin using XML, though, take a quick look at its history.

A Brief History of XML

There are earlier variations of markup languages, but this historic review starts with SGML, the Standard Generalized Markup Language.

SGML and XML's Evolution

SGML was adopted as an international standard (ISO 8879) in 1986. Tools and processes for working with SGML were developed, though not adopted as widely as was hoped.

A markup language like SGML is a text language that enables you to describe your content in a way that is independent of hardware, software, formats, or operating system. Markup language documents are designed to be interchangeable between tools and systems. SGML paved the way for its scaled-down descendant, XML.

The SGML standard, and now the XML standard, enables companies to take information such as the following:

```
Melvin Winery "Muscadine Scupp" Wine,
Vintage 1998
Available in 750ml only.
Our complex purple Muscadine grape lends an assertive aroma and flavor, with a
semi-sweet velvety smooth finish.
```

and put markup information around the data so that it is more specifically identified. To mark up content, you simply surround each element with descriptive tags, most often with a beginning tag and an end tag. Here's the syntax:

```
<element>content</element>
```

where `<element>` represents the beginning of the markup. Here, `element` is a placeholder for whatever your markup element's name right be. Then `</element>` represents where the markup ends, after the content.

For example, the markup of the preceding information looks like this:

```
<wine id="Muscadine_750ml">
<name>Muscadine</name>
<varietal>Scupp</varietal>
<vintage>1998</vintage>
<winery>Melvin</winery>
<bottlesize>750ml</bottlesize>
<description>Our complex purple Muscadine grape lends an assertive aroma and ↩
flavor, with a semi-sweet velvety smooth finish.</description>
</wine>
```

If you are not familiar with the angle brackets, slashes, and other odd pieces of markup in this example, do not worry; all will be explained in detail and soon.

Design of XML

In the mid-1990s, SGML's capability to make sets of markup elements was used to create HTML (Hypertext Markup Language), which provided many with the capability to create markup and display it using browser technologies. But HTML could only mark data as headings or lists or paragraphs or other simple format-oriented content. It could not semantically describe what the content was. Something more powerful was needed.

XML was designed with a narrower scope than SGML so that lighter-weight processors and parsers could be utilized to serve up content via the Internet (and other venues).

The W3C's "XML 1.0 Recommendation" described the initial goals for XML. These design goals, as listed on the W3C site, are:

- XML shall be straightforwardly usable over the Internet.
- XML shall support a wide variety of applications.
- XML shall be compatible with SGML.
- It shall be easy to write programs that process XML documents.
- The number of optional features in XML is to be kept to the absolute minimum, ideally zero.
- XML documents should be human-legible and reasonably clear.
- The XML design should be prepared quickly.

- The design of XML shall be formal and concise.
- XML documents shall be easy to create.
- Terseness in XML markup is of minimal importance.

XML was designed to fit where HTML was falling short (partly in extensibility and reusability) and where SGML had been more difficult than the average user could manage.

Understanding XML Basics

The basic unit of markup is an element. Elements can contain text, graphics paths, table data, and even other elements.

When you create an information model, you define an information hierarchy. The hierarchy describes the way in which elements can be used and how they can fit together. Your content is contained within this hierarchy and controlled somewhat by the elements used. As elements are nested hierarchically inside other elements, they take on a relationship to the elements that contain them. This relationship becomes useful in retrieving and sorting the data. Rules regarding the hierarchical nesting of elements include the following:

- The main element that is hierarchically around all other elements is called the root element.
- An element that has other elements hierarchically between its beginning and ending tags is the parent element to all elements immediately inside it, which are its child elements. (Elements a further level in would not be its child elements but its descendants.)
- An element can be a parent of other elements while being a child of one element. (Any parent of its parent, and so forth, would be considered its ancestors.)
- Child elements within the same parent are sibling elements. (There are no aunt, uncle, or cousin designations for elements.)

In an XML instance (document) representing a chapter of a book, for example, you might design a hierarchy in which a `<chapter_title>` child element always begins a `<chapter>`, where `<chapter>` is the root element. Structurally set as a sibling to the `<chapter_title>` element you might have an `<intro>` element followed by a `<numbered_list>` element. These siblings would be positioned beneath the `<chapter_title>` element, ensuring that the title information always appears first. The following XML markup example illustrates the structured hierarchy just described:

```
<chapter>
<chapter_title>Changing the Battery</chapter_title>
<intro>In this chapter, we review the procedures for changing a battery.</intro>
<numbered_list>
<item>Open the rear panel of the device.</item>
<item>Using a screwdriver, pry the old batteries out.</item>
<item>Insert the new batteries, using a hammer as needed to fit.</item>
</numbered_list>
.
.
[the rest of the document would be here]
.
</chapter>
```

In this example, <chapter> is parent to <chapter_title>, <intro>, and <numbered_list>. All the child elements of <chapter> are siblings. The <chapter> element is not a parent to any of the <item> elements; their parent is <numbered_list>. Position-wise it is more their "grandparent," but that isn't an official designation in XML, so you would refer to the <item> elements as "descendants" of the <chapter> element.

Because there is a hierarchy — relationship — between the chapter and its title, and between the intro and the chapter, those pieces of content could be retrieved and managed as a whole later on by using tools that can manipulate the markup. Then if a search tool found the chapter title and provided it in the search results, the person accessing the results could easily see that it was part of a chapter. You could even have an interface that showed the introductory paragraph, from the <intro> element, in search results before searchers retrieved the entire chapter.

Some elements appear as empty elements rather than as beginning and ending tags. These elements have no text content, but serve some purpose within the markup. For example,

```
<img src="imemine.jpg" />
```

is considered an empty element because the ending slash is inside the tag rather than in a separate end tag. An image is a fairly common example of an empty tag because there is generally a path to the image without any text content, only the tag and attribute data (as in this case).

Attributes are examined more later, but briefly an attribute is extra information about the element and is placed inside the beginning tag or in the empty tag. Attributes have a name, followed by a value in quotation marks. You will see more examples in the XML markup to come.

Exploring the Winery Markup Example

Take a closer look at the winery markup shown earlier:

```
<wine id="Muscadine_750ml">
<name>Muscadine</name>
<varietal>Scupp</varietal>
<vintage>1998</vintage>
<winery>Melvin</winery>
<bottlesize>750ml</bottlesize>
<description>Our complex purple Muscadine grape lends an assertive aroma and ⮐
flavor, with a semi-sweet velvety smooth finish.</description>
</wine>
```

The markup is the angle-bracketed items (tags) placed around the content. The first line is the beginning tag of the root element <wine>:

```
<wine id="Muscadine_750ml">
```

For now, just ignore the id="Muscadine_750ml" metadata. The next line identifies the name of the wine:

```
<name>Muscadine</name>
```

The <name> beginning tag shows where the content begins, and the </name> end tag closes the element.

The varietal markup further identifies the wine and might be used later in sorting and selecting the wines for display:

```
<varietal>Scupp</varietal>
```

The vintage is critical data because wines are often selected based on their age:

```
<vintage>1998</vintage>
```

Assuming data from your winery and other wineries will be included in some master list by a partner or tourism agency, the winery name is included in the markup:

```
<winery>Melvin</winery>
```

This also enables sharing with directory publishers. Within the winery itself, this information most likely serves little purpose.

Listing the bottle size(s) available could be helpful in data sorting or business inventory management:

```
<bottlesize>750ml</bottlesize>
```

The <description> tag provides a marketing snippet describing the wine:

```
<description>Our complex purple Muscadine grape lends an assertive aroma and ⮐
flavor, with a semi-sweet velvety smooth finish.</description>
```

This might help those who use this data to select the wine. It may be used directly in marketing pieces, or displayed in a web browser to reach those reading online. Potentially this could be combined with some keyword information to provide better searches and to better help searchers locate the best wine for them.

Finally, the end tag for the wine element that appeared as the very first line of the example closes out the document:

```
</wine>
```

That's enough XML markup information to get you going, and you'll better recognize the XML code to come. Now let's take a look at the winery example XML in more detail.

Determining an Information Model for the Winery XML

As you're learning, element markup in XML documents provides descriptive information about the content. It enables you to formalize your information models and create rules specific to the your content.

When you create an information model for your data, you identify all the pieces that compose the structure of your documents, and any hierarchical relationships between the pieces of content. In the preceding example, the markup identifies the content as parts of the <wine> element.

XML Elements

XML enables you to name and define each element you need and to assign additional pieces of metadata — attributes — to these elements. You can name these elements whatever you like. This highly descriptive markup then can be used to retrieve, reuse, and deliver content.

```
Here is an example of an XML document using element names defined for accounting
data.
<accounting>
<invoice>
<inv_number>8559</inv_number>
<inv_recipient>
<company_name>Mad Melvin Inc.</company_name>
<contact_name>Melvin Brock</contact_name>
<address1>100 Brockway Hill, Suite 1</address1>
<city>Kenmore</city>
<state>NY</state>
<zip>14223</zip>
</inv_recipient>
<amount>199.00</amount>
<due_date>2006/11/02</due_date>
</invoice>
</accounting>
```

Accounting data is quite different from the winery catalog data and may give you some idea of the endless possibilities for element naming and hierarchical arrangement. In this example, the `<invoice>` element is the only child of the `<accounting>` element, and is the parent of the `<inv_number>`, `<inv_recipient>`, `<amount>`, and `<due_date>` elements. The `<inv_recipient>` is parent to the elements `<company_name>`, `<contact_name>`, `<address1>`, `<city>`, `<state>`, and `<zip>`. All of the child elements of `<invoice>` and `<inv_recipient>` are descendants of the `<accounting>` element. These tags make it easy to call out all invoice amounts or due dates, or the recipient's address information.

When determining the best information model for your content, consider what information you have, how you want to use it, and what additional information must be added to your data set. Then create element markup and XML documents that meet your needs.

Do not strive to create a perfect structure because that may never be attained. You may not create a structure completely wrong or completely right; just aim for a structure that is logical and will do what you need it to do. Down the road, you may find it necessary to adjust the structure, and that's fine and planned for within the extensible design of XML.

To ensure that your data is as complete as it needs to be, you need to analyze the situation not only before you begin but also periodically afterward. Whenever you find it necessary, you can modify your element set by removing elements, adding elements, renaming elements, or adjusting the hierarchy. Points for analysis are covered throughout this book.

XML Declaration

An XML document may begin with an XML declaration, which is a line that lets processors, tools, and users know that the file is XML and not some other markup language. Declarations are optional and need not be used. Here's what it looks like:

```
<?xml version="1.0"?>
```

If a declaration is used, it must be at the top of the XML file, above the root element's beginning tag, like this:

```
<?xml version="1.0"?>
<accounting>
<invoice>
<inv_number>8559</inv_number>
<inv_recipient>
<company_name>Mad Melvin Inc.</company_name>
<contact_name>Melvin Brock</contact_name>
<address1>100 Brockway Hill, Suite 1</address1>
<city>Kenmore</city>
<state>NY</state>
<zip>14223</zip>
</inv_recipient>
<amount>199.00</amount>
<due_date>2006/11/02</due_date>
</invoice>
</accounting>
```

If you are producing XML instances that are small chunks of reusable data, you probably won't use declarations because they might end up elsewhere in the file as chunks are combined, and an XML declaration anywhere but first in the file will throw an error. If you have XML that will stand alone, and that might be handled by automated processes that verify if the files are XML, then you may want to include the XML declaration to ensure proper recognition of the files as XML documents.

Attributes and Information Modeling

XML elements can contain more than just their name inside their angle brackets. Elements can have *attributes,* which are additional bits of information that go with the element. The attributes appear inside the element's beginning tag.

For instance, the `<chapter>` element from an example earlier in the chapter can have an attribute of `author`. This means that the author's name, although not part of the document content, can be retained within the XML markup. The author's university affiliation could also be included. Attributes in the structure can be either required or optional. While there might always be an author named in the markup, some authors may not be affiliated with a university. In those cases, the name attribute would have a value (a name), but no university attribute would be added. These attributes will then enable you to locate information by searching the data for specific authors or universities. Here's an XML markup using the `author` attribute:

```
<chapter author="William Penn">
```

The end tag is still `</chapter>`. No attribute data is included in it.

Elements with multiple attributes have spaces between the attributes. Here's a `<chapter>` element with both `author` and `university` attributes:

```
<chapter author="William Penn" university="Duquesne">
```

Elements and their corresponding attributes are markup that enable you to create content with the structure you need. You can design elements and attributes the way you need them to be, creating dynamic content for delivery to multiple formats via various media, based on the preferences of your users.

Create an XML Document

Open Notepad or another text editor, and enter the following data:

```
<?xml version="1.0"?>
<wine id="Muscadine_750ml" type="dessert">
<name>Muscadine</name>
<varietal>Scupp</varietal>
<vintage>1998</vintage>
<bottlesize>750ml</bottlesize>
<description>Our complex purple <keyword>Muscadine</keyword> grape lends an ↵
<keyword>assertive</keyword> aroma and flavor, with a semi-sweet velvety ↵
<keyword>smooth</keyword> finish.</description>
</wine>
```

Remember, the book's pages aren't always wide enough for an entire code line. The ↵ symbol indicates that you should not press Enter yet, but continue typing the following line(s). Press Enter at the end of the first line thereafter that does not have the ↵ symbol.

For now, follow the example precisely. Chapter 3 explores the rules you must follow to create an XML document, after which you will know the basic syntax and can create your own XML documents from scratch. Following the rules results in your document being well-formed XML so that a parser — or browser — can use it.

Save your file as `muscadine.xml`. Your document will look much like the one shown in Figure 1-1.

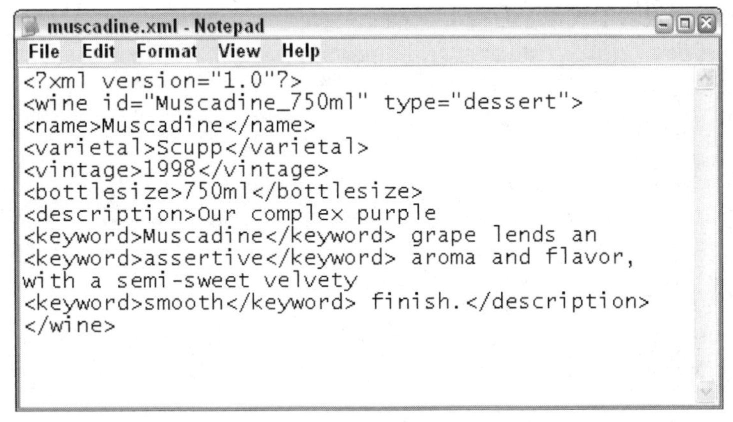

Figure 1-1

If your text editor adds `.txt` *extension instead of an* `.xml` *extension, rename the file with an* `.xml` *extension before proceeding.*

Now open your file in an XML-savvy web browser such as Microsoft Internet Explorer. You should see your elements in a tree view, with the hierarchical nesting clearly shown in each level. Your document should look similar to the one shown in Figure 1-2.

This is the first step in ensuring that your XML document is usable. If you cannot view it in a browser, it may have errors in the markup.

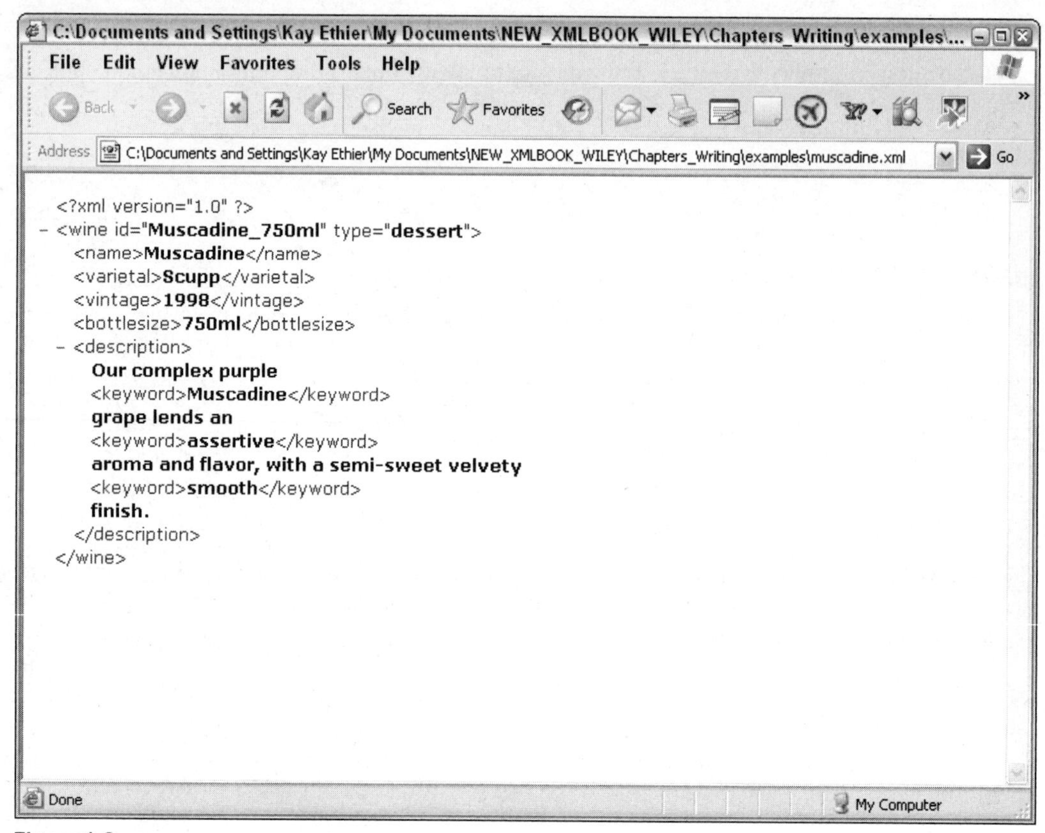

Figure 1-2

On your screen, you can see small minus signs next to the wine and description markup's beginning tags. All elements that have descendants appear with these minus signs next to them. You can click on these minus signs to hide the descendants. Once the descendents are hidden, the minus sign appears as a plus sign, which you can click to show the descendants and return the sign to a minus.

You may want your XML to be displayed a certain way. Most certainly, you will want it to look better than the tree view — unless it is being used by processes rather than being displayed.

XML can be formatted so that it looks good in a browser, using fonts, colors, and images instead of just showing in a tree view like the Internet Explorer view of Figure 1-2. You can make XML look good by using style sheets, such as the Cascading Style Sheets (CSS) used frequently for HTML. There is also an XML formatting and transformation language — XSLT (the Extensible Stylesheet Language Transformation — which you can use to produce XML or turn XML into another type of text-based document (you'll learn more about this later in the book).

Problems That XML Addresses

To better understand how XML can help your business projects, take a look at some of the ways it's used:

- Reusing content to multiple outputs or devices
- For text in multiple languages, as a way of tracking or managing translation among languages
- Enforcing structured authoring processes
- Enforcing data consistency standards
- Sharing nonproprietary data

Reusing Content (Multiple Outputs, Multiple Media)

If one of your goals is structured authoring, with or without added requirements for reusing your content or revision management, then XML authoring is a logical choice. XML authoring tools can help authors ensure that content rules are followed. XML documents can interact with databases, or even act as a database or repository for content chunks, so that structured content can be sorted, processed, extracted, and even automatically linked in for reuse in separate documents.

Content management software vendors are leading companies into XML by providing systems that enable you to accomplish what you want — and need — to do with your content. Content in the XML format is more easily managed than content in a basic text format or a word processing format because the XML is not bogged down with proprietary coding or formatting. Additionally, the XML information is identified by the elements used around the content. Content management systems enable those who want to create structured content to interface with more than one XML authoring tool, simplifying corporate purchases by avoiding protracted arguments over the "one tool" that must be used. With interfaces capable of interacting with multiple authoring tools, authors can create and share content without conversion, transformation, or other magic.

For example, a structured document can be saved to XML by the authoring tool, providing as a finished product an XML file with a complex hierarchy of data. Using a scripting language or stylesheet, chunks of the XML content can be pulled from one document and used to produce other documents. Additionally, data can be sorted and retrieved to create custom web pages, database content, or handheld device files. When changes are made to each linked content chunk, all of the documents that contain that chunk can be automatically updated.

Once your information is in XML and accessible, stylesheets and XSLT can be used to push your information to the web, PDF, cellular phones, iPod (PodCasts), and to some handheld devices. Publishing is not just for print anymore.

Managing Translated Content

Companies that publish in multiple languages often work with translation agencies. In many cases, word processor files are provided to the translation house, which translates each word into the target language(s) and formats the files for distribution. Service costs include translation and formatting (word processing) services. As an alternative, XML that can be translated without the need for additional formatting, which can amount to significant savings.

Because XML documents can include metadata — descriptive information about the document and the individual chunks that compose it — saving revision and language information within attributes or elements becomes straightforward. When sending an XML document for translation, metadata can be added by the client or the translation agency to indicate which pieces of the document require translation. In long documents, considerable savings can be realized by translating only new information in the document, rather than translating entire documents over and over.

Authoring with Enforced Structure and Automated Formatting

Authors working on the same document or document set can introduce inconsistencies due to different working styles. Even the same author sometimes makes different decisions about formatting. Additionally, multiple authors can choose to organize their content in slightly different fashions. Implementing a structured authoring environment based on XML provides an extra level of control—and hands-off formatting—that style guides and authoring "suggestions" cannot come close to duplicating.

Structured authoring guides authors to follow the content model of the structure being used. This type of enforcement eliminates the need for authors to make decisions about layout, format, and the order of things. Structured authoring enables you to formalize and enforce authoring, branding, and style guidelines, ensuring that the documents created are structurally correct and properly formatted.

In short, authors can write content with guidance and without concern for formatting.

Enforcing Consistency of Data

XML documents are consistently organized. Elements are named, defined, and tagged, and as a result, can be processed by other software applications that can read XML content. XML documents make content more easily retrievable and reusable.

XML documents can contain metadata designed to identify when an element was created, and by whom, thus improving your ability to ensure that you are providing the most up-to-date, accurate information available. When you spot an inaccuracy, you can fix it.

If, for example, an XML document outlines the menu items to be displayed in a software tool, the developers can consistently update the listing without fear of missing a location within the code. Similarly, strings of data used in error messages and other parts of the software interface can be controlled from a central point or be found easily by tracking within certain element structures.

Changes you later make to the source will be reflected immediately and automatically in all other areas of the product or product line that utilize that piece of information. In a perfect process, this information would also find its way to marketing.

The winery project includes many details for the wines listed. To ensure that this data is consistent and complete throughout, a data structure is created that checks the XML. Missing bits of data can be flagged in authoring or editing tools that understand or display XML. Data that is out of place or added can also be flagged, making error checking and correcting easier. This type of identification enables you to easily fix the data and begin using it again.

> *There are many tools on the market that allow the authoring or editing of XML. Tools used by the authors are mentioned briefly in the remaining chapters.*

Sharing Information

To facilitate the exchange of information, some industries have adopted common structures that formalize the structure of their information. By sharing common structures, industries' players are able to use a common vocabulary, which makes it easier, faster, and less expensive to exchange information with partners or clients.

Several industries were early adopters of structured authoring and shared structure; they have been reaping benefits for years already. Because these industry organizations shared data, and have invested heavily in structured content processes, they can insist that partners, affiliates, and customers integrate with their systems.

Airlines, for example, must integrate content provided by airplane parts manufacturers with their own documentation. While the parts manufacturers document the pieces of the airplane, the airlines create new information for pilot-training guides, user manuals, and the like, yet can integrate information about maintenance of parts easily by following a common structure. Airline parts manufacturers using a structured authoring approach can share their XML (or SGML) with their airline partners to ensure that both parties are using the same element names, metadata, and revision data.

Following is a sample of the type of information your winery could have about a partner company. This XML has more detail, including keywords marked up with a <keyword> element, than the simple examples shown earlier in this chapter.

```
<catalog>
<section subject="Wines">
<winery id="Melvin">
   <name>Mad Melvin's Muscadine Wines</name>
   <region>New York</region>
   <country>United States</country>
      <wine id="Nags_Head_Carlos_WHT_750ml">
         <name>Nags Head Carlos WHT</name>
         <varietal>Scupp</varietal>
         <vintage>1994</vintage>
         <bottlesize>750ml</bottlesize>
         <description>Aged in Carolina Willow Oak, this velvety ⮐
         <keyword>red</keyword> wine is highly complex, with a flavor of red ⮐
         <keyword>cherries</keyword>, <keyword>apricots</keyword> ⮐
          and <keyword>grapefruit</keyword>.</description>
      </wine>
      <wine id="Muscadine_750ml" type="dessert">
          <name>Muscadine</name>
          <varietal>Scupp</varietal>
          <vintage>1998</vintage>
          <bottlesize>750ml</bottlesize>
          <description>Our complex purple <keyword>Muscadine</keyword> grape⮐
           lends an <keyword>assertive</keyword> aroma and flavor, with⮐
           a semi-sweet velvety <keyword>smooth</keyword> finish.</description>
      </wine>
</winery>
</section>
</catalog>
```

The preceding markup is certainly helpful, although perhaps not as detailed as is needed for enterprise-wide use. However, because the structure provides basic information about each wine and includes the winery designation, it may be possible to access a partner's catalog, share your own winery catalog, and even combine the two catalogs. Assume that the winery data also must be shared with the tourism organizations that spread the word about wineries in the Finger Lakes region.

For this project, assume that the preceding markup is standard for the data your winery has made available.

To share this information properly, your company and any partner companies not only need the same XML document, but they would also ideally have the same structure or similar structures to allow sharing of information with little loss of dissimilar data or unused extra data.

To design a solution for combining the catalogs, you first review what you have and what your partner has, and then determine a plan for merging your data.

Here's a selection of the XML content of your partner's XML catalog of wine:

```
<?xml version="1.0" encoding="UTF-8"?>
<catalog>
   <section subject="Wines">
<distributor id="" name=""/>
      <distributor id="Aeg" name="Aegean Imports, INC."/>
      <distributor id="Cla" name="Classic"/>
      <distributor id="Cou" name="Country Vintner"/>
      <distributor id="Emi" name="Eminent Domains"/>
      <distributor id="Emp" name="Empire"/>
      <distributor id="Fran" name="Franklin Selection"/>
      <region name="Western Cape"/>
<winery id="">
         <region>Burgundy</region>
         <country>France </country>
      </winery>
      <winery id="ALong">
         <region>Chablis</region>
         <country>France</country>
      </winery>
    <wine id="Cabernet_Sauvignon_1992_750ml">
         <name>Cabernet Sauvignon</name>
         <varietal>Cabernet Sauvignon</varietal>
         <vintage>1992</vintage>
         <winery>Caskone</winery>
         <distributor>Aeg</distributor>
         <bottlesize>750ml</bottlesize>
      </wine>
      <wine id="Chardonnay_1994_750ml">
         <name>Chardonnay</name>
         <varietal>Chardonnay</varietal>
         <vintage>1994</vintage>
         <winery>Caskone</winery>
         <distributor>Aeg</distributor>
         <bottlesize>750ml</bottlesize>
      </wine>
      <wine id="Sauvignon_Blanc_1994_750ml">
         <name>Sauvignon Blanc</name>
         <varietal>Sauvignon Blanc</varietal>
         <vintage>1994</vintage>
         <winery>Caskone</winery>
         <distributor>Aeg</distributor>
         <bottlesize>750ml</bottlesize>
      </wine>
      <wine id="Zinfandel_15L">
         <name>Zinfandel</name>
         <winery>CorbetCanyon</winery>
```

```
            <distributor>Emp</distributor>
            <bottlesize>1.5L</bottlesize>
         </wine>
         <wine id="The_Cabernet_1996_750ml">
            <name>The Cabernet</name>
            <varietal>Cabernet Sauvignon</varietal>
            <vintage>1996</vintage>
            <winery>Cosentino</winery>
            <distributor>Emp</distributor>
            <bottlesize>750ml</bottlesize>
         </wine>
      </section>
   </catalog>
```

Take a closer look at the data available to you in this XML. The first line is, of course, the XML declaration:

```
<?xml version="1.0" encoding="UTF-8"?>
```

The second line begins the company's catalog:

```
<catalog>
```

The end tag for the catalog element comes at the end of all the listings.

Although not particularly descriptive, `<section>` elements break the catalog information down by product, so that the wine-related data appears here and other nonwine products might be included at another point in the XML:

```
   <section subject="Wines">
```

Distributor data may help you reach distributors, and you may be pleasantly surprised to see that your partner company shared this data in its XML catalog:

```
      <distributor id="" name=""/>
      <distributor id="Aeg" name="Aegean Imports, INC."/>
      <distributor id="Cla" name="Classic"/>
      <distributor id="Cou" name="Country Vintner"/>
      <distributor id="Emi" name="Eminent Domains"/>
      <distributor id="Emp" name="Empire"/>
      <distributor id="Fran" name="Franklin Selection"/>
```

The `<region>` element is a sibling to the distributor data, and names the region; structurally, this is not well tied to the distributors or other data to come:

```
      <region name="Western Cape"/>
```

Multiple wineries are listed within the source, each with child element data designating the region and country. These `<winery>` elements are also siblings to the `<distributor>` elements.

```
      <winery id="">
         <region>Burgundy</region>
         <country>France </country>
      </winery>
```

```
<winery id="ALong">
   <region>Chablis</region>
   <country>France</country>
</winery>
```

After the winery data are the details of each wine, which include relational data back to the winery and distributor data:

```
<wine id="Cabernet_Sauvignon_1992_750ml">
   <name>Cabernet Sauvignon</name>
   <varietal>Cabernet Sauvignon</varietal>
   <vintage>1992</vintage>
   <winery>Caskone</winery>
   <distributor>Aeg</distributor>
   <bottlesize>750ml</bottlesize>
</wine>
<wine id="Chardonnay_1994_750ml">
   <name>Chardonnay</name>
   <varietal>Chardonnay</varietal>
   <vintage>1994</vintage>
   <winery>Caskone</winery>
   <distributor>Aeg</distributor>
   <bottlesize>750ml</bottlesize>
</wine>
<wine id="Sauvignon_Blanc_1994_750ml">
   <name>Sauvignon Blanc</name>
   <varietal>Sauvignon Blanc</varietal>
   <vintage>1994</vintage>
   <winery>Caskone</winery>
   <distributor>Aeg</distributor>
   <bottlesize>750ml</bottlesize>
</wine>
<wine id="Zinfandel_15L">
   <name>Zinfandel</name>
   <winery>CorbetCanyon</winery>
   <distributor>Emp</distributor>
   <bottlesize>1.5L</bottlesize>
</wine>
<wine id="The_Cabernet_1996_750ml">
   <name>The Cabernet</name>
   <varietal>Cabernet Sauvignon</varietal>
   <vintage>1996</vintage>
   <winery>Cosentino</winery>
   <distributor>Emp</distributor>
   <bottlesize>750ml</bottlesize>
</wine>
```

Some of the wines have more details included in the data than other wines have.

For the most part, your data structure matches that of your partner's catalog. Aside from including notations on distributors, the other markup uses the same element and attribute names as your snippets. It will be fairly easy to consolidate the like data so that your winery and this partner can share information.

At the end of the XML document is the closing information for the section (which included all wine product data) and the entire catalog:

```
    </section>
</catalog>
```

There is only one section in this file, so at this point the company has only structured its wine product data and not any peripheral offerings (apparel, foods, tours, and the like).

Solution

Starting with what you know of your winery content, expand the data beyond the basic information about the wines and add data necessary for enterprise use plus partner distribution. You change the XML content model in the next chapter.

Later, you will create a web interface to display the existing data and provide a form-based entry system for your wine data, which will enable you to fill in missing content and revise existing data easily.

Summary

XML is a format-free way to share information. Marking up content with XML enables you to identify what makes up your documents, and to identify each component potentially for reuse, sorting, or formatting. It is becoming more widespread for enterprise use as the tools and technologies expand.

You've been introduced to a number of concepts in this chapter, including:

- The basics of XML
- How to begin an information model
- How XML can resolve content and consistency problems
- Why XML is so helpful in sharing information

In Chapter 2, you learn the rules of XML markup and explore the concept of well-formed XML.

2

Well-Formed XML

Now that you have a basic understanding of the overall structure of XML markup, it's time to examine the rules of XML markup and to explore the concept of well-formed XML. In this chapter, you:

- Learn more about creating XML documents.
- See what can be done with well-formed XML.
- Learn how to name elements.
- Describe your own content.

Problem

One of the issues with your catalog data is merging the data between your catalog and your partners' without losing data the does not match — or inadvertently sharing more data than you want to share with a partner. Another issue is ensuring a logical hierarchy that can be followed without error. A good starting point is to step back and ensure that your winery's data fits all of your enterprise needs, while still remaining capable of being merged with your partner's data, before mistakes are made in the data structure and transmission media.

Design

Start by reviewing the records provided by the previous winery owner, augment this data as you think necessary, and organize the data so that you can use it in the ways you need for the business and marketing activities. At the outset, you know that you want to do the following:

- Track orders at least for your best customers (or distributors).
- Share your data with partners and tourism agencies, and use their data to augment your own.
- Prepare information for the winery web site, which is currently a single HTML page with a large image overlaid with the address and phone number — ugly and unsearchable!
- Prepare marketing pieces to hand out to winery visitors or to distribute to local restaurants.

With your winery ramping up, you have the potential to use your wine data to interact with distributors, magazine publishers, and internal business centers (accounting, marketing, distribution). To move forward, at least some cleanup of the winery content is needed.

Your content should be adjusted to include enterprise data such as:

- Inventory count
- Distributor name

Some additional data that you may want to incorporate to support other business usage include:

- U.S. and Canadian pricing (supporting Internet sales across the nearby border)
- Keywords (to allow better retrieval for clients and distributors seeking details)
- Category (for sorting of table wines versus dessert wines, for example)
- Purchaser contact details (to allow the mailing of flyers)

Now, all these wines must have their XML modified. New data is needed for the elements plan to add.

Producing a Well-Formed XML Document

Well-formed XML is XML that is following all of the "rules of an XML document," which are outlined below. These rules dictate how your markup should be placed around your content, how hierarchical elements should be nested, how attributes need to be punctuated, and what element names are acceptable.

Rules of an XML Document

When creating XML documents, there are some basic guidelines to follow so that the resulting documents can be referred to as "well formed." This means that your XML elements are properly written, following the rules of XML. Here are the rules:

- An XML document must have a root tag, which is a single element whose beginning and ending tags wrap around the rest of the elements and content in the document.
- The XML markup must have matching beginning and end tags for each element. XML is case-sensitive so, for example, <vintage>1994</vintage> works, but `<vintage>1994</Vintage>` does not.
- Element names can include letters, numbers, and underscores; they cannot start with a number or include spaces.
- Empty elements — elements without content — must have a single tag with an ending slash. For example, <image file="branding.png" />.

- Attribute values must always be quoted. Single or double quotation marks can be used, but consistency is recommended. In the preceding rule's example, file is the attribute name, and branding .png is the attribute value. You will have a name and value pair for each of your attributes.
- Entities and special characters must be used properly. For example, special characters in the content of an XML document, such as a greater-than symbol (<), appear in markup as a code or entity. The greater-than symbol would be shown in your XML code as `>` and an XML parser would recognize it and display the proper character.

If you follow all these rules, your XML documents will be well formed, and most tools and browsers will be able to parse them fully.

Well-formed XML is the lowest-quality XML that can be used. A higher-quality, valid form of XML, is introduced later in this book.

Element Naming

The element names available for your use are almost unlimited. You can create a wide variety of XML documents to perfect your skills through practice. Here are some example XML instances—documents. For the best understanding of the rules of XML documents, open Notepad or another text-editing tool and enter these document examples. Practice really does help!

In the first example, the root tag is <grocery_list>. Spaces and line breaks are used to help you see the beginning and end tags, although they are not required. In fact, some tools don't like the extra spaces and breaks and may remove them.

```
<grocery_list>
   <produce>
      <item>banana</item>
      <item>apple</item>
   </produce>
   <meat>
      <item>chicken breast</item>
   </meat>
   <dairy>
      <item>milk</item>
   </dairy>
</grocery_list>
```

In the second example, the root tag is <game>. Only line breaks (created by pressing the Enter key) are used here to help you see the beginning and ending tags; no extra spaces are added. Line breaks are optional and generally only good for human editors (parsers do not need them).

```
<game>
<poker type="Omaha Hi Lo">
<players>
<player standing="17">Denis Ethier</player>
<player standing="23">Nancy Mallett</player>
<player standing="112">Kim Beaver</player>
<player standing="411">Leslie Thomas</player>
<player standing="517">Leatta Welch</player>
<player standing="711">Davie Dilts</player>
<player standing="720">Juli Allentine</player>
<player standing="809">Riley Dillon</player>
```

```
<player standing="905">Nadia Grace</player>
<player standing="1217">Eddie Cidade</player>
<player standing="2741">Pamela Harris</player>
<player standing="2977">Bernard Aslan</player>
</players>
<rules src="play.pdf" />
</poker>
</game>
```

The third line from the bottom—`<rules src="play.pdf" />`—is an empty element (discussed in Chapter 1), meaning that it doesn't have content between two tags. An empty element does not have beginning and ending tags, only a single tag with an ending slash just inside the closing angle bracket.

The last example shows you some different tags; the root tag is <party>. Also, spaces and line breaks, although optional, are used:

```
<party>
   <date>
      <month>October</month>
      <date>29</date>
      <year>2005</year>
   </date>
   <time>
      <start>7:30 <pm /></start>
      <end>1:00 <am /></end>
   </time>
   <theme>Halloween</theme>
   <guests costumes = "Yes">
      <guest>Eric<costume>prisoner</costume></guest>
      <guest>Sue<costume>ghoul</costume></guest>
      <guest>Tom<costume>ghoul</costume></guest>
      <guest>Mark<costume>Grim Reaper</costume></guest>
      <guest>George<costume>Doctor Death</costume></guest>
      <guest>Dianne<costume>Morticia Adams</costume></guest>
      <guest>Steve<costume>Lurch</costume></guest>
   </guests>
   <guests costumes = "No">
   </guests>
</party>
```

Using the XML rules, you can create a simple XML document. For now, construct an XML document using whatever element names you can think of and in whatever hierarchy you make up as you go along.

Now, what can you do with your XML document?

If you have made up your XML correctly, you can open your document in a browser, such as Microsoft Internet Explorer. You will see a fairly plain document in a tree view with collapsible sections where you have nested elements, similar to what was shown in Figure 1-2 in Chapter 1.

What else can you do with this XML instance? Well, quite honestly if you do not have a specific structure or information model in mind, it does not matter what elements you include in your XML. You need to have an idea what elements will work for your needs and ensure that the markup hierarchy makes sense for how you need to retrieve information. What you do have is a well-formed XML document that can be used by any tool or process that accesses well-formed XML.

Introducing Valid XML

You may want to attain a "higher-quality" XML that is even more predictable — and therefore may be more usable. XML that follows a predictable structure is called *valid* XML. Valid XML is well-formed XML that uses elements, attributes, and hierarchical nesting according to a file that defines its structure. This file can be a schema or a DTD:

- A schema is an ASCII text format file using XML markup to create elements, attributes, and content models.
- A Document Type Definition (DTD) is an ASCII text format file using specific syntax to create elements, attributes, and content models.

You can use the rules of an XML document to create well-formed XML as you did in Chapter 1 by typing it in Notepad. Your document can then be used by tools, including Microsoft Internet Explorer.

This book's examples use schemas or DTDs and work with XML that is valid.

Developing Your Structure

Design essentials are selecting the elements needed in your structure. In Chapter 4, you will put the structure of the data into a DTD or schema so that you can properly check your data against the desired structure.

For now, consider that the type of structures needed to augment the existing winery and wine data can include some or all of these:

- Inventory
- Price (U.S. and Canadian)
- Client data (address, phone, email)
- Client type (distributor, end user)
- Category
- Keywords
- Business details (hours of operations, days open to the public, physical address, certifications)

Solution

Based on the design information, the solution to designing a complex markup for the winery XML markup is to create the appropriate elements.

To enable management of wines as inventory, basic details regarding the wine `name`, `varietal`; the containers (`bottlesize`) categorized by sizes available; the number of bottles counted per `case`; and any internal encoding (such as an `id` attribute) should all be created as elements within the structure.

To ensure proper management of inventory, and to work with the accounting system for profit-and-loss data, an element for `price` is needed.

For use with shipping and accounting systems, any sales to clients should record the client-specific contact data: `address`, `phone`, `email`, `fax`, and so forth. For clients that also act as distributors, an element for client `type` (with attribute values such as `distributor`, `enduser`) would ensure proper tracking.

Add to this some more specific markup for the winery sales, such as `category`, and you may have a structure that weathers business expansions. For example, all sales now are wines, but later sales may include apparel, sports equipment, or wine accessories. These might be set up as attributes, or as additional elements, now or at a later point.

Used to some degree in the earlier examples, providing keyword markup will not only assist internal use of the data but may also allow for modified displays when the content is retrieved by end users through media like the winery web site.

Also to enable positioning of the content for internal and external use, an element set that includes business details (operating hours, days open, winery contact information (address, phone, email, fax) should be stored with all the other winery data.

> *As mentioned in Chapter 1, do not strive for a perfect structure but instead for one that seems to work and cover specific needs. The elements proposed herein are just one of many possible solutions for a business such as this.*

These elements will serve as a starting point for this enterprise. Take a few moments and think of other elements that might useful for expanding the structure of this data. Examples later in the book will expand upon this foundation.

Summary

Starting with basic knowledge of elements, this chapter expanded on how element hierarchies are created and the importance of proper element naming and nesting. The data needed by the winery was reviewed, and a solution to the markup issues considered.

More about your implementation, and its testing and troubleshooting, is covered in Chapter 4. Expect to encounter a few issues and to have to rethink your information modeling at some point. You will ultimately end up with better data, a more defined structure, and better plans for how to use your data.

3

Creating and Distributing a Structure for Shared Information

The XML elements proposed at the end of the previous chapter are designed to allow creation of XML that will be usable by the winery for both internal and external needs. In this chapter, you:

- Learn how a structure can be documented.
- Discover new types of documents.
- Explore details of syntax used to define structure.
- Examine tools for verifying structures.

Just having elements marked up around your content and following the rules of XML, give you well-formed XML. To ensure consistency of your XML, however, you want to check that the basic markup is done correctly and that elements are in a recognizable order. In this chapter, you review a document type definition (DTD) and schema for the winery data. They provide you with the ability to verify the element hierarchy, and you will create new structure variations based on needed enhancements.

Problem

After you've decided on the elements and hierarchy of your structure, allocate time to create a document type definition (DTD) or schema, which enables you to validate your XML documents against a fixed structure.

The information in the DTD or schema identifies the elements, what they can contain, and any attributes. This structure can be used by authoring tools, search tools, and transformation files.

Knowing the elements and attributes you want to use in your markup, you then move into the phase of development and testing of your DTD or schema. While the initial file can come together quickly, be prepared for days, weeks, or even longer for complete testing of an enterprise-level system. The more complex the system, the more elements there are, the more testing is required. The time and money needed to prepare for and implement the structure can be significant. A rudimentary structure, however, can be pulled together, tested, and used within a matter of hours or days.

As an alternative, some industry-standard structures are available to shorten this time. You can Google industry standards, including DocBook, DITA, and ATA.

Design

While you will examine both a starter DTD and a schema so that you can compare their syntax, in the real world you need only select one of these — the one that works best with your tools of choice or partners' processes — and then move forward with it.

DTDs are older technology; schemas are newer and — because they are written in XML — more easily handled by automated processes. Many tool vendors are building with schemas in mind, and the future may bow to schemas. Consider the long-term plans of your company in addition to the short-term requirements of existing tools.

You create each element and give it a rule regarding its structure. This is called the *content model*, the model for what the element is allowed to contain. Some elements can contain text (#PCDATA, or parsed character data). Other elements are allowed to contain elements or, more specifically, to be the parent elements to child elements.

The child elements (or text) inside an element are named in the content model along with special symbols to signify the order and frequency of the child elements. When the content model is written, it becomes the model against which all structure is checked, and the model that must be followed when XML documents are created.

Creating a Document Structure (Information Model)

Both the schema and the DTD are a list of the elements you plan to use, the corresponding attributes, and information about how they fit together hierarchically. One major difference between them is that the DTD is an ASCII text file with a simple syntax, while the schema is an ASCII text file made using XML markup. Because the schema has the added benefit of being an XML document, processes can be run on it as well. As of this writing, DTDs are more widely used and supported than schema; however, schemas may become the method of choice in the future because of their capability of being treated as other XML documents.

In an accounting document's markup, for example, you'd have many elements designed to contain the text of an invoice. These elements might include <number>, <amount>, and <due_date> among others. In an ideal situation, you would have a list of these in advance, and as the XML documents were created, you'd follow the element structure. The list of elements and nesting rules would be available for authors, or for processes that are making use of the XML for you (eliminating errors made by human editors).

Examining the Structure at the Outset

Here is an example DTD for the winery data:

```
<!ELEMENT catalog (section)+>
<!ELEMENT section (distributor*,region*,winery*,wine+)>
<!ATTLIST section  subject (Wines) #REQUIRED>
<!ELEMENT distributor (#PCDATA)>
<!ATTLIST distributor
  id ID #IMPLIED
  name CDATA #IMPLIED>
<!ELEMENT region (#PCDATA)>
<!ATTLIST region  name CDATA #IMPLIED>
<!ELEMENT name (#PCDATA)>
<!ELEMENT country (#PCDATA)>
<!ELEMENT winery (#PCDATA|name|region|country)*>
<!ATTLIST winery  id ID #IMPLIED>
<!ELEMENT wine (name,varietal,vintage,winery,distributor,bottlesize,description)>
<!ATTLIST wine  id ID #REQUIRED>
<!ELEMENT bottlesize (#PCDATA)>
<!ELEMENT description (#PCDATA)>
<!ELEMENT varietal (#PCDATA)>
<!ELEMENT vintage (#PCDATA)>
```

Certain DTD syntax needs to be explained before proceeding. The following table describes the syntax for frequency (if an element may be used more than once).

Symbol	Example	Required or Optional
(None)	`section`	The child element is required, and only one can be used.
Question mark	`section?`	The element is optional and can be used once or not at all.
Plus sign	`section+`	The child element is required for the structure to be valid and can be used once or repeatedly.
Asterisk	`section*`	The element is optional and can be used once, repeatedly, or not at all.

Your content models can also use symbols for the order of child elements within the parent element. These symbols, described in the following table, are used between the child elements' names.

Symbol	Example	Meaning
comma	`winery, region`	The elements must occur in the order given.
pipe	`winery|region`	You can choose only one of these elements. Thinking of this as an OR, as in "this element OR that element" can be helpful.

Parenthesis can be used to group elements, enabling you to hone the rule so that child elements are controlled the way you want. For example, you might want to have a rule something like this:

```
region*, (winery|distributor)
```

Knowing this simple syntax, you can proceed to review the DTD line by line.

The first line declares an element called `catalog`. On that same line, the rule states that `catalog` can contain one or more `section` child elements (because `section` is followed by the plus sign, meaning required and repeatable):

```
<!ELEMENT catalog (section)+>
```

The second line creates the `section` element. Its rule first allows an optional and repeatable `distributor` child element (because the asterisk is used), followed by an optional and repeatable `region`, and an optional and repeatable `winery`. The last child element, `wine`, is the only one that is required, and it is also repeatable.

```
<!ELEMENT section (distributor*,region*,winery*,wine+)>
```

The next line creates an attribute for the `section` element. The attribute's name is `subject`:

```
<!ATTLIST section subject (Wines) #REQUIRED>
```

`#REQUIRED` denotes that the attribute must be given a value before the XML document is considered valid.

Then the distributor element is created; it can contain text (parsed character data):

```
<!ELEMENT distributor (#PCDATA)>
```

`#PCDATA` is short for parsed character data. This means that the element will contain text content between its beginning and ending tags.

The next three lines create two attributes for the distributor element:

```
<!ATTLIST distributor
  id ID #IMPLIED
  name CDATA #IMPLIED>
```

The attribute names are `id` and `name`. The id is an ID type (used in linking and referencing), and `name` is character data (text strings).

The region element, which can contain text, is created:

```
<!ELEMENT region (#PCDATA)>
```

A `name` attribute of the type `CDATA` (character data)—so its value will be expressed as character data (text strings)—is defined:

```
<!ATTLIST region name CDATA #IMPLIED>
```

`#IMPLIED` denotes that the attribute does not have to be given a value before the XML document is considered valid.

The next two lines create the name and country elements, which can contain text:

```
<!ELEMENT name (#PCDATA)>
<!ELEMENT country (#PCDATA)>
```

The `winery` element has a mixed content model. That means that it can contain a mix of text and child elements; in this case, `name`, `region`, or `country`—repeatable and in whatever order is desired.

```
<!ELEMENT winery (#PCDATA|name|region|country)*>
```

The following line creates an attribute `id` of type `ID` for the winery element:

```
<!ATTLIST winery id ID #IMPLIED>
```

The next part of the DTD creates the wine element. It is required to have these child elements in this specific order (because of the commas): `name`, `varietal`, `vintage`, `winery`, `distributor`, `bottlesize`, `description`. If any of these were to be missing, the wine element would not be valid. As was seen in an earlier subset of the winery XML, some of the wines do not have all of these bits of data; this can be part of the adjustments made to the structure later in this chapter.

```
<!ELEMENT wine (name,varietal,vintage,winery,distributor,bottlesize,↩
    description)>
```

The `wine` element gets an `id` attribute of type `ID`:

```
<!ATTLIST wine id ID #REQUIRED>
```

The next four lines create the elements `bottlesize`, `description`, `varietal`, and `vintage`, all of which can contain text:

```
<!ELEMENT bottlesize (#PCDATA)>
<!ELEMENT description (#PCDATA)>
<!ELEMENT varietal (#PCDATA)>
<!ELEMENT vintage (#PCDATA)>
```

This is a fairly small and simple DTD example. Now take a look at how the same structure is created as a schema:

```
<?xml version="1.0" encoding="UTF-8"?>
<xs:schema xmlns:xs="http://www.w3.org/2001/XMLSchema" ↩
elementFormDefault="qualified">
  <xs:element name="catalog">
    <xs:complexType>
      <xs:sequence>
        <xs:element ref="section"/>
      </xs:sequence>
    </xs:complexType>
  </xs:element>
  <xs:element name="section">
```

```
    <xs:complexType>
      <xs:sequence>
        <xs:element minOccurs="0" maxOccurs="unbounded" ref="distributor"/>
        <xs:element minOccurs="0" maxOccurs="unbounded" ref="region"/>
        <xs:element minOccurs="0" maxOccurs="unbounded" ref="winery"/>
        <xs:element maxOccurs="unbounded" ref="wine"/>
      </xs:sequence>
      <xs:attribute name="subject" use="required">
        <xs:simpleType>
          <xs:restriction base="xs:token">
            <xs:enumeration value="Wines"/>
          </xs:restriction>
        </xs:simpleType>
      </xs:attribute>
    </xs:complexType>
  </xs:element>
  <xs:element name="wine">
    <xs:complexType>
      <xs:sequence>
        <xs:element ref="name"/>
        <xs:element ref="varietal"/>
        <xs:element ref="vintage"/>
        <xs:element ref="winery"/>
        <xs:element ref="distributor"/>
        <xs:element ref="bottlesize"/>
        <xs:element ref="description"/>
      </xs:sequence>
      <xs:attribute name="id" use="required" type="xs:ID"/>
    </xs:complexType>
  </xs:element>
  <xs:element name="varietal" type="xs:string"/>

  <xs:element name="vintage" type="xs:integer"/>
  <xs:element name="bottlesize" type="xs:NMTOKEN"/>
  <xs:element name="description" type="xs:string"/>
  <xs:element name="distributor">
    <xs:complexType mixed="true">
      <xs:attribute name="id" type="xs:ID"/>
      <xs:attribute name="name"/>
    </xs:complexType>
  </xs:element>
  <xs:element name="region">
    <xs:complexType mixed="true">
      <xs:attribute name="name"/>
    </xs:complexType>
  </xs:element>
  <xs:element name="winery">
    <xs:complexType mixed="true">
      <xs:choice minOccurs="0" maxOccurs="3">
        <xs:element ref="name" maxOccurs="1"/>
        <xs:element ref="region" maxOccurs="1"/>
        <xs:element ref="country" maxOccurs="1"/>
      </xs:choice>
      <xs:attribute name="id" type="xs:ID"/>
    </xs:complexType>
```

```
    </xs:element>
    <xs:element name="country" type="xs:string"/>
    <xs:element name="name" type="xs:string"/>
  </xs:schema>
```

Let's examine this schema one chunk at a time. Unlike the DTD, the schema is an XML document. It starts with an XML declaration. This declaration is different from the one shown earlier in this book in that it includes the optional encoding data, which enables you to identify whether the file uses Unicode content or other encoding that relates to the language used in the XML document.

```
<?xml version="1.0" encoding="UTF-8"?>
```

The markup declares the `schema` namespace. A namespace is an optional part of XML markup, and allows for recognition of elements as part of a particular element set. Using namespaces can be helpful when you're combining elements from multiple structures by allowing you to identify the structure with which each element is associated. An `address` element, for instance, might be part of a client database as well as part of a corporate contact information document. Adding a namespace in front such as `xs:address` ensures that the right structure is associated with the element. The `schema` namespace has been declared in the winery example, so the markup can use the `xs:` designation on the elements.

After the `xs:` designation, you will see many Extensible Stylesheet Language (XSL) elements used in this XML document. The XSL elements and syntax are described in more detail later in the book.

```
<xs:schema xmlns:xs="http://www.w3.org/2001/XMLSchema" ➥
elementFormDefault="qualified">
```

The following group of lines creates the `catalog` element, which can contain section child elements.

```
  <xs:element name="catalog">
    <xs:complexType>
      <xs:sequence>
        <xs:element ref="section"/>
      </xs:sequence>
    </xs:complexType>
  </xs:element>
```

These lines create the `section` element and allow for the optional-and-repeatable `distributor`, `region`, and `winery` elements, just as the DTD did. The `wine` child is required and can be repeated (`"unbounded"`). If the elements are optional, then the `minOccurs` is set to `0`.

```
  <xs:element name="section">
    <xs:complexType>
      <xs:sequence>
        <xs:element minOccurs="0" maxOccurs="unbounded" ref="distributor"/>
        <xs:element minOccurs="0" maxOccurs="unbounded" ref="region"/>
        <xs:element minOccurs="0" maxOccurs="unbounded" ref="winery"/>
        <xs:element maxOccurs="unbounded" ref="wine"/>
      </xs:sequence>
```

Then a `subject` attribute is created for the `section` element. Notice that the `section` element's closing tag does not appear until after the attribute is defined:

```
        <xs:attribute name="subject" use="required">
          <xs:simpleType>
            <xs:restriction base="xs:token">
              <xs:enumeration value="Wines"/>
            </xs:restriction>
          </xs:simpleType>
        </xs:attribute>
      </xs:complexType>
    </xs:element>
```

A wine element is created. It's required to have the following child elements in this specific order: name, varietal, vintage, winery, distributor, bottlesize, and description. This chunk of code also creates an id attribute of the ID type.

```
    <xs:element name="wine">
      <xs:complexType>
        <xs:sequence>
          <xs:element ref="name"/>
          <xs:element ref="varietal"/>
          <xs:element ref="vintage"/>
          <xs:element ref="winery"/>
          <xs:element ref="distributor"/>
          <xs:element ref="bottlesize"/>
          <xs:element ref="description"/>
        </xs:sequence>
        <xs:attribute name="id" use="required" type="xs:ID"/>
      </xs:complexType>
    </xs:element>
```

The varietal element can contain text:

```
<xs:element name="varietal" type="xs:string"/>
```

The vintage element can contain a number (this is a bit different from the DTD):

```
<xs:element name="vintage" type="xs:integer"/>
```

The bottlesize element comes next and is set as a number (NMTOKEN) so that the attribute value can be treated as a number in sorting or adding quantities:

```
<xs:element name="bottlesize" type="xs:NMTOKEN"/>
```

The description element can contain text strings because of the type that's set in the schema:

```
<xs:element name="description" type="xs:string"/>
```

The following lines create the distributor element, which can contain text and subelements (mixed type). This element has attributes id and name, just as in the DTD.

```
    <xs:element name="distributor">
      <xs:complexType mixed="true">
        <xs:attribute name="id" type="xs:ID"/>
```

```
    <xs:attribute name="name"/>
  </xs:complexType>
</xs:element>
```

The `region` element gets a `name` attribute:

```
<xs:element name="region">
  <xs:complexType mixed="true">
    <xs:attribute name="name"/>
  </xs:complexType>
</xs:element>
```

The following chunk of the schema creates the `winery` element, which has a mixed content model (`mixed="true"`, in this case). It can contain a mix of text and child elements; in this example, `name`, `region`, or `country`—repeatable and in whatever order is desired.

```
<xs:element name="winery">
  <xs:complexType mixed="true">
    <xs:choice minOccurs="0" maxOccurs="3">
      <xs:element ref="name" maxOccurs="1"/>
      <xs:element ref="region" maxOccurs="1"/>
      <xs:element ref="country" maxOccurs="1"/>
    </xs:choice>
    <xs:attribute name="id" type="xs:ID"/>
  </xs:complexType>
</xs:element>
```

Then the `country` and `name` elements are created; both can contain text:

```
<xs:element name="country" type="xs:string"/>
<xs:element name="name" type="xs:string"/>
```

Finally, the closing tag for the schema ends the XML document:

```
</xs:schema>
```

Revising the Structure

Now you'll see how to modify the DTD to include certain elements desired for the enterprise-wide use. To keep this example simple, only the `winetype` information will be added to the DTD and schema; you can continue modifying the code as you like to get closer to the more complete structure additions discussed in the "Developing Your Structure" section of Chapter 2.

- Inventory
- Price (U.S. and Canadian)
- Client data (address, phone, email)
- Client type (distributor, customer)
- Category

- Keywords
- Business details (your own hours of operations, days open to the public, physical address, certifications)

One of the changes needed in your structure is the addition of a wine type. Varietal information gives some categorization of the wine, but knowing the type of the wine will be even more helpful. With `winetype`, you will be able to specify whether a wine is a dessert wine, a table wine, or another type.

You can add this extra information to the structure as a new element or as an attribute on one of the existing elements. For this example, add a `winetype` attribute to the existing `varietal` element. This is not necessarily the only way or the best way, but it is one of the options and will work for your purposes here.

Here's how to add the attribute in the structure of the DTD:

```
<!ATTLIST varietal winetype CDATA #IMPLIED>
```

An equal change in the schema involves adding content that give us an additional attribute and defines its type:

```
    <xs:element name = "varietal">
        <xs:complexType>
            <xs:simpleContent>
                <xs:extension base = "xs:string">
                    <xs:attribute name = "winetype" type = "xs:string"/>
                </xs:extension>
            </xs:simpleContent>
        </xs:complexType>
    </xs:element>
```

The corresponding change in the XML data is shown in bold for one wine:

```
<wine id="Muscadine_750ml">
<name>Muscadine</name>
<varietal winetype="dessert">Scupp</varietal>
<vintage>1998</vintage>
<winery>Melvin</winery>
<bottlesize>750ml</bottlesize>
<description>Our complex purple Muscadine grape lends an assertive aroma and
flavor, with a semi-sweet velvety smooth finish.</description>
</wine>
```

The final stage is to tie your XML document to the DTD or schema by including a `DOCTYPE` declaration within the XML. Note the position of the `DOCTYPE` beneath the XML declaration (the DTD path is shown in this example):

```
<?xml version="1.0"?>
<!DOCTYPE wine SYSTEM "wines.dtd">
<wine id="Muscadine_750ml">
<name>Muscadine</name>
```

```
<varietal winetype="dessert">Scupp</varietal>
<vintage>1998</vintage>
<winery>Melvin</winery>
<bottlesize>750ml</bottlesize>
<description>Our complex purple Muscadine grape lends an assertive aroma and ⮐
flavor, with a semi-sweet velvety smooth finish.</description>
</wine>
```

With the `DOCTYPE`, the root element is named, followed by the word `SYSTEM` if the DTD or schema is on your computer, or the word `PUBLIC` if the DTD or schema is located on a URL. Then you put the name of the DTD or schema in quotation marks.

The reference changes to reference a schema instead of a DTD:

```
<?xml-stylesheet href="wine.xsl" type="text/xsl"?>
```

Solution

Ta da!

You have a fairly solid structure for your winery data. You have a DTD and a schema (that are at this point essentially equal). These files will be used in future chapters to do validation of your data and ensure your XML follows all of the structure rules set down for it as the XML is modified.

Here's the revised DTD:

```
<!ELEMENT catalog (section)>

<!ELEMENT section (distributor*, region*, winery*, wine+)>

<!ATTLIST section subject (Wines) #REQUIRED >
<!ELEMENT wine (name,varietal,vintage,winery,distributor,bottlesize,description⮐
,inventorycount?,price?)>
<!ATTLIST wine  id ID  #REQUIRED >
<!ELEMENT varietal (#PCDATA)>
<!ATTLIST varietal  winetype CDATA #IMPLIED >
<!ELEMENT vintage (#PCDATA)>
<!ELEMENT bottlesize (#PCDATA)>
<!ELEMENT description (#PCDATA)>
<!ELEMENT distributor (#PCDATA)>
<!ATTLIST distributor id  ID   #IMPLIED
                      name CDATA  #IMPLIED >
<!ELEMENT region (#PCDATA)>
<!ATTLIST region  name CDATA  #IMPLIED >
<!ELEMENT winery (#PCDATA|name|region|country|address1|address2|⮐
city|state|zip)*>
<!ATTLIST winery id ID  #IMPLIED >
<!ELEMENT country (#PCDATA)>
<!ELEMENT name (#PCDATA)>
<!ELEMENT inventorycount EMPTY>
<!ELEMENT price (us|canada|other)>
```

```
<!ELEMENT us (#PCDATA)>
<!ELEMENT canada (#PCDATA)>
<!ELEMENT other (#PCDATA)>
<!ELEMENT address1 (#PCDATA)>
<!ELEMENT address2 (#PCDATA)>
<!ELEMENT city (#PCDATA)>
<!ELEMENT state (#PCDATA)>
<!ELEMENT zip (#PCDATA)>
```

And here's the revised schema:

```
<?xml version = "1.0" encoding = "UTF-8"?>

<!--Generated by Turbo XML 2.4.1.100. Conforms to w3c ⮐
    http://www.w3.org/2001/XMLSchema-->
<xs:schema xmlns:xs = "http://www.w3.org/2001/XMLSchema"
     elementFormDefault = "qualified">
    <xs:element name = "catalog">
        <xs:complexType>
            <xs:sequence>
                <xs:element ref = "section"/>
            </xs:sequence>
        </xs:complexType>
    </xs:element>
    <xs:element name = "section">
        <xs:complexType>
        <xs:sequence>
         <xs:element ref = "distributor" minOccurs = "0" maxOccurs = "unbounded"/>
         <xs:element ref = "region" minOccurs = "0" maxOccurs = "unbounded"/>
         <xs:element ref = "winery" minOccurs = "0" maxOccurs = "unbounded"/>
         <xs:element ref = "wine" maxOccurs = "unbounded"/>
        </xs:sequence>
            <xs:attribute name = "subject" use = "required">
                <xs:simpleType>
                    <xs:restriction base = "xs:token">
                        <xs:enumeration value = "Wines"/>
                    </xs:restriction>
                </xs:simpleType>
            </xs:attribute>
        </xs:complexType>
    </xs:element>
    <xs:element name = "wine">
        <xs:complexType>
            <xs:sequence>
                <xs:element ref = "name"/>
                <xs:element ref = "varietal"/>
                <xs:element ref = "vintage"/>
                <xs:element ref = "winery"/>
                <xs:element ref = "distributor"/>
                <xs:element ref = "bottlesize"/>
                <xs:element ref = "description"/>
                <xs:element ref = "inventorycount" minOccurs = "0"/>
                <xs:element ref = "price" minOccurs = "0"/>
            </xs:sequence>
            <xs:attribute name = "id" use = "required" type = "xs:ID"/>
```

```
        </xs:complexType>
    </xs:element>
    <xs:element name = "varietal">
        <xs:complexType>
            <xs:simpleContent>
                <xs:extension base = "xs:string">
                    <xs:attribute name = "winetype" type = "xs:string"/>
                </xs:extension>
            </xs:simpleContent>
        </xs:complexType>
    </xs:element>
    <xs:element name = "vintage" type = "xs:integer"/>
    <xs:element name = "bottlesize" type = "xs:NMTOKEN"/>
    <xs:element name = "description" type = "xs:string"/>
    <xs:element name = "distributor">
        <xs:complexType mixed = "true">
            <xs:choice/>
            <xs:attribute name = "id" type = "xs:ID"/>
            <xs:attribute name = "name" type = "xs:string"/>
        </xs:complexType>
    </xs:element>
    <xs:element name = "region">
        <xs:complexType mixed = "true">
            <xs:choice/>
            <xs:attribute name = "name" type = "xs:string"/>
        </xs:complexType>
    </xs:element>
    <xs:element name = "winery">
        <xs:complexType mixed = "true">
            <xs:choice minOccurs = "0" maxOccurs = "3">
                <xs:element ref = "name"/>
                <xs:element ref = "region"/>
                <xs:element ref = "country"/>
                <xs:element ref = "address1"/>
                <xs:element ref = "address2"/>
                <xs:element ref = "city"/>
                <xs:element ref = "state"/>
                <xs:element ref = "zip"/>
            </xs:choice>
            <xs:attribute name = "id" type = "xs:ID"/>
        </xs:complexType>
    </xs:element>
    <xs:element name = "country" type = "xs:string"/>
    <xs:element name = "name" type = "xs:string"/>
    <xs:element name = "inventorycount">
        <xs:complexType>
            <xs:sequence/>
        </xs:complexType>
    </xs:element>
    <xs:element name = "price">
        <xs:complexType>
            <xs:choice>
                <xs:element ref = "us"/>
                <xs:element ref = "canada"/>
                <xs:element ref = "other"/>
```

```
            </xs:choice>
        </xs:complexType>
    </xs:element>
    <xs:element name = "us" type = "xs:string"/>
    <xs:element name = "canada" type = "xs:string"/>
    <xs:element name = "other" type = "xs:string"/>
    <xs:element name = "address1" type = "xs:string"/>
    <xs:element name = "address2" type = "xs:string"/>
    <xs:element name = "city" type = "xs:string"/>
    <xs:element name = "state" type = "xs:string"/>
    <xs:element name = "zip" type = "xs:string"/>
</xs:schema>
```

You'll find more details regarding the schema language later in the book.

Summary

This chapter explored the DTD and schema, and the role they play in validating XML documents. To ensure that your XML content is consistently structured, and that the hierarchy follows a specific pattern, you need either a DTD or schema. Choose the one most appropriate to your publishing situation, with an eye toward using schema long term.

Presenting XML Directly

Your catalog isn't going to sell itself — you have to get products placed in front of an audience, and in a reasonably attractive package. The next few chapters explain how to take XML-based information and present it in usable and pleasing ways. This chapter focuses on making the product line accessible to online shoppers, with a minimum of change to the XML.

In the preceding chapter, you verified that the product catalog met certain constraints, expressed as a schema. You know, for instance, that the catalog is well-formed XML and that it contains details about bottled wines. Yet the raw XML seems obviously unsuitable for displaying to the end user. Angle brackets are angle brackets after all, and they don't lend themselves to promotional displays.

Or do they? With a few caveats, the XML catalog can be presented online directly with very little (or no) modification to the original data. In this chapter, you explore the use of a standard web technology — Cascading Style Sheets — to serve up the XML wine data directly to a web browser.

Problem

Products need to be seen in order to sell. This section explores the requirements and limitations of sending XML directly to a browser, and results in a list of objectives to meet in the remainder of the chapter.

Promoting Product Online

If you are going to be selling to the general public, you need to let customers know what you're offering. This works best if you anticipate the kinds of questions that customers may have and include the answers in your presentation. The first such question might be: Which wines are available from a particular winery?

The traditional way to answer this question is by way of a wine list, which is more or less a form of product line card. Many, if not most, include images of the product as a way of enticing customers. Product line cards are widely used to promote a vendor's or distributor's products. To get an idea of what the wine list should look like, it is helpful to sketch the desired result.

One style option is to use a compact form of *breadcrumb*, which uses hyperlinked key terms to provide a compact index. This layout is frequently seen in online technical references. Here's an example:

> **CSS** - **DOM** - **HTML** - **HTTP** - **InkML** - **MathML** - **OWL** - **PICS** - **PNG** - **RDF** - **SMIL** - **SOAP/XMLP** - **SPARQL** - **SVG** - **TAG** - **URI/URL** - **WebCGM** - **XForms** - **XHTML** - **XLink** - **XML** - **XML Query** - **XML Schema** - **XML Signature** - **XPath** - **XPointer** - **XSL** - **XSLT**

A scan of wine sellers on the web reveals that this isn't a popular form, and it isn't difficult to see why. For one thing, unlike the technical acronyms in the example just given, wine names vary from winery to winery. The wine names don't represent general categories, but unique products. Another reason is that terseness isn't particularly useful when selling wines. You need a more open layout that allows for added effects, such as including pictures of the bottled wines and comments on the flavor.

A top-to-bottom menu of wines is more in keeping with the spirit. Given a winery, a prospective buyer can quickly view the wines it produces and get additional information on a wine selection. To start with, the prospect should be given a wine name, a vintage, and, if available, the size of the bottling. The wine catalog has other elements that might be presented as well, should the prospective buyer select a wine of interest. The description element in particular can guide the buyer in making a selection, but the flowery, drawn-out prose should be displayed carefully to avoid muddying up the layout. Here's an example:

```
Mad Merlin Merlot     2005   1.5L
   Reward your desires with this intensely colored red wine. Delightful
   sweet finish with an intense aroma, reminiscent of freshly cut limes.

Mad Merlin Champagne  2005   750ml
   Velvety smooth semi-dry champagne with delicate aromas of mangos and berries.
   A premium champagne developed at Great North University with Krakau White grape.

Muscadine Wine 2005 2L
   ...
```

. . . and so on.

To publish this wine list, refer to the XML structures you learned about earlier. It is a straightforward problem, with a straightforward solution, and is easy to accomplish. You need to consider which elements apply, and that's the subject of the next section.

Pertinent Product Data

How can you isolate the wines of a particular winery? The XML catalog contains several different elements describing, among other things, the distributors, wineries, regions, and wines. The particular elements of interest are <winery> and <wine>; here is an example of each:

```
<winery id="Melvin">
   <name>Mad Melvin's Muscadine Wines</name>
   <region>North Carolina</region>
```

```
        <country>United States</country>
    </winery>

    <wine id="Smoky_Scupp_750ml">
        <name>Smoky_Scupp</name>
        <varietal>Scupp</varietal>
        <vintage>1992</vintage>
        <winery>Melvin</winery>
        <distributor>Dri</distributor>
        <bottlesize>750ml</bottlesize>
        <description>A dry red muscadine with hints of oak. A delicious wine ⮐
produced from a unique mix of Carlos and Magnolia Scuppernong grapes. ⮐
Blackberry aromas lead to fat, smoky flavors and long spicy ⮐
finish.</description>
    </wine>
```

One concern in feeding XML straight to a browser is that files often contain large amounts of data. The wine catalog is no exception — many different wineries and wines are included, not to mention information about the distributors and regions. Choose a winery to use in the following exercises, rather than attempt to illustrate the entire catalog at once. For the purposes of the exercises in the remainder of this chapter, Mad Melvin's Muscadine Wines is the winery of choice.

Extracting Requirements

An objective is set: displaying a wine list for prospective buyers interested in Mad Melvin's Muscadine Wines. You have a rough idea of what the output should look like, and have identified the elements from which the information is sourced. Further, by extracting a well-defined chunk of the catalog into the `wine.xml` file, the catalog won't overwhelm the capacity of a web browser. In practice, this filtering would be automated using scripts, queries, and/or XSLT.

This chapter can be viewed as working backward from the end of an information delivery process. Automating the manual editing steps is the subject of technologies discussed in subsequent chapters.

Because XSLT technology hasn't yet been discussed, another constraint is that no automated transformations can be used at this point. One of the objectives is to display XML directly, so minimal editing is desirable.

Design

Common web browser technology can present readable and navigable XML directly. You can use ordinary web browsers to style XML. Modern browsers such as Internet Explorer, Netscape, and Mozilla/Firefox have XML features built in. But perhaps you're wondering, "Why format XML with a browser?"

Technical Motivation

Unlike HTML, which has elements that imply document formatting, XML is data-oriented and implies very little about how it should be processed. In its raw form, the wine catalog — the skeletal XML source — isn't particularly conducive to the sales process. The next step is to associate formatting semantics with the XML structures in the catalog, so a browser can display it.

Cascading Style Sheets (CSS) provides a means of doing just that. CSS is widely supported (if not always well implemented) in commodity web browsers today. CSS provides a box model in which elements can be mapped to boxes and positioned as blocks or as lines of content. It also provides style properties to affect numerous presentational aspects including fonts and colors.

CSS conformance is defined by the World Wide Web Consortium in terms of levels. CSS Level 1 is widely supported, and it can be used to display HTML and XML in Internet Explorer 6. CSS Level 2 builds upon this with many new formatting features but is less widely supported. CSS Level 2 Revision 1 (CSS 2.1) was introduced to correct errors in CSS Level 2, bring the specification more in line with actual browser implementations, and ease the transition to CSS Level 3. CSS 2.1 is not fully supported, either, but many of its features are available in Internet Explorer and even more in Firefox. CSS Level 3 is not yet available in either Internet Explorer– or Mozilla-based browsers.

Browsers aren't always the best way to format XML. Other ways to format XML include XSLT transforms into XHTML or XSL Formatting Objects, writing an import filter for a suite application such as OpenOffice Writer, or even binding the XML elements to vector graphic primitives in a Standard Vector Graphics (SVG) viewer. While there are legitimate reasons for going down those paths, they involve considerably more coding (or an understanding of another graphic language in the case of SVG). Using CSS directly also provides a means of prototyping output for these other automation methods.

With the advent of key XML features in modern browsers, another headline-grabbing method is AJAX (Asynchronous JavaScript and XML). AJAX is a development technique for delivering interactive user interfaces based on XML. AJAX relies on four key features: HTML (or XHTML) with CSS, a programmable Document Object Model (DOM) interface, event handling in JavaScript, and a special object (`XMLHttpRequest`*) that allows scripts to exchange XML data with a web server. AJAX moves away from using the browser as a thin client in web applications to using it as a so-called "rich client" by implementing more application logic on the browser.*

The principle reason for using a browser to format XML is that, from the user's viewpoint, it provides a seamless web experience. In general, people can't tell that the wines they are browsing are described using XML. A more subtle reason is that a large base of potential customers has immediate access to browsers such as Internet Explorer and Firefox. Delivering XML directly to their browsers, with CSS for style, is a simple, direct means of reaching these people without requiring additional technology.

Structure of the Design

The formatted wine list consists of at least two resources: the XML wine list and Cascading Style Sheets. Conceptually, the stylesheet consists of a set of rules that apply to a particular *target media type*. The CSS processor (in this case, a browser) determines values that apply for the formatting properties applicable to a particular output media, and annotates the XML element tree accordingly. The annotated tree structure is used to generate a formatting structure that is transferred to the output media. Figure 4-1 illustrates this process.

One feature of the CSS formatting model is the tree annotation process, which minimally affects the arrangement of elements in the tree. The structure of the output is quite similar to the structure of the input. Although the formatting structure may omit elements and allows for independently positioned areas and minor decorative additions, the order and number of elements is substantially unchanged throughout the process.

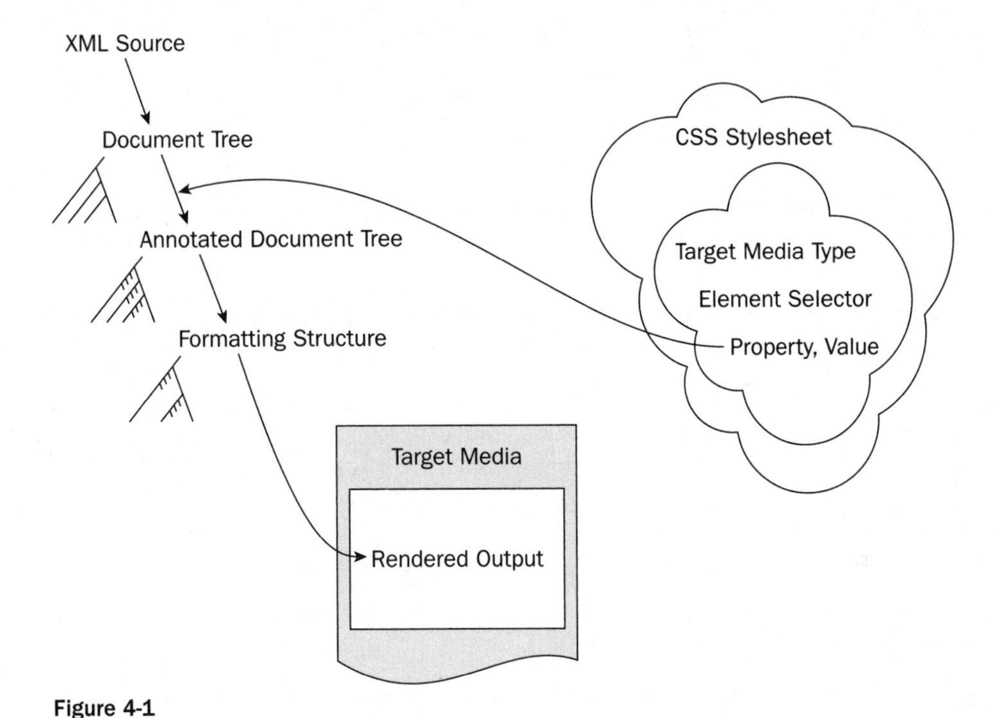

Figure 4-1

The XML is to be parsed and styled by a web browser much as any HTML file. The wine list is a simple XML file on disk, but it could as well be generated on a server as a result of a database query. The process is virtually the same as a typical web page retrieval.

The syntax of CSS is quite different from that of XML. Rather than using angle brackets as markup delimiters, CSS uses a notation similar to programming languages like JavaScript. In particular, curly braces are used to denote style blocks for selectors and media types. The following sections provide the basic syntax.

Selectors

CSS Level 1 defines *selectors* as simple strings that determine the scope of application of a corresponding style rule. A selector is a kind of generic identifier that matches a set of elements in the document. Take, for example the following XML, an oversimplified order for a bag of hammers:

```
<order id="k9000">
   <customer>
      <name>John Doe</name>
   </customer>
   <lineitem>
      <product>
         <name>Hammer</name>
      </product>
      <unit>bag</unit>
      <quantity>1</quantity>
   </lineitem>
</order>
```

A simple CSS type selector to style all the names in a 12-point, bold-faced serif font is:

```
name {
   font-size: 12pt;
   font-weight: bold;
   font-family: serif;
}
```

There are a few simple syntax rules to follow in CSS:

- Property declarations are terminated with a semicolon (;). Technically, the semicolon separates the property declarations, and the last semicolon can be omitted on the last property in the rule.
- White space can be used liberally to make the code more readable.
- Property names and values are case-insensitive, so `Serif` means the same thing as `serif`. (But watch out for XML element and attribute names, which are case-sensitive.)
- Comments can be inserted by `/* wrapping them in C-style comment delimiters */`.

Simple selectors in CSS 2.1 may be combined in various ways, as summarized in the following table:

Selector	Usage

A, B	A comma-separated list of selectors sharing the same style declarations.
	Example:
	`name, unit {`
	`font-family: sans-serif;`
	`}`

A > B	Child selector. The selector B indicates an immediate child of A.
	Example:
	`product > name {`
	`font-family: fantasy;`
	`}`

A B	Descendant selector. The selector B indicates an element contained at any level of nesting within its ancestor A.
	Example:
	`lineitem name {`
	`font-weight: bold;`
	`}`

A + B	Adjacent sibling selector. The selector B indicates the element immediately following element A.
	Example:
	`product + unit {`
	`text-decoration: underline;`
	`}`

There are a number of other selector types, but a more extensive treatment is beyond the scope of this book. Two additional selectors should be mentioned, however. First, the *universal selector*, written as an asterisk (the * symbol) in place of an element name, acts as a wildcard matching any element type in the document. Second, a *pseudo-classes* or *pseudo-element* can be appended to a simple selector to qualify the selection based on a predetermined condition. For instance, the selector `A:hover` applies whenever the mouse pointer is placed over an `A` element.

Style Properties

A major part of the CSS formatting process is to annotate the XML tree with style properties. A CSS style property has the form:

```
property : value;
```

As with the many selector types, coverage of even a fraction of the proposed CSS style properties is beyond this book's scope. Some of the visual properties that may be useful in laying out the wine list are shown in the table below:

Property	Example	Description
`border`	`border: solid thin grey;`	Shorthand to set several border properties at once; draw a border around a formatted element.
`font`	`font: normal 12pt Times;`	Shorthand to set several font properties at once.
`background-image`	`background-image: url(bg.png)`	Place an image as the background of an element.
`background-repeat`	`background-repeat: repeat;`	Tile an image along x, y, or both x and y dimensions.
`background-color`	`background-color: #FFFFFF;`	Fill an element's background with a color.
`float`	`float: right;`	Position an element's box by shifting it left or right on the current line, flowing remaining content to the right or left.
`display`	`display: block;`	Determine the kind of box generated for an element, and how it is flowed in formatting.
`margin`	`margin: 12px;`	Shorthand to set several margin properties at once.
`height`	`height: 10em;`	Set the height of a box.
`width`	`width: 50%;`	Set the width of a box.

There are far too many style properties to cover in this book. The CSS specifications, available at the W3C links mentioned earlier, are the definitive source for the properties. Because browser support varies, it is important to consult browser compatibility tables such as those at QuirksMode (`www.quirksmode.org`) and Web Devout (`www.webdevout.net`). The properties used within this chapter deal with visual formatting and fall into just a few groups: fonts, text effects, the box model, and positioning. These are covered as encountered in the project.

Stylesheet Processing Instruction

The stylesheet *processing instruction* (PI) allows an HTML, XHTML, or XML document to embed an association with a CSS or XSL stylesheet. This instruction is placed in the prolog of the XML, after the `<?xml version="1.0"?>` and before the document element, like this:

```
<?xml version="1.0"?>
<?xml-stylesheet type="text/css" href="somestylesheet.css"?>
<catalog>
```

The `xml-stylesheet` processing instruction informs the browser that a stylesheet is available to be used when presenting a formatted version of the document. The browser reads the stylesheet, applies the formatting properties contained in it, and renders the result to the display. Multiple associations can be made by including multiple `xml-stylesheet` PIs, but for this project, one is sufficient.

Applicable Technologies

The key technologies used in this chapter are CSS and the `xml-stylesheet` processing instruction. Of the two, CSS warrants the most attention.

CSS is part of the W3C's Style activity. The W3C recommendations and drafts, as well as supporting materials, can be found at the Cascading Style Sheets Home Page at `www.w3.org/Style/CSS`. At present the CSS has three *levels*:

- CSS Level 1 is a W3C recommendation. It defines properties for basic style properties such as fonts, the box model, colors, margins, borders, and other styles originally motivated by HTML.
- CSS Level 2, revision 1, is a candidate recommendation. (As a candidate recommendation, it is currently being reviewed by the W3C, but vendors are encouraged to implement its features.) It allows absolute positioning of elements, and provides pagination properties and some control over text direction.
- CSS Level 3 includes levels 1 and 2. It's under development as of this writing.

The "Associating Style Sheets with XML Documents" recommendation can be found at `www.w3.org/TR/xml-stylesheet`. The project in this chapter uses the `xml-stylesheet` processing instruction specified in the "Associating Style Sheets with XML Documents" recommendation to link the XML to the wine list stylesheets.

Finally, XML and CSS don't exist in a vacuum. You need a browser with good XML and CSS support such as Mozilla/Firefox or Opera. The project should work with Internet Explorer, but as you go farther many of IE's CSS limitations will be evident. Users of IE5/IE6 who want to use CSS may want to consider Dean Edward's IE7 workaround at `http://dean.edwards.name/IE7`.

Design Consequences

Using a browser with CSS capabilities to format XML has several consequences, some good and some not so good.

CSS allows, to a degree, a separation of style characteristics from the structure of the XML. This separation is limited by the dependence of the formatting process upon the original document structure and semantics. Style concerns tend to bleed over into the structure of the XML. It is very common for a XHTML/CSS layout task to rely more on rearranging XHTML structures than on changes to the CSS rules.

If the XML is already prepared for a specific display purpose, it is possible to use CSS to deliver a formatted presentation with minimal modifications to the XML. The formatting process itself makes little rearrangement of the original ordering of the document tree and is fast enough for use in web browsing.

It is frequently the case, however, that XML is *not* optimally arranged for direct formatting through CSS. The content may be out of order with respect to the best display arrangement, or it may be too voluminous for efficient displaying by a web browser. For the practical purpose of formatting, the use of additional technologies to marshal and stage the data is essential.

At a minimum, the XML still needs to be associated with a stylesheet. The only practical means of doing so in a web environment is to use client-side scripting of styles or to embed an `xml-stylesheet` processing instruction in the XML document. Both of these approaches imply logic on the server to make the association and perform the editing, either prior to accessing the XML or just in time as the XML resource is retrieved.

By itself, XML lacks the semantics you might associate with browsing hypertext, and CSS doesn't address link semantics. There are W3C recommendations to address the need for linking, including XHTML (`www.w3.org/MarkUp`) and the XLink Recommendation (`www.w3.org/TR/xlink`). XLink defines special attributes to implement HTML `href`-like links in XML. While some browsers, such as Mozilla/Firefox, implement simple XLinks, others offer no support. An alternative is to modify the XML to incorporate XHTML elements (which would be fine if it weren't the subject of another chapter). Internet Explorer takes a similar, though nonstandard, approach by allowing you to incorporate older-style HTML links.

While it is a goal to produce a "browsable" wine list, and XML is a web technology, web browsers are neither the most efficient nor the most consistent formatting engines. CSS 2.1 implementations are currently incomplete to the point that heavy reliance on browser version-specific workarounds is commonplace.

Having considered the consequences of what you are about to do, the wine list still needs to be developed. Later chapters deal with several of the challenges discussed, and they won't interfere with the wine list.

Solution

Having reviewed the problem, a proposed design approach, and applicable technologies, it is time to get down to the nuts and bolts of constructing the solution. In the rest of the chapter, you sketch a layout for the wine list, identify the XML content that is needed to fill in the layout, and finally apply CSS rules to bring the wine list together.

Product Line Sketch

Drawing on the requirements stated earlier, here is a more developed sketch of the product line card, illustrated as if the prospective buyer selected the first wine:

```
Cabernet Sauvignon
   Varietal: Cabernet Sauvignon
   Vintage: 1992
    Bottle Size: 750ml
      A highly complex wine with flavors of dark cherry, cedar, tobacco,
         and black currant.
      Aged in French oak barrels for the finest and most complex red wine possible.
      One of the most popular choices. Goes well with grilled meats and
         pasta dishes.
Spumante
Barolo "La Muerto"
Gigante Classico
Cabernet Bolillo
Lithuanian Hill Merlot
```

Product Data — Raw XML

Right now, the only means you have to access Mad Melvin's elements is to edit the XML file manually and pick out a selection of wines. This is obviously a suboptimal method, but it demonstrates steps that are automated in following chapters.

Use the techniques you learned in previous chapters to pick out Melvin's Muscadine Wines elements. The catalog element, the winery element for Melvin's, and the wine elements that specify Melvin as the winery, are required for the project. The other elements — distributors, regions, and the other wines and wineries included in the catalog — may be useful for answering interesting questions but they are not relevant here. Under ordinary circumstances, this kind of chunking would be automated, but doing it manually illustrates the objective better. (You'll automate the task in Chapter 5.)

XML and Mismatched Structures

The fact that information is made available in XML does not mean that the data is immediately suitable for a specific use, or that it is feasible to use it at all. Even if you've taken great care to analyze your processes, ideal XML content for one purpose is probably suboptimal for other objectives. Like software, XML often mirrors an ongoing business concern, and any fixed interface to a continuously adapting business is likely to drift out of phase with its business reality. XML doesn't preclude such impedance mismatches. Because manually slicing and dicing the data is not an effective means for delivering information on a regular basis, other methods must be employed. Much of the XML Starter Kit speaks to these methods. This chapter's project, though, focuses on consuming the XML as is . . . raw or uncooked as it were.

Open the XML wines catalog with your text editor or XML-editing tool. The start of the XML wines catalog file is shown in Figure 4-2. The XML file is included as `wines.xml`, along with the rest of the code for this chapter. Save this to a new file called `wines.xml` (in Notepad, select File➪Save As.)

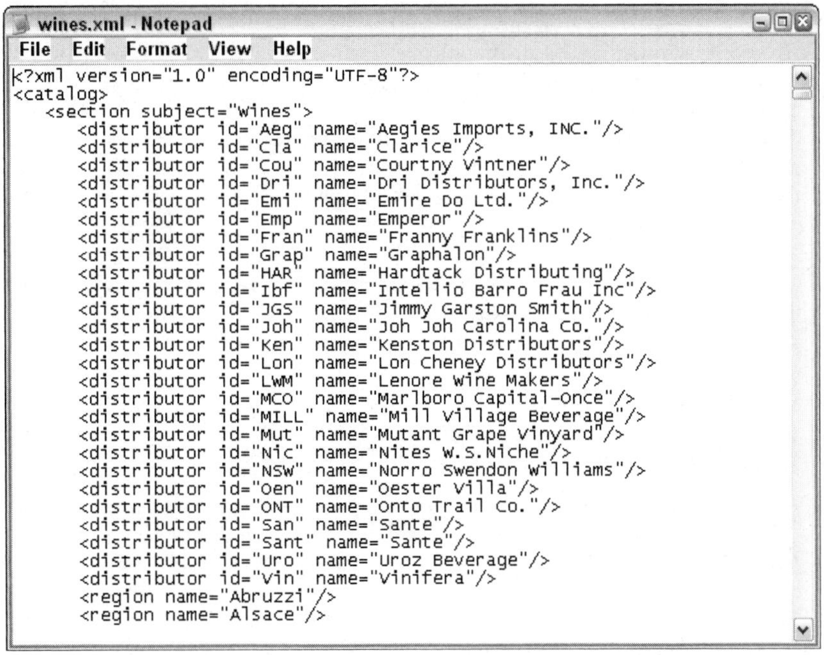

wines.xml - Notepad

File Edit Format View Help

```
<?xml version="1.0" encoding="UTF-8"?>
<catalog>
   <section subject="wines">
      <distributor id="Aeg" name="Aegies Imports, INC."/>
      <distributor id="Cla" name="Clarice"/>
      <distributor id="Cou" name="Courtny Vintner"/>
      <distributor id="Dri" name="Dri Distributors, Inc."/>
      <distributor id="Emi" name="Emire Do Ltd."/>
      <distributor id="Emp" name="Emperor"/>
      <distributor id="Fran" name="Franny Franklins"/>
      <distributor id="Grap" name="Graphalon"/>
      <distributor id="HAR" name="Hardtack Distributing"/>
      <distributor id="Ibf" name="Intellio Barro Frau Inc"/>
      <distributor id="JGS" name="Jimmy Garston Smith"/>
      <distributor id="Joh" name="Joh Joh Carolina Co."/>
      <distributor id="Ken" name="Kenston Distributors"/>
      <distributor id="Lon" name="Lon Cheney Distributors"/>
      <distributor id="LWM" name="Lenore Wine Makers"/>
      <distributor id="MCO" name="Marlboro Capital-Once"/>
      <distributor id="MILL" name="Mill Village Beverage"/>
      <distributor id="Mut" name="Mutant Grape Vinyard"/>
      <distributor id="Nic" name="Nites W.S.Niche"/>
      <distributor id="NSW" name="Norro Swendon Williams"/>
      <distributor id="Oen" name="Oester Villa"/>
      <distributor id="ONT" name="Onto Trail Co."/>
      <distributor id="San" name="Sante"/>
      <distributor id="Sant" name="Sante"/>
      <distributor id="Uro" name="Uroz Beverage"/>
      <distributor id="Vin" name="Vinifera"/>
      <region name="Abruzzi"/>
      <region name="Alsace"/>
```

Figure 4-2

After you have saved the file, begin removing the elements that won't be needed. Start with the distributor elements; delete all except:

```
<distributor id="Dri" name="Dri Distributors, Inc."/>
```

Then delete all of the regions except the following:

```
<region name="North Carolina"/>
```

Finally, remove all wineries except the Mad Melvin winery. For reference, here is what Melvin's winery element looks like:

```
<winery id="Melvin">
   <name>Mad Melvin's Muscadine Wines</name>
   <region>North Carolina</region>
   <country>United States</country>
</winery>
```

Following the winery elements are many wine elements. You only want to keep those wines produced by Melvin, or, to put it in XML, those `<wine>` elements that have a `<winery>Melvin</winery>` child. The first such wine is Smoky Scupp:

```
<wine id="Smoky_Scupp_750ml">
   <name>Smoky_Scupp</name>
   <varietal>Scupp</varietal>
   <vintage>1992</vintage>
   <winery>Melvin</winery>
   <distributor>Dri</distributor>
   <bottlesize>750ml</bottlesize>
</wine>
```

Keep most (if not all) of Melvin's `<wine>` elements, and discard the rest.

Do not delete the `</section>` and `</catalog>` end tags at the bottom of the file. If you do, the file will no longer be well-formed XML.

The resulting catalog has one winery (Mad Melvin's Muscadine Wines), its wines, its distributor, and region. Figure 4-3 shows how the file begins.

wines.xml - Notepad

File Edit Format View Help

```
<?xml version="1.0" encoding="UTF-8"?>
<?xml-stylesheet type="text/css" href="winelist.css"?>
<catalog>
   <section subject="Wines">

      <distributor id="Dri" name="Dri Distributors, Inc."/>


      <region name="North Carolina"/>
      <winery id="Melvin">
         <name>Mad Melvin's Muscadine Wines</name>
         <region>North Carolina</region>
         <country>United States</country>
      </winery>


      <wine id="Smoky_Scupp_750ml">
         <name>Smoky Scupp</name>
         <varietal>Scupp</varietal>
         <vintage>1992</vintage>
         <winery>Melvin</winery>
         <distributor>Dri</distributor>
         <bottlesize>750ml</bottlesize>
         <description>A dry red muscadine with hints of oak. A delicious
wine produced from a unique mix of Carlos and Magnolia Scuppernong
grapes. Blackberry aromas lead to fat, smoky flavors and long spicy
finish.</description>
      </wine>
```

Figure 4-3

Using the methods you learned in Chapter 3, verify that the file is still well-formed XML. If you are using an XML editor, you should have caught any editing errors already. Once you are done, you are ready to begin working on the presentation.

For the examples that follow, the wine list used actually consists of only three wines. The only difference is that a very short list prevents the bottom border from scrolling off the bottom, allowing both the top and bottom borders to show and making screen shots nice and tidy.

Wine List, First Draft

Load the raw XML wine catalog into a browser. The browser may show a tree view of the unstyled XML source, as shown in Figure 4-4, but it may also just show the raw source code.

```
  <?xml version="1.0" encoding="UTF-8" ?>
- <catalog>
  - <section subject="Wines">
      <distributor id="Dri" name="Dri Distributors, Inc." />
      <region name="North Carolina" />
    - <winery id="Melvin">
        <name>Mad Melvin's Muscadine Wines</name>
        <region>North Carolina</region>
        <country>United States</country>
      </winery>
    - <wine id="Smoky_Scupp_750ml">
        <name>Smoky Scupp</name>
        <varietal>Scupp</varietal>
        <vintage>1992</vintage>
        <winery>Melvin</winery>
        <distributor>Dri</distributor>
        <bottlesize>750ml</bottlesize>
        <description>A dry red muscadine with hints of oak. A delicious wine produced from a
          unique mix of Carlos and Magnolia Scuppernong grapes. Blackberry aromas lead to
          fat, smoky flavors and long spicy finish.</description>
      </wine>
    - <wine id="Raspberry_750ml">
        <name>Raspberry</name>
```

Figure 4-4

Add an `xml-stylesheet` processing instruction to the file, before the `<catalog>` start tag:

```
<?xml-stylesheet type="text/css" href="winelist.css"?>
```

Now if you reload the browser, you see the text content minus the XML tags. This is normal. You have taken control of the formatting, and all the elements are appearing as inline text by default.

Starting with the catalog element, refine this default appearance by editing the stylesheet. Open your favorite editor, and begin by saving an empty file as `winelist.css`, the name used earlier in the `xml-stylesheet href` pseudo-attribute. Then enter the following rule to select all the elements:

```
* {
   display: inline;
}
```

If you reload the browser now, the page should be a run-on block of text. What you've just done is taken a sledgehammer to the content and knocked out all the element delimiters. In the next few steps, you'll selectively add styles to the elements.

The catalog element acts as a top-level container for all of the others, so it makes sense to use this element to provide some common style options and to frame up the appearance. First, specify that the catalog needs to generate a box, and the box width should be about 33 characters wide. The CSS to do this looks like this:

```
catalog {
   display: block;
   width: 33em;
}
```

Don't stop now . . . the appearance is still run-on text, so there's still nothing much to see. You are also not done providing defaults. To "frame up" the wine list, add a default font, margin, and a border,

```
catalog {
   display: block;
   width: 33em;
   font: normal 12pt serif;
   margin: 120px;
   border: solid 2px gray;
}
```

The wine list should now look a bit more like it's the proper size and shape. However, the text content is still crammed together unattractively. Consider the first bit of text—Mad Melvin's Muscadine Wines—and that it comes from the `<winery><name>` element. The CSS selector to pick out this element is `winery > name` (a less specific selector is `winery name`, which works with IE6). You want the name to appear in a slightly larger font size:

```
winery name {
   font-size: 18pt;
}
```

However, the winery name is still crammed together with the text that follows. To prevent this from happening, treat the winery name as a block:

```
winery name {
   font-size: 18pt;
   display: block;
}
```

Much of the XML is contained in wine elements, so specify them as blocks as well:

```
wine {
   display: block;
}
```

This improves the appearance somewhat (see Figure 4-5). Text content is still crammed together, but at least the wine descriptions aren't a single run-on block of text.

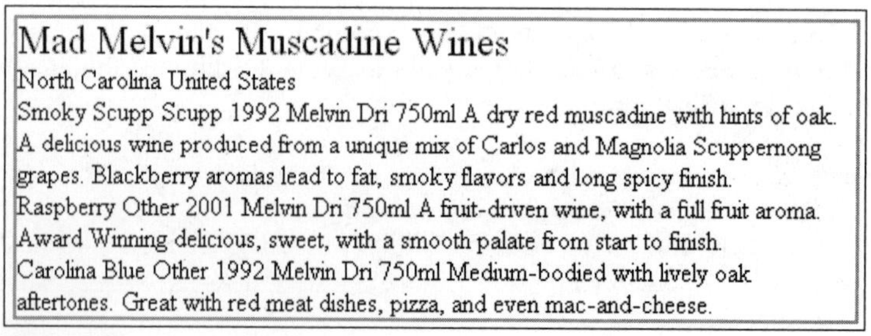

Mad Melvin's Muscadine Wines
North Carolina United States
Smoky Scupp Scupp 1992 Melvin Dri 750ml A dry red muscadine with hints of oak.
A delicious wine produced from a unique mix of Carlos and Magnolia Scuppernong
grapes. Blackberry aromas lead to fat, smoky flavors and long spicy finish.
Raspberry Other 2001 Melvin Dri 750ml A fruit-driven wine, with a full fruit aroma.
Award Winning delicious, sweet, with a smooth palate from start to finish.
Carolina Blue Other 1992 Melvin Dri 750ml Medium-bodied with lively oak
aftertones. Great with red meat dishes, pizza, and even mac-and-cheese.

Figure 4-5

There are still a few obvious improvements to make. First, make the wine varietal, country, region, vintage, and bottle size are displayed as blocks, and deemphasize the text by making the `font-size` smaller:

```
wine varietal, wine country, wine region,
wine vintage, wine bottlesize {
   display: block;
   font-size: 8pt;
}
```

Second, indent the description a bit on either side to make it easier to read:

```
wine description {
   display: block;
   margin-left: 2em;
   margin-right: 2em;
}
```

Reloading the page, you might notice the ragged right edge on the description text. This can be reduced by setting the `text-align` property to `justify`. Browsers sometimes interpret this by placing unattractive gaps between a small number of words, so using this property is left to your discretion.

Third, there are some things that a wine just doesn't want to advertise too loudly. Things like the wine's distributor, the winery (doesn't have to be repeated), and the bottle and case prices don't have to be displayed at all. To omit them, include a selector that sets the `display` property to `none`:

```
wine distributor, wine winery,
wine bottleprice, wine caseprice {
   display: none
}
```

Reload the page and take a peek. You should see something like Figure 4-6.

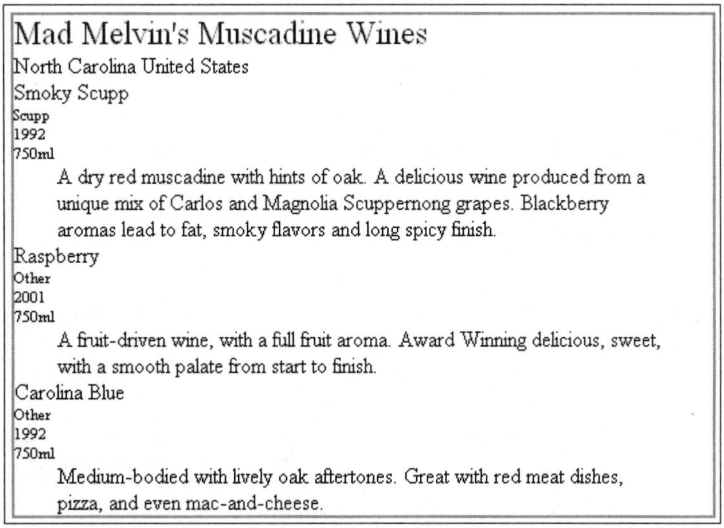

Mad Melvin's Muscadine Wines
North Carolina United States
Smoky Scupp
Scupp
1992
750ml
A dry red muscadine with hints of oak. A delicious wine produced from a unique mix of Carlos and Magnolia Scuppernong grapes. Blackberry aromas lead to fat, smoky flavors and long spicy finish.
Raspberry
Other
2001
750ml
A fruit-driven wine, with a full fruit aroma. Award Winning delicious, sweet, with a smooth palate from start to finish.
Carolina Blue
Other
1992
750ml
Medium-bodied with lively oak aftertones. Great with red meat dishes, pizza, and even mac-and-cheese.

Figure 4-6

The format of the Wine catalog file illustrates an issue in exchanging information using XML. Languages such as CSS that directly bind properties to existing structures are of limited use in dealing with the problems that arise from XML structures being misaligned with objectives. For that, two other closely related XML technologies apply: the XSL Transformation language (XSLT) and XQuery. They aren't silver bullets, but they do help mitigate the work involved in realigning content to fit expectations. XQuery is discussed in Chapters 8–10. XSLT and XSL are the subjects of the next few chapters.

Wine List, Second Draft

Reviewing the current form of the wine list, you might notice that the format is dependant upon the order and relative nesting of the original XML element structures. That is both a feature and a limitation of formatting with CSS directly. It is frequently impossible to achieve a particular layout without going back into the structure and making changes. But I digress. Make a list of issues to address, like this:

- The winery's name would look better centered.
- The region and country of the winery isn't really necessary.
- The name of the wine doesn't particularly stand out.
- There is too little padding around the inside of the border.

In CSS, padding is a space between the inside of the border and the content of a box. This sets a uniform gap between the border set earlier and all of the elements contained within it.

- Each wine's name is too close to the description above it.
- The varietal, year, and bottle size are a bit out of place and take up more space than necessary.
- The background looks rather plain and uninviting.

Starting with the winery region and country, deal with each item in turn. Centering the winery's name is just a matter of adding a `text-align` property to the existing `winery name` rule:

```
winery name {
   text-align: center;
}
```

If you haven't guessed already, you can remove elements from the wine list by setting the `display` property to `none`:

```
winery region, winery country {
   display: none;
}
```

Do something special to the wine name to make it stand out. Increasing the font size would make it compete with the winery's name, but it is easy to make the wine name bold and underline it:

```
wine name {
   font-weight: bold;
   text-decoration: underline;
}
```

The padding problem with the border is a little different. You can't just tweak every single element to increase its margin — it would be tedious and error prone to get the results just right. The answer is to go to a containing element, such as the catalog, and increase the padding:

```
catalog {
   padding: 0.8em;   /* a little less than one character space */
}
```

Similarly, the space between the description and the next wine name could be handled in terms of padding around the wine. However, that would push everything inward. Assuming that the description content is always relatively short, a more attractive alternative is to set a fixed height for the box. That would give the wine list a more open and consistent spacing, while not interfering with the space above the first wine name. Adding the following rule provides a fixed space for about eight lines of text:

```
wine description {
   height: 8em;
}
```

You could deal with the varietal, year, and bottle size simply by making them `display: inline`, but this presents a good opportunity to show yet another CSS feature: a *float*. Floats are boxes that are positioned as if they were inline, but are shifted off to the left or right side until they hit the edge of an absolutely positioned box or another floated box. Floats can quickly become quite complicated in practice, but the needs here are simple: `float` the bottle size and vintage off to the right. To set them off a bit, you can also provide a border on the bottom:

```
wine vintage, wine bottlesize {
   float: right;
   border-bottom: solid thin red;
}
```

Note that the year and bottle size now run together, and in some cases get uncomfortably close to the right edge of the description text. The space can be increased by padding both to the left. Add the `padding-left` property to the previous style rule:

```
wine vintage, wine bottlesize {
   float: right;
   border-bottom: solid thin red;
   padding-left: 1em;
}
```

That completes the basic layout of the wine list. If you have followed along, your wine list should look similar to Figure 4-7.

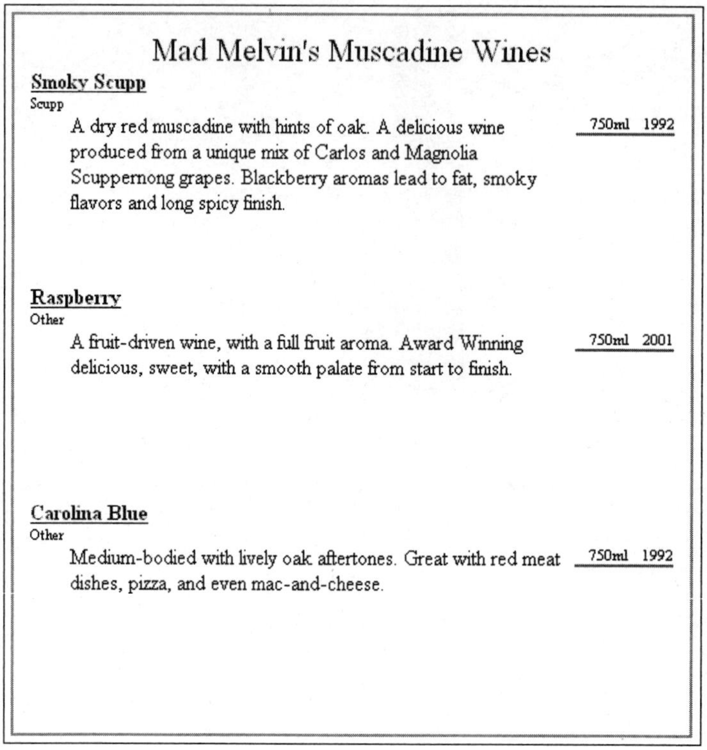

Mad Melvin's Muscadine Wines

Smoky Scupp
Scupp
A dry red muscadine with hints of oak. A delicious wine produced from a unique mix of Carlos and Magnolia Scuppernong grapes. Blackberry aromas lead to fat, smoky flavors and long spicy finish. 750ml 1992

Raspberry
Other
A fruit-driven wine, with a full fruit aroma. Award Winning delicious, sweet, with a smooth palate from start to finish. 750ml 2001

Carolina Blue
Other
Medium-bodied with lively oak aftertones. Great with red meat dishes, pizza, and even mac-and-cheese. 750ml 1992

Figure 4-7

It is admittedly a bit plain, but you aren't completely finished yet—there is still some decorating to be done.

Final Cut

There is one final touch to make before you're done. The wine list looks reasonably clean, but somewhat sterile. An almost universal practice when pitching the fruit of the grape is to show pictures of grapevines, or wine bottles and glasses. It should be something elegant and suggestive, to make the palate thirst in anticipation. It so happens that a small background image is available just for that purpose. To keep the text readable, the image in Figure 4-8 (`wine.png`) was deliberately prepared as a background image by giving it a washed out look.

CSS provides a special syntax for accessing external resources. In this case, the image URL can be specified in the `background-image` property as `url("wine.png")`. The `background-repeat` property determines whether the image is tiled, and how. The value `repeat` means it is tiled both horizontally and vertically. Here's the rule that sets the background image:

```
catalog {
    background-image: url("wine.png");
    background-repeat: repeat;
}
```

This final style rule completes the wine list. Figure 4-9 shows the result.

Figure 4-8

Mad Melvin's Muscadine Wines

Smoky Scupp
Scupp

A dry red muscadine with hints of oak. A delicious wine produced from a unique mix of Carlos and Magnolia Scuppernong grapes. Blackberry aromas lead to fat, smoky flavors and long spicy finish. 750ml 1992

Raspberry
Other

A fruit-driven wine, with a full fruit aroma. Award Winning delicious, sweet, with a smooth palate from start to finish. 750ml 2001

Carolina Blue
Other

Medium-bodied with lively oak aftertones. Great with red meat dishes, pizza, and even mac-and-cheese. 750ml 1992

Figure 4-9

The wine list presentation is finished, ready to be dropped into the decorated body of a web site, printed on delicate papers, or virtually imprinted in PDF files. Many other features can be added to the wine list, ranging from hover effects to hyperlinks, but that's all left as an exercise for you. Examples of some of these additional effects can be found in the files provided for this chapter.

This also represents the limit of what you can achieve in Internet Explorer without using additional supporting technologies such as Dean Edward's IE7 scripts or similar Internet Explorer–specific custom code.

Summary

The constraints imposed on the exercises in this chapter were deliberate. While providing an interesting experiment in page layout and a basis for a formatting model, CSS does not specifically address transformational requirements such as altering content, adapting structures, or computing complex arrangements. Still, it allows a separation of the concerns of style properties from concerns regarding the way information is expressed in XML. Due to this separation, the appearance of the wine list can be adapted with minimal or no need to change the XML. Conversely, element structures in the XML can be extended and modified, with little impact on the CSS styles. The model is successful enough to be adopted not only by web browsers but also other W3C recommendations, including the subject of a following chapter, XSL — the Extensible Stylesheet Language.

5

Converting XML Content Online

You just manually partitioned the wine product catalog to isolate the wines of one winery, Melvin's Muscadine Wines, and applied a non-XML syntax — Cascading Style Sheets — to alter the appearance of the elements for displaying. Now you'll see how to accomplish the partitioning automatically using an XML-based syntax called XSLT, the Extensible Stylesheet Transformations Language. You'll also discover how to enhance the output with XHTML (Extensible HyperText Markup Language), effectively bypassing some of the limitations of browsing straight XML using CSS alone.

Along the way, you'll also pick up some exposure to XPath, a concise expression syntax for specifying the parts of the XML that you want to process. Don't worry about getting bogged down in details: this chapter's project provides just enough XPath for you to get by. (There's a deeper discussion of XPath, and more-developed projects, in Chapters 8–10.)

Problem

The more distinctive a wine, the more it merits a unique presentation. A winery wants to highlight its achievements and characteristics with fidelity to the brand image. Unmodified XML structures can take you only so far in reaching those goals. In this chapter, you take your information delivery to the next step by changing the XML structure to serve the needs of a target audience. The focus is on automating changes to the XML, providing an increasingly refined look and feel to the presented information.

Presenting a Comprehensive View

The wine list in Chapter 4 leaves something to be desired. Specifically, although it can be delivered to a web browser, it lacks active hypertext links. There are also no documents to target with those hypothetical hyperlinks. The first problem, that of inserting hyperlinks, is used to illustrate the first XSLT stylesheet in the following section. You'll remedy the second problem by creating a data sheet, a kind of promotional card for a particular wine, in the final section. This section frames up the objectives and resources you'll need to accomplish this goal.

At the end of the chapter, you will have the means of recreating the original wine list as well as pages to promote individual wines through XSLT transformations. Hyperlinks should be utilized to allow the reader to navigate from the wine list to a wine of interest, and back again. The graphical depiction of the site map in Figure 5-1 shows the navigation enabled by adding hyperlinks.

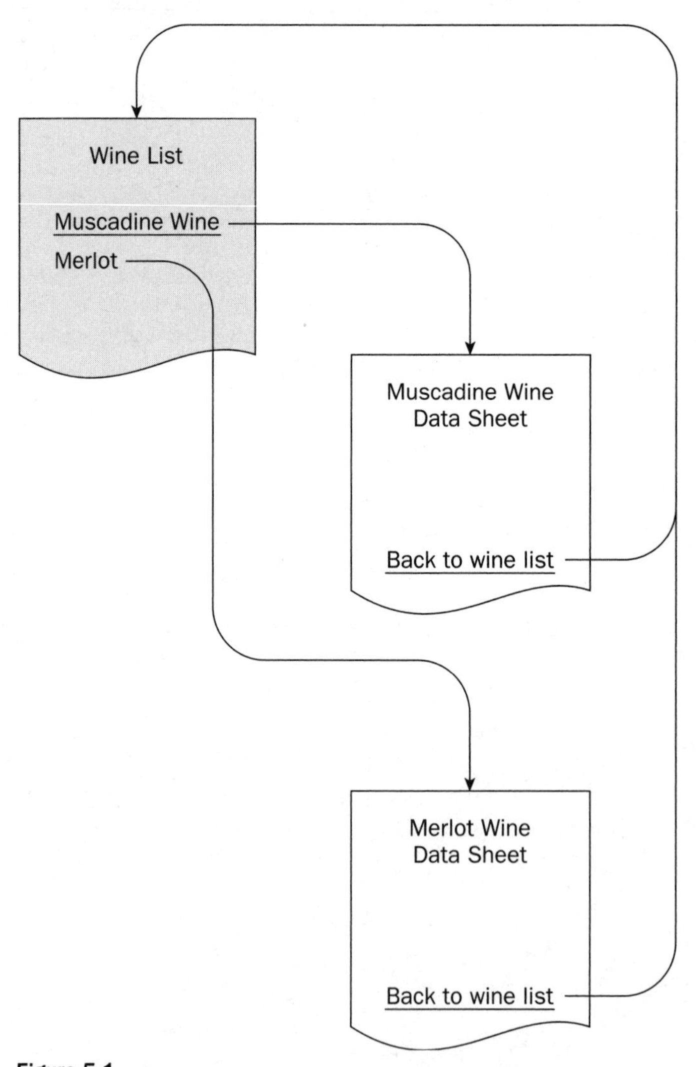

Figure 5-1

The promotional pages will act in a role similar to product data sheets, with enough information for the reader to make an informed buying decision. Approaching the problem as a data sheet strikes a middle ground between pure advertisement and an educational piece, making it more appealing to novices. Twists on the data sheet theme can also be used for in-store displays and in instruction manuals.

An example may be useful at this point to illustrate the objective. Figure 5-2 is a piece from a hypothetical cheese distributor named Black Forke. This cheese profile looks as if it is intended for inclusion in a sales agent's marketing kit. For demonstrating the XML transformations, the style is less important than the content. Indeed, as you'll see, the transformation process is devoid of style — it relies on the semantics of an external language to produce the final appearance.

It is evident from a careful inspection of the Black Forke cheese profile that there are several bits of information needed. Several decisions must be made about what to include, what to leave out, and how to compose the final winery piece. Also, because the data sheet is to be displayed in a web browser, a few XHTML techniques will be needed to accomplish the composition effectively. The next section, "Pertinent Wine Data," looks at the information you'll need.

Pertinent Wine Data

You can deduce several bits of information from the Black Forke promo piece that aren't evident in the XML wine catalog used in Chapter 4:

- The distributor's logo is featured prominently.
- The distributor's name and address are styled in a specific font.
- Informational disclosures notes regarding food coatings and nut allergen exposure are included (small print at bottom).
- In addition to objective characteristics of the product, subjective advice is included regarding usage.
- An image or portrayal of the product is featured as well.
- The background is set with a three-color blend to convey the distributor's brand image.

Some of these bits such as setting the background or font face for the distributor's name are purely stylistic. These topics are properly the domain of CSS, and are covered in Chapter 4. Graphic work such as blends and vector artwork are beyond the scope of this chapter. For simplicity, you can omit the background. Other graphics are introduced as they are needed by the text.

It is important to keep the piece simple, because people frequently scan more often than they read in depth. As much as reconfiguring the information in the XML, the transform must mask out unnecessary data. The kinds of information you can find in a wine element include:

- Wine name
- Varietal
- Bottle size and price
- Case price
- Description

Black Forke

Fine American Cheeses

Black Cow Smoked Jack

Style: Firm/Hard

Texture Profile: Moderately elastic

Taste Profile: Mellow; smoky; nutty overtones

Best for: Slicing; course grating for salads

Melting: Smooth melting characteristics

Available In 5lb rounds and 1lb wedges.

Call today for prices and specials.

Product of Black Cow Homestead Cooperative.

Black Forke
555 Mockingbird Lane
Rolesville, NC
(919) 555-1212

Coated with food grade wax.
Processed at a facility that also process nuts, including peanuts.

 Figure 5-2

It probably isn't wise to throw prices out in front of the consumer too early, so the bottle price and case price should be hidden. If you know the wine, you can look up the corresponding winery to find these kinds of information indirectly:

- Winery name
- Country
- Region

Most of the information is available in the `wine.xml` file. Rather than isolating these elements manually as you did in Chapter 4, let XSLT do the job. XSLT can pick out the elements as part of the transformation process, provided that you give it some hints. Specifying those hints is the purpose of XPath — but more on that in the next section.

There are a few bits of information that *aren't* present in the `wines.xml` file you've been using up to this chapter. This includes a wine label image and a winery logo. It isn't obvious how the images would fit in the present `wines.xml`. Wine label images and winery logos are graphical files most often found in a binary format. An example of a wine label is that of Americana Vineyards' Dry Riesling shown in Figure 5-3 (used with permission).

Figure 5-3

Used with the permission of Americana Vineyards & Winery

An example winery logo for Americana Vineyards is shown in Figure 5-4. Both graphic files have a non-XML binary format. It is possible to add attributes or child elements to `wines.xml` to point to these files, but it isn't necessary — given a consistent naming convention, XSLT can be made to compute the filename for you.

Figure 5-4

There is one more piece of information you need to consider. Like the Black Forke data sheet, the wine label includes warnings that are required by statute. Looking closely at the label in Figure 5-3, you will notice the presence of government warnings in the upper-right corner:

> **GOVERNMENT WARNING: (1) ACCORDING TO THE SURGEON GENERAL, WOMEN SHOULD NOT DRINK ALCOHOLIC BEVERAGES DURING PREGNANCY BECAUSE OF THE RISK OF BIRTH DEFECTS. (2) CONSUMPTION OF ALCOHOLIC BEVERAGES IMPAIRS YOUR ABILITY TO DRIVE A CAR OR OPERATE MACHINERY AND MAY CAUSE HEALTH PROBLEMS. *CONTAINS SULFITES.***

This is common on wine labels sold in the United States. The label already contains the proper warnings and need not be duplicated to meet the statute. Such warnings may well be included for health reasons. The last sentence in the wine label warning cautions that the product contains sulfites. Including the warnings enables people with chemical sensitivities to make intelligent choices.

For this chapter's project, the image names and warnings will be hard-coded in the XSLT. This is far less general because the image and logo apply only to one wine and winery and the sulfite caution may not apply to some wines, but it makes the project more straightforward. It should work well enough for the usage scenario of responding to a mouse click on a link to a specific wine data sheet. Parameters, which can be used to generalize information such as the image names and warnings, are discussed in more detail in Chapter 7.

Objective

The objective of the exercise is to rearrange the XML in such a way as to present a moderately good representation of a data sheet for use in an online display. Many of the XML elements in the wine catalog must be omitted, and some additional information added in the process.

The output of the transformation won't be the same old XML you've been dealing with in previous chapters. It includes hyperlinks between pages and is structured strictly for the purposes of presentation. HTML and CSS already serve that presentational purpose on a wide variety of browsers. The transform can generate well-formed HTML, allowing the largest possible audience access to the information.

Design

Raw XML is rarely suitable for direct presentation, and frequently must be reorganized, or *transformed*, to suit the needs of a specific output device. Ignoring for the moment the limitations of specific output devices, XML structures often need to be remodeled to suit the needs of specific audiences or process integration purposes. For instance, the wine list presented in Chapter 4 lacks any sort of web hyperlinks — they aren't present in the wine catalog XML, and CSS lacks the capability to insert them.

XSLT was developed with such requirements in mind. This chapter utilizes XSLT to provide a more refined wine list and data sheet than was possible with simple XML and CSS alone. An XSLT process consumes XML, applies a series of rules to construct an output tree (or trees), and provides the result in the form of XML or text.

Technical Motivation

Languages such as CSS lack the computational power to repurpose XML. Compiled languages such as Java, C#, and C++ require more time and consideration to deploy. Scripted languages such as Active Server Pages (ASP), PHP, and Perl similarly present a set of design considerations and trade-offs. XSLT presents a targeted solution to the specific problem of XML transformations. XSLT is also more approachable for nontechnical professionals than traditional programming languages are.

XSLT provides an effective procedure — a tree transformation process — for manipulating XML at the level of elements and attributes. A special-purpose language, XSLT has features that simplify the task of defining transformations of XML. Though it does not attempt to be a general-purpose programming language, XSLT addresses a broad and interesting range of XML manipulation problems.

Structure of Design

The process enabled by XSLT harks back to a mathematical construct known as a Turing machine, which is basically a model for an effective procedure that reads input from a tape, interprets instructions, and writes output. The process can be likened to duplicating audio or video tapes by connecting the output of a player to the input of a recorder.

This discussion is somewhat simplified and addresses XSLT 1.0 behavior. It applies to XSLT 2.0 as well, with the caveat that XSLT 2.0 provides more flexibility in how it manages the various trees used in the process. In some instances XSLT 2.0 also uses different terminology.

In the case of XSLT, the process takes an XML document as input and one or more XSLT stylesheet modules to provide the instructions that control what is output. Figure 5-5 illustrates the components in the process graphically. The XML input (on the left) is fed into an XML parser, resulting in a tree structure. Similarly, the XSLT instructions (at the top) are parsed as XML into a tree. Together, the two trees are used to guide and control the XSLT engine, which constructs a third tree, the result tree. The result tree is then serialized into an output in a text or XML syntax. The graphic depicts HTML output, which is a special method provided in XSLT for backward compatibility with older, non-XML-compliant HTML tools.

The central block in Figure 5-5 is an XSLT engine. In some programming environments, the XSLT engine consists of a library accessible through an application programming interface (API). An alternative that avoids fussing with programming is to use a command line XSLT tool. Many good open source tools, as well as commercially licensed XSLT systems, are available. The examples make use of Saxon, a leading XSLT engine developed by Michael Kay.

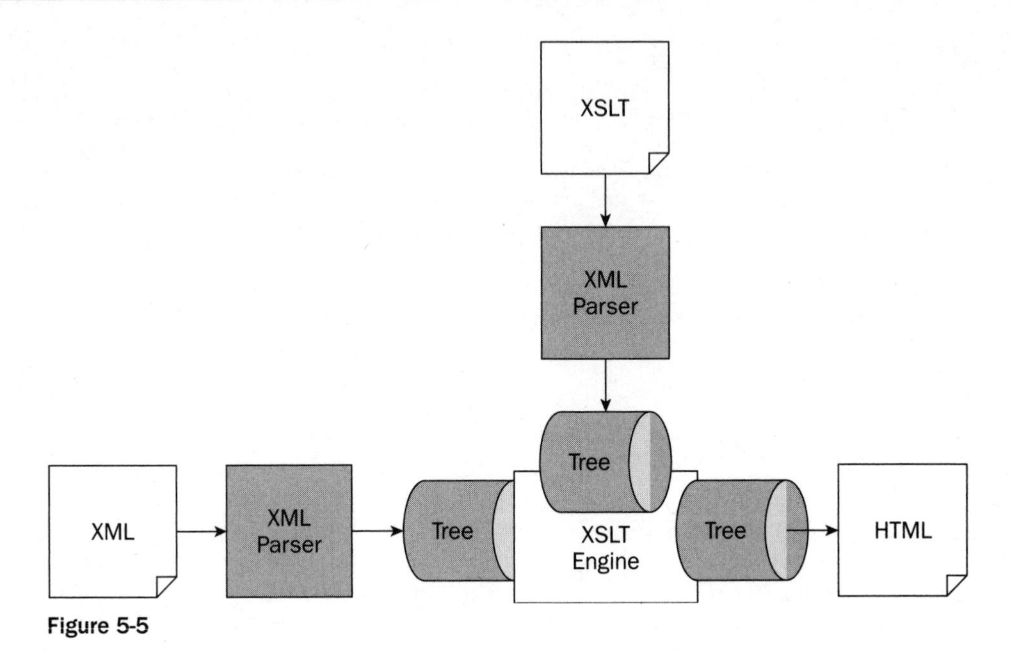

Figure 5-5

One XSLT Engine

Saxon currently comes in two variations. An advanced XML Schema–aware version, Saxon-SA, provides enhanced performance and is available under a commercial license. The version used in this book, Saxon-B, conforms to the basic level of XSLT 2.0, and is available under an open source license. The example command lines are written for Saxon-B (although Saxon-SA should work equally well).

Saxon can be downloaded for free from `http://saxon.sourceforge.net`. Saxon relies on Java, which you can download from `http://java.sun.com/j2se/1.5.0/download.asp`. After installing Java and Saxon, you'll need to set the `CLASSPATH` variable to include the `saxon8.jar` file. Under Windows XP, this can be done at the command line by using the `SET` command. In this example, `saxon8.jar` is installed under `C:\saxon`:

```
SET CLASSPATH=C:\saxon\saxon8.jar
```

Invoking Saxon from the command line is easy. You invoke `java`, providing the class name `net.sf.saxon.Transform`. The two required arguments are the name of the XML file and XSLT file. The `-o` option allows you to redirect output to a file rather than the screen:

```
java net.sf.saxon.Transform -o mynewwinelist.xml wines.xml winelist.xsl
```

Saxon may generate a warning that you are running an XSLT 1.0 stylesheet with an XSLT 2.0 processor. It does not affect the result of the transformation. To turn off the warning, use the `-w0` option in Saxon:

```
java net.sf.saxon.Transform -w0 -o mynewwinelist.xml wines.xml winelist.xsl
```

Chunky or GUI

A number of graphical XML editors and integrated development environments provide support for creating and running XSLT transformations. Examples include SyncRO Soft's Oxygen XML, DataDirect's Stylus Studio, and Altova's XML Spy. You won't need to install or use the command line XSLT engine if you use such a tool, but you will have to translate the command-line operations into the corresponding graphical mouse and menu actions.

Knowing how the components come together from a high level provides limited understanding of what's going on inside a transformation. Before working on the wine data sheet, take a look at what goes on under the covers and how XPath fits into solution.

XSLT Unwrapped

The final XML wine list in Chapter 4 suffers from a grievous shortfall with respect to online presentation: it lacks hyperlinks. This isn't a problem with the XML but reflects the reality that some popular browsers have limited or no XML capabilities. XSLT could be applied to mitigate the lame-duck browser problem by translating the original wine list into HTML . . . but that's jumping ahead a bit too far. For now, the objective is simply to illustrate how XSLT uses XPath to transform XML.

The following XSLT stylesheet can be applied to `wines.xml`, to duplicate it. This is a variation on a well-known XSLT idiom known as the *identity transform*. As with all well-formed XML, the XSLT file contains one top-level document element, `xsl:stylesheet`. The key part to focus on is the `xsl:template` element, shown in bold.

```
<xsl:stylesheet version="1.0" xmlns:xsl="http://www.w3.org/1999/XSL/Transform">

   <xsl:output method="xml" />

   <xsl:template match="* | @* | processing-instruction()">

      <xsl:copy>
         <xsl:apply-templates select="* | @* | text() | processing-instruction()"/>
      </xsl:copy>

   </xsl:template>

</xsl:stylesheet>
```

The identity transform can seem pretty arcane, but it demonstrates an important aspect of XSLT. Unlike many other computer languages, XSLT does a little bit of hand-holding by looking at the input XML and invoking templates that match the input to construct the output tree. The transformation process can be thought of as having a "loop" set into motion by structures found in the input XML.

Drawing upon the tape-duplication metaphor, consider what happens when music is remixed in a studio, or when soundtracks for movies are dubbed. Dubbing is a stepwise procedure in which the tape is moved to a particular point, and sounds are inserted or removed to form a new recording. XSLT's templates enable you to "dub" the XML by specifying the structures to be created at each stopping point. This internal activity is illustrated in Figure 5-6.

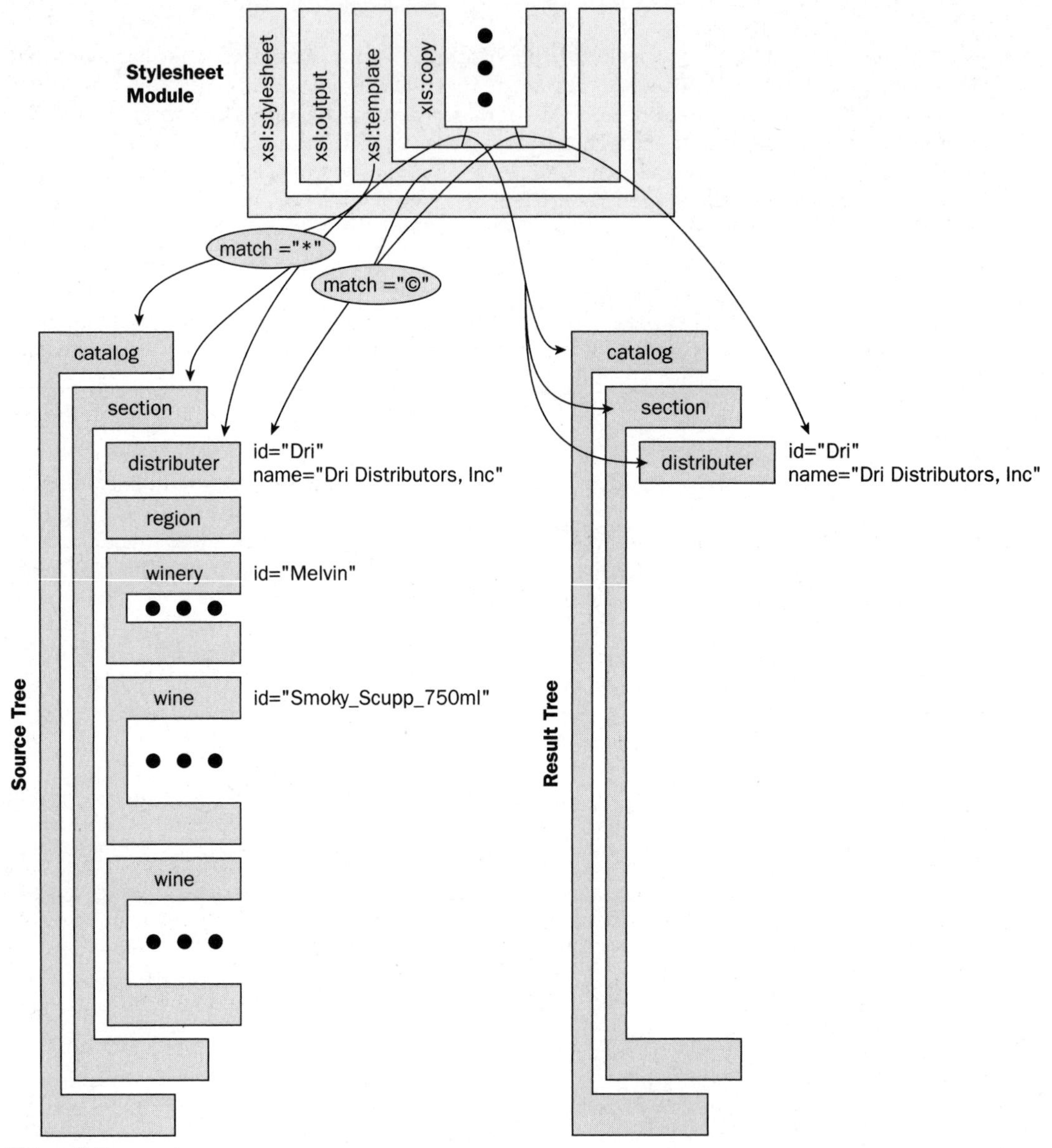

Figure 5-6

The template's `match` attribute specifies where the engine will stop. The `apply-templates` element is used to get the engine to look for more templates invoke, whereas the `select` attribute specifies the input XML at which the engine should continue. The `match` and `select` attributes are both kinds of XPath expressions.

> *Technically, the* `match` *attribute contains an XSLT pattern. Patterns are expected to refer only to child elements, descendants, or attributes. Certain kinds of XPath expressions, such as numeric expressions or string constants, also don't serve the purpose of matching XML structures.*

XPath Exposed

XPath expressions form a sort of connective tissue that ties the input and output to the backbone that is the XSLT process. It is a fairly concise syntax, meant for use within XML attributes. XPath is worthy of its own book, and only enough to cover what this project requires can be presented here. The following table provides a simplified summary of the XPath expressions used in this chapter. Bear in mind that some of these expressions may have more general interpretations with a more precise technical definition — the meanings given in the table apply to the limited usage you will see here.

XPath Expression	Meaning
`*`	Matches elements, like a wildcard
`@*`	Matches attributes, like a wildcard
`/`	Used alone or as the leftmost character, matches the document root; used between other expressions it separates steps along the path
`Wine`	Matches an element named `wine`
`@id`	Matches an attribute named `id`
`wine/name`	Location path; matches a name element, as a child of a wine element
`processing-instruction()`	Matches a PI (like the `<?xml-stylesheet` ... syntax used to connect a CSS stylesheet to the document)
`Text()`	Matches text content
`..`	Matches the parent element (if there is one)

Running a Transform

You can run a transform now to copy the `wines.xml` file, but that wouldn't be too interesting. What makes the identity transform interesting is that XSLT gives priority to templates that it judges to be better matches. You can use this to your advantage by adding a template that matches the wine `name` element and recreates `the wines.xml` file, with an XHTML <a> link inside of it:

```
<xsl:stylesheet version="1.0" xmlns:xsl="http://www.w3.org/1999/XSL/Transform">

   <xsl:output method="xml" />

   <xsl:template match="* | @* | processing-instruction()">

      <xsl:copy>
         <xsl:apply-templates select="* | @* | text() | processing-instruction()"/>
      </xsl:copy>

   </xsl:template>

   <xsl:template match="wine/name">
     <name>
      <a xmlns="http://www.w3.org/1999/xhtml"
         href="{../@id}.xhtml">
          <xsl:value-of select="."/>
      </a>
```

```
        </name>
    </xsl:template>

</xsl:stylesheet>
```

The XPath introduced here, `wine/name`, is known as a *location path*, which in this case consists of two element names separated by a slash character. The path indicates that the template should match any `name` elements that are also children of some `wine` element. This is a much more selective pattern than the wildcard `*` used in the first template, so when XSLT comes across wine names, it invokes the second template rather than the first.

Another special feature of XSLT is that it interprets curly braces inside literal XML as XPath expressions to be substituted in place. This syntax is known as an *attribute value template*. The expression inserts the wine `id` for the first part of the data sheet filename in the link's `href`. Remember this little bit of mapping for later; it is what you'll have to name the data sheets.

With the addition of the template to match the wine name, the transform is complete. Assuming that the XSLT stylesheet is saved as `winelist.xsl`, the command line given previously should still work:

```
java net.sf.saxon.Transform -o mynewwinelist.xml wines.xml winelist.xsl
```

Here is a fragment of the XML/XHTML output:

```
        <wine id="Smoky_Scupp_750ml">
            <name>
                <a xmlns="http://www.w3.org/1999/xhtml"
href="Smoky_Scupp_750ml.html">Smoky Scupp</a>
            </name>
            <varietal>Scupp</varietal>
            <vintage>1992</vintage>
            <winery>Melvin</winery>
            <distributor>Dri</distributor>
            <bottlesize>750ml</bottlesize>
            <description>A dry red muscadine with hints of oak. A delicious wine
produced from a unique mix of Carlos and Magnolia Scuppernong grapes. Blackberry
aromas lead to fat, smoky flavors and long spicy finish.</description>
        </wine>
```

Browsing the `mynewwinelist.xml` file using an XHTML-aware browser such as Mozilla/Firefox shows that the link is recognized (see Figure 5-7).

> *When a file is provided through a web server, the server usually (but not always) tells the browser how the type of data it contains should be displayed. When loading from a local file, browsers make a guess based on the file extension, perhaps interpreting the file as HTML and ignoring most of the markup, leaving the text crammed together.*

With more work, the entire XML file could be converted to XHTML (or to HTML suitable for Internet Explorer). One of the nicer aspects of working with XSLT is that changes can often be made in small increments, with little unintentional interaction between templates to hamper progress. As more templates are added to match the XML elements, you could even remove the wildcard template. That's left as an exercise for you.

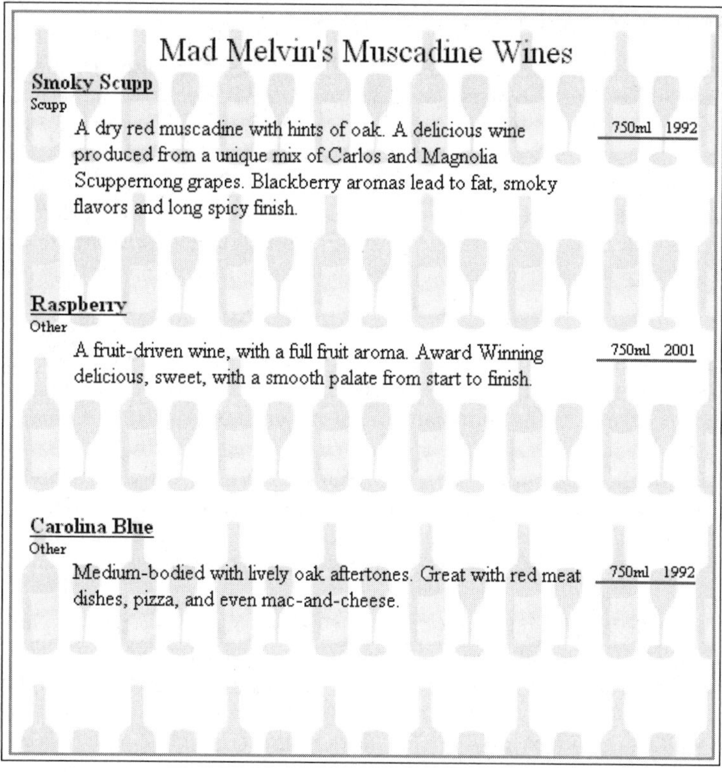

Figure 5-7

Applicable Technologies

The key technologies used in this chapter are XSLT transformations (also called XSLT stylesheets), and the XPath expression language. Bits of HTML and XHTML are useful to know as well, but the choice of which to use is somewhat coincidental (and to a large extent determined by who you expect to receive the output).

For the purposes of the project in this chapter, refer to the 1.0 versions of each of the following W3C Recommendations:

- XSLT 1.0 — `www.w3.org/TR/xslt`
- XPath 1.0 — `www.w3.org/TR/xpath`
- XHTML 1.0 — `www.w3.org/TR/xhtml1`

XSLT 2.0 (`www.w3.org/TR/xslt20`) and XPath 2.0 (`www.w3.org/TR/xpath20`) are candidate recommendations Because they are candidate recommendations, some features of XSLT 2.0 and XPath 2.0 may change, but leading XSLT vendors such as Saxonica and Oracle are implementing the new features in their products.

Design Consequences

Introducing a transformation process — whether XSLT or not — has a number of technological and logistical consequences. Chief among such issues is that you need to decide on a platform on which to deploy the code. Fortunately, XSLT is provided as a feature in a great many server platforms and browser clients.

There are downsides to the aspect of built-in behavior in the XSLT engine, particularly as it concerns developers who are unfamiliar with the history of similar languages. Developers who code in a procedural style may find the application of template rules a stumbling block rather than a welcome addition to their toolkit.

Many XSLT engines read in all of the XML and all of the XSLT transform modules, prior to execution. The dual effects of this are that large, naive transformations can have a fairly long lag time prior to output being evident, and large XML inputs can use up an enormous amount of memory. Certain XPath expressions such as `//`, `following-sibling`, and `preceding-sibling`, act like loops, forcing an XSLT engine to search through a large number of XML elements. A little analysis can help you steer clear of resource bottlenecks, and various optimized implementations are available to address special performance needs. For more advice on performance, look at the performance topic in section 4 of Dave Pawson's XSL FAQ page at `www.dpawson.co.uk/xsl/sect4/index.html`.

XSLT implies a separate processing step (or multiple processing steps), in which information can be culled, masked out, merged, or otherwise manipulated. This also holds true for general-purpose programming languages, although XSLT seems to bring about greater separation of presentational concerns from storage and retrieval concerns. Some XSLT server implementations also encourage more modular designs and better partitioning of functionality, leading to increased flexibility and a better capability to respond to business needs.

You haven't learned everything there is to know about XSLT, but the next section provides you with a better understanding of the details.

Solution

First, take a look at the template for the desired data sheet, shown in Figure 5-8. Documents displayed in a browser can be scrolled, so the implied pagination is coincidental — the page can be as long as it needs to be to fit the data.

It is worth noting that several of the visual elements are positioned with quite a bit of blank space in between. This is intentional and requires that the output use either HTML tables or CSS for positioning. Tables are somewhat painful to compose properly, so the project relies on CSS positioning for the layout effects.

Next, let's review the data from which the data sheet is constructed.

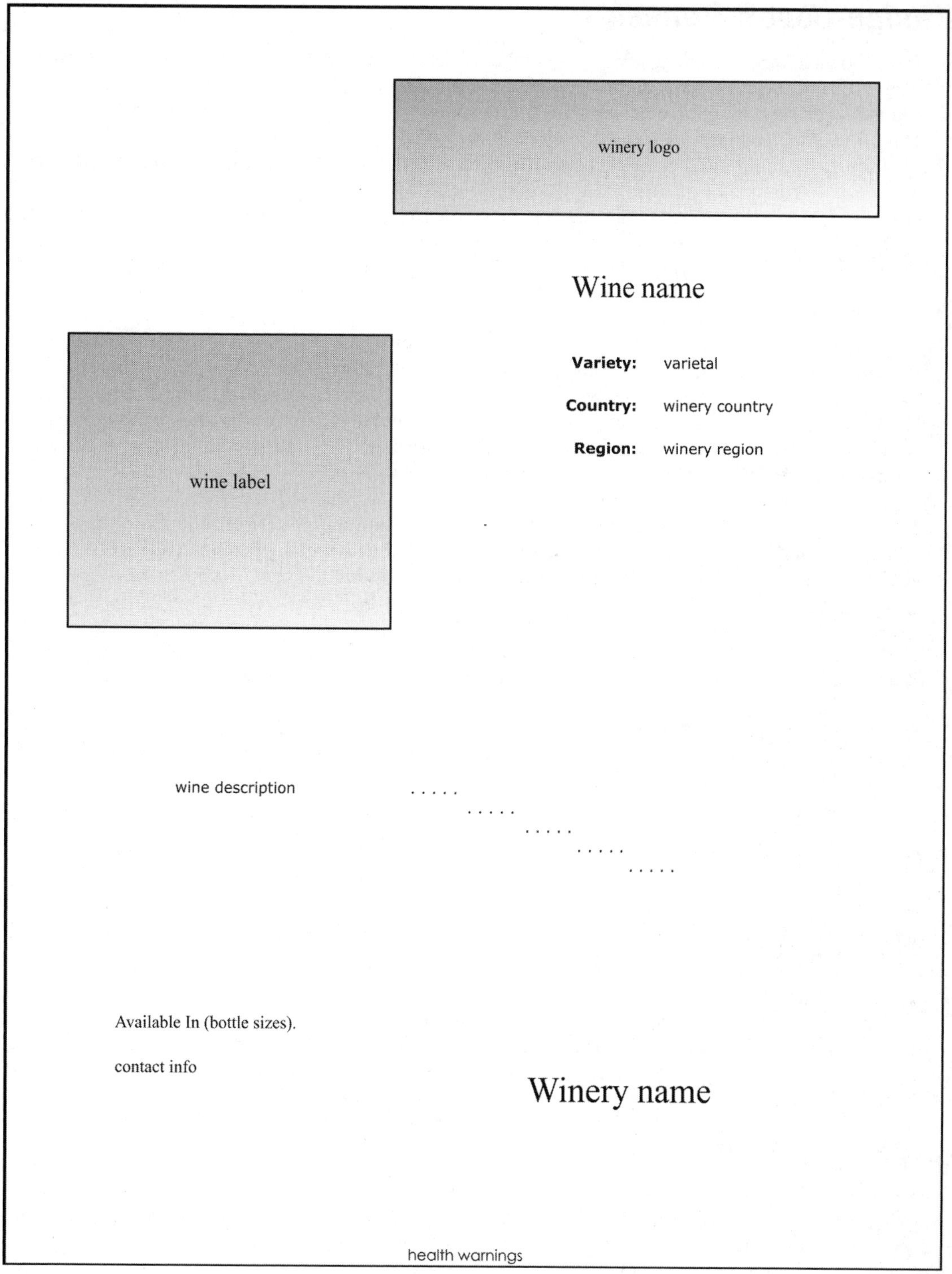

winery logo

Wine name

wine label

Variety: varietal

Country: winery country

Region: winery region

wine description . . . . .
. . . . .
. . . . .
. . . . .
. . . . .

Available In (bottle sizes).

contact info

Winery name

health warnings

Figure 5-8

Product Data: Raw XML

There isn't actually a lot to say about the raw XML, because it hasn't changed from the wine catalog XML used in Chapter 4. Most of the elements have already been identified. Two additional bits are needed: warnings, and image filenames.

To simplify the handling of warnings, include them as text within the XSLT transform.

The wine label and winery logo filenames must be determined. Recall from the earlier discussion how the wine list stylesheet used the wine `id` attribute to compute an HTML filename:

```
<a ... href="{../@id}.xhtml">
```

The way the filename used within the `href` attribute is constructed — concatenating the wine `id` with the suffix `.xhtml` in this case — is completely up to you as the stylesheet designer. It is highly unlikely that an external supplier providing wine labels and winery logos follows that method of naming its files. However, it is not unreasonable to expect that for images extracted from a database or content management system the names have some predictable format. (If not, the names would have to be included explicitly in any XML that referenced the images.)

The project assumes that logos and labels follow a similar naming convention, and that they are located in a subdirectory called images. Further assuming that all the images are provided as PNG files, an attribute value template to format one of these filenames would look very much like the following:

```
<a ... href="images/{../@id}.png">
```

Here's the list of the information you need:

- Wine name
- Varietal
- Bottle size and price
- Case price
- Description
- Winery name
- Country
- Region
- Wine label
- Winery logo
- Warnings

Online Data Sheet

You've seen bits of XSLT and XPath, and even used a stylesheet to articulate the wine list with XHTML hyperlinks. The identity transform (`winelist.xsl`) may seem obscure, but it is an important item in your toolkit. The next stylesheet has a bit more of a procedural style.

Preparing a Transform

As you saw earlier, an XSLT module, called a *stylesheet module*, is frequently also called a *transform*. Begin by editing a new file, `datasheet.xsl`. The `xsl:stylesheet` element is the document element representing the transform:

```
<?xml version="1.0">
<xsl:stylesheet
```

```
    version="1.0"
    xmlns:xsl="http://www.w3.org/1999/XSL/Transform"
    >

</xsl:stylesheet>
```

XSLT is well-formed XML, so you need the XML declaration, but not a DOCTYPE declaration. The version attribute identifies this module as an XSLT 1.0 stylesheet.

Many processors now support version 2.0 as well. It makes little difference which version is used for this project.

xmlns:xsl looks like an attribute but isn't treated like one. It is the namespace declaration for the prefix xsl, which is used in this file for all of the XSLT elements. What is required is that the string http://www.w3.org/1999/XSL/Transform be assigned, and that the xsl part of xmlns:xsl correspond to the prefixes used on the XSLT elements. The choice of the xsl prefix is somewhat arbitrary, but it follows a convention used in the XSLT 1.0 Recommendation. Besides, using the xsl convention makes it easier to cut and paste sample code.

The xsl:stylesheet element is only the start of the basic skeleton that you need for writing transforms. The next decision you must make is what method the XSLT engine should use when the result tree is output. This is controlled through the xsl:output element.

xsl:output is only allowed as a child of the top-level xsl:stylesheet (or xsl:transform) element. There are a variety of attributes that can be set for various options, including whether a DOCTYPE is output (doctype-public, doctype-system), how the output is indented (indent), and the preferred character encoding (encoding). You can omit most of them and work with the defaults. Because the intent is to create XHTML, you should make sure it outputs well-formed markup by setting the method attribute to xml:

```
<xsl:stylesheet
    version="1.0"
    xmlns:xsl="http://www.w3.org/1999/XSL/Transform"
    >

    <xsl:output method="xml" />

</xsl:stylesheet>
```

To Template or Not to Template

XSLT provides two other means of creating transformation modules. The first, xsl:transform, is merely an alternative element with the same attributes and meaning as xsl:stylesheet. Which element you use, xsl:stylesheet or xsl:transform, is a matter of taste.

The second method of creating a stylesheet known as *Literal Result Element as Stylesheet* (or Simplified Stylesheet Module in XSLT 2.0 nomenclature). The simplified form lacks template rules, being the equivalent of a single, top-level template applied against the document root. It can be useful for design-by-example or for fill-in-the-blanks scenarios in which values are plugged into a boilerplate design (report writers, for example). Michael Kay's excellent *XSLT 2.0 Programmer's Reference* (Wrox) book has a good example of a fill-in-the-blanks stylesheet using this method.

An output method of `html` *is also available. Don't use it unless you are targeting an older HTML browser because the output uses the older style HTML syntax, which allowed elements like* `<br>`, `<img>`, *and* `<p>` *to omit their end tags. In other words, the* `html` *output method is a concession to older browsers, but the output is not well formed.*

The XHTML output belongs in a particular namespace. Just as you declared the XSLT namespace, you need to include a declaration for XHTML. You can use a prefix, and that is probably a good idea, but for the sake of simplicity this stylesheet doesn't use one. Because all of the XSLT elements are already explicitly qualified, you can just declare the XHTML namespace as the default. Then any literal elements you include that do not have prefixes pick up the XHTML namespace by default. The namespace declaration is placed within the `xsl:stylesheet` element:

```
<xsl:stylesheet
   version="1.0"
   xmlns:xsl="http://www.w3.org/1999/XSL/Transform"
   xmlns="http://www.w3.org/1999/xhtml"
   >

   <xsl:output method="xml" />

</xsl:stylesheet>
```

Believe it or not, this is a complete stylesheet module, just waiting to be executed. Remember that XSLT does a little facilitation of the processXSLT also implicitly defines default templates that process nodes such as the document root, elements, and text in the absence of user-defined code. The result of running this stylesheet:

```
java net.sf.saxon.Transform wines.xml datasheet.xsl | more
```

is that the text content is stripped of its enclosing markup tags (but not the white space). Note that XSLT provides an XML declaration as well, because the `xsl:output` element tells it to do so. The default templates allow the transformation process to navigate through the entire XML input tree and construct a (more or less) significant result tree. Here's an example of the output (white space has been trimmed for brevity):

```
<?xml version="1.0" encoding="utf-8"?>
            Mad Melvin's Muscadine Wines
         North Carolina
         United States
         Smoky Scupp
         Scupp
         1992
         Melvin
         Dri
         750ml
         A dry red muscadine with hints of oak. A delicious wine produced from a
unique mix of Carlos and Magnolia Scuppernong grapes. Blackberry aromas lead to
fat, smoky flavors and long spicy finish.
```

The output is actually quite meaningful, although not very pretty. However, it isn't well-formed XML, and it doesn't include any XHTML presentational elements. Also, it includes much more information than is needed by the data sheet. Let's try to trim it town. What you need are some templates of your own to override the defaults.

Navigating the XML Tree

The principle organizing element in an XSLT transformation is `xsl:template`. Templates can be called like functions (more on that later on), but a more common practice is to let the XSLT engine apply templates that can be matched against XML input structures. The `match` attribute holds the pattern used to determine whether a template should apply. While the data sheet is a two-dimensional layout, the XHTML from which it is to be constructed is a hierarchical, well-formed XML document. It makes sense then, to start from the top, or the root, of the document, and the match pattern for the top is a single forward-slash (`/`):

```
<xsl:template match="/">

</xsl:template>
```

Insert this new template in the `datasheet.xsl` stylesheet, and run it. Did you get the same output? If you didn't get an error, then you should see a lonely XML declaration, with no other output:

```
<?xml version="1.0" encoding="utf-8"?>
```

You killed the transformation process! By defining a template that matches the root of the tree, you blocked the default template that would have been applied. The default template is equivalent to this:

```
<xsl:template match="* | /">
   <xsl:apply-templates/>
</xsl:template>
```

The default template basically tells the XSLT engine not to stop, but to keep looking for more templates that match the input. The default rule makes it look like some invisible force is navigating all of the branches of the XML source tree. When your template doesn't call `xsl:apply-templates`, that navigation stops, effectively "pruning" the branches below the element(s) in the XML tree that had matched the template. Because the document root is at the conceptual top of the tree, above even the document element, your template pruned the whole tree.

It is pretty easy to correct that sort of mistake. First, put in some basic XHTML document structure:

```
<xsl:template match="/">
   <html>
   <body>

   </body>
   </html>
</xsl:template>
```

Then, ask the engine to `apply-templates`. Place `apply-templates` within the body element so that the result tree that is generated is properly nested in the XHTML document:

```
<xsl:template match="/">
   <html>
   <body>
      <xsl:apply-templates/>
   </body>
   </html>
</xsl:template>
```

The result of running this version of the stylesheet is a well-formed XHTML document. Other than the XHTML wrapping the output, it should look very much the same as the plain-text result prior to adding the `/` template. Now you can begin checking the results of each transformation with a good XHTML-aware browser. This is enough to begin navigating down the XML source tree.

Parameterizing a Transform

Continuing down the tree, you can leave the catalog element to the default template rule. The next element nested within the catalog is the section that contains the interesting elements: the region, winery, and wine. Check the design sketch in Figure 5-8. The objective is to compose a data sheet for a single wine.

The wine catalog structure allows for multiple wines and wineries. The goal here is a one-shot process, so what is needed is a way to parameterize the stylesheet, to make XSLT process only one winery. It happens that XSLT allows stylesheet parameters, using a top-level element called `xsl:param`:

```
<xsl:stylesheet
   version="1.0"
   xmlns:xsl="http://www.w3.org/1999/XSL/Transform"
   xmlns="http://www.w3.org/1999/xhtml"
   >

   <xsl:output method="xml" />

   <xsl:param name="wineid">Nags_Head_Scuppernong_750ml</xsl:param>

   <xsl:template match="/">
      <html>
      <body>
         <xsl:apply-templates/>
      </body>
      </html>
   </xsl:template>

</xsl:stylesheet>
```

It isn't necessary to have a default value, but it will save a bit of typing later on. To override the default from the saxon command line, append a simple assignment following the stylesheet argument:

```
java net.sf.saxon.Transform wines.xml datasheet.xsl wineid=@@
Nags_Head_Scuppernong_750ml
```

Parameters are not much good unless you can use them to control conditional behavior. XSLT has a number of ways to provide conditional behavior. As you saw in the wine list example, XPath can also be used to select what is processed. One XPath expression that applies here is the predicate, which acts as a filter on the list of nodes returned.

Predicates are appended to an XPath expression using square brackets. Inside the brackets, another expression is evaluated within the context of the part of the expression immediately to the left. Simple comparisons that evaluate to `false` cause nodes to be filtered out.

The `apply-templates` command invoked in the section template then uses a predicate to compare the value of the `wineid` parameter to the wine's `id` attribute. Parameters are referenced by prefacing them with a single dollar sign (`$`):

```
<xsl:template match="section">
   <xsl:apply-templates select="wine[@id=$wineid]"/>
</xsl:template>
```

Run the transform again (you don't need to include the `wineid` parameter on the command line because it was also set as the default):

```
java net.sf.saxon.Transform wines.xml datasheet.xsl
```

The output should be much smaller now, showing only the data for the Nags Head Scuppernong product. This is what you want, because the CSS absolute positioning method used would otherwise run all of the wines on top of one another. Using JavaScript techniques, there might be an advantage to doing that — one could flip the `display` property on and off without having to reload the data sheets page by page — but that isn't XML- or XSLT-specific and is left as an exercise for you. There is enough fun to be had in positioning the Nags Head product.

Document or Root?

The `"/"` pattern may seem to match the `catalog` element (the top-level document element in the project), but it actually matches the root of the source tree, a node introduced by the XPath data model that sits above the document element. If this node weren't present, things that precede the document element such as comments, processing instructions, and `DOCTYPE` declarations would be difficult to attach to the tree. You can test the difference with a template that matches `catalog` but that doesn't invoke `apply-templates`:

```
<xsl:template match="catalog"/>
```

The XHTML wrapper still comes out — an indication that the root (/) match still occurred — but the rest of the catalog is pruned off.

Formatting

As noted earlier, XSLT lacks any built-in style semantics. To format an output, you have to pick an application format or language with which to express the layout. This chapter targets a simple XHTML format using inline CSS styles. Don't confuse XSLT with the characteristics (and limitations) of XHTML or CSS. The XSLT transformation is not limited to creating XHTML output. Other formats and languages that can be expressed as text or in XML syntax can be created as well. XHTML and CSS are simply convenient means to an end.

CSS supports formatting methods called absolute positioning and floats. The XSLT transformation uses the CSS properties as values for XHTML style attributes. Rather than create a separate CSS stylesheet as was done in Chapter 4, the styles are included inline with the XHTML code. You're free to tweak the styles, but if you don't completely grok CSS, just copy the values provided. The particulars of CSS are incidental to the transformation process.

Having invoked `apply-templates` for the Nags Head Scuppernong wine element (and only that element), you need a template to match. It isn't necessary to use a pattern to match just the Nags Head Scuppernong wine. In XSLT 1.0, the predicate used earlier isn't even possible, because patterns aren't allowed to contain references to parameters. The predicate used earlier to filter `apply-templates` is sufficient. A template that matches wines is all that is needed:

```
<xsl:template match="wine">

</xsl:template>
```

Here's where things get interesting from a style perspective. Note in the Figure 5-8 template sketch that the wine label is supposed to appear about a quarter of the way down the page. On a 1024x768 screen, that's 192 pixels down. A quick guess puts the left edge at about 50 pixels in. The style for this is:

```
position: absolute; left: 50px; top: 200px;
```

The wine label may be slightly oversized for your needs; that can (and should) be fixed with a graphical editor, but a quicker fix is simply to constrain one dimension to a maximum size. A width of 288 pixels looks pretty good.

Because CSS is incidental to the XSLT transformations, style calculations won't be discussed anymore.

Recall that the labels are located in an images subdirectory. The names are derived directly from the wine `id` attribute. An XHTML `img` tag is needed, and as with the wine list, you can use an attribute value template for the `src` attribute to compose the filename:

```
<xsl:template match="wine">

    <img src="images/{@id}.png" style="position: absolute; left: 50px; top: ⮐
200px; width: 288px;" />

</xsl:template>
```

To the right of the wine label and slightly higher on the page is the winery logo. The logos are located in an images subdirectory, and the names are derived directly from the `id` attribute. In the `wines.xml` file are two elements named winery, each with its own purpose. One represents a winery, while the other, a child of the wine element, represents a reference. The value of the latter is identical to the `id` attribute of the former. That's enough information to create a template and an `img` to display the logo:

```
<xsl:template match="wine">
    <img src="images/{@id}.png" style="position: absolute; left: 50px; top:
200px; width: 288px;" />

    <img src="images/{winery}.png" style="position: absolute; top: 50px; ⮐
left: 380px; height: 72px;" />

</xsl:template>
```

Notice the difference in the attribute value templates for each image? The second image references the content of the winery that is a child of the wine element. Both expressions are XPath expressions.

Beside the wine label, the design sketch shows a slightly more complicated arrangement, with the wine name displayed as a subheading, aligned on the left side with a group of fields and their labels aligned along a center line. The effect can be achieved by positioning a `div` and then nesting the vertically aligned labels and field values together. Here's the basic structure:

```
<xsl:template match="wine">

    <img src="images/{@id}.png" style="position: absolute; left: 50px; top:
200px; width: 288px;" />

    <img src="images/{winery}.png" style="position: absolute; top: 50px; left:
380px; height: 72px;" />

    <div style="position: absolute; left: 455px; top: 150px;">
        <h2> </h2>

        <div>
            <div style="float: left; text-align: right; font-weight: bold; ⮐
line-height: 2em;">Variety:<br/>
                Country:<br/>
                Region:<br/>
            </div>
            <div style="float: left; text-align: left; margin-left: 20px; ⮐
line-height: 2em;">

            </div>
        </div>
    </div>
</xsl:template>
```

The wine name heading, and field values need to be plugged in. You can use `apply-templates` with `select` for that, as in:

```
<xsl:template match="wine">

    <img src="images/{@id}.png" style="position: absolute; left: 50px; top: ⮐
200px; width: 288px;" />

    <img src="images/{winery}.png" style="position: absolute; top: 50px; ⮐
left: 380px; height: 72px;" />

    <div style="position: absolute; left: 455px; top: 150px;">
```

```
        <h2><xsl:apply-templates select="name"/></h2>

        <div>
           <div style="float: left; text-align: right; font-weight: bold; ⮐
line-height: 2em;">Variety:<br/>
              Country:<br/>
              Region:<br/>
           </div>
           <div style="float: left; text-align: left; margin-left: 20px; ⮐
line-height: 2em;">

           </div>
        </div>
     </div>
  </template>
```

Recall that XSLT defines default templates that allow the XSLT processor to navigate through the entire XML document tree. The default template will plug the wine name into the `h2` heading, which is fine. Had there been a template specifically for the wine name, the XSLT processor would have invoked that template instead, inserting the result into the `<h2>` tags. That isn't always what you want. For instance, after looking at the output you may want to insert a template that shows the wine name in a small font somewhere else on the page. If the result from the new template were to end up inside the `<h2>` tags, the output inside the heading would change in an unexpected way. To avoid this potential problem, bypass XSLT's template matching altogether by using the `xsl:value-of` element.

Using xsl:value-of

The `xsl:value-of` element is used to extract values directly from XML elements and attributes. No templates are called when `xsl:value-of` is invoked, so the value inserted can't be changed accidentally (or on purpose) by adding or changing other templates. Like `xsl:apply-templates`, it has a `select` attribute that takes an XPath expression. The result of evaluating the expressing is placed in the result tree at that point.

The varietal is a simple example:

```
  <xsl:template match="wine">

     <img src="images/{@id}.png" style="position: absolute; left: 50px; top: 
200px; width: 288px;" />

     <img src="images/{winery}.png" style="position: absolute; top: 50px; left: 
380px; height: 72px;" />

     <div style="position: absolute; left: 455px; top: 150px;">
        <h2><xsl:apply-templates select="name"/></h2>

        <div>
           <div style="float: left; text-align: right; font-weight: bold; ⮐
line-height: 2em;">Variety:<br/>
              Country:<br/>
              Region:<br/>
           </div>
```

```
            <div style="float: left; text-align: left; margin-left: 20px; ↵
line-height: 2em;">
                <xsl:value-of select="varietal"/><br/>

            </div>
        </div>
    </div>
</template>
```

Getting the value of the country or the region is more complicated. Neither is a child of the wine element. Both `country` and `region` are nested under the `winery` element: a winery has a country and a region. Both the `winery` and the `wine` elements are nested within the same `section` element. The XPath expression `..` can be used within the template matching `wine` to refer to the `section`, and a `country` or `region` relative to the `section`. The `..` is an abbreviated syntax, short for `parent::node()`, which selects the parent of the element (or attribute) currently being processed. Here is an example of how to use the `..` syntax to access the region.

```
<xsl:value-of select="../winery/region"/>
```

The problem is that this gets all of the wineries, not just the one you need. You need to cross-reference the two winery elements, so that you can get access to the winery's country and region. There are workable solutions using predicates, but you can let the XSLT engine do the work for you by declaring a key.

Using Keys

A *key* is a method of cross-referencing by means of a value that can be found or computed from the structures to be referenced. A key is essentially an index into the XML structures created by the XSLT engine in response to a top-level `xsl:key` element. After a key is declared with `xsl:key`, the `key()` function can be used in XPath expressions to obtain elements (or attributes or text nodes) that match a key value. The basic form is:

```
<xsl:key name="keyname" match="pattern" use="valueexpression" />
```

The `use` attribute determines the key value for the structure matched by the pattern. The `key()` function can be called to find all structures that fit the pattern and that possess a given value. `key()` gets two parameters: the name of the key (declared using `xsl:key`) and an expression evaluating to a value to use as a cross-reference. The second parameter can be a string or nodes that can be converted to a string for the comparison:

```
key( keyname, valueexpression)
```

Because there are two different winery element types, the pattern could pick up winery elements that represent the cross-references. In the `wines.xml` data, the `use` expression will marginalize these false hits, but the match pattern should be written so as to exclude them. Because `xsl:key` is a top-level element, it must be placed as a direct child of `xsl:stylesheet` rather than inside an `xsl:template`:

```
<xsl:stylesheet
   version="1.0"
   xmlns:xsl="http://www.w3.org/1999/XSL/Transform"
   xmlns="http://www.w3.org/1999/xhtml"
```

```
   >

   <xsl:output method="xml" />

   <xsl:param name="wineid">Nags_Head_Scuppernong_750ml</xsl:param>

   <xsl:key name="wineries" match="section/winery" use="@id" />
```

The key established, it is now possible to revisit the <div> inside of the wine template, and use key() to dereference the winery and obtain the country and region:

```
   <xsl:template match="wine">

      <img src="images/{@id}.png" style="position: absolute; left: 50px; top:
200px; width: 288px;" />

      <img src="images/{winery}.png" style="position: absolute; top: 50px; left:
380px; height: 72px;" />

      <div style="position: absolute; left: 455px; top: 150px;">
         <h2><xsl:apply-templates select="name"/></h2>

         <div>
            <div style="float: left; text-align: right; font-weight: bold; ⮐
line-height: 2em;">Variety:<br/>
               Country:<br/>
               Region:<br/>
            </div>
            <div style="float: left; text-align: left; margin-left: 20px; ⮐
line-height: 2em;">
               <xsl:value-of select="varietal"/><br/>
               <xsl:value-of select="key('wineries',winery)/country"/><br/>
               <xsl:value-of select="key('wineries',winery)/region"/><br/>
            </div>
         </div>
      </div>
</xsl:template>
```

The stylesheet, with the parameter, the key, and a few templates, looks like this:

```
<xsl:stylesheet
   version="1.0"
   xmlns:xsl="http://www.w3.org/1999/XSL/Transform"
   xmlns="http://www.w3.org/1999/xhtml"
   >

   <xsl:output method="xml" />

   <xsl:param name="wineid">Nags_Head_Scuppernong_750ml</xsl:param>

   <xsl:key name="wineries" match="section/winery" use="@id" />

   <xsl:template match="/">
```

```
        <html>
        <body>
           <xsl:apply-templates/>
        </body>
        </html>

   </xsl:template>

   <xsl:template match="section">
      <xsl:apply-templates select="wine[@id=$wineid]"/>
   </xsl:template>

   <xsl:template match="wine">

      <img src="images/{@id}.png" style="position: absolute; left: 50px; ⮐
top: 200px; width: 288px;" />

      <img src="images/{winery}.png" style="position: absolute; top: 50px; ⮐
left: 380px; height: 72px;" />

      <div style="position: absolute; left: 455px; top: 150px;">
         <h2><xsl:apply-templates select="name"/></h2>

         <div>
            <div style="float: left; text-align: right; font-weight: bold; ⮐
line-height: 2em;">Variety:<br/>
               Country:<br/>
               Region:<br/>
            </div>
            <div style="float: left; text-align: left; margin-left: 20px; ⮐
line-height: 2em;">
               <xsl:value-of select="varietal"/><br/>
               <xsl:value-of select="key('wineries',winery)/country"/><br/>
               <xsl:value-of select="key('wineries',winery)/region"/><br/>
            </div>
         </div>
      </div>

   </xsl:template>

</xsl:stylesheet>
```

To test the stylesheet, execute it with `saxon` and store the result in `Nags_Head_Scuppernong_750ml.xhtml`. (Any name would do, but that filename happens to correspond to the link it was assigned in the `winelist.xml` transformed earlier.):

```
java net.sf.saxon.Transform -o Nags_Head_Scuppernong_750ml.xhtml
 wines.xml datasheet.xsl
```

The data sheet is more than halfway done (see Figure 5-9), and most of the more complicated features are complete. All that remains is to place several text fragments.

Muscadine Wines

Nags Head Scuppernong

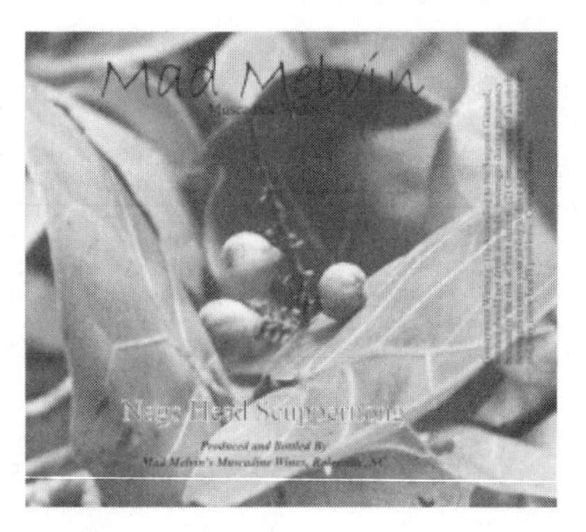

Variety:	Scupp
Country:	United States
Region:	North Carolina

Figure 5-9

Online Data Sheet, Second Draft

While there are several other elements to place in the data sheet, the coding is fairly straightforward. Tackle the `description` next. A child of the `wine` element, the text of the `description` should flow evenly across the page. You could use another `<div>` with an `xsl:value-of`, but it is possible that some descriptions would be omitted, leaving empty blocks. This won't have much effect on the appearance, but it is a bit sloppy. If you use a template instead, the surrounding `<div>` will be output only if the description is also present. The same holds true for the bottle size. Here's the fragment, in context of the wine template:

```
<xsl:template match="wine">

    <img src="images/{@id}.png" style="position: absolute; left: 50px; top:
200px; width: 288px;" />

    <img src="images/{winery}.png" style="position: absolute; top: 50px; left:
380px; height: 72px;" />

    <div style="position: absolute; left: 455px; top: 150px;">
        <h2><xsl:apply-templates select="name"/></h2>

        <div>
            <div style="float: left; text-align: right; font-weight: bold; ⮐
line-height: 2em;">Variety:<br/>
                Country:<br/>
                Region:<br/>
            </div>
            <div style="float: left; text-align: left; margin-left: 20px; ⮐
line-height: 2em;">
                <xsl:value-of select="varietal"/><br/>
                <xsl:value-of select="key('wineries',winery)/country"/><br/>
                <xsl:value-of select="key('wineries',winery)/region"/><br/>
            </div>
        </div>
    </div>

    <xsl:apply-templates select="description"/>
    <xsl:apply-templates select="bottlesize"/>

</xsl:/template>
```

Add a couple of new templates following the wine template to handle the description and bottle size (as noted earlier, the elements are positioned in absolute coordinates, estimated from the data sheet sketch). The new templates can be inserted after the template you just entered to match the `wine` element:

```
<xsl:template match="description">
    <div style="position: absolute; width: 540px; left: 130px; top: 520px;
        font-size: 14pt;
        line-height: 1.35em; text-align: justify;">
    <xsl:value-of select="."/>
    </div>
</xsl:template>

<xsl:template match="bottlesize">
    <div style="position: absolute; left: 100px; top: 640px;">
        <xsl:text>Available in </xsl:text>
        <xsl:value-of select="."/>
        <xsl:text> bottles.</xsl:text>
    </div>
</xsl:template>
```

The winery name requires a bit of a twist. Because it is a shortened string that is stored in the wine/winery element, you need to look up the proper name for the winery in the section/winery/name element. Fortunately, the wineries key is already defined for this kind of cross-reference. All you have to do is look up the name relative to the key. Put an `xsl:apply-templates` instruction in just before the end of the template used to match the `wine` element.

```
      <xsl:apply-templates select="description"/>
      <xsl:apply-templates select="bottlesize"/>

      <xsl:apply-templates select="key('wineries',winery)/name"/><br/>

   </xsl:template>
```

You also need to place the `name`. As with the `description` and `bottlesize`, just provide a template that matches the element and wraps the value in a positioned `<div>`:

```
   <xsl:template match="name">
      <div style="position: absolute; left: 380px; top: 670px;">
         <h2><xsl:value-of select="."/></h2>
      </div>
   </xsl:template>
```

The new template matching the name element can be placed near the bottom of the file following the other templates. The stylesheet should now look like this:

```
<xsl:stylesheet
   version="1.0"
   xmlns:xsl="http://www.w3.org/1999/XSL/Transform"
   xmlns="http://www.w3.org/1999/xhtml"
   >

   <xsl:output method="xml" />

   <xsl:param name="wineid">Nags_Head_Scuppernong_750ml</xsl:param>

   <xsl:key name="wineries" match="section/winery" use="@id" />

   <xsl:template match="/">
      <html>
      <body>
         <xsl:apply-templates/>
      </body>
      </html>

   </xsl:template>

   <xsl:template match="section">
      <xsl:apply-templates select="wine[@id=$wineid]"/>
   </xsl:template>

   <xsl:template match="wine">

      <img src="images/{@id}.png" style="position: absolute; left: 50px; ⮐
```

```
top: 200px; width: 288px;" />

      <img src="images/{winery}.png" style="position: absolute; top: 50px; ⮐
left: 380px; height: 72px;" />

      <div style="position: absolute; left: 455px; top: 150px;">
         <h2><xsl:apply-templates select="name"/></h2>

         <div>
            <div style="float: left; text-align: right; font-weight: bold; ⮐
line-height: 2em;">Variety:<br/>
               Country:<br/>
               Region:<br/>
            </div>
            <div style="float: left; text-align: left; margin-left: 20px; ⮐
line-height: 2em;">
               <xsl:value-of select="varietal"/><br/>
               <xsl:value-of select="key('wineries',winery)/country"/><br/>
               <xsl:value-of select="key('wineries',winery)/region"/><br/>
            </div>
         </div>
      </div>

      <xsl:apply-templates select="description"/>
      <xsl:apply-templates select="bottlesize"/>

      <xsl:apply-templates select="key('wineries',winery)/name"/><br/>

   </xsl:template>

   <xsl:template match="description">
      <div style="position: absolute; width: 540px; left: 130px; top: 520px;
         font-size: 14pt;
         line-height: 1.35em; text-align: justify;">
      <xsl:value-of select="."/>
      </div>
   </xsl:template>

   <xsl:template match="bottlesize">
      <div style="position: absolute; left: 100px; top: 640px;">
         <xsl:text>Available in </xsl:text>
         <xsl:value-of select="."/>
         <xsl:text> bottles.</xsl:text>
      </div>
   </xsl:template>

   <xsl:template match="name">
      <div style="position: absolute; left: 380px; top: 670px;">
         <h2><xsl:value-of select="."/></h2>
      </div>
   </xsl:template>

</xsl:stylesheet>
```

The last few items on the sketch present a problem. The `contactinfo` and warnings don't have corresponding elements in the input XML. How can you apply a template for a structure that doesn't yet exist? One way is to give a template a name and call it explicitly using `xsl:call-template`. Place two `xsl:call-template` instructions near the bottom of the template that matches the `name` element, just after the last `xsl:apply-templates` invocation:

```
        <xsl:apply-templates select="description"/>
        <xsl:apply-templates select="bottlesize"/>

        <xsl:apply-templates select="key('wineries',winery)/name"/><br/>

        <xsl:call-template name="contactinfo"/>
        <xsl:call-template name="warnings"/>

    </xsl:template>
```

While `xsl:call-template` bypasses the built-in XSLT pattern-matching behavior, calling named templates is frequently indispensable when output structures do not parallel the input XML. For this to work, you need templates, but the old standby of using a match pattern won't do any good. Instead, you have to give a name to each called template, `contactinfo` and `warnings`. Insert the `warnings` template toward the bottom of the file following the template matching the `name` element. The warnings template is simple because it is just a static line of text:

```
    <xsl:template name="warnings">
        <div style="position: absolute; width: 540px; left: 130px; top: 720px;
            text-align: center;">
            <xsl:text></xsl:text><br/>
            <xsl:text>May contain sulfites</xsl:text><br/>
        </div>
    </xsl:template>
```

The `contactinfo` template is a bit like the winery lookup in that the distributor name is an attribute of a `distributor` element contained outside of the wine element. As with the winery, the distributor can be indexed with an `xsl:key`:

```
<xsl:stylesheet
    version="1.0"
    xmlns:xsl="http://www.w3.org/1999/XSL/Transform"
    xmlns="http://www.w3.org/1999/xhtml"
    >

    <xsl:output method="xml" />

    <xsl:key name="wineries" match="section/winery" use="@id" />
    <xsl:key name="distributors" match="section/distributor" use="@id" />
```

and cross-referenced with a `key()` expression:

```
<xsl:template name="contactinfo">
   <div style="position: absolute; left: 100px; top: 670px;">
      <xsl:value-of select="key('distributors',distributor)/@name"/><br/>
      <xsl:text>Call to place an order today!</xsl:text>
   </div>
</xsl:template>
```

The transformation now conforms to the design sketch. The data sheet isn't quite complete, though. A few final touches are needed.

Final Cut

The design sketch omitted an important element needed to enable the navigational objectives of this project. For a user to get back to the wine list requires some form of back link. A link can be added simply by adding another named template:

```
<xsl:template name="backlink">
   <div style="position: absolute; width: 54px; right: 20px; top: 720px;
      text-align: center;">
      <a href="mynewwinelist.xml">Back to Wine List</a>
   </div>
</xsl:template>
```

The new template could be called with an `xsl:call-template` instruction inserted at the end of the wine template or in the section template, or invoked from the top-level template that matches the `/` XPath. While you're looking at the top-level template, you might have noticed that it didn't set a page title, either. Let's make both changes here:

```
<xsl:template match="/">
   <html>
      <head>
         <title>Data Sheet - <xsl:value-of select="catalog/section/wine
[@id='Nags_Head_Scuppernong_750ml']/name"/>
         </title>
   </head>
   <body>
      <xsl:apply-templates select="catalog/section"/>
      <xsl:call-template name="backlink"/>
   </body>
   </html>
</xsl:template>
```

The transformation is now finished. Here's the completed stylesheet:

```
<xsl:stylesheet
   version="1.0"
   xmlns:xsl="http://www.w3.org/1999/XSL/Transform"
   xmlns="http://www.w3.org/1999/xhtml"
```

```
>

<xsl:output method="xml" />

<xsl:param name="wineid">Nags_Head_Scuppernong_750ml</xsl:param>

<xsl:key name="wineries" match="section/winery" use="@id" />
<xsl:key name="distributors" match="section/distributor" use="@id" />

<xsl:template match="/">
   <html>
      <head>
         <title>Data Sheet - <xsl:value-of select="catalog/section/wine
[@id='Nags_Head_Scuppernong_750ml']/name"/>
         </title>
   </head>
   <body>
      <xsl:apply-templates/>
      <xsl:call-template name="backlink"/>
   </body>
   </html>

</xsl:template>

<xsl:template match="section">
   <xsl:apply-templates select="wine[@id=$wineid]"/>
</xsl:template>

<xsl:template match="wine">

   <img src="images/{@id}.png" style="position: absolute; left: 50px;
top: 200px; width: 288px;" />

   <img src="images/{winery}.png" style="position: absolute; top: 50px;
left: 380px; height: 72px;" />

   <div style="position: absolute; left: 455px; top: 150px;">
      <h2><xsl:apply-templates select="name"/></h2>

      <div>
         <div style="float: left; text-align: right; font-weight: bold;
line-height: 2em;">Variety:<br/>
            Country:<br/>
            Region:<br/>
         </div>
         <div style="float: left; text-align: left; margin-left: 20px;
line-height: 2em;">
            <xsl:value-of select="varietal"/><br/>
            <xsl:value-of select="key('wineries',winery)/country"/><br/>
            <xsl:value-of select="key('wineries',winery)/region"/><br/>
         </div>
      </div>
```

```
      </div>

      <xsl:apply-templates select="description"/>
      <xsl:apply-templates select="bottlesize"/>

      <xsl:apply-templates select="key('wineries',winery)/name"/><br/>

   </xsl:template>

   <xsl:template match="description">
      <div style="position: absolute; width: 540px; left: 130px; top: 520px;
         font-size: 14pt;
         line-height: 1.35em; text-align: justify;">
      <xsl:value-of select="."/>
      </div>
   </xsl:template>

   <xsl:template match="bottlesize">
      <div style="position: absolute; left: 100px; top: 640px;">
         <xsl:text>Available in </xsl:text>
         <xsl:value-of select="."/>
         <xsl:text> bottles.</xsl:text>
      </div>
   </xsl:template>

   <xsl:template match="name">
      <div style="position: absolute; left: 380px; top: 670px;">
         <h2><xsl:value-of select="."/></h2>
      </div>
   </xsl:template>

   <xsl:template name="warnings">
      <div style="position: absolute; width: 540px; left: 130px; top: 720px;
         text-align: center;">
         <xsl:text></xsl:text><br/>
         <xsl:text>May contain sulfites</xsl:text><br/>
      </div>
   </xsl:template>

   <xsl:template name="contactinfo">
      <div style="position: absolute; left: 100px; top: 670px;">
         <xsl:value-of select="key('distributors',distributor)/@name"/><br/>
         <xsl:text>Call to place an order today!</xsl:text>
      </div>
   </xsl:template>

</xsl:stylesheet>
```

Executing the transform one last time:

```
java net.sf.saxon.Transform -o Nags_Head_Scuppernong_750ml.xhtml
 wines.xml datasheet.xsl
```

The final piece is shown in Figure 5-10.

Mad Melvin
Muscadine Wines
Nags Head Scuppernong
Variety: Scupp
Country: United States
Region: North Carolina
Blends notes of Chardonnay with the natural sweetness of juicy peaches. Featuring mango and sweet pineapple undertones, it is enriched with hints of ripe guava. A *must have* for casual summer picnics.
Available in 750ml bottles.
Dri Distributors, Inc.
Call to place an order today!
Mad Melvin's Muscadine Wines
May contain sulfites
Back to Wine List

Figure 5-10

Summary

This chapter covers a lot of ground. Although it doesn't provide complete coverage of either XSLT or XPath, you have the basics for preparing and executing a transformation. XSLT coding frequently features a blend of coding styles, often distinguished as "push" or "rule-based" (transformations with heavy, almost universal reliance on template matching to drive the process) or "pull" processing (transformations thick with the imperatives of `xsl:value-of` and `xsl:call-template`). The worse your XML structure is, or the more divergent the output, the less likely you are to meet such ideals. The coding style presented here is certainly not the most elegant, nor does it claim to be completely uniform, but it does show a number of important features of the language.

XSLT presents itself as a special-purpose language for transforming XML. The term "transforming XML" applies to a great variety of problem domains — certainly much broader than formatting a wine brochure. While its built-in behaviors lend it to certain coding styles better than others, XSLT provides both a well-structured language environment and a great deal of flexibility and extensibility in deploying solutions. In later chapters, you'll see some of these other application areas.

6

Rendering XML to Print

In Chapter 5, you learned basic steps to manipulate XML using XSLT transformations, rearranging the wine catalog into an XHTML data sheet. In this chapter, you redirect your effort into producing more refined output than is otherwise possible using an HTML browser. Upgrading to this capability requires an advanced formatting and layout model, and XSL fits this need nicely.

XSL (Extensible Stylesheet Language) is a syntax and formatting model for constructing high-fidelity page layouts. Using XSL Formatting Objects, your transforms can lay out pages in much the same way as a word processor such as Microsoft Word or a desktop publishing suite such as Quark Xpress. This chapter can't cover all of the ins and outs of XSL, but it shows one way to construct pages using its Formatting Objects.

Problem

The needs of a target audience frequently dictate that information be provided in printed form, or at least in a form that is highly predictable in appearance. In this project, customers need printable data sheets. The marketing needs of a wine business are also well served by predictable print materials — brochures, handouts, mailers, and so forth. This chapter demonstrates the use of the XSL vocabulary for basic pagination and layout. Rather than repeat the transforms of Chapter 5, the XSL Formatting Objects syntax is shown directly. It is left as an exercise for the reader to adapt the XSLT transform for outputting XSL Formatting Objects (FO) syntax rather than XHTML.

Presenting a High-Fidelity Image

To provide a more refined image, consider the Black Forke brochure from Chapter 5 (see Figure 5-2). Even when delivered as fully rendered bitmaps, images often exhibit a layered presentation structure. Implicit in such an image are the operations that preceded it in the formatting and rendering process: image positioning, text justification, flowing and line breaking, font selection, page breaking, repeated elements, and so on. CSS addresses some of these properties (some were used in Chapter 5), but in the case of XHTML, a browser is required to render a visible output.

Contrast the use of print media to the online presentation of XHTML/CSS. Printed materials present no navigational interface—no hyperlinks, pop-ups, balloon help, Back button, history, or active cursor. There is no animation. Color handling, an unfinished puzzle piece of World Wide Web screen display, is a hard requirement for professional print output. Professional printers color-calibrate their displays and printers, a process used to ensure that colors are reproduced accurately across different types of output devices. Most systems used to browse Web pages are not properly color-calibrated. (The International Color Consortium has more information on color management at `www.color.org`.) Pages represent the fixed dimensions of the output medium, not the relatively scrolled areas of a graphical user interface (GUI) window. Simple browser technology suffices for only the simplest of print renditions.

What is needed is an expanded formatting model, and technology component(s) to substitute for the browser, so that you can target specific presentational media. The choice of writing one transform or many depends on the need for reuse and simplicity of design, and the time available.

Objectives

The objective of this project is to produce print-ready documents in a form that can be repurposed to both electronic and print media. The underlying requirements of the appearance are assumed to be consistent with the brochure of Chapter 5. Unlike Chapter 5, you won't be using a transform, but keep in mind that this is done only to simplify the project—the formatting object syntax used here was designed to be used as the target format for XSLT transforms.

As XML, an XSL document is not only intended to be an output of an XSLT transform but can also be postprocessed as input to subsequent transforms.

While the XSL is XML, it isn't the kind of XML you'd use to manage information. Rather, it targets a generic model of a page-oriented output device. The goal is a stream of XML data that can drive an effective print process, emulated screen display, or cross-conversion into the slightly different formatting model of a browser.

Design

CSS provides a number of properties needed for both display and print media layout, yet the combination of XHTML and CSS provides semantics that cannot be reproduced in print. XSL adopts many of the CSS properties and provides a more comprehensive process and object model for standardized page layout.

In this chapter, you apply XSL to the problem of creating output suitable for print rendering. XSL's Formatting Objects provide better control over several aspects of layout, a few of which are:

- Pagination, including page masters
- Writing direction and orientation
- Hyphenation
- Blocks and inline areas

Expressed in terms of XSL Formatting Objects, a composition can be converted into instructions specific to the output device. The formatting engine is responsible for doing the conversion or raster image processing, which is outside the scope of XSL.

Structure of Design

The typical process of creating XSL using XSLT is virtually identical to any other XSLT-based transform—only the format targeted by the transform changes. XSL isn't much good in and of itself, though—you need a formatter to render the final page images. While XHTML is typically viewed with a browser, XSL is most often processed through an XSL Formatting Objects processor, sometimes called an FO processor.

The conceptual formatting process is illustrated in Figure 6-1. Following an XSLT tree transformation process, the result tree consists of XSL elements. The result tree specifies a set of XSL Formatting Objects and their properties. Within the formatter, the objects are refined so that various XSL semantics are applied, mapping the properties into formatting constraints (called *traits* in the XSL 1.0 Recommendation).

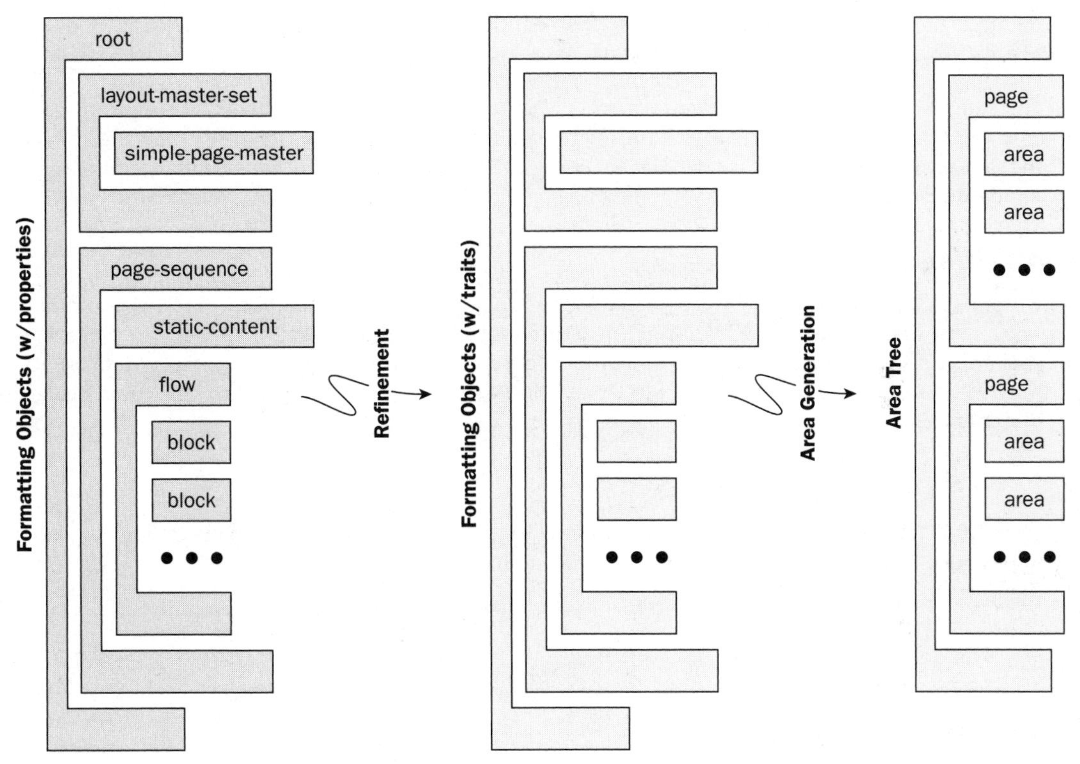

Figure 6-1

Exactly how the area tree is serialized into a device-specific representation is defined by an implementation. The Apache Project's FOP (Formatting Objects Processor) implementation provides back ends to generate PDF, Java AWT (2-D graphics), MIF, RTF, TIFF, PNG, PCL, PostScript, text, SVG, and a raw XML representation of the area tree.

Processing FO into PDF

The project makes use of the Apache FOP. The beta 0.91 version of FOP is used in this project. It can be downloaded for free from `http://xmlgraphics.apache.org/fop/download.html`, which redirects you to a download mirror. Be sure to get a 0.91 binary distribution, not a source distribution. Also avoid the older 0.20 versions, which lack some of the XSL features used in the project. (The distributions labeled "current" were version 0.20.5 at the time this chapter was being written.) FOP relies on Java, which you can download from `http://java.sun.com/j2se/1.5.0/download.jsp`.

Running an XSL formatting process is no more difficult than executing an XSLT transformation. Processors provide options to execute an XSLT transform and point the XSL FO result tree directly to an FOP. This chapter's project avoids that step by working with the FO document directly. For users of Windows environments with Java already installed, FOP provides a batch file that conveniently sets up the necessary library paths. To run an FO document through FOP, serializing to Acrobat/PDF output, simply provide the FO file and an output file name with a `.pdf` extension:

```
fop brochure.fo brochure.pdf
```

The Apache FOP project is not the only FO processor. Several commercial FO processors exist; some are even offered as web services.

Formatting Objects

Unlike XSLT, the Formatting Object syntax does not represent a transformation—at least not in the XSLT sense of converting an XML input into a different XML or text structure. Rather, it represents the semantics of a formatting process. The high-level element structures in an XSL-FO document reflect this purpose. Let's explore the basic structure of an XSL-FO document and look at how the constructs relate to one another.

Basic FO Skeleton

The XSL-FO document starts out with a standard XML declaration. Being XML, the document also has to have one, and only one, document-level element. In the case of XSL, this document level element is the *root*:

```
<?xml version="1.0"?>
<fo:root xmlns:fo="http://www.w3.org/1999/XSL/Format">

</fo:root>
```

XSL uses the namespace `http://www.w3.org/1999/XSL/Format` *to identify its elements. The prefix* `xsl:` *or* `fo:` *is often associated with the XSL namespace. This is only a convention; as with any other namespace-aware processor, you can use other prefixes as long as the URI (Uniform Resource Identifier) mentioned remains the same.*

Page Masters and Page Regions

In XSL, unlike most word processors and desktop publishing applications, there is no default or implicit page layout. The designer must specify configurations for each type of page that is to be created in the formatting process. The XSL 1.0 Recommendation provides one model of a page master, represented by the `simple-page-master` element. You need to specify one `simple-page-master` element for each of the different kinds of page layouts used in the final output. The formatter later uses these page masters to determine how content is flowed into pages.

While you might think that the specification of a page master could be defaulted, the formatting process has no way of determining appropriate layout constraints for your projects. In the simplest cases, all pages are laid out in the same manner and only one `simple-page-master` element is needed. For instance, a technical research journal may format research papers so that all of the pages are two columns and page numbers are at the bottom, centered on the page. Simple business documents such as invoices and purchase orders may also require only one page master.

Additional page masters are used to vary the layout as pages are formatted. For instance, the technical journal might use one page master for right-hand pages, and another for left-hand pages, to position the page number at the edge of each page.

The following FO fragment is an example of a simple page configuration using `layout-master-set`. The `layout-master-set` enables you to specify one or more page masters. The `simple-page-master` specifies a 3 x 5 index card format, with alignment set to vertically center areas on the page.

```
<fo:layout-master-set>
   <fo:simple-page-master master-name="master1"
       page-height="3in" page-width="5in" >
      <fo:region-body display-align="center"/>
   </fo:simple-page-master>
</fo:layout-master-set>
```

> **Block and Inline Progression**
>
> Technically, the `display-align` property doesn't align vertically; it aligns along the direction in which blocks progress as they are flowed into an area. The block progression direction depends upon the writing mode implied by the language of the document. To better support international languages, XSL allows the writing mode to be specified explicitly.
>
> The initial writing mode is from left to right, from top to bottom, making the default suitable for Western languages. In left-to-right, top-to-bottom mode, the block progression direction is from the top down along the 11-inch length of a portrait page. In contrast, the inline progression direction is to the right along the 8.5-inch width. XSL's property refinement rules govern how width and height properties are mapped onto block and inline progression dimensions. For an English-language document, `block-progression-dimension` usually equates to "height" (vertical) and `inline-progression-dimension` to "width." (horizontal).

A page master determines the geometry of regions into which areas produced by Formatting Objects are placed. Regions provide constraints on the areas into which static pieces of information and dynamically formatted areas are laid out. A `simple-page-master` divides a page up into five regions, as shown in Figure 6-2. Of these regions, the Body region is the most versatile for general layout, and can cover the whole page or a small part of it. Many common formatting semantics—headers, footers, sidebars, and the like—are best specified using one of the other regions.

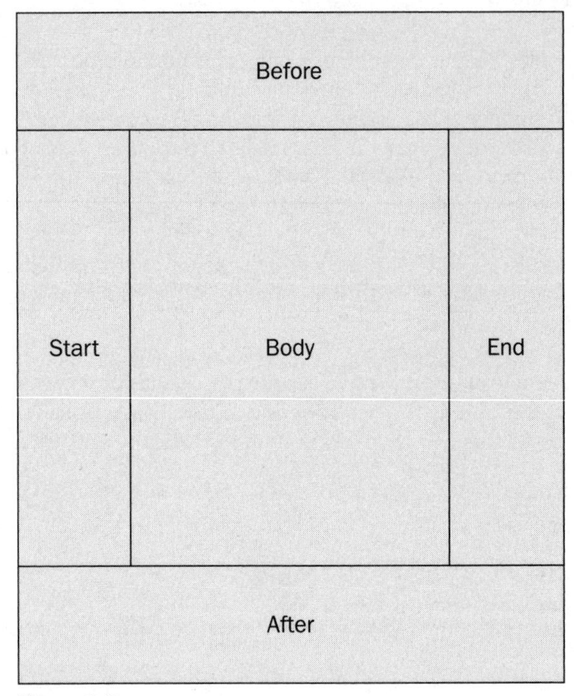

Figure 6-2

The dimensions and margins of the Body region must be set explicitly to avoid overlap. The Before and After regions may extend to the corners of the page if their respective `precedence` attributes are set to `true` (as is suggested by the figure). The Start and End regions' upper and lower edges are determined by whether the Before and After regions extend to the corners. XSL won't try to second-guess the Body region's dimensions; it overlaps the other regions by default—you need to set its margins to avoid the overlap. For the other regions, the `extent` attribute determines the corresponding height (Before, After) or width (Start, End) of the region.

At least one page master is needed to create a formatted page.

A `page-sequence-master` provides greater control over how page masters are used during the formatting process. The `page-sequence-master` elements are children of the `layout-master-set` and contain references to page masters. The order and constraints specified with a `page-sequence-master` allow the formatter to choose between different page masters during the formatting process. For documents with differing geometries for left (verso) and right (recto) pages in two-page spreads, the page sequence master allows the appropriate symmetries to be configured on different page masters. For the project in this chapter, this isn't necessary.

Page Sequences, Flows, and Blocks

Page sequences are the real "roots" of the formatted information. A `page-sequence` specifies the flows that are composed onto pages, as constrained by a given page master. Within a page sequence, a `flow` maps a series of areas — blocks and lines — into a given region. The following fragment shows this structure with a "Hello World" example:

```
<fo:page-sequence master-reference="master1">
   <fo:flow flow-name="xsl-region-body">
      <fo:block text-align="center" >Hello World</fo:block>
   </fo:flow>
</fo:page-sequence>
```

In the context of the previously defined page master (`master1`), the block containing "Hello World" is centered both vertically and horizontally on a 3 x 5–inch page. The `flow-name` of `xsl-region-body` is a name reserved in the XSL 1.0 Recommendation, which maps to the Body region of the `simple-page-master`. Corresponding names are reserved for the Start (`xsl-region-start`), End (`xsl-region-end`), Before (`xsl-region-before`), and After (`xsl-region-after`) regions. These defaults are for your convenience. You can also give an explicit `region-name` to each of the region elements and refer to those names instead.

The Before and After regions are often used to implement headers and footers, respectively. Similarly, the Start and End regions are used for sidebars. Headers, footers, and sidebars often contain the same or similar information, so the `fo:static-content` objects are repeated from page to page. XSL `fo:static-content` elements are placed before the `fo:flow`, to provide content for these regions. The following example places a header and footer on the Hello World page:

```
<fo:page-sequence master-reference="master1">
   <fo:static-content flow-name="xsl-region-before">
      <fo:block text-align="start">HELLO WORLD EXAMPLE</fo:block>
   </fo:static-content>

   <fo:static-content flow-name="xsl-region-end">
      <fo:block text-align="end">END OF EXAMPLE</fo:block>
   </fo:static-content>

   <fo:flow flow-name="xsl-region-body">
      <fo:block text-align="center" >Hello World</fo:block>
   </fo:flow>
</fo:page-sequence>
```

Static content is repeated across pages, so if (and when) static content overflows the region, unlike the `fo:flow` object, the overflow doesn't cause new pages to be created. The `overflow` attributes of the respective region elements (`fo:region-start`, `fo:region-end`, `fo:region-before`, `fo:region-after`) determine whether the content should be hidden (clipped) when it overflows the extent of the region, or if it should overlap the adjacent regions' areas. Setting `overflow` to `hidden` hides any content that would otherwise fall outside of the extent.

It isn't an error to refer to one of the four side regions even when there is no corresponding region defined in the page master. In fact, FO processors may not even support these regions (they are specified by XSL 1.0 as part of the extended conformance level).

In addition to blocks, FO provides two container structures to serve as overarching reference areas for the blocks contained within. The `fo:block-container` is treated like a block but enables you to set characteristics such as positioning, size, and orientation. The following fragment has a block container to place a 2-inch x 2-inch blue border around the words Hello World:

```
<fo:block-container border="solid thin blue" width="2in" height="2in">
   <fo:block>Hello World</fo:block>
</fo:block-container>
```

The `fo:inline-container` by comparison is used to allow blocks to be included inline, as if they were fragments of text. The "inline" in `fo:inline-container` doesn't refer to its content—it must contain blocks—the name merely indicates how the contained blocks get formatted as a result of being placed inside of the inline container. Because it isn't implemented in the FOP beta at the time this is being written, the inline container isn't included in the project.

Inlines

XSL has several formatting object elements that are referred to as *inline-level objects*. These objects cause line breaks only when no more space is available to fit them on the line. Think of how characters inserted into your text editor cause lines to wrap, and you'll understand the way inlines are formatted by XSL. The inline Formatting Objects used in the project include:

- `fo:inline`
- `fo:external-graphic`

While a block corresponds to things like paragraphs and headings in XHTML, an `fo:inline` most closely corresponds to a `SPAN`. The `SPAN` element is commonly used as a point of attachment so that document authors can achieve effects such as underlining words or phrases. Similarly, `fo:inline` is commonly used to associate style properties with a fragment of text. It is a chunk of information to be formatted along the current line, in the inline progression direction, without forcing a line break to automatically occur. The `fo:inline` structure allows application of additional formatting characteristics, such as adjustments to the baseline, background, or border. The following fragment illustrates this:

```
<fo:block>
   <fo:inline border="solid thin red">Hello World w/ Red Border</fo:inline>
</fo:block>
```

As an inline object, the `fo:external-graphic` must be inside of a block. As with other inlines, the graphic is placed as if it were just another string included on a line. If you want it to be positioned as a block, you can wrap it inside of a block alone, like this:

```
<fo:block>
   <fo:external-graphic src="url(images/BlackForke.png)" />
</fo:block>
```

The syntax for the `src` attribute is a URI specification of the form `url(uri-reference)`.

URI stands for Universal Resource Identifier, the definition of which includes the more web-specific term URL (Universal Resource Locator). The IETF RFC 3986 defines a URL as a URI that specifies a resource as well as a primary access mechanism (its network location). The differences are subtle and have no practical impact on this project.

Note how the `url(uri-reference)` as a value in an XML attribute has to be surrounded by double quotation marks. This means that if a URI reference itself contains a query string with double quotation marks, you'll need to escape those quotation marks. For instance, if you have:

```
<fo:block>
   <fo:external-graphic
      src="url(http://somehost.com/find?image="BlackForke")"/>
</fo:block>
```

The double quotation marks cause the XML parser to flag an error. Double quotation marks also seem to be required by the XSL 1.0 Recommendation in cases where the URI reference contains an embedded apostrophe (although your FOP may not flag failure to do so as an error). Double quotation marks can be included around the URI reference through use of the predefined XML entity """ (or apostrophes using "'"):

```
<fo:block>
   <fo:external-graphic
      src="url( http://somehost.com/find?image=&quot;BlackForke&quot;)"/>
</fo:block>
```

The Rest

There are many, many other Formatting Objects and properties . . . even a brief sketch of their function is beyond the scope of this book. This list of Formatting Objects includes markers, tables, lists, color profiles, floats, and leaders to name but a few. Most of the properties won't be needed for the page layout project. Some aspects of the XSL 1.0 Recommendation, such as the aural properties, aren't commonly implemented in current FO processors. Yet it isn't necessary to have all of XSL 1.0 to get interesting layouts.

Applicable Technologies

XSLT was designed as an enabling technology, to produce XSL FO syntax as input to an FO processor. The means and methods of doing this are virtually the same as when XSLT is used to generate any other output format.

XSL 1.0 (`www.w3.org/TR/xsl`) is a W3C recommendation. At the time of this writing, XSL version 1.1 is a working draft and, as previously mentioned, several features of the 1.0 Recommendation have yet to be implemented in Apache's newest FOP beta (0.91).

While the FOP project has made significant progress, the most complete implementations are still found in commercial offerings such as Antenna House's XSL Formatter or RenderX's XEP.

XSL frequently uses properties derived from CSS. However, the way in which XSL uses those properties is often somewhat different, and understanding the CSS derivation is relatively unimportant. The main focus is on the XSL Formatting Objects and the rendered result.

Design Consequences

It is frequently the case that a concrete language such as XHTML/CSS is the target of a transformation-based process. Aside from the fact that such combinations are destined for a specific class of browsers, choosing to go with an HTML variation can lead to device-specific tweaks becoming entangled with the logic needed to meet user requirements. XSL is designed so that Formatting Objects specify constraints, while formatters provide their own implementations of formatting algorithms. Device-specific instructions are therefore compartmentalized to the formatter implementation.

Consider the formatter implementation as a black box. In the ideal case, the semantics of your data are mapped into the presentational structures of Formatting Objects, which the formatter compiles into a device-specific instruction stream. In the not-so-ideal case, the formatter provides insufficient options for controlling the device-specific instruction stream. For instance, a generation of high-end printers uses specialized PostScript coding conventions to allow a digital press to run at or near capacity. Attempting to use a plain, old PostScript stream would result in a monolithic document of many gigabytes of data, which simply couldn't be processed fast enough to feed pages into a printer. How you would work around such stumbling blocks would depend on whether there is a good application program interface (API) (or any API), whether the problem can be addressed through postprocessing of the device-specific stream, and the resources you have to expend.

The Apache FOP implementation currently relies on a postprocessing solution to provide several PDF features such as watermarks, security, and document metadata properties.

Confronted by a declarative language such as XSL, the lack of procedural code, and access to global variables can be a stumbling block for some developers. For instance, you might want to include the quantity presented on a page out of the total count, where the total quantity that will fit on a page is variable and a function of the pagination process. Workarounds are sometimes necessary to meet such requirements. Solutions to obstacles like this may involve postprocessing an XML serialization of the area tree or relying on a preprocessing step in another language such as XSLT to divide and conquer the problem.

Beyond such details, XSL-FO provides a coherent model and community standard for page formatting. While individual implementations and the model itself may have shortcomings, XSL-FO serves as a common means of specifying formatting semantics, and a focal point for further improvements.

Solution

Basically, the solution is to create a generic FO layout and use it to output Acrobat PDF (Portable Document Format), as well as some other formats of the data sheet, easily printable by the customer. The first step in recreating the data sheet is to consider the layout requirements. Rather than repeating the XSLT transforms of Chapter 5, you'll express the same intent directly in FO syntax. Recreating XSLT templates to output FO is left as an exercise for the reader. The XML inputs are precisely the same as in Chapter 5 and won't be repeated here.

Product Data — Layout

The layout is almost identical to that used in Chapter 5, but the scroll metaphor no longer applies — for PDF output, you want to target a fixed page size. For reference, the layout is repeated in Figure 6-3.

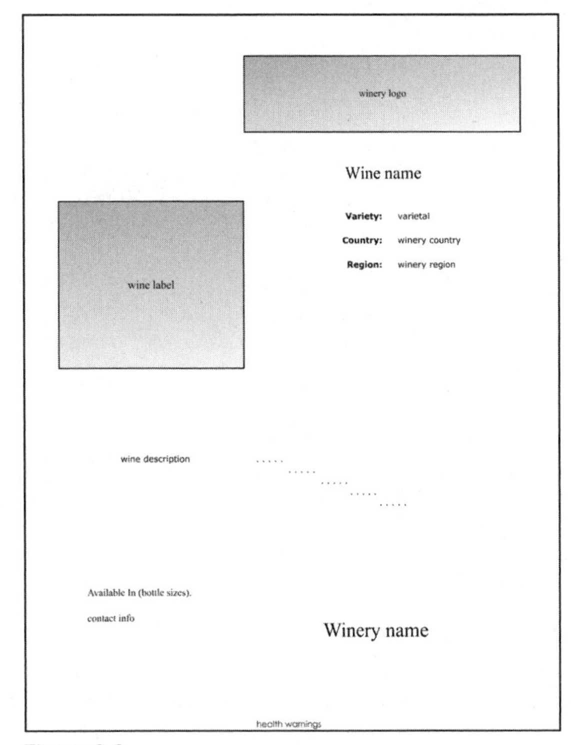

Figure 6-3

Next, you'll apply FO objects to reproduce this layout. As with XHTML, FO tables could be used for positioning, but that doesn't really illustrate XSL's features. The project relies more on fixed and normally flowed blocks for positioning. The methods are the same for tables: you can place tables within blocks and block or inline containers.

Multiple-Output Formatting

One of the selling points of XSL is that, having written a stylesheet to generate FO syntax, the same formatting semantics can be rendered to different output systems. For example, FOP can generate PDF, but it also has back ends for PostScript, Rich Text Format, PNG, MIF, SVG, and several other formats. It can even reduce the FO input to plain text, or directly drive a Java AWT preview.

With such different rendering mechanisms, you should expect the image to vary slightly (or a lot!). One reason for this in FOP is that different back ends may get font information from different sources.

Wine Brochure Formatting Objects

So, you're ready to assemble an FO document to reproduce the wine brochure layout, this time for paginated media. Don't try to understand every facet of XSL-FO — at more than 370 pages formatted, not including the appendices, the full XSL 1.0 Recommendation is a lot to grok — but you can use the brochure here as a starting point.

Although you're using XSL-FO to describe a printed page, FO also supports the semantics of scrolled areas through the overflow property. The usefulness of scrolling depends on whether your FO processor supports a suitable output.

Remember, the project focuses on XSL-FO only. No XSLT or XPath is required. That said, the breakdown roughly follows a pattern in which each subsection can be expressed as one or two XSLT templates.

If you're eager to apply your knowledge of XSLT, consider the match pattern that could be used in a template rule. For instance, the next subsection sets the FO document root. The XSLT template to output this fragment would reasonably be specified with a `match="/"` *attribute.*

An FO Blank

To start the Wine Brochure FO document, simply follow the format described previously. Because FO documents are also XML, the XML declaration begins the file. All FO documents start out with a `root` element as the document element:

```
<?xml version="1.0"?>
<fo:root xmlns:fo="http://www.w3.org/1999/XSL/Format">

</fo:root>
```

As with all namespace prefixes, the `fo` prefix is simply an accepted convention. The namespace URI `http://www.w3.org/1999/XSL/Format` is specified by the XSL 1.0 Recommendation. The rest of the FO elements that follow are nested within the `fo:root` element.

Again, following the skeletal format laid out previously, the next thing to consider is the page layout, described using an `fo:layout-master-set`. Even for multiple wine brochures, a single-page format suffices. Give it a straightforward name, such as `master1`, that you won't confuse with any of the XSL-FO element names or predefined attribute values, and set the `size` to `"portrait"`:

```
    <fo:layout-master-set>
       <fo:simple-page-master master-name="master1" size="portrait">
          <fo:region-body />
       </fo:simple-page-master>
    </fo:layout-master-set>
```

You could get away with just using the Body region to accomplish the layout, but that would make it difficult to extend the example to other applications. Standard boilerplate content (like the sulfite warning message discussed in Chapter 5) also would fit quite nicely into a header, footer, or sidebar. So, rather than put it off until later and possibly have to rearrange the layout, add the rest of the page regions and make the adjustments up front.

Referring to the sketch in Figure 6-2, the logo at the top could go into a header. A quick guess puts the header at a little less than 1.75 inches — about an inch or so of margin and a logo a little smaller than an inch high. Similarly, the winery name and sulfite warning could fit into a footer of about 1.5 inches. `fo:region-before` corresponds to the header and `fo:region-after` to the footer. Give `region-before` a 1.72-inch extent, and `region-after` a 1.5-inch extent. `fo:region-start` and `fo:region-end` correspond to sidebars on the left and right, respectively. Give them each 1 inch, just to reserve the space (and remind you that they are there, if and when you want to use them). The simple page master now looks like this:

```
<fo:simple-page-master master-name="master1" size="portrait">
   <fo:region-body />
   <fo:region-before extent="1.72in"/>
   <fo:region-after extent="1.5in"/>
   <fo:region-start extent="1.0in"/>
   <fo:region-end extent="1.0in"/>
</fo:simple-page-master>
```

Notice that the Body region is going to overlap the other four regions. Set the `fo:region-body`'s `margin` attributes to solve that. Figure 6-4 illustrates the relationship of region extents to the Body region's margins. In the figure, the Before, After, and Start regions' extents are set lower than the Body's respective margin settings, but the End region extent is set larger than the body's `margin-right` and thus the areas overlap. As the figure suggests, you can tweak the margins to provide "gutters" between the body region and the other regions. For instance, by rounding the top margin to 2 inches, you will leave at least a 0.28-inch gap between the header and any content placed in the body.

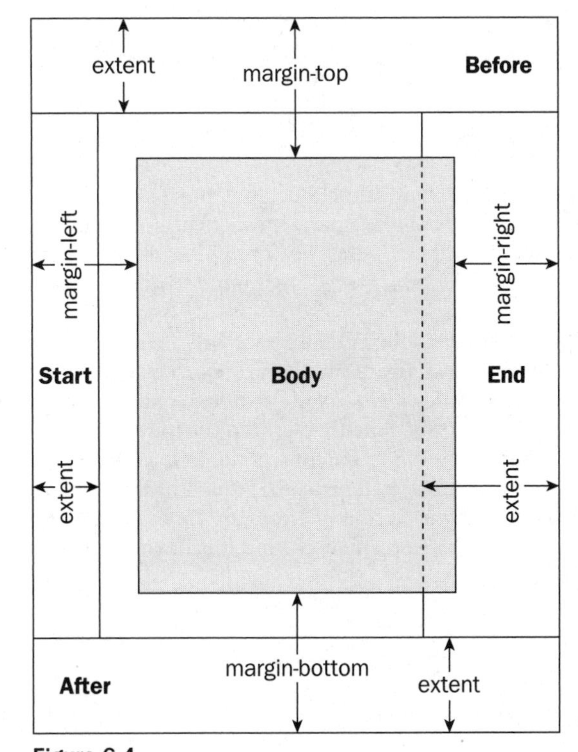

Figure 6-4

```
<fo:simple-page-master master-name="master1" size="portrait">
   <fo:region-body
      margin-left="1.0in" margin-right="1.0in"
      margin-top="2.0in" margin-bottom="1.5in"
   />
   <fo:region-before extent="1.72in"/>
      <fo:region-after extent="1.5in"/>
      <fo:region-start extent="1.0in"/>
      <fo:region-end extent="1.0in"/>
</fo:simple-page-master>
```

It wouldn't make much sense to put a margin over a margin, so the four outer regions (Before, After, Start, and End) don't get to have margins. If you want to set a margin within one of those areas, use a block container to adjust the placement of its contents.

Unfortunately, you still don't have a working FO document. To complete the skeleton, at least enough to get it to render, you need to establish a page sequence and flow blocks of content into the regions you've just defined.

Establishing a Page Sequence

Start with the basic boilerplate fragment of FO that includes the minimum needed to create a sequence of pages: an `fo:page-sequence`, with an `fo:flow`. In turn, the `fo:flow` is parent to one or more blocks or block containers, which you will insert later. Put this fragment after the simple page master (not inside of it):

```
<fo:page-sequence master-reference="master1">
   <fo:flow flow-name="xsl-region-body">

   </fo:flow>
</fo:page-sequence>
```

The value of the `master-reference` attribute must match the `master-name` attribute of the simple page master defined earlier. The `flow-name` names a sequence of Formatting Objects that provide content to be paginated. The flow is implicitly mapped onto a region, which is the part of the `flow-name` value that follows the `xsl-` prefix. In the preceding fragment, the flow is mapped to the body region.

The brochure should specify a font, or the FO processor will be forced to make the choice for you. Settings such as the font family and size are common properties that can be applied to most FO elements. The easiest way to set them for the body of the document is to add the necessary attributes to the flow element. Any objects added to the flow then inherit the font specifications automatically and can override them as needed. The following fragment sets the font to Times New Roman. If Times New Roman is not present, Times Roman is used instead. If neither font is present, the formatter uses the default serif font, which is typically a version of Times, or Times New Roman in the case of PDF. (In the FOP beta, this mechanism isn't fully implemented, and it is likely to choose the first font listed.) The font is size is then set to 12 points:

```
<fo:page-sequence master-reference="master1">
   <fo:flow flow-name="xsl-region-body"
```

```
            font-family="Times New Roman, Times Roman, Serif" font-size="12pt">

        </fo:flow>
    </fo:page-sequence>
```

Flowed Content

The skeletal structure is almost ready. After this step, the minimal FO document can be processed. The flow needs Formatting Objects — at least one to put something on the page. Because the logo is going to be put in the header, start with the wine label image. (The logo and label images are included with this chapter's download files.) Recall that an external graphic is placed inside of a block, and uses the `src` attribute with the `uri()` specification syntax.

```
    <fo:page-sequence master-reference="master1">
        <fo:flow flow-name="xsl-region-body" font-family="Times New Roman, ⮐
Times Roman, Serif" font-size="12pt">

            <fo:block>
                <fo:external-graphic
                    src="url(images/Nags_Head_Scuppernong_750ml.png)"
                />
            </fo:block>

        </fo:flow>
    </fo:page-sequence>
```

The brochure is finally ready for processing. Run it through FOP:

```
fop brochure.fo brochure.pdf
```

View the output in a PDF viewer such as Acrobat Reader or Ghostview. The resulting PDF should have the green label about 2 inches down the page to the left, as shown in Figure 6-5.

At this point in the layout, the thing to notice is that the image is a bit too large to allow the wine name and varietal information to fit properly. In fact, FOP picked up the raw size of the image and placed it on the page as is. One way to fix this is to ensure that all images are of a known, fixed size prior to processing. A quicker-and-dirtier way is to use the FO processor to do the scaling for you, giving it one of the dimensions and asking it to scale both dimensions uniformly. The label(s) are rectangular and close to being square, so this strategy should work well enough. The `content-height` and `scaling` attributes of the external graphic achieve this end. While you're making those changes, set the block's `margin-left` attribute to `0.25in`:

```
    <fo:page-sequence master-reference="master1">
        <fo:flow flow-name="xsl-region-body"
            font-family="Times New Roman, Times Roman, Serif" font-size="12pt">

            <fo:block margin-left="0.25in" >
                <fo:external-graphic
                    src="url(images/Nags_Head_Scuppernong_750ml.png)"
                    content-height="2.25in"
                    scaling="uniform"
```

```
            />
        </fo:block>

      </fo:flow>
    </fo:page-sequence>
```

If you run FOP now, you'll notice that the image is smaller and is jogged to the right by .25 inch.

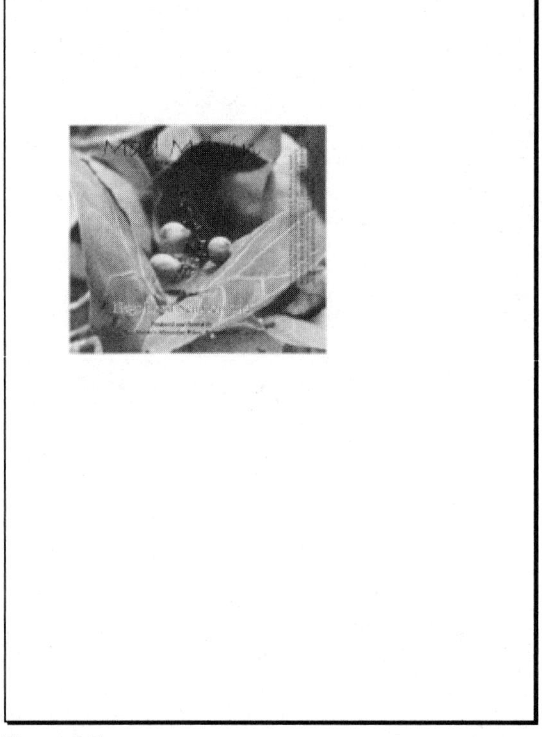

Figure 6-5

From this point on, objects are positioned with respect to the objects that preceded them. The FO processor keeps track of how the objects are stacked along the line and down the page. You can get around the automatic flowing behavior by using absolute positioning properties, which will be covered in the next section. Right now, you just need to add a few more normally flowed Formatting Objects.

A Debugging Tip

Placing an unusual border on the blocks or block containers can help you visualize how the reference areas and blocks are sized and positioned. Think of it as an FO equivalent of a debugging `print` statement. For instance, include an attribute such as `border="dashed thick red"` on a block to make its actual formatted size and position stand out. Note that a border may slightly offset the position because it has thickness.

More Flowed Content

Blocks that participate in the normal flow aren't totally at the mercy of the formatter for positioning. Just as you adjusted the left margin on the first block, you can adjust all four margins to ensure that sufficient white space remains even when one object is placed up against another. Add another block to the flow, after the block containing the Scuppernong label image, this time using `fo:inline` to provide the wine description:

```
<fo:page-sequence master-reference="master1">
   <fo:flow flow-name="xsl-region-body"
      font-family="Times New Roman, Times Roman, Serif" font-size="12pt">

      <fo:block margin-left="0.25in" >
         <fo:external-graphic
            src="url(images/Nags_Head_Scuppernong_750ml.png)"
            content-height="2.25in"
            scaling="uniform"
         />
      </fo:block>

      <fo:block>
         <fo:inline>Blends notes of Chardonnay with the natural sweetness of ⮐
juicy peaches. Featuring mango and sweet pineapple undertones, it is enriched ⮐
with hints of ripe guava. A *must have* for casual summer picnics. </fo:inline>
      </fo:block>

   </fo:flow>
</fo:page-sequence>
```

The `padding` *properties can also be used to fine-tune the space within the area generated by an object. This is useful to provide space between a border and content of a block.*

Bring the right and left edges in by an inch, and provide a little more space between the description and the wine label just above:

```
<fo:block
   margin-top=".875in"
   margin-left="1in"
   margin-right="1in"
   >
   <fo:inline>Blends notes of Chardonnay with the natural sweetness of ⮐
juicy peaches. Featuring mango and sweet pineapple undertones, it is enriched ⮐
with hints of ripe guava. A *must have* for casual summer picnics. </fo:inline>
</fo:block>
```

The description is the same size as the rest of the text. Make it 14 points by adding a `font-size` attribute to the inline or block. The entire block is also ragged edged on the right. To fix this, add a `text-align` attribute to the block:

```
<fo:block
   margin-top=".875in"
   margin-left="1in"
   margin-right="1in"
   text-align="justify"
```

```
      >
      <fo:inline font-size="14pt">Blends notes of Chardonnay with the natural
sweetness of juicy peaches. Featuring mango and sweet pineapple undertones,
it is enriched with hints of ripe guava. A *must have* for casual summer
picnics.</fo:inline>
   </fo:block>
```

It isn't evident from this example, but multiple Formatting Objects can be run together inside of a block. In this case, it would be easier to grab the chunk of wine description text and format it as a single `fo:inline`. Aside from the omitted font size, the following fragment provides the same result as the preceding single `fo:inline`:

```
<fo:inline>Blends notes of Chardonnay with the natural sweetness of juicy
peaches. </fo:inline>
<fo:inline>Featuring mango and sweet pineapple undertones, it is enriched
with hints of ripe guava. </fo:inline>
<fo:inline>A *must have* for casual summer picnics.</fo:inline>
```

Run the brochure FO document through FOP, and preview the output again:

```
fop brochure.fo brochure.pdf
```

Figure 6-6 shows the result: the text block follows the wine label, offset from either side by a 2-inch gap.

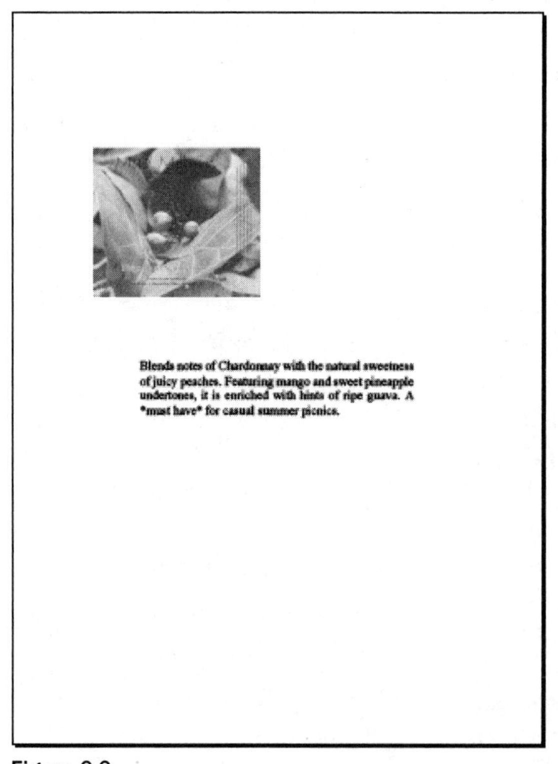

Figure 6-6

There is just a little bit more to add to the normal flow before moving on to other modes of placing content. A few lines make note of the available sizes, the distributor, and a brief sales pitch. These can be included by simply adding blocks to the flow. To line up the blocks, you can either set their left margins or embed the blocks within an `fo:block-container` and set its margins as needed:

```
<fo:block
   margin-top=".875in"
   margin-left="1in"
   margin-right="1in"
   text-align="justify"
   >
   <fo:inline font-size="14pt">Blends notes of Chardonnay with the natural ⮐
sweetness of juicy peaches. Featuring mango and sweet pineapple undertones, ⮐
it is enriched with hints of ripe guava. A *must have* for casual summer ⮐
picnics.</fo:inline>
</fo:block>

<fo:block-container
   margin-top="1.375in"
   margin-left="0.375in"
   >
   <fo:block>
      <fo:inline>Available in 750ml bottles.</fo:inline>
   </fo:block>
   <fo:block margin-top="1em">
      <fo:inline>Dri Distributors, Inc.</fo:inline>
   </fo:block>
   <fo:block>
      <fo:inline>Call to place an order today!</fo:inline>
   </fo:block>
</fo:block-container>
```

With more blocks, eventually the formatter would run out of space on the current page and create a new one. Page breaks can also be induced through the `page-break-before`, `page-break-inside`, *or* `page-break-after` *properties. This might be used by an XSLT stylesheet to force a page break on each new wine entry.*

But enough of the so-called normal flow! By now you get the idea. Blocks stack on top of one another, and inlines stack from left to right within an area (in the default writing mode). The processor keeps track of how areas created by the Formatting Objects are flowed onto the page. To make things more interesting, you can position blocks fixed with respect to a page, absolutely with respect to an area, and statically to be repeated on multiple pages. The following sections explore these options.

Fixed Positioning

XSL flows objects by stacking them in these two progression dimensions according to the writing mode. You can also express formatting in terms of items with respect to a page, or positioned relative to a fixed block container. Much of XSL is oriented toward formatting of what might be called narrative text layouts. With some creative interpretation, the same Formatting Objects can be used for layout designs for marketing materials such as mailers, brochures, or newsletters.

To position a block with respect to a page, use the `absolute-position` property on an `fo:block-container`, and place the block inside of the positioned block container. It helps to know the general constraints on the amount of space you need for the blocks you are placing into the container. If you don't have a good feel for how it will look, make an estimate of position and size based on the layout sketch, and then refine the properties by looking at the output.

Actual data may vary greatly, and the manner in which you position and size a block may lead to unintended line wrapping or clipping. For the wine brochure project, you can assume that the wine names are all relatively short. With that in mind, and a few estimates taken from the sketch in Figure 6-3, here is a fragment to place the wine name:

```
<fo:block-container
   absolute-position="fixed"
   height="20pt"
   width="3in"
   top="2.125in"
   left="4.32in"
   >
   <fo:block>
      <fo:inline>Nags Head Scuppernong</fo:inline>
   </fo:block>
</fo:block-container>
```

This fragment makes no use of margins. The `fixed` value indicates that the block container is placed with respect to the page in which its area would have appeared in the normal flow. This means, among other things, that it appears on just one page.

Fixed does not mean static: static areas are used to repeat the same or similar content across multiple pages. A fixed area is placed on one page.

That should place the wine name to the right of the wine label. However, in the sketch and the HTML output of Chapter 5, the wine name was presented as a heading. XSL-FO has no elements to represent headings, instead relying purely upon style properties to give the right appearance. Simply increase the font size and weight of the `fo:inline`, as you might do in CSS, and you've got your heading:

```
<fo:block-container
   absolute-position="fixed"
   height="20pt"
   width="3in"
   top="2.125in"
   left="4.32in"
   >
   <fo:block>
      <fo:inline font-size="18pt" font-weight="bold">Nags Head ⮐
Scuppernong</fo:inline>
   </fo:block>
</fo:block-container>
```

After fiddling with implementation limitations, absolute positioning turned out to be quite useful for emulating the float behavior used in Chapter 5 to position the winery information. Absolute positioning is yet another twist on taking blocks out of the normal flow.

Absolute Positioning

In absolute positioning, a block container is positioned in terms of the area that contains it. Like fixed areas, once an area is placed absolutely it does not affect how other objects are positioned in the normal flow. However, a block container serves to coordinate the placement of its children. By absolutely positioning the children, you can get their contents to align along a common edge, emulating the way in which floats were used in Chapter 5.

First, establish a fixed block container to provide a reference area. The following fragment places the block container to the right of the wine label image, below the wine name heading.

```
<fo:block-container
   absolute-position="fixed"
   height="9em"
   width="2in"
   top="2.5in"
   left="4.32in"
   line-height="2em"
   >

</fo:block-container>
```

Next, use an absolutely positioned block container as a wrapper to place the field labels for the wine and winery information within a fixed size area:

```
<fo:block-container
   absolute-position="fixed"
   height="9em"
   width="2in"
   top="2.5in"
   left="4.32in"
   line-height="2em"
   >
   <fo:block-container
      absolute-position="absolute"
      width="0.625in"
      height="8em"
      top="0in"
      left="0in"
      text-align="right"
      >
      <fo:block>Variety:</fo:block>
      <fo:block>Country:</fo:block>
      <fo:block>Region:</fo:block>
   </fo:block-container>

</fo:block-container>
```

Follow up with another absolutely positioned block container to hold the field values. This time the container is placed sufficiently to the right to avoid overlapping the field labels (and provide a little space in between):

```
<fo:block-container
   absolute-position="fixed"
   height="9em"
   width="2in"
   top="2.5in"
   left="4.32in"
   line-height="2em"
   >
   <fo:block-container
      absolute-position="absolute"
      width="0.625in"
      height="8em"
      top="0in"
      left="0in"
      text-align="right"
      >
      <fo:block>Variety:</fo:block>
      <fo:block>Country:</fo:block>
      <fo:block>Region:</fo:block>
   </fo:block-container>

   <fo:block-container
      absolute-position="absolute"
      top="0in"
      left="0.645in"
      width="1.355in"
      height="8em"
      >
      <fo:block>Scupp</fo:block>
      <fo:block>United States</fo:block>
      <fo:block>North Carolina</fo:block>
   </fo:block-container>
</fo:block-container>
```

Someone might stop at this point and wonder why `fo:inline-container` *was not used instead. That would be a good question. At the time of this writing, the FOP beta does not support the inline container object.*

Note that the `top` and `left` attributes are not measured relative to the page, but relative to the fixed block container in which the absolutely positioned block containers are nested.

The FO document now produces the results shown in Figure 6-7.

It isn't perfect, but it is getting much closer. All that is left to deal with are the header and footer areas.

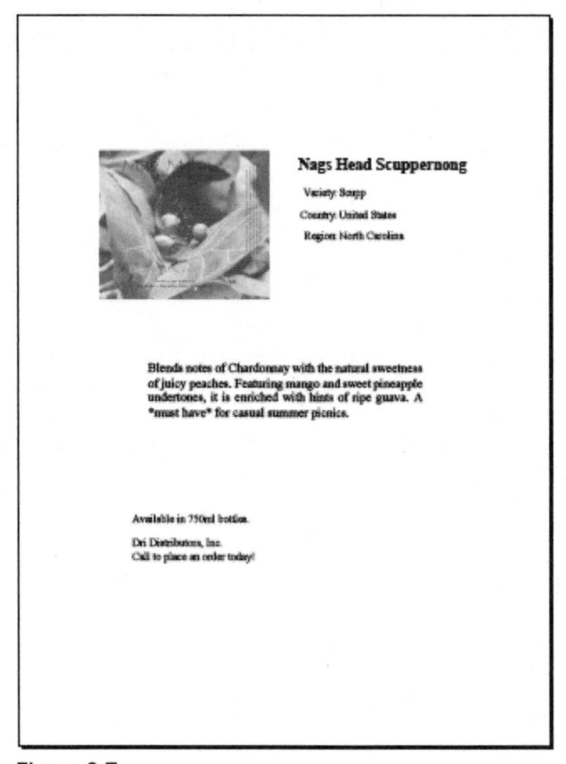
Nags Head Scuppernong
Variety: Scupp
Country: United States
Region: North Carolina
Blends notes of Chardonnay with the natural sweetness of juicy peaches. Featuring mango and sweet pineapple undertones, it is enriched with hints of ripe guava. A *must have* for casual summer picnics.
Available in 750ml bottles.
Dri Distributors, Inc.
Call to place an order today!

Figure 6-7

Headers and Footers

XSL's simple page master provides four regions along the boundaries of the page in which to place content. A common use of those areas is to provide content that does not change from page to page. The `fo:static-content` element is used for this purpose. Static content elements, if present, are included as children of the page sequence before the `fo:flow` element. Like `fo:flow`, the `flow-name` attribute refers to one of the regions in the page master. The following code snippet shows the tags to create the static content; for context, the `fo:page-sequence` and `fo:flow` start tags are shown as well.

```
<fo:page-sequence master-reference="master1">

   <fo:static-content flow-name="xsl-region-before">

   </fo:static-content>

   <fo:flow flow-name="xsl-region-body"
      font-family="Times New Roman, Times Roman, Serif" font-size="12pt">
```

Note again that while `fo:static-content` elements are optional, if present they must be placed within the `fo:page-sequence` element before the `fo:flow`.

fo:static-content is populated similarly to fo:flow. Blocks and block containers placed within the static content are flowed within the region. The following fragment positions the Mad Melvin logo within the static content:

```
<fo:static-content flow-name="xsl-region-before">
        <fo:block text-align="right">
     <fo:external-graphic src="url(images/Melvin.png)"
         content-width="3.36in"
         scaling="uniform" />
   </fo:block>
</fo:static-content>
```

If the static content overflows down the page, the formatter doesn't create a subsequent page to catch the overflow. Static content elements just overflow into the adjoining areas or are hidden, based on the setting of the overflow property of the region with which it is associated. However, given that it still flows blocks (in the default writing mode) from top to bottom, the graphic above in your project would appear right on the top edge of the page. That's not at all what you want. You could set a margin, or, better still, tweak the fo:region-before so that blocks align with the bottom of the region. To do that, go back to the fo:simple-page-master and add a display-align attribute to the fo:region-before:

```
<fo:simple-page-master master-name="master1" size="portrait">
   <fo:region-body
      margin-left="1.0in" margin-right="1.0in"
      margin-top="2.0in"  margin-bottom="1.5in"
   />
   <fo:region-before extent="1.72in" display-align="after"/>
   <fo:region-after extent="1.5in"/>
   <fo:region-start extent="1.0in"/>
   <fo:region-end extent="1.0in"/>
</fo:simple-page-master>
```

The footer is handled in a similar manner. The following code places the Mad Melvin's byline on the bottom right of the page and locates the sulfite warning further down toward the center.

```
<fo:static-content flow-name="xsl-region-after" >
   <fo:block-container text-align="right">
      <fo:block>
         <fo:inline font-size="18pt"
            font-weight="bold">Mad Melvin's Muscadine Wines</fo:inline>
      </fo:block>
      <fo:block text-align="center" margin-top=".375in">
         <fo:inline font-size="10pt">May contain sulfites</fo:inline>
      </fo:block>
   </fo:block-container>
</fo:static-content>
```

With the footer added, the wine brochure is done. Running FOP one more time creates the PDF shown in Figure 6-8.

```
fop brochure.fo brochure.pdf
```

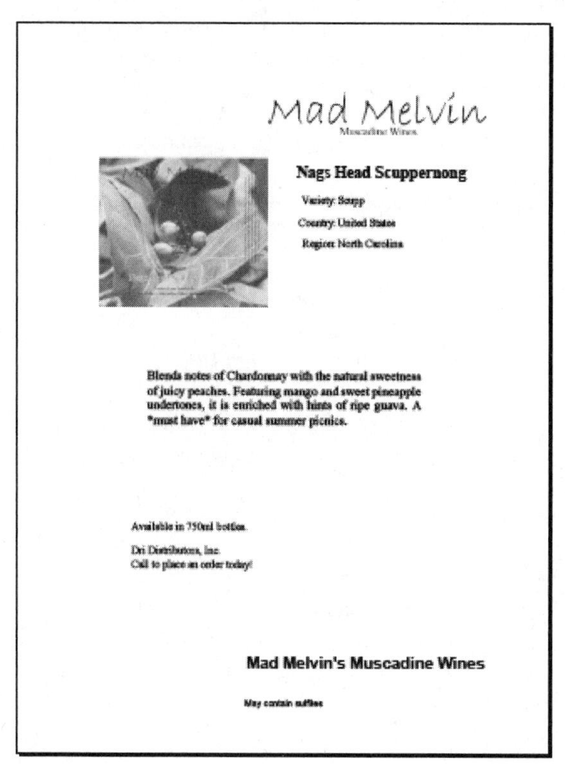
Mad Melvin
Nags Head Scuppernong
Variety: Scupp
Country: United States
Region: North Carolina
Blends notes of Chardonnay with the natural sweetness of juicy peaches. Featuring mango and sweet pineapple undertones, it is enriched with hints of ripe guava. A "must have" for casual summer picnics.
Available in 750ml bottles.
Dri Distributors, Inc.
Call to place an order today!
Mad Melvin's Muscadine Wines

Figure 6-8

The PDF version is a pretty good approximation of the XHTML page of Chapter 5 and much more likely to print out the same way, over and over and over again.

Alternative Formats

What if you're a dyed-in-the-wool anti-PDF activist? Many XSL-FO processors seem to support PDF as a baseline. Because of its obvious connection to PDF, PostScript output is also very common. Other formats are less well supported.

As mentioned earlier, aside from PDF and PostScript, Apache's FOP supports several other outputs. Reflecting its open source background, FOP seems to have a lot of options: MIF, RTF, PNG, TIFF, PCL, TXT, and SVG. (The FOP beta version referred to in this chapter still had problems with several of the back ends.)

You can get an output of the brochure using the format as an output option. For instance, to get an RTF output, use `-rtf filename.rtf`; to get a PNG image, use `-png filename.png`:

```
fop brochure.fo -rtf brochure.rft
fop brochure.fo -png brochure.png
```

Some of these formats lack the capability to precisely represent the formatting information. With others, the formatter back end loses something in the translation. For instance, the RTF version of the brochure is distorted in both MS Word and OpenOffice.

Some of the FOP back ends vary in the way fonts are handled. For example, the PNG output from the FOP beta looks pretty good overall, but the wine description isn't properly justified, and the variety/country/region fields run into their labels. If you're willing to tweak it until both the PDF and PNG are "good enough," this might not matter. Of course, you could also use another application to render the PDF version as a PNG image.

Summary

XSL FO is not a silver bullet for producing identical formatting results, just a helpful tool. Still, it is a very useful tool for producing printed materials, and electronic versions of printed materials, based on XML inputs. You used XSL FO to produce a special-purpose printed piece, and have a basic framework on which to construct FO outputs of greater complexity.

XSLT is a natural fit for XSL-FO. Now that you've completed this chapter, you may want to review Chapter 5 with an eye toward how the transform could output FO syntax.

7

Targeting Your Audience

In Chapter 6, you saw how to use XSL's formatting objects to produce a paginated document (albeit with one page). You might have noticed that FO processors often support multiple back-end rendering features. Using these features, you could target multiple output formats. This chapter considers the other aspect of targeting XML — using information inside and outside of the XML to target a demographic audience.

Rather than working through a single example, this chapter calls out much smaller fragments of XML, XSLT, and XPath. You won't need to be an expert in any of the technologies, but knowing something about XSLT will help to put the fragments in context.

Problem

Customers have peculiar needs, preferences, and capabilities. Prospects differ in income level, geographic regions, age, and so forth. Many businesses market their goods and services to "targeted" segments — that is, to populations identified as most likely to purchase those goods and services. Depending on the wine catalog's use in importing and exporting, you may find that the information also needs to be directed toward audiences who differ substantially in language.

The following problem/design/solution is not a treatise on multiple-language support. In many cases, development platforms provide toolkits to support multiple languages and other aspects of internationalization. Rather, it calls out features of XML and its related technologies that may be useful for tweaking XML to address different audiences based on demographics.

The preceding chapters took for granted that people who might buy the wine are all uniformly speakers of American English. One clue was dropped while discussing XSL for formatting documents: XSL supports languages whose scripts do not follow the English left-to-right, top-to-bottom mode. This raises a questions like "What features does XML provide to directly address language issues?" and "How would an XSLT transform know to select a suitable writing mode?"

Literal translation can sometimes complicate the problem, and while that's out of the scope of this book, it warrants some pointers and links, which can be found toward the end of the chapter.

More fundamentally, you might ask whether your system can process and display the characters required for different languages. XML parsers are required, at a minimum, to be capable of reading ISO10646 UTF-8 and UTF-16 encodings. That requirement may not apply to the rest of your toolchain—you may have to go through some hoops to get the data to display properly. For instance, many (if not most) fonts include only enough glyphs (symbols) to display characters commonly used in ASCII, an earlier encoding standardized by the American National Standards Institute (ANSI). Also, some older software (including some XML tools and core libraries) assumed that data was only expressed as ASCII.

If you see small square blocks or "??" in your XML document, you may need to load a font capable of displaying the characters and ensure that any older tools you use correctly support the character encoding.

Internationalization (I18N) and localization are ways of adjusting such things as publications and software for non-native environments, especially other nations and cultures. In localization, information is adapted to target a specific group, usually on the basis of language and culture. A similar practice is to target an audience based on market demographics. For instance, an insurance agency might use geographic region and age to assemble greetings, articles, and byline elements into a newsletter designed to appeal to older executives. Personalization involves creating marketing collateral material with personal information. Your XML must incorporate structures to deal with such problems.

Legal jurisdictions such as cities, counties, and states may also be a source of customization requirements. Consider the wine label introduced in Chapter 5 (see Figure 7-1). The U.S. government requires the health warning on labels of wine sold in the U.S. Labels like this can be expressed using XSL-FO, SVG (Standard Vector Graphics), or a combination of the two. Small businesses selling wine products in different jurisdictions might need to use different regulatory messages, bilingual portions, and/or personalized components to the label.

Figure 7-1

By the end of the chapter, you'll understand some basic XML features that can help you address the catalog information to specific audiences. XSLT examples are thrown in for good measure. The features are not an end in themselves; supporting technologies and techniques such as SQL databases and Cocoon pipelines are discussed in other chapters. As noted, many application development environments provide resource toolkits for implementing multiple-language support. XML doesn't preclude using these tools when they are needed, but there are hooks and techniques that can be useful in tying everything together.

Design

The first thing to consider is what changes to make to the XML document type definitions or schemas. In other words, let's explore how to adapt the XML to resolve language and personalization problems, starting with the built-in features provided by XML 1.0.

XML let the cat out of the box in terms of multiple-language support. By requiring ISO 10646 (Unicode) support and divorcing the procedural instructions from the information content, XML promoted a view of data that no longer assumed that all the world was using U.S. English in ASCII. Despite this, the features it offers are not very elaborate.

xml:lang

One built-in XML 1.0 language feature is the `xml:lang` attribute. It attaches a code to an element, telling a processor the intended language of its contents.

> `xml:lang` *is one of two attributes reserved for special use in XML. (The XML Namespaces Recommendation actually reserves the* `xml: prefix` *or any case-insensitive equivalent for use by XML related specifications.) The other is* `xml:space` *for whitespace handling.*

To define the value of `xml:lang`, XML 1.0 points to IETF RFC 3066, which in turn refers to language codes interpreted according to ISO 639, "Code for the representation of names of languages." The language tag represents a human language as spoken, not a computer language. Basically, `xml:lang` is an attribute that contains a language code (or a composite language-region code).

The value of `xml:lang` applies to the element to which it is attached, as well as to the content and attributes of that element, and any element children it may have. This can be overridden on child elements by attaching another `xml:lang` attribute to the child element. Because there is only one `xml:lang` per element, it can't be used to specify the languages of individual attributes or children — the attribute isn't that complicated.

The `xml:lang` code value is typically in the form `"aa"` or `"aa-bb"`, where `aa` is the language code and `bb` the country code. Sometimes, instead of or in addition to the country code, other codes are appended to indicate the dialect or regional identification. The following example adds French and Spanish descriptions to the Smoky Scupp `wine` element, so that three descriptions are available: one in Canadian French, one in Spanish (region unspecified), and one in U.S. English.

> *Excuser mon français et espagnol, s'il vous plaît. The alternative descriptions are both machine translations, so they may read strangely to those fluent in French or Spanish.*

```
<wine id="Smoky_Scupp_750ml">
    <name>Smoky Scupp</name>
    <varietal>Scupp</varietal>
    <vintage>1992</vintage>
```

```
    <winery>Melvin</winery>
    <distributor>Dri</distributor>
    <bottlesize>750ml</bottlesize>
    <description xml:lang="es"> Una uva moscatel roja seca con insinuaciones de
roble. Un vino delicioso produjo de una combinación extraordinaria de Carlos y uvas
de Magnolia Scuppernong. Las aromas de la zarzamora llevan a la grasa, smoky
condimenta y el fin picante largo.</description>
    <description xml:lang="fr-CA">Un muscadine rouge sec avec les allusions de
chêne. Un vin délicieux a produit d'un mélange unique de Carlos et les raisins de
Scuppernong de Magnolia. Les arômes aux mûres menent au gras, smoky parfume et la
fin épicée longue.</description>
    <description xml:lang="en-US">A dry red muscadine with hints of oak. A
delicious wine produced from a unique mix of Carlos and Magnolia Scuppernong
grapes. Blackberry aromas lead to fat, smoky flavors and long spicy
finish.</description>
</wine>
```

Codes that begin with `x-` are reserved so that private, experimental language codes can be created without going through a registration process. You might use such codes to support language usage within a specialized professional field, for development and testing, or for less than serious purposes. For instance, science fiction fans might want to refer to `x-klingon` or `x-romulan` codes to refer to those fictional languages. If you rely on such codes, you limit the interoperability of the markup. If you use a few southeastern U.S. words in your texts, it is probably self-defeating to call it `x-en-NC` rather than `en-US`.

Part 2 of ISO 639 can be found at `www.loc.gov/standards/iso639-2/normtext.html`; its tables of language codes include both three-character and two-character codes. A FAQ is also available at `www.loc.gov/standards/iso639-2/faq.html`. The RFC gives preference to the ISO 639 two-character codes rather than the three-character codes. Some languages have more than one three-character code, and the two-character code avoids questions about which code to use. For cases in which a language has no two-character code, the three-letter code is allowed. The guideline also ensures better interoperability with older systems that only use two-character language codes. The country codes, including codes for regional subdivisions, are defined in ISO 3166; more information can be found at `www.iso.org/iso/en/prods-services/iso3166ma/index.html`.

The code lists themselves can be useful, serving as lookup tables in transforms and validation. The ISO 3166 web site offers the country lists free in XML format, for private or noncommercial use. The Library of Congress site also has links to the ISO 639 language code lists (not in XML). Check the licensing status before incorporating such lists into a commercial product.

The Internet Assigned Numbers Agency (IANA) also serves as a registration authority for language tags. Some that are registered by IANA itself are prefixed with `i-`. *Some might be considered silly (*`i-klingon` *?), while others are straightforward. Not all of the IANA-registered codes use the* `i-` *prefix. These codes don't quite have the same status as the ISO counterparts, although several of them may coincide.*

Structural Changes for xml:lang

If you use a DTD or Schema, you need to declare `xml:lang` as an attribute on any elements on which you want the indicated language used. The noted wine/description element would require an `ATTLIST`. You can leave the specification open ended by using a `NMTOKEN` type, or constrain the codes to those you know you can support to a fixed list of tokens. XML DTDs provide a special value type, called an enumerated token list, to do just that. Here's an example of declaring an `xml:lang` attribute for the `description` element, allowing only U.S. English (`en-US`), Canadian French (`fr-CA`), and Spanish (`es`):

```
<!ATTLIST description xml:lang (en-US|fr-CA|es) #IMPLIED>
```

This fragment can be added to the DTD from Chapter 3 to allow `xml:lang` on the `description` element only.

The same sort of declaration is needed for any other element that should allow an `xml:lang` attribute. This can become tedious, and XML DTDs adopt (or partially adopt) an SGML method known as Parameter Entities to help manage repeated definitions within a DTD. Like regular entities that refer to characters or strings for reference within a document, you can refer to parameter entities within a DTD to substitute the parameter entity's text at the point of reference. Here's an example of using a parameter entity for the `xml:lang` attribute, so that the same definition may be reused consistently throughout the DTD:

```
<!ENTITY % commonattr.xmllang "xml:lang (en-US|fr-CA|es) #IMPLIED">
<!ATTLIST description  %commonattr.xmllang; >
```

Some industry-defined document types go to great lengths to chunk the DTD into fragments using parameter entities, with the result that the DTD becomes very difficult to read. You need not go that far with your own DTDs. Neither W3C XML Schema nor RelaxNG use parameter entities, so if you maintain your schemas in one of those forms you can use their features to organize and reuse definitions. Tools can help bootstrap the conversion and reorganization. The open source trang tool from James Clark, used to convert schemas between different schema syntaxes (including DTD, W3C Schema, Relax NG), tries to carry over the implicit structure of parameter entities into high-level structures. This is helpful to port the original organization of a DTD into other schema languages. Trang is available at `http://thaiopensource.com/relaxng/trang.html`.

The schema presented in Chapter 3 has an additional difficulty with the description element. Take, for instance, the schema declaration:

```
<xs:element name="description" type="xs:string"/>
```

Validating the wine description against the schema produces an error. The description element, being a simple type (`xs:string`), does not allow attributes other than those corresponding to the XML Schema namespace. The solution is to give the description a complex content model:

```
<xs:element name = "description">
   <xs:complexType mixed = "true">

   </xs:complexType>
</xs:element>
```

However, this leaves the attribute and namespace undeclared. The prefix `xml` is associated with the string `"http://www.w3.org/XML/1998/namespace"`, and shouldn't need to be declared. The special XML 1.0 attributes can be imported from `"http://www.w3.org/2001/xml.xsd"`, or a similar local copy of that schema. (Trang generates a copy of the `xml.xsd` file when converting schemas or DTDs containing any of the special attributes to XML Schema.) The following fragment shows how to import the special XML attributes schema file (the schema document element is shown for context):

```
<xs:schema xmlns:xs = "http://www.w3.org/2001/XMLSchema"
    elementFormDefault = "qualified">

    <xs:import
       namespace="http://www.w3.org/XML/1998/namespace"
       schemaLocation="xml.xsd" />
```

After this import, it is a simple matter of referencing the attribute definition:

```
<xs:element name = "description">
   <xs:complexType mixed = "true">
      <xs:attribute ref="xml:lang" />
   </xs:complexType>
</xs:element>
```

This isn't quite the same as the DTD, which uses an enumeration. The `xml.xsd` *definition uses the simple type "language" for* `xml:lang`.

The wine document with the `xml:lang` in the description should now . . . still be rejected. The `xml:lang` no longer causes an error, but there is a subtle shift in the structural assumption that a wine has one description. With the inclusion of descriptions for other languages, that assumption is broken. The solution is to throw it away—it was a bad assumption anyway. You can allow zero or more or require at least one description, as in this modified declaration:

```
<!ELEMENT wine
(name,varietal,vintage,winery,distributor,bottlesize,description+,inventorycount?,
price?)>
```

The XML Schema change is similar (the changed part is in bold):

```
<xs:element name = "wine">
     <xs:complexType>
         <xs:sequence>
             <xs:element ref = "name"/>
             <xs:element ref = "varietal"/>
             <xs:element ref = "vintage"/>
             <xs:element ref = "winery"/>
             <xs:element ref = "distributor"/>
             <xs:element ref = "bottlesize"/>

             <xs:element ref = "description"
                minOccurs = "1" maxOccurs = "unbounded"/>

             <xs:element ref = "inventorycount" minOccurs = "0"/>
             <xs:element ref = "price" minOccurs = "0"/>
         </xs:sequence>
         <xs:attribute name = "id" use = "required" type = "xs:ID"/>
     </xs:complexType>
  </xs:element>
```

The DTD and XML schema are now able to validate the XML, with the new attribute and altered assumptions about the number of description elements. But wait—there's more!

Consequences of xml:lang

The altered structure has further implications for the results of XPath expressions. Paths that should have matched a single (English) description node are going to match multiple descriptions. By extension, there's an impact on the logic of XSLT transformations. For a situation such as the descriptions, the visible effect provides clues; a worse outcome is for results to silently succeed or fail with unobvious results.

Remember, too, that XPath and XSLT are often used in situations other than page formatting. While it is fairly easy to adjust a DTD or XML schema, the consequences of these changes flow over into any code that made the same flawed assumption. If you don't test the results, any output is — technically — valid output.

`xml:lang` is a fairly simple hook. Only one language code can be contained in an `xml:lang` attribute. When used on a document element, it isn't necessarily the exclusive language used throughout the document. Other elements may override the language setting. The code in `xml:lang` can be validated with an enumeration in a DTD, but the validation process won't check whether the language used in content actually matches the language code. For instance, the following `description` element claims to have French language content, but actually has Spanish. You can't rely upon the XML parser to catch this kind of error.

```
<description xml:lang="fr">Una uva moscatel roja seca con insinuaciones de roble.
Un vino delicioso produjo de una combinación extraordinaria de Carlos y uvas de
Magnolia Scuppernong. Las aromas de la zarzamora llevan a la grasa, smoky
condimenta y el fin picante largo.</description>
```

Entities

XML adopts SGML's method of defining a replaced character string, referred to as an "entity." You've seen the predefined XML entities:

Entity	Reference
`<`	`<`
`>`	`>`
`&`	`&`
`"`	`"`
`'`	`'`

XML also provides numeric character references that allow you to include Unicode characters by their numeric code. For instance, the character representing the copyright symbol (©) can be included using the numeric reference "`©`" in decimal. The same character can be expressed in hexadecimal as "`©`".

You can't define new numeric character entities — they are derived from the ISO10646 set. You can define new entities using your own names, but only if you use a DTD (or local section). The declarations can even refer to other entities, including numeric references, allowing names to be assigned to international language characters. This can be useful if your editor does not make it easy to type in the characters, or to make the use of the characters more explicit.

The syntax is similar to that for parameter entities (but loses the %). To give a name to the copyright character, use the declaration:

```
<!ENTITY copyright "&#169;" >
```

Entities also allow a string of such characters:

```
<!ENTITY copyright.message.en "Copyright &#169; 2006 by John Doe" >
```

Names for commonly used characters can be found in various places around the web, particularly at standards organizations' web sites. The XHTML Latin-1 entity declarations can be found at `www.w3.org/TR/xhtml1/dtds.html#h-A2`, and the recommendation links to files containing entity declarations for other special characters.

XPath Features for xml:lang

The `lang()` function returns true if the `xml:lang` value in effect for the context node matches the given language code. Based on the changes to the description element, if you write the following into an XPath toolbar (available in many XML development environments), the result will be false for the first two descriptions and true for the last:

```
/catalog/section/wine/description/lang("en-US")
```

Why not just test the node with a simple predicate? Take for example:

```
/catalog/section/wine/description[ @xml:lang = 'en-US' ]
```

First, the `lang()` function doesn't just test equality. The "`en`" matches "`en-GB`" and "`en-US`", but `"en-US"` given as an argument does not match a node with `xml:lang="en"`. That is, `lang()` tests whether the language in effect on a node is the same as, or a subset of, the given argument. In keeping with the RFC, the comparison is also case-insensitive, so "`EN`" matches "`en`" (or "`eN`" or "`En`").

Second, `xml:lang` is given special treatment by XML. It isn't just an attribute; it is an attribute whose value effectively propagates down the tree of nodes from parent to child, from element to nested elements, their attributes, and so on. Due to this inheritance, the preceding XPath could filter out legitimate nodes. The `xml:lang` attribute doesn't actually have to be literally present on an element for a test with `lang()` to work properly. (You can use the `ancestor-or-self::` axis to emulate the inheritance, but `lang("en")` is a lot shorter to write, less prone to error, and easier to understand.)

Pertinent XML Data

Making the preceding changes, with a little help from machine translation, provides a modified wines catalog. As amended, the wines now carry multiple descriptions, each with a target language, and possibly a region code. A sample of the Smoky Scupp wine includes English, French (mechanically translated), and Spanish (just as mechanical):

```
<wine id="Smoky_Scupp_750ml" >
    <name>Smoky Scupp</name>
    <varietal>Scupp</varietal>
    <vintage>1992</vintage>
```

```
    <winery>Melvin</winery>
    <distributor>Dri</distributor>
    <bottlesize>750ml</bottlesize>
    <description xml:lang="en-US">A dry red muscadine with hints of oak. A
delicious wine produced from a unique mix of Carlos and Magnolia Scuppernong
grapes. Blackberry aromas lead to fat, smoky flavors and long spicy
finish.</description>
    <description xml:lang="fr">Un muscadine rouge sec avec les allusions de chêne.
Un vin délicieux a produit d'un mélange unique de Carlos et les raisins de
Scuppernong de Magnolia. Les arômes aux mûres menent au gras, smoky parfume et la
fin épicée longue.</description>
    <description xml:lang="es">Una uva moscatel roja seca con insinuaciones de
roble. Un vino delicioso produjo de una combinación extraordinaria de Carlos y uvas
de Magnolia Scuppernong. Las aromas de la zarzamora llevan a la grasa, smoky
condimenta y el fin picante largo.</description>
</wine>
```

Applicable Technologies

In this chapter's project, you'll use some of the less well-known features of technologies referred to in earlier chapters: XML 1.0, XSLT transformations, and XPath expressions.

The project uses the 2.0 versions of each of the XSLT and XPath recommendations. At the time of this writing, XSLT 2.0 (`www.w3.org/TR/xslt20`) and XPath 2.0 (`www.w3.org/TR/xpath20`) are candidate recommendations. As candidate recommendations, some features of XSLT 2.0 and XPath 2.0 may change, but leading XSLT vendors such as Saxonica and Oracle are implementing its features in their products.

A familiar XSL transformation from Chapter 5 is reintroduced in the final section, "Solution," and the identity transform will help bring into focus how parameters can be used to adapt the output for specific audiences.

Solution

As you know, XSLT provides special stylesheet parameters. In Chapter 5, you used a parameter to cherry-pick a wine selection from the catalog. But there's more to parameters than the one-off problem of the wine brochure could expose. Whether you pass them as arguments at a command line, set them in an XML editor's user interface, or control them as part of a Java API to invoke a transformation, parameters are key to personalizing the output.

Parameterizing a Transform

Parameters are your window of opportunity for controlling the logic in an XSLT transformation. You saw stylesheet-level parameters in Chapter 5, but XSLT also allows parameters at lower levels of the transformation, in templates (and in XSLT 2.0, in functions). By using template parameters and variables, you can tweak the logic of the transformation.

The following code shows the basic syntax in XSLT 2.0. Parameters are declared at either the level of the stylesheet, or within an `xsl:template`. This code specifies both stylesheet parameters and template parameters. The XSLT 2.0 parameters allow other options that are discussed later.

```
<xsl:stylesheet xmlns:xsl="http://www.w3.org/1999/XSL/Transform" version="2.0">

<xsl:param name="top_level_param" select=" 'somestring' " />

<xsl:template match="some_elem">
   <xsl:param name="template_level_param" select=" 'someotherstring' " />
</xsl:template>

</xsl:stylesheet>
```

The stylesheet version attribute is set to `"2.0"`*, indicating an XSLT 2.0 transformation, which will be needed later when tunnel parameters are discussed.*

Variables can be specified in the same manner, using the `xsl:variable` element. Unlike variables, parameters can be passed into a transform and into template invocations. The manner in which stylesheet parameters are passed depends upon your environment (GUI tool, command-line, Java program, ANT build script, etc.) and upon the XSLT implementation. To pass the `top_level_param` parameter in via the Saxon command line, use a line like the following:

```
java net.sf.saxon.Transform inputfile.xml transformfile.xsl ⮐
top_level_param=some_other_string
```

XSLT implementations provide various methods to set the parameters. The JAXP `Transformer` class provides a `setParameter()` method. (Saxon supports the JAXP interface.) Microsoft's MSXML uses a typed argument ("`XsltArgumentList`") to the `XslTransform` class's `Transform` method. Firefox's Transformix interface provides a `setParameter` method. All of them require a namespace qualified name (which is what the `xsl:param` specifies). In the example, the namespace is defaulted. If the parameter name is qualified (has a namespace prefix), you need to locate the corresponding namespace URI and pass it along in the call. (The API documentation should tell you how.)

The parameter can also use a result tree fragment—its element content—as its value. In this case, the select attribute can't be used. The parameter then holds the result tree nodes:

```
<xsl:param name="param_name">result tree nodes</xsl:param>
```

These nodes aren't limited to literal text and result elements. You can also include XSLT instructions, including calls to `xsl:call-template` and `xsl:apply-templates`. (If you're tempted to do this a lot, you may want to consider the pipelines discussed in Chapter 10, and rethink the structure of your transformations.)

Some parameters defined in terms of result tree elements are subtly different from those using a `select`. The result tree equivalent of a simple XPath numeric expression such as `select="1"` is actually a node and may evaluate as a Boolean true in test expressions later in the code.

To provide a parameter to a template, you use the `xsl:with-param` element, within an `xsl:call-template` or `xsl:apply-templates` instruction:

```
<xsl:call-template name="some_template">
   <xsl:with-param name="param_name" select=" 'some string value' " />
</xsl:call-template>
```

or

```
<xsl:apply-templates match="some_pattern">
   <xsl:with-param name="param_name" >some result tree</xsl:with-param>
</xsl:apply-templates>
```

As with the `xsl:param` element, the result tree form can include other instructions, to pull in the results of other templates as the parameter value. This can cause problems if you assume that default values are always defaulted: if an empty node set is passed, the default value specified in `xsl:param` no longer applies. You can avoid passing result trees as parameters, or you can guard the default using a conditional variable within the template that is invoked:

```
<xsl:template name="my_template">
   <xsl:param name="someparam" />
   <xsl:variable name="defaulted_var">
      <xsl:if test="string-length($someparam) = 0">
         <xsl:text>Some default</xsl:text>
      </xsl:if>
   </xsl:variable>
</xsl:template>
```

There are a lot of extra bits there just for setting a default value. If the defaults are that important, another option is to use the `xsl:message` element in a way reminiscent of the `assert()` function to trigger a static error when an unacceptable condition is detected:

```
<xsl:template name="my_template">
   <xsl:param name="someparam" select="' Some default'"/>

      <xsl:if test="string-length($someparam) = 0">
         <xsl:message terminate="yes">Error: the my_template/someparam
           parameter was passed as empty while processing
           <xsl:value-of select="name()"/>
      </xsl:if>
</xsl: template>
```

A Stage in the Pipe

Your marketing guru tells that the mailings to Quebec should be bilingual in French and English, but that mailings to Mexico are always in Spanish. When the region is the United States, which is usually the case, only English should appear in the primary listings. She also says that for the bilingual marketing collaterals, as a general rule of thumb, English is placed after the other language. You decide that while the requirements can be handled elsewhere, a few small changes to the identity transform can make it easier to accommodate the requirements, and easier to back out changes when the marketing gurus change their minds.

Starting with the identity transform, let's take a look at a simple filter that tweaks the wine catalog so that it only contains elements suitable for a specific language and region-specific. This might be used to prepare XML containing `xml:lang` references for stylesheets that only expect one language, such as the transforms developed in Chapter 5. A filter like this might also be used in a build script or as a stage in a pipeline. For reference, following is the identity transform. Save it as `filter_lang.xsl`.

```
<xsl:stylesheet version="20"
   xmlns:xsl="http://www.w3.org/1999/XSL/Transform"
   >
   <xsl:output method="xml" indent="yes" />
   <xsl:template match="@*|*|processing-instruction()|comment()">
      <xsl:copy>
         <xsl:apply-templates select="*|@*|text()|processing-
instruction()|comment()"/>
      </xsl:copy>
   </xsl:template>

</xsl:stylesheet>
```

The marketing guru is going to give you the region, but wants you to map it to a language. For the time being, you decide to provide the logic in the stylesheet, and give it a parameter to read the region. Start by adding a top-level parameter to the identity transform:

```
<xsl:stylesheet version="20"
   xmlns:xsl="http://www.w3.org/1999/XSL/Transform"
   >

   <xsl:output method="xml" indent="yes" />

   <xsl:param name="target_region" />

   <xsl:template match="@*|*|processing-instruction()|comment()">
      <xsl:copy>
         <xsl:apply-templates select="*|@*|text()|processing-
instruction()|comment()"/>
      </xsl:copy>
   </xsl:template>

</xsl:stylesheet>
```

There is no default set, so throw an error if the stylesheet is not passed a suitable value. Remember that `xsl:if` can't be put in as a top-level element, so you have to add another template. Make it a named template so that it can be taken into another module and reused if needed. (From this point on, most of the listing is omitted for brevity.)

```
   <xsl:template name="check-target-region">
      <xsl:if test="string-length($target_region) &lt; 2">
         <xsl:message terminate="yes">Error: The target region must be
            at least a two character string! Instead it is
            "<xsl:value-of select="$target_region"/>".</xsl:message>
      </xsl:if>
   </xsl:template>
```

Then add a template to match the document root, so your transform can call the template once to check the new precondition prior to doing any worthless processing. Be sure to put in an `xsl:apply-templates` so that the other template rules are invoked after the check. Here's the code:

```
<xsl:template match="/">
   <xsl:call-template name="check-target-region"/>
   <xsl:apply-templates/>
</xsl:template>
```

Globals are often frowned on, however. The `check-target-region` template is now dependant on the name of the top-level parameter. Use a template parameter to define the interface better; note that the references to the top-level parameter are changed as well as the delimiters on the `xsl:call-template` instruction:

```
<xsl:template name="check-target-region">
   <xsl:param name="region" />
   <xsl:if test="string-length($region) &lt; 2">
      <xsl:message terminate="yes"> Error: The target region must be ↩
         at least a two character string! Instead it is ↩
         "<xsl:value-of select="$region"/>".</xsl:message>
   </xsl:if>
</xsl:template>

<xsl:template match="/">
   <xsl:call-template name="check-target-region">
      <xsl:with-param name="region" select="$target_region" />
   </xsl:call-template>
   <xsl:apply-templates/>
</xsl:template>
```

Here's what the transform should look like:

```
<xsl:stylesheet version="20"
   xmlns:xsl="http://www.w3.org/1999/XSL/Transform"
   >

   <xsl:output method="xml" indent="yes" />

   <xsl:param name="target_region" />

   <xsl:template match="@*|*|processing-instruction()|comment()">
      <xsl:copy>
         <xsl:apply-templates select="*|@*|text()|processing-↩
           instruction()|comment()"/>
      </xsl:copy>
   </xsl:template>

   <xsl:template name="check-target-region">
      <xsl:param name="region" />
      <xsl:if test="string-length($region) &lt; 2">
   <xsl:message terminate="yes">Error: The target region must be ↩
            at least a two character string! Instead it is ↩
            "<xsl:value-of select="$region"/>".</xsl:message>
```

```
        </xsl:if>
    </xsl:template>

    <xsl:template match="/">
        <xsl:call-template name="check-target-region"/>
        <xsl:apply-templates/>
    </xsl:template>

</xsl:stylesheet>
```

If you run the transform now without setting the parameter, you should get an error message:

```
java net.sf.saxon.Transform  wines.xml filter_lang.xsl

Error: The target region must be a two character string! Instead it is "".
```

At this point, you could set the parameter, but the transform isn't yet using the parameter. The transform still needs to map the regions into a language code and apply that to filter the output. You could ask your database administrators if they've already set up an interface to query this information, or just use a quick XML file of your own.

Lookup Tables

The languages that you know about at present in the wine catalog include English, French, and Spanish. The regions for which you know the marketing department has an interest in are the United States, Canada (specifically Quebec), and Mexico. The mapping isn't one-to-one because Quebec is bilingual, and the country codes don't quite match the marketing department's breakdown. A small structure to drive the logic might help to clarify things. You can call this `regionmap.xml`:

```
<?xml version="1.0" encoding="UTF-8"?>
<region-map>
    <region id="unitedstates">
        <country>US</country>
        <lang>en</lang>
    </region>
    <region id="quebec">
        <country>CA</country>
        <lang>fr</lang>
        <lang>en</lang>
    </region>
    <region id="canada">
        <country>CA</country>
        <lang>en</lang>
        <lang>fr</lang>
    </region>
    <region id="mexico">
        <country>MX</country>
        <lang>es</lang>
    </region>
</region-map>
```

This is just a well-formed XML file. The country codes and language codes are standard, but the file itself is simply a gap filler for business logic to fulfill the requirement. Given a proxy for the marketing department's term for a region (`"unitedstates"`, `"quebec"`, `"canada"`, `"mexico"`), the transform can now look up the region by ID, the principal language as the first `lang` element in document order within the region, and any other languages that should be included.

The transform can use variables to stage the proper language codes prior to the transformation. The XSLT 1.0 `document()` function is useful for looking up data such as this. Using `document()`, the transform can pull in the lookup table and bind variables to the language codes it needs. This should be placed near the top of the stylesheet:

```
<xsl:param name="target_region" />

<xsl:param name="region_map_file" select="'regionmap.xml'" />
<xsl:variable name="region_map" select="document($region_map_file)" />
```

The file can be placed in a well-known location if it needs to be shared (or you can look into using Oasis Open catalogs, which aren't covered here but are good for defining the locations of resources). An assertion could be put in to ensure that the map is always set explicitly, but that point has been made — the map is simply defaulted to `regionmap.xml`.

There are ways to embed the information in a stylesheet module, rather than exposing it as a separate XML file. Your own elements can be placed inside of variables and referenced as result tree fragments, or placed in the stylesheet module under your own extension namespace and accessed with a path such as `"document('')/xsl:stylesheet/myns:myelem"`. This information is probably best extracted from the stylesheet, but sometimes it can be useful to make self-contained examples, and to embed manifest constants that are specific to a transform.

The `region_map` variable now contains the nodes parsed from the `regionmap.xml` content. The region map provides a way to express the primary language for a region, and any other languages needed. The language codes can be determined by looking up the region, using the `target_region` parameter as the ID:

```
<xsl:param name="target_region" />

<xsl:param name="region_map_file" select="'regionmap.xml'" />
<xsl:variable name="region_map" select="document($region_map_file)" />

<xsl:variable name="language_codes"
   select="$region_map/region-map/region[@id=$target_region]/lang"/>
```

The language codes can be broken out in document order. The region map presupposes that the first such `lang` element represents the principal language:

```
<xsl:variable name="language_codes"
   select="$region_map/region-map/region[@id=$target_region]/lang"/>

<xsl:variable name"principal_language_code" select="$language_codes[1]"/>
<xsl:variable name="other_language_codes"
    select="$language_codes[ position() != 1]"/>
```

The exercise makes the simplifying assumption that either a single description with a generic language code is used (`"en"` for English) or the descriptions use country-specific codes (`"en-GB"` or `"en-US"`), but not both. This is because a code like `"en"` will match all three, and subsequent descriptions will need to be eliminated. (That is, ignore the country codes and use the language codes alone to drive the output.)

Filtering

Taking these codes, it is now possible to tweak the identity transform to filter and arrange the descriptions. Add another template to match the wine element, processing most of its children normally but diverting the processing for the description elements:

```
<xsl:template match="wine">
   <xsl:copy>

      <xsl:apply-templates select="*[
         local-name()!= 'description'
        ] | @* | text() | processing-instruction()|comment()"/>

   </xsl:copy>
</xsl:template>
```

The principal language can be handled in a straightforward manner—simply apply templates to descriptions for which `lang()` indicates it is the corresponding language:

```
<xsl:template match="wine">
   <xsl:copy>

      <xsl:apply-templates select="*[
         local-name()!= 'description'
        ] | @* | text() | processing-instruction()|comment()"/>

      <xsl:apply-templates
         select="description[ lang($principal_language_code) ]"/>

   </xsl:copy>
</xsl:template>
```

The subsequent languages in the list are not so easy to process with `lang()`. For one thing, `lang()` expects a string, not a node list, so while you could pass it the `$other_language_codes` variable, the output would be deceptive. The first node in the list would serve as the argument, and the rest of the nodes would be ignored.

What about an `xsl:for-each`? The `for-each` changes the context node, but `lang()` relies on the context node for the inherited value of `xml:lang`. So, looping over the codes in a `for-each` results in no output. You need to use a variable to stuff away the wine element (the context node) for use in the `apply-templates` select expression. Use `current()` inside the filter expression, because within the `[]` the "`.`" no longer points to the language code:

```
<xsl:template match="wine">
   <xsl:copy>

      <xsl:apply-templates select="*[
```

```
         local-name()!= 'description'
        ] | @* | text() | processing-instruction()|comment()"/>

      <xsl:apply-templates
         select="description[ lang($principal_language_code) ]"/>

      <xsl:variable name="mywine" select="."/>

      <xsl:for-each select="$other_language_codes">
          <xsl:apply-templates
              select="$mywine/description[lang( current() )]" />
      </xsl:for-each>

   </xsl:copy>
</xsl:template>
```

Here's the completed transform:

```
<xsl:stylesheet version="2.0"
   xmlns:xsl="http://www.w3.org/1999/XSL/Transform"
   xmlns:myns="tag:mitch.amiano@agilemarkup.com,2006:namespace#xmltoolkit"
   >
   <xsl:output method="xml" indent="yes" />

   <xsl:param name="target-region" />
   <xsl:param name="region_map_file" select="'regionmap.xml'"  />

   <xsl:variable name="region_map" select="document($region_map_file)"  />
   <xsl:variable name="language_codes"
      select="$region_map/region-map/region[@id=$target_region]/lang"/>
   <xsl:variable name="principal_language_code" select="$language_codes[1]"  />
   <xsl:variable name="other_language_codes"
       select="$language_codes[ position() != 1]" />

   <xsl:template name="check-target-region">
      <xsl:param name="region" />
      <xsl:if test="string-length($region) &lt; 2">
         <xsl:message terminate="yes">Error: The target region
            must be at least a two character string! Instead it
            is "<xsl:value-of select="$region"/>".</xsl:message>
      </xsl:if>
   </xsl:template>

   <xsl:template match="/">
      <xsl:call-template name="check-target-region">
         <xsl:with-param name="region" select="$target_region" />
      </xsl:call-template>
      <xsl:apply-templates/>
   </xsl:template>

   <xsl:template match="@*|*|processing-instruction()|comment()">
      <xsl:copy>
         <xsl:apply-templates
            select="*|@*|text()|processing-instruction()|comment()"/>
```

```
      </xsl:copy>
   </xsl:template>

   <xsl:template match="wine">
      <xsl:copy>
         <xsl:apply-templates select="*[local-name()!=
            'description']|@*|text()|processing-instruction()|comment()"/>
         <xsl:apply-templates
            select="description[lang($principal_language_code)]"/>
         <xsl:variable name="mywine" select="."/>
         <xsl:for-each select="$other_language_codes">
             <xsl:apply-templates
                select="$mywine/description[lang( current() )]" />
         </xsl:for-each>
      </xsl:copy>
   </xsl:template>
</xsl:stylesheet>
```

Run the transform again:

```
java net.sf.saxon.Transform wines.xml filter_lang.xsl target_region=quebec
```

A small fragment, one of the wine elements in the output, follows. (This fragment omits the XML declaration and encoding.) You'll see that the descriptions have been reordered so that the French description is first, and the Spanish description has been omitted:

```
<wine id="Smoky_Scupp_750ml">
   <name>Smoky Scupp</name>
   <varietal>Scupp</varietal>
   <vintage>1992</vintage>
   <winery>Melvin</winery>
   <distributor>Dri</distributor>
   <bottlesize>750ml</bottlesize>
   <description xml:lang="fr">Un muscadine rouge sec avec les allusions de chêne.
Un vin délicieux a produit d'un mélange unique de Carlos et les raisins de
Scuppernong de Magnolia. Les arômes aux mûres menent au gras, smoky parfume et la
fin épicée longue.</description>
   <description xml:lang="en-US">A dry red muscadine with hints of oak. A delicious
wine produced from a unique mix of Carlos and Magnolia Scuppernong grapes.
Blackberry aromas lead to fat, smoky flavors and long spicy finish.</description>
</wine>
```

Verify it by preparing the stream for Mexico:

```
java net.sf.saxon.Transform wines.xml filter_lang.xsl target_region=mexico
```

The corresponding wine element in the resulting output XML:

```
<wine id="Smoky_Scupp_750ml">
    <name>Smoky Scupp</name>
    <varietal>Scupp</varietal>
    <vintage>1992</vintage>
    <winery>Melvin</winery>
```

```
    <distributor>Dri</distributor>
    <bottlesize>750ml</bottlesize>
    <description xml:lang="es"> Una uva moscatel roja seca con insinuaciones de
roble. Un vino delicioso produjo de una combinación extraordinaria de Carlos y uvas
de Magnolia Scuppernong. Las aromas de la zarzamora llevan a la grasa, smoky
condimenta y el fin picante largo.</description>
</wine>
```

And for the United States:

```
java net.sf.saxon.Transform wines.xml filter_lang.xsl ⮐
target_region=unitedstates
```

Again, the corresponding wine element in the resulting XML follows. Note that each of the descriptions are present in the output because the lookup table specified that all three languages should be included for the `unitedstates` region:

```
<wine id="Smoky_Scupp_750ml">
    <name>Smoky Scupp</name>
    <varietal>Scupp</varietal>
    <vintage>1992</vintage>
    <winery>Melvin</winery>
    <distributor>Dri</distributor>
    <bottlesize>750ml</bottlesize>
    <description xml:lang="en-US">A dry red muscadine with hints of oak. A
delicious wine produced from a unique mix of Carlos and Magnolia Scuppernong
grapes. Blackberry aromas lead to fat, smoky flavors and long spicy
finish.</description>
    <description xml:lang="fr">Un muscadine rouge sec avec les allusions de chêne.
Un vin délicieux a produit d'un mélange unique de Carlos et les raisins de
Scuppernong de Magnolia. Les arômes aux mûres menent au gras, smoky parfume et la
fin épicée longue.</</description>
    <description xml:lang="es"> Una uva moscatel roja seca con insinuaciones de
roble. Un vino delicioso produjo de una combinación extraordinaria de Carlos y uvas
de Magnolia Scuppernong. Las aromas de la zarzamora llevan a la grasa, smoky
condimenta y el fin picante largo.</description>
</wine>
```

Refinements

Similar uses of parameterized transforms can be used to achieve stepwise refinements, forming a stream of data directed toward a particular audience. In the context of selling into a particular region, the `winery` and `region` elements provide structures on which to key further processing:

```
<region name="North Carolina"/>

<winery id="Melvin">
    <name>Mad Melvin's Muscadine Wines</name>
    <region>North Carolina</region>
    <country>United States</country>
</winery>
```

Perhaps the wine seller should target a region by advertising wines from the geographic area. This can be accomplished using a parameter to match against the target `region`, applying templates to the wineries associated with that region, and those wineries' wines in turn. The `region` as expressed in the wine catalog could also be extracted using another stylesheet to initially populate the `regionmap.xml` file.

The XSLT code presented earlier conforms to the XSLT 1.0 Recommendation. An astute observer might note that when using parameters you are effectively coupling templates. To a programmer, having to rely on top-level parameters seems a bit suspicious, even if they can't be assigned to and changed during processing. Top-level parameters look, feel, and smell like globals (well, almost). Programmers want clearly defined interfaces.

Look what happens to a template that relies on parameters:

```
    <xsl:template match="wine">
      <xsl:param name="lang_code" />
      <xsl:param name="oth_codes" />

      <xsl:copy>

         <xsl:apply-templates select="*[
            local-name()!= 'description'
           ] | @* | text() | processing-instruction()|comment()"/>

         <xsl:apply-templates
            select="description[ lang($lang_code) ]"/>

         <xsl:variable name="mywine" select="."/>

         <xsl:for-each select="$oth_codes">
              <xsl:apply-templates
                   select="$mywine/description[lang( current() )]" />
         </xsl:for-each>

      </xsl:copy>
   </xsl:template>

   <xsl:template match="@*|*|processing-instruction()|comment()">
      <xsl:copy>
         <xsl:apply-templates select="*|@*|text()|processing-
instruction()|comment()"/>
      </xsl:copy>
   </xsl:template>
```

Whoops! Without further changes, the catchall template (the one that matches `"@*|*|processing-instruction()|comment()"`) doesn't bother passing the parameter along, so the wine template gets neither the `lang_code` or `oth_codes` parameter. You can add the parameters to the catchall template, but that just pushes the problem back by one template in the calling sequence, and there is no guarantee that is the only one that is invoking the wine template. Well-defined interfaces in XSLT 1.0 could give rise to some very tight, and unwarranted, coupling between templates.

XSLT 2.0 addresses this problem by introducing *tunnel parameters*, which are much like ordinary parameters but do not need to be passed explicitly through every call to `xsl:call-template` or `xsl:apply-templates`. A tunnel parameter is passed on by default templates and by user-defined templates, even when those templates don't explicitly define or pass on a parameter of the same name. To use tunnel parameters, add the `tunnel` attribute to the `xsl:with-param` and `xsl:param` elements:

```
<xsl:template match="/">
    <xsl:call-template name="check-target-region">
        <xsl:with-param name="region" select="$target_region" />
    </xsl:call-template>
    <xsl:apply-templates>
        <xsl:with-param name="principal_language_code"
            select="$principal_language_code" tunnel="yes"/>
        <xsl:with-param name="other_language_codes"
            select="$other_language_codes" tunnel="yes"/>
    </xsl:apply-templates>
</xsl:template>

<xsl:template match="@*|*|processing-instruction()|comment()">
    <xsl:copy>
        <xsl:apply-templates select="*|@*|text()|processing-⮐
instruction()|comment()"/>
    </xsl:copy>
</xsl:template>

<xsl:template match="wine">
    <xsl:param name="principal_language_code"  tunnel="yes"/>
    <xsl:param name="other_language_codes"  tunnel="yes"/>

    <xsl:copy>
        <xsl:apply-templates select="*[local-name()!= 'description'] ⮐
|@*|text()|processing-instruction()|comment()"/>

        <xsl:apply-templates select="description⮐
[lang($principal_language_code)]"/>


        <xsl:variable name="mywine" select="."/>

        <xsl:for-each select="$other_language_codes">
            <xsl:apply-templates select="$mywine/description[lang( current() )]" />
        </xsl:for-each>

    </xsl:copy>
</xsl:template>
```

Although the root element provides two named parameters, it isn't the root template that eventually passes the values on. Tunnel parameters help reduce complexity in monolithic "big ball of mud" transforms. They also provide a means of decoupling the interfaces of intermediary templates, which may have (should have) been designed to work without knowing the internal details of other templates.

Domain-Specific Languages

The small region-map file was created to describe the languages of various regions from the perspective of a particular marketing department. In the evolution of this scenario, you might expect the file to either dead end and be absorbed into a relational database implementation, or grow to encode other facets of business information as expressed by the marketing experts. The latter case can lead to a domain-specific language, a small programming language that more closely matches the business person's own terminology. While personalization handles the needs of external clients, such domain-specific languages (DSLs) often target the needs of internal stakeholders.

Very often, XML development spawns efforts to encapsulate all facets of knowledge and practice within an organization into a domain language. Some XML languages emerge into the community and become open standards and consortium recommendations. Others serve as inward, retrospective models of proprietary information. It may not be fair to refer to these proprietary uses as domain-specific because, by comparison with DSLs developed with a professional or industry domain in mind, they represent the knowledge and practices of only one or a small number of interested parties. Still, they serve a similar role, albeit with different sets of stakeholders. The audience is more or less inconsequential to whether a language is domain-specific.

DSLs have been around for quite a long time. Some, like YACC (a compiler-compiler), are highly coherent, having a well-defined purpose and expressive capability, and remain relatively small and stable. Others like PHP grow into full-featured general-purpose programming languages. The problem for an enterprise is in dealing with the cases in between, where the DSLs are not as coherent and stable as YACC, nor supported by a community with sufficient resources to keep the mind share alive. When the initial developers move on, die, or simply tire of their inventions, IT departments often refuse or are unable to provide support. Because the tools that implement the DSLs often require someone with scripting skills, developers who serve as configuration managers are often the "stuck-ees." In the meantime, the organization may loose an opportunity to learn from the experience, and the expertise encoded in the orphaned DSL.

As XML has spurred interest in DSLs, XSLT has given developers a new appreciation for the concept of compiler-compilers. New special-purpose template languages seem to spring up every day. Frequently they are implemented using XSLT transforms as an interpreter, but may also be cross-translated into XSLT or into a general-purpose language.

A common shortcoming in initial versions of these template systems is a lack of expressiveness. DSLs are often designed to address very specialized problem areas, and may even be focused on a single task. Many simple templates use empty elements as placeholders, replaced with simple substitution:

```
The items for <CRFL:ORDERNO/> have been shipped in <CRFL:NUMPKG/> packages. They
should arrive in <CRFL:LAGTIME/> days.
```

This is fine when the needs are limited, but as the needs grow, so does the complexity of the templates and their proprietary interpreters or translators. The method falls apart altogether when there is a significant design aspect to the template users' role in the process. If you've thought of going down this road, consider a strategy of allowing XPath expressions inside of your templates instead of fixating the element names based on field names. The template instances can be compiled into XSLT using XSLT. The use of XPath decouples the structure of the DSL template elements from the data.

Note that there are a couple of security risks in this strategy. First, as anyone who as developed "query-by-example" interfaces can tell you, the technique is vulnerable to code injection attacks. This may not mean much to you if you're working within a trusted environment, but for scenarios involving over-the-web transactions, this may be an unacceptable risk. Remember that most XSLT engines are capable of communicating over the network, and weak or nonexistent verification of a customized DSL template's contents constitutes a major hole.

One method of mitigating the risk of code injection is to use symbolic XPaths rather than literal paths. Just as simple element names must be interpreted, such paths would need to be dereferenced through a lookup strategy. If the lookup fails, the paths are illegal. Another method is to provide a design template, also in XML, that serve as a metadata role to guide the creation of, and later validation of, template instances.

For example, consider the preceding DSL fragment. A design template serving in a metadata role would define each of the allowable tags:

```
<desn:metatemplate>
   <desn:pathnames>
      <desn:name  shortname="orderno" base="orders"
         path="header/order_number">Order Number</desn:name>
      <desn:name  shortname="numpkg" base="shipment"
         path="packaging/@shipparcels">Number of Packages</desn:name>
      <desn:name  shortname="lagtime" base="shipment"
         path=".">Expected Shipping Time</desn:name>
   </desn:pathnames>
</desn:metatemplate>
```

Such meta-template templates allow aspects of the design to take place within a more coherent execution model. Meta-templates act like object-oriented classes, and can serve as lookup tables for valid symbolic paths, and to guide GUI user interfaces. In this sense, a meta-template may also be considered a domain-specific schema. A downside is that someone must design the design template.

Second, while most general-purpose languages and languages based on open standards are thoroughly vetted, the execution models of domain specific languages (almost by definition) are generally not so well analyzed. With some DSLs this isn't a problem because they simply aren't meant to be executed, but simply transformed into other passive forms of information. Theoretically, other more actively executed DSLs may expose their users to denial of service attacks, but that is no more a risk than code injection. The real risk here is of opportunity costs: a lot of resources can be frittered away as engineers futz with diagnosing and debugging execution models that were not coherent to begin with.

TheExtreme Programming camp has a good software practice that applies to DSLs as well: drive the development by testing first. Test early and test often, and remember — when you're tempted to add new features — consider whether the YAGNI principle applies (You Aren't Going to Need It).

Resources and Further Reading

How would an XSLT transform know to select a suitable writing mode? A lookup table strategy could be applied, but you still have to design it and build the logic to navigate the table. Just as with the difference between the marketing department's idea of a region and the country code, there aren't hard-and-fast rules that can be mechanically applied to magically determine the writing direction from the language. Many languages have multiple, equally legitimate scripts for writing the same language. Western scripts seem to be more of an exception than the rule. This chapter barely scratched the surface of internationalization. If you want to look at internationalization issues further, the W3C's Web Architecture Domain has an excellent resource at `www.w3.org/International/resource-index`.

Vocabularies also are too complex an issue to fit within the scope of this chapter. However, if they interest you, there are a few technology areas that you should consider researching further. Two stand out: DITA and Topic Maps.

DITA (Darwin Information Typing Architecture) is an XML-based architecture for authoring. It is rapidly gaining acceptance in organizations that rely heavily on documentation and documentation authoring teams. A key concept in DITA is topic-oriented authoring, in which chunks of information are created as small, highly coherent units. The DITA topics can be combined and specialized to address the needs of a particular audience. DITA is maintained by the Oasis Open organization. More information on DITA can be found at the Technical Committee FAQ page at `www.oasis-open.org/committees/dita/faq.php`.

The Topic Maps standard is an ambitious and potentially far-reaching foundation for creating and managing conceptual views of information resources. In the simplest case, a topic map itself may be a container for vocabulary terms, but even then it has the potential to relate the terms to one another and to publicly maintained subject lists. Two key aspects, from the point of view of this chapter, are that the topic map allows multiple language terms to be represented and that maps can be merged. The Topic Maps standard is maintained by the ISO as ISO/IEC 13250:2000. Oasis also has formed technical committees to create and publish subject lists suitable for use as Topic Maps subject indicators. More information on Topic Maps can be found at `www.topicmaps.net`, and the consortium site `www.topicmaps.org`.

Summary

This chapter considered features of XML technologies in approaching internationalization, revisiting the XSLT transforms from previous chapters to illustrate parameterized templates in detail. The identity transform was illustrated as a virtual stage in a pipeline. Parameter values were used to perform lookups, and the result of the look-up was used to direct language-specific processing. Along the way, you picked up more details about XML entities, the XPath `lang()` function (and its equivalent path), and the `tunnel` parameter feature from XSLT 2.0.

As you move on to the following chapters, you'll begin to consider higher-level strategies, looking more at pipelines, merging, and querying from a business process integration perspective.

8

Searching and Merging XML Documents

In the earlier chapters, you saw how XML can structure information and how you can transform XML for presentation. This chapter explains how you can search the data in your XML as well as merge data across XML documents. The discussion focuses primarily on a language called XQuery, which was designed and built especially to accomplish tasks like these. Along the way, you'll also see other approaches to searching and merging problems. One of the other tools that you'll examine is the language you've been learning: XSLT.

Problem

Your catalog has come a long way so far. So far, in fact, that people are starting to see the value in the information that it contains. Inside and outside of your organization, people are beginning to ask questions whose answers are contained in the catalog, such as:

- What wines of a certain varietal are available?
- What wines of a certain vintage are available, ordered by price?

You can certainly find those answers manually, but you really need an automated method for retrieving answers to these and other frequent questions. You also require a way to rearrange and merge the data in the catalog. It's impossible to design a single XML schema that is going to be a perfect fit for every need, nor is it practical to put all of your data into a single XML document. You need to reach across documents to create new documents, create new structures, and merge documents. Consider the following problems that require these capabilities:

- Create a document that, starting at country, represents a geographical hierarchy of available wines
- Create a document that gives the address that returns should be shipped to for any wine

These are all problems that XQuery can solve, as you'll learn in this chapter. The "Design" section develops your understanding of XQuery as well as its alternatives. In the course of design, you'll explore how you can adopt XQuery for these uses.

Design

The problems discussed here are common anytime you have a large amount of data. SQL and other languages were invented to deal with exactly these kinds of problems. In the XML world, several languages have been suggested and implemented to address querying across XML documents. XSLT, which you learned in the previous chapters as a transformation language, can also be used for querying and merging. How you can perform these tasks with XSLT will be discussed briefly, but the focus of this chapter is XQuery.

How XQuery Works

There are many different programming languages, and they don't all work the same way. As the name implies, XQuery is a query language. It works most similarly to Structured Query Language (SQL). It isn't the same as procedural languages like Pascal and C, or object-oriented languages such as Java, C#, and C++.

Figure 8-1 shows, at a high, abstract level, how XQuery works. At the left are the source XML documents. The XQuery query chooses the information that you want from the various source documents. The result of the query is a new XML document.

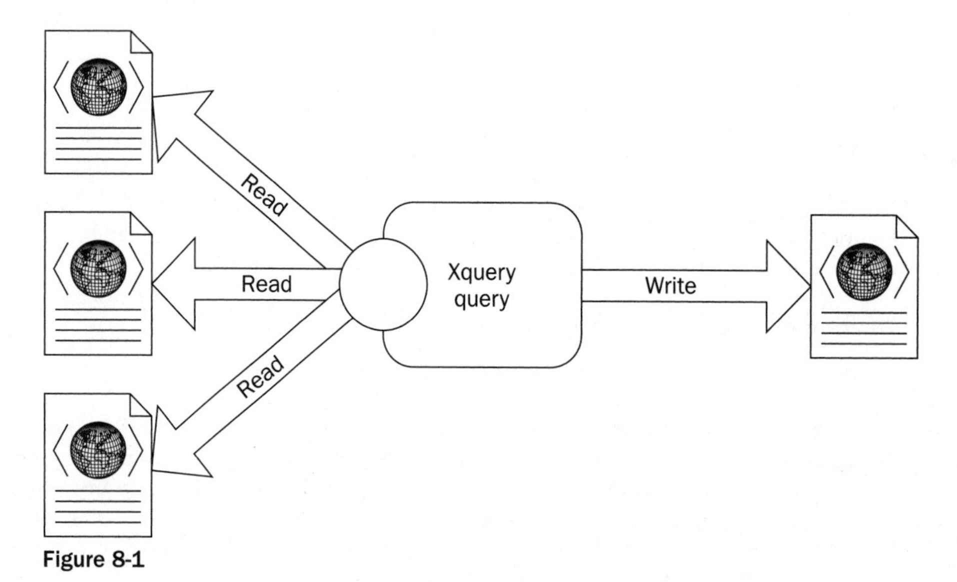

Figure 8-1

The query must be processed by some sort of application. The sophistication of the application varies—some are true multiuser servers, while some are simple libraries that are really meant as tools for building your own applications from scratch.

Following is an example of a typical query. This query returns the Cabernet Sauvignon wines in the catalog.

```
<wines>
     {
      for $wine
        in doc("wines.xml")//wine
        where $wine/varietal = "Cabernet Sauvignon"
      return
        $wine
     }
</wines>
```

Like SQL, one of the goals for XPath is to make it easy to read. For this one, you read the statement as "for each `wine` element in `wines.xml` where the `varietal` element is Cabernet Sauvignon, return the `wine` element." Here's the result of the query:

```
<wines>

 <wine id="Cabernet_Sauvignon_1992_750ml">
 <name>Cabernet Sauvignon</name>
 <varietal>Cabernet Sauvignon</varietal>
 <vintage>1992</vintage>
 <winery>Caskone</winery>
 <distributor>Aeg</distributor>
 <bottlesize>750ml</bottlesize>
    <price>
     <us>42.33</us>
    </price>
 </wine>

 <wine id="The_Cabernet_1996_750ml">
  <name>The Cabernet</name>
  <varietal>Cabernet Sauvignon</varietal>
  <vintage>1996</vintage>
  <winery>Cosentino</winery>
  <distributor>Emp</distributor>
  <bottlesize>750ml</bottlesize>
     <price>
      <us>56.74</us>
     </price>
    </wine>

</wines>
```

That's how XQuery works in a nutshell. In the "Solution" section of this chapter, you'll see XQuery in action against the wine catalog. Before solving the problem, let's first examine some alternatives and how they compare to XQuery.

Some Alternatives

By the end of this chapter, hopefully you'll see that XQuery is the best choice for querying across XML documents and merging content contained in documents. But it's worth looking at some alternatives.

The main purpose in considering these options is to provide some insight into the problems typically encountered. But these alternatives aren't completely without merit, and in some situations you might want to use them.

Text Searching

The problems posed at the beginning of this chapter involve searching for text across separate XML files. On one hand, simply searching for certain words or phrases in a set of XML files can be easy. XML, after all, is text, and because the files are text, you can search across the files by using common tools such as Windows Explorer, shown in Figure 8-2. It's easiest to do if the files are all in the same directory.

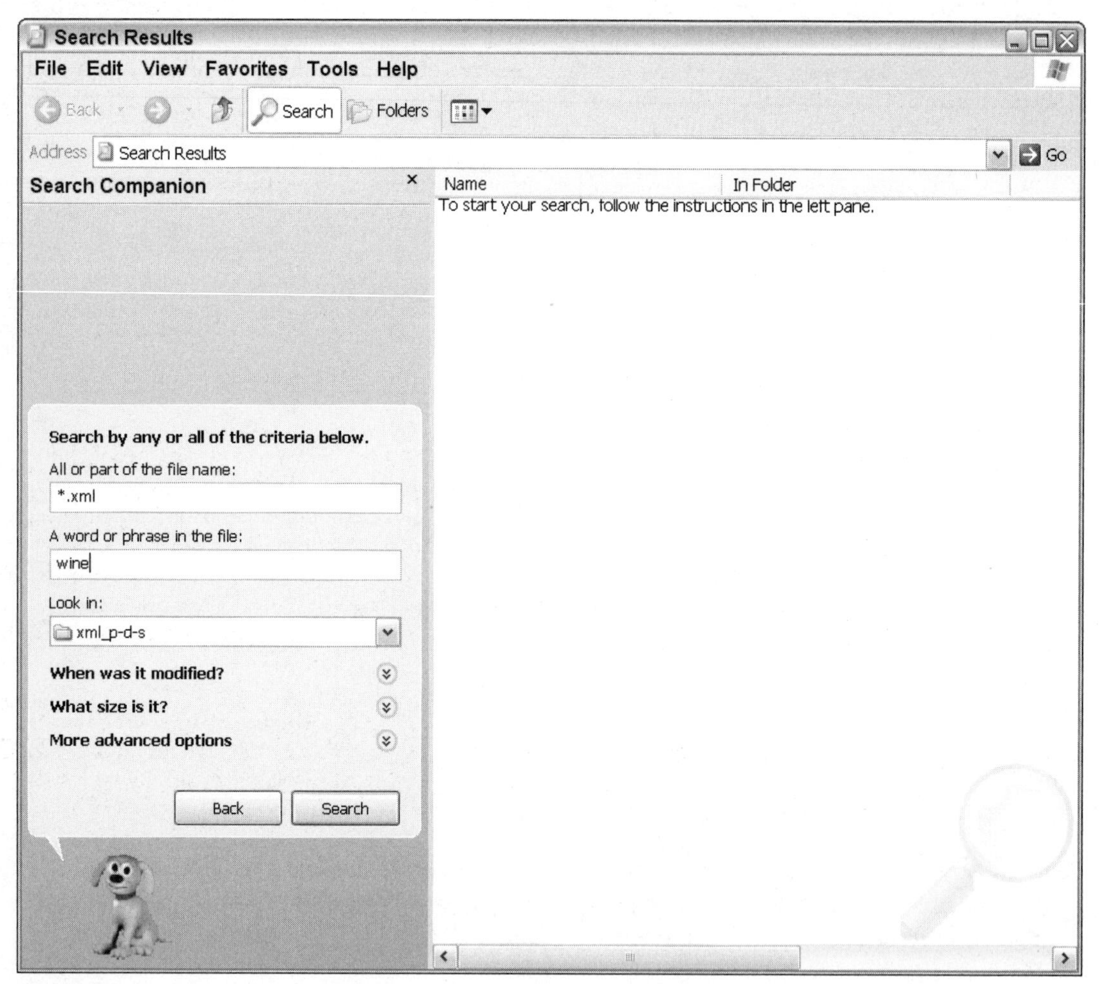

Figure 8-2

With this approach, you would get a list of files that contain the text that you are searching for. For example, a search for "Scuppernong" might return the list of files, and then you would then have to open each file in turn to determine if it had the information you are looking for. Though you may find what you are looking for, the text search makes no distinction between the data, structure, and metadata of the XML. This can cause searches that are less than efficient at best and misleading or inaccurate at worst.

For example, let's say that you perform a search for the greater than sign (>). In the data of your XML, this isn't a common character. Maybe you are using it as a search character precisely because it only appears in statements like `where cost > price` in your actual data. But XML uses the > in every element, so you are guaranteed to get a hit on every single XML file. That's not much of a search at all.

The > and other structurally significant characters aren't very typical searches, but you can see how a text search makes no distinction between XML syntax and your data. More common problems occur with element and attribute names. Consider the following XML:

```
<wine name="Nagg Merlot" winery="Melvins">
    <price>
      <us>21.43</us>
    </price>
    <qty>43</qty>
</wine>
```

In this situation, a full-text search returns hits on "winery" and "wine" because they are element names and attribute names. As with >, your simple text searches is blind to the structure of XML and the different layers that are obvious to anyone familiar with XML. Specifically, the text search doesn't see the difference between the metadata and the data. These strings describe the data, and hence the name metadata — "data about data."

So, the full-text search is blind to the structure and metadata of XML. Depending on what you are searching on, that may not be so bad. But the fundamental problem with full-text searching is that it doesn't leverage the rich structure and semantics built into every XML document. Imagine that you go to a lot of trouble organizing all of your files. You've bought filing cabinets and lots of folders, labeled all of the folders, and spent hours getting your papers into the correct folders. Then, you ask your colleague to find a particular item, such as a utility bill from last year. You watch in horror as the colleague searches for the bill by starting in the first cabinet drawer and examining each paper in sequence, completely ignoring all of your painstaking organization.

A full-text search against XML is very much like your clueless colleague. But in the case of the text search, it isn't just your individual efforts that are being ignored. It takes a lot of work for an organization to put data into XML. Treating XML documents as just text ignores all of that effort. By taking advantage of the structure of XML, you can perform much more refined searches.

Although you may be successful with full-text searches for finding data in some cases, you still have the problem of merging to consider. The work of merging data between documents is a manual process. Again, there are problems in treating XML as just text. In the course of copying and pasting, it's very likely that you'll make errors in how you grab the XML and transfer it into the new XML document. If you make such errors, the new XML document won't be valid and won't be usable in your catalog.

Text Search Engines

Instead of using Windows Explorer's search facility, you could use an elaborate search engine designed for an enterprise intranet. In that case, you would feed all of the files into the search engine and the users would employ a web front end to perform the same kind of searches. Such a solution offers more accessibility and probably more functionality. It also likely has enough intelligence to avoid searching inside the markup tags. But as long as the search engine just sees the XML as text, it isn't using the catalog to its fullest advantage.

XML and SQL Queries

When talking about querying large amounts of data, SQL often comes to mind. SQL is used to query databases such as Oracle, SQL Server, DB2, and mySQL. SQL databases underlie a huge number of systems and are very popular for management of large amounts of structured data.

As you'll see in the next chapter, modern SQL databases have many mechanisms for integrating structured business data with loosely structured XML data. But it's important to note that there is a gap between the XML and SQL worlds. SQL is a very powerful query mechanism. SQL databases are generally oriented toward more structured data. Because SQL is well known and popular, it's tempting to look to it as a solution for querying your XML catalog, yet the differing nature of SQL and XML data often makes these attempts problematic.

There are some common patterns that when attempting to leverage XML and regular, standard SQL— that is, statements without specialized XML extensions. But when using regular SQL without specialized XML extensions, using SQL as an XML query mechanism can become complex and unwieldy very quickly.

SQL extensions that are specific to XML are discussed in the next chapter. In fact, the problems identified here motivated the development of the XML-specific extensions that bridge the gap between SQL XML, and you'll see that XML SQL extensions can actually offer good alternatives to the XQuery approach covered in this chapter.

As you may already know, SQL is designed to query tables. Consider the following example of a standard SQL statement:

```
select id, employee_name from emp_table
```

To use it to query XML, you first have to get the XML data into tables. SQL databases can easily load large amounts of text into a column, so a common approach is to create a table like the one shown in Figure 8-3. In this case, the text (content) of the XML document is added as character data to the column.

Then you perform searches for words and phrases with SQL statements like this, where `xml_doc` is a column containing XML documents:

```
SELECT xml_doc FROM doc_table WHERE xml_doc LIKE '%wine%'
```

But that's really just the same as the full-text search discussed earlier. You have all of the same problems because you're treating XML as just text. Unlike full-text searches, SQL provides the mechanism to divide the data across columns. For instance, if all of your XML documents have elements called `name` and `description`, then you could make columns in your table called Name and Description, as is shown in Figure 8-4.

Doc_Id	XML_Doc
winery01	
winery02	
winery03	
winery04	
winery05	

Figure 8-3

Doc_Id	Name	Description	XML_Doc
winery01			
winery02			
winery03			
winery04			
winery05			

Figure 8-4

Now, you could do searches that are more precise. By issuing a SQL query, you can isolate your searches to just `name`, or just `description`, or some combination of the two. Here is a SQL statement that returns documents that contain the text, wine:

```
SELECT xml_doc FROM doc_table WHERE name LIKE '%wine%'
```

That's the beginning of better, targeted queries, although you are achieving them by breaking your XML document into a table one column at a time. Setting aside the amount of work involved, it's important to ask: can the approach really work? In the preceding example, there was an important assumption: each document had only one `name` element and one `description` element. What if that isn't true? What if there are multiple `name` elements? They won't all fit into one column in such a way that you could distinguish between them. More importantly, you need a way to relate attributes to their elements and to describe the relationship between child elements and their parent elements.

To correctly recreate XML data in a SQL database, you can't map an XML document to a table. Rather, you have to map at the element level — that is, create tables at the element level. You need a table for each type of element. At a minimum, the tables require:

- Fields for each attribute of an element
- A field that references the parent element
- A field that references a second table that describes the child elements and text

With a document mapped into tables, you can now perform arbitrary queries that target precise fields and locations in the documents. Indeed, if these queries are easy to write and execute, this would be an acceptable solution. Building the tables might be painful, but the process can be automated and you get what you want — a way to query across XML documents. As you can guess, this isn't the case. Because XPath is built to query XML, XPath is a clear winner in the case where you are only querying a single document. Of course, as previously mentioned, XPath isn't capable of looking across multiple documents. A SQL approach would work across multiple documents — you just have to map all of those different documents into SQL schemas. The SQL approach only gets more complex with each additional document, which involves the creation of many more tables and more and more complex SQL queries.

Regarding XPath versus SQL on a single table, it's worth asking: why is a relatively new language (XPath) so dominant over a venerable standard of querying SQL? This question cuts to the core theme in any discussion of the integration of the XML and SQL database worlds. XML is based on the concept of trees, and SQL is based on tables. These are fundamentally different data structures.

XPath is built for trees, and SQL is built for tables. In this example, the two different data structures can organize the data effectively, but only because the data is really a better fit for a table. In fact, a table can always be represented as a tree, but a tree cannot always be represented as a table. Because XML is a poor fit for SQL databases, XPath yields much easier queries. Unfortunately, XPath is limited to only a single document. In a world without XQuery, you might be forced to fit your XML document into the SQL world view just so that you can do queries. But XQuery extends the capability of XPath so that multiple documents, or trees, can be joined.

Fortunately, the story on merging documents is better with SQL. A new standard, SQL/XML, gives you tools that can be used inside of your SQL queries so that XML can be produced. It is a powerful mechanism for creating XML from relational data, and puts a SQL-based approach ahead of full-text searching. In Chapter 9, SQL/XML is discussed thoroughly as a way to integrate XML and relational data.

It's important to remember that a SQL approach requires you to transform your data into tables. This isn't a trivial process and can be very costly. In the end, you can have the capability to perform precise queries and create XML output, but it isn't a straightforward solution to implement. Although SQL is a powerful query language, it is best focused on relational data.

Later in the book, you learn more about how to integrate these two worlds and explore proprietary database extensions that can overcome some of the problems discussed here.

XSLT

The earlier chapters of this book focused on XSLT as a transformation language, and you saw ways to transform source documents into documents that are more presentable. Are querying and merging really that different from the concept of transformation? And if they aren't — if you can create transformations that can act like queries and merge operations — then maybe XSLT can do the job just fine.

In fact, XSLT can accomplish all of the query and merge tasks that were suggested at the beginning of the chapter. It's an open debate as to when to use XQuery instead of XSLT. XQuery is the topic here, but if you are more comfortable with XSLT than XQuery, rest assured that you will be able to find query and merge solutions with XSLT. First, you need to understand how XSLT can be used for querying and merging.

Using XSLT for queries is really fairly simple and doesn't require any deeper understanding of XSLT — you just have to make something of a conceptual leap. All you need to do is think of a query as a type of transformation. It's a transformation that throws all of the source data away except for what you need. You may have already noticed that transformations tend to ignore large amounts of the source data. For instance, a transformation that displays wines might not make any use of the `distributor` elements and the `winery` elements. If your query is meant to locate just one or two wines, you can think of your query as a transformation that ignores all of the other wines.

The mechanism for getting such a query to work is XPath, and the real secret is XPath predicates. XPath predicates are reviewed in more detail later in the chapter, so for now just consider the following example:

```
<xsl:apply-templates
     select="//wine[vintage > 2000 and price/us > 40]"/>
```

The predicate of the path expression (the part in square brackets) limits the `wine` elements to only those with a vintage greater than 2000 and a price greater than 40. By simply adding this predicate, a stylesheet previously used to display all of the wines can be used to query the catalog for specific wines and display only those. You can even use XSLT's `xsl:param` parameters to control the query from outside the stylesheet. In this way, the query the stylesheet performs can be controlled when the transformation is executed. This enables you to use a single stylesheet to handle a query for any vintage or any price, for instance.

To merge multiple documents with XSLT, use the document function. Here's a simple example:

```
<someElement>
   <xsl:apply-templates select="document('anotherDoc.xml')"/>
 </someElement>
```

In this case, `anotherDoc.xml` is brought in via the XPath expression and templates are applied to its root node. You can also use the document function as part of an XPath expression, like this:

```
<someElement>
   <xsl:apply-templates select="document('anotherDoc.xml')/catalog/section/wine"/>
</someElement>
```

The preceding examples use relative URIs. You can also use absolute URIs to access a document from anywhere:

```
<someElement>
   <xsl:apply-templates select="document('http://some.server/anotherDoc.xml')"/>
</someElement>
```

XSLT and XQuery are overlapping languages. They both share XPath and they both can handle transformation problems as well as query and merge problems. They are usually interchangeable for any particular problem, yet each has its own sweetspot as well as weaker areas. Their respective sweetspots are spelled out in their names — XSLT is better oriented toward transformation problems, and XQuery is better pointed toward complex queries.

XSLT can perform queries, but XQuery really outshines XSLT on complex queries because of its FLWOR expressions, which you'll read about more later in the chapter. In short, FLWOR expressions provide a concise and powerful way to perform very complex queries across any number of documents. XQuery is also better at problems involving multiple source documents

Although XQuery can be used for transformations of one source document to an output document, you'll probably find it too complicated for simple chores. For instance, XSLT really shines when you are essentially decorating the source XML, often as XHTML, without having to deeply consider the content of the data or relate data from one document to another. In those cases, you can think about the transformation as pushing the XML document through a simple, elegant stylesheet. In contrast, the XQuery to solve the exact same problem is likely to be quite long and complex, because instead of having templates that decorate certain node types throughout the XML tree, you have to query the document for elements and then process them. Thus, XQuery always acts in pull mode, where it is pulling data from the source documents.

In the end, the choice between XQuery and XSLT is specific to the practitioner, the organization, and the problem at hand. Where two technologies overlap, there are always experts on both sides who see no reason for the other technology to be used at all. So the decision is more about which is the best fit — both for the problem and for the aptitudes of the developers. It's also important to remember that they can be used together. For instance, an XQuery query can synthesize a result XML document from several XML source document, and then XSLT can be used to transform it into XHTML.

Traditional Programmatic Approaches

If your organization isn't already using XQuery, developers will have to learn it before you can take advantage of it. Learning a new language requires overcoming a sometimes steep learning curve and can be costly. Managers and developers alike will make the argument that it is better to stay with the languages that are already known rather than be distracted by yet another language.

To make the leap to a new language, there needs to be compelling reasons why current tools aren't getting the job done. In the case of XML querying, popular programming languages such as Java, C#, C++,

VB, and Perl are well built for searching through XML documents and handling merges. XQuery may be specialized for the specific task, but is it worth investing in a specialized tool when a broader, commonly known language may be capable of handling the tasks?

The answer depends partly on the personalities of individual developers and organizations. Some developers would rather stick with what they know rather than branch into newterritory, while others jump at learning a new technique — even if they could stand more study of the ones they already use. Likewise, some organizations are more willing to take a new programming language for a spin, while others won't pull in a new tool until well after its need is apparent.

The most important part of the equation should be the capability of a new tool to get the job done quicker and with less pain. In the alternatives studied so far, the different approaches offered so much pain that anything new promised to be better. But in the case of broad programming languages, you always encounter die-hards who say, "I can just do it in <my favorite programming language here>." And, for popular programming languages, they would be right.

The questions, though, are, can you amortize the cost of adopting a new tool against the potential benefit, and how long will it take to see a return on the investment? In this case, it's a matter of whether the upfront pain in adopting XQuery yields productivity gains quickly.

To evaluate this, you must first understand how general programming languages can solve the problem of querying and merging of documents. The top programming language all have libraries for dealing with XML, so programmers don't need to worry about low-level mechanics such as parsing out all of those angle brackets and identifying elements and attributes. Instead, an entire XML document can be loaded into memory, typically in just a few lines of code. In the case of object-oriented languages, you then have a set of connected objects that represent the XML document. From there, the task of querying and merging documents is a programming effort of traversing those sets of connected objects, finding what you want, and creating a new model of objects. Then, with just a couple lines of code, you can write the object back out to disk.

Eventually, a developer in the organization may start looking at ways to increase reuse so that the same effort isn't required for every single problem that comes along. This might include setting up a way to say what elements should be queried and could even involve the development of some kind of syntax to describe what the core code should do.

The ultimate end of this direction is something like XQuery — something that acts as shorthand for a larger more complex operation. This is similar to what SQL does in the relational world — it describes in a short statement how to perform a query against a document. That directive is turned over to application code in a language like C++ or Java that then grinds through all of the data. Likewise, XQuery enables you to say only what needs to be done, without getting bogged down in the details of how to do it.

XQuery Concepts

The following sections teach you the key concepts — the basics — of XQuery, after which you'll know how to create useful queries and how and when XQuery can be used. The next few pages aren't enough to make you an expert on XQuery — you'll need to gain more experience with practice and invest in further study.

Very Simple XQuery

Most tutorials on programming start with a "Hello World!" example. The idea is to show the simplest possible code that can produce simple output. In the case of XQuery, the Hello World program is really simple. Here it is, and it isn't a trick:

```
<SimpleQuery>
  Hello, World!
</SimpleQuery>
```

Looking at this code, you are probably thinking: wait, that's just XML. One of the benefits of XQuery is that it is very closely integrated with XML. Any XML document is, in fact, a valid XQuery. It isn't an interesting XQuery because it doesn't actually query any documents, but it has an important implication: it is easy to create XML documents with XQuery. As you'll see, you can use an XQuery statement as a template for the document you want to create.

An XQuery query isn't necessarily valid XML. Unlike XSLT, XQuery isn't an XML-based language. Just as there are benefits of being XML-based for XSLT, there are advantages to not being XML-based for XQuery. For XQuery, being free of the requirements of XML makes it easier to attack more complicated query problems. If XSLT is more naturally attuned to simple transformations, while still being capable of very complicated queries, XQuery is more tuned for complicated queries.

The next query is more useful:

```
<distributors>
  {
   for $someDistributor
     in doc("wines.xml")/catalog/section/distributor
   return
     $someDistributor
  }
</distributors>
```

It queries the `wines.xml` file and returns all of the wine elements.

There are many ways to execute an XQuery query like this, or any XQuery query. For instance, you could execute it through a programming language such as Java or C# that handles the query through an XQuery library (a design that is discussed further in the "Solution" section of this chapter). Or you could use a desktop tool like Stylus Studio to create and execute an XQuery. To use Stylus Studio, select File⇨New⇨XQuery File, and enter your XQuery in the top pane, as shown in Figure 8-5.

For this query to execute as written, the `wines.xml` file must be in the same directory as the XQuery file. When it isn't practical to have the XQuery file and the source XML files in the same directory, you can just specify an absolute path instead of a relative path. The `doc` function takes a URI as an argument, so the source XML files can also reside on different machines entirely.

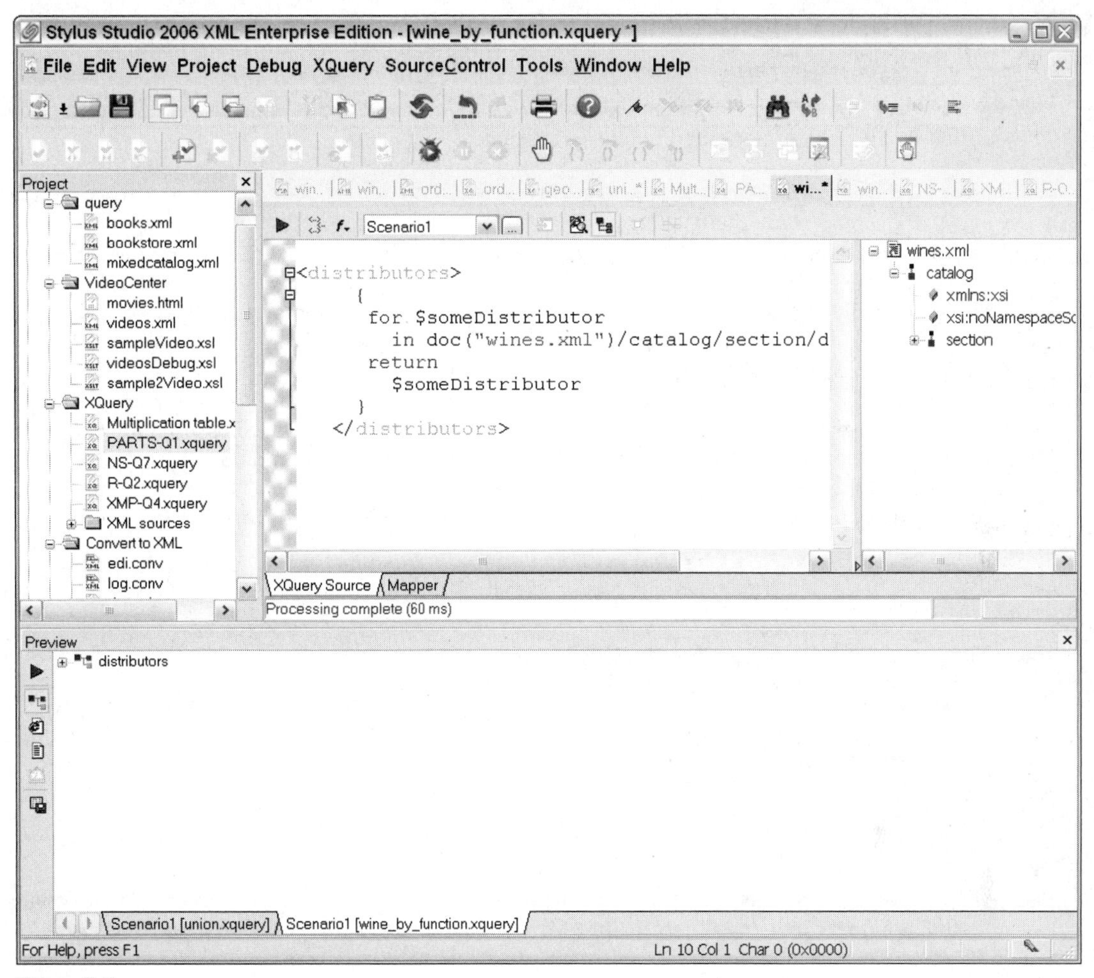

Figure 8-5

To execute the query, click the green arrow in the upper-left corner of the pane. The query executes and displays its output in the bottom pane. You have several options for how the output can be displayed, including in a tree format, as straight text, or in Internet Explorer. You can run all of the examples from this chapter through XQuery in the way described. The result of the example query is:

```
<distributors>
 <distributor id="Dri" name="Dri Distributors, Inc."/>
 <distributor id="Aeg" name="Aegean Imports, INC."/>
 <distributor id="Cla" name="Classic"/>
 <distributor id="Cou" name="Country Vintner"/>
 <distributor id="Emi" name="Eminent Domains"/>
 <distributor id="Emp" name="Empire"/>
 <distributor id="Fran" name="Franklin Selection"/>
</distributors>
```

Notice that the top-level element of the resulting XML document is `distributors`. The query expression itself is enclosed by the `distributors` element. Thus, the query behaves like a template.

What is the query doing? The `for` statement specifies a sequence of nodes to be processed, one at a time. That sequence of nodes is determined by the expression:

```
doc("wines.xml")/catalog/section/distributor
```

The first part of the expression is actually an XQuery function. Think of it as loading the XML document. More precisely, it specifies the document node of `wines.xml` as the beginning of the expression. Then, the expression simply looks down the tree and finds all distributor elements in `wines.xml` whose parent element is `section` and whose grandparent element is `catalog`. Each of these `distributor` elements is assigned to the variable `someDistributor`.

The next part of the expression is the return clause. As you could guess, it specifies what the expression is to return. This one simply says that the `$someDistributor` variable should be returned. That means that each distributor element will be returned exactly as it exists in `wines.xml`. If you want just the name of the distributor returned in its own element, you can do that with a query like this one:

```
<distributors>
     {
      for $distributor
        in doc("wines.xml")/catalog/section/distributor
      return
       <distributorName>
        {xs:string($distributor/@name)}
       </distributorName>

     }
   </distributors>
```

Because XQuery isn't XML-based, you can easily generate non-XML output if you want. The following example shows a query that doesn't create an XML document. As you can see, the query itself isn't XML either.

```
for $distributor
        in doc("wines.xml")/catalog/section/distributor
      return
         xs:string($distributor/@name)
```

The output of this query is a simple list:

```
Dri Distributors, Inc.
Aegean Imports, INC.
Classic
Country Vintner
Eminent Domains
Empire
Franklin Selection
```

Some Definitions

Before going much further, it's important to understand a few key definitions. These concepts aren't unique to XQuery; they're seen in other parts of the XML universe as well. If you've worked with XML a while, this section is more of a review.

Node

A *node* is essentially anything in an XML document. It is the most abstract concept in XML. Elements, attributes, comments, and even documents are all different types of nodes. Nodes can contain nodes. For instance, the following XML snippet contains two processing instructions, one comment, six elements, two attributes, and four text nodes.

```
<?xml version="1.0" encoding="UTF-8"?>
<?xml-stylesheet type="text/xslt" href="somestylesheet.xsl"?>
<!-- Last updated, 12/04/2005 -->
<catalog name="my catalog">
  <description language="en_US">
    <paragraph>
      This is my <bold>BIG, BIG</bold> catalog!
    </paragraph>
    <paragraph>
     <italics>I'm really excited!</italics>
    </paragraph>
  </description>
</catalog>
```

Of all these different types of nodes, the text node is the most often overlooked and misunderstood. Text nodes are uninterrupted text, such as "This is my" and "BIG, BIG" in the preceding code. Text nodes might not look like anything special, yet they are an especially important concept for XQuery. Look at the text nodes in the preceding snippet text — there are four. The first `paragraph` element has two, the `bold` element has one, and the `italics` element has one. The second `paragraph` element doesn't have any child text nodes, but it does have one child element, `italics`, which has a text node. With text nodes, it's also important to understand that:

- An element may have more than one child text node.
- All of the text contained within an element is not necessarily contained in the child text nodes of an element.

Sequence

XQuery expressions return sequences of nodes. In XQuery:

- There can be any number of nodes.
- The order of the nodes is significant.
- A sequence might not contain any nodes at all.

Sequence is a mathematical term that isn't as popular as its cousin term, set. Set isn't precise enough for XQuery's purposes, though, because sets don't define order. For instance, the sets (1,2,3,4) and (4,3,2,1) are equivalent, but as sequences, they are not.

Document Order

Document order simply means the order of nodes in the XML document. Document order isn't particularly interesting in a static XML document, but when you start querying XML and merging documents, document order becomes very important.

In document order, the `document` node is always first and the order of the rest of the nodes is established by considering the position of the first character of the node in relation to the position of the other nodes. For instance, if an element starts on line 40 of a document, then it is before an element that starts on line 65. Because the first character of attributes and child nodes have to follow the first character of the nodes that contain them, it follows that:

- Parent elements precede child nodes, such as child elements and child text nodes.
- Elements precede their attributes.

Consider the following XML document:

```
<Doc>
  <ParentElementA attribA="valueA">
    <ChildElementA/>
    <ChildElementB>
      text node 1
        <ChildElementC>
         text node 2
        </ChildElementC>
      text node 3
    </ChildElementB>
  </ParentElementA>
  <ParentElementB/>
</Doc>
```

The nodes of this document in document order are:

1. The `document` element, which is an imaginary node containing all of the document
2. The `Doc` element
3. The `ParentElementA` element
4. The `attribA` attribute
5. The `ChildElementA` element
6. The `ChildElementB` element
7. The text node `text node 1`
8. The `ChildElementC` element
9. The text node `text node 2`
10. The text node `text node 3`
11. The `ParentElementB` element

Multiple Source Documents

One of XQuery's strengths is its capability to easily handle multiple source documents, and the doc function used in the previous section plays a key role. This section introduces multiple source documents. This section explores a couple of simple merges of multiple documents. The first example simply concatenates two documents and wraps them into a top-level document element. The second example is your first true joining of the data between two documents.

Before being able to concatenate two documents, a second document is needed. The second document that the query will use is one that contains the shipping and office addresses for the distributors. To save room, only a couple of elements are shown here, but you can imagine that each winery would have its own winery element.

```
<?xml version="1.0"?>
<distributors>
 <distributor id="Dri" name="Dri Distributors, Inc.">
  <address type="shipping">
   <street>1000 Industrial Drive</street>
   <city>Newark</city>
   <state>NJ</state>
   <zipcode>07103</zipcode>
  </address>
  <address type="shipping">
   <street>1000 Dri Way</street>
   <city>Newark</city>
   <state>NJ</state>
   <zipcode>07106</zipcode>
  </address>
 </distributor>
 <distributor id="Aeg" name="Aegean Imports, INC.">
  <address type="shipping">
   1000 Industrial Drive
   Dritown, NJ, 07103
  </address>
  <address type="billing">
   1000 Dri Way
   Dritown, NJ, 07103
  </address>

 </distributor>
[ . . . additional distributor elements here ]
</distributors>
```

The following query expression concatenates two documents and includes both of them under a top-level element. The top-level element is necessary because without a single root element, a concatenation of the elements of two XML documents wouldn't result in a valid XML document.

```
let $winesDoc := doc("wines.xml")
let $distributorsDoc := doc("distributor_addresses.xml")
return
    <combinedDoc>
```

```
    {$winesDoc}
    {$distributorsDoc}
  </combinedDoc>
```

Figure 8-6 shows the result of this query in Internet Explorer, which enables you to collapse the XML tree. As you can see, the elements of both documents are grouped together under the `combinedDoc` root element.

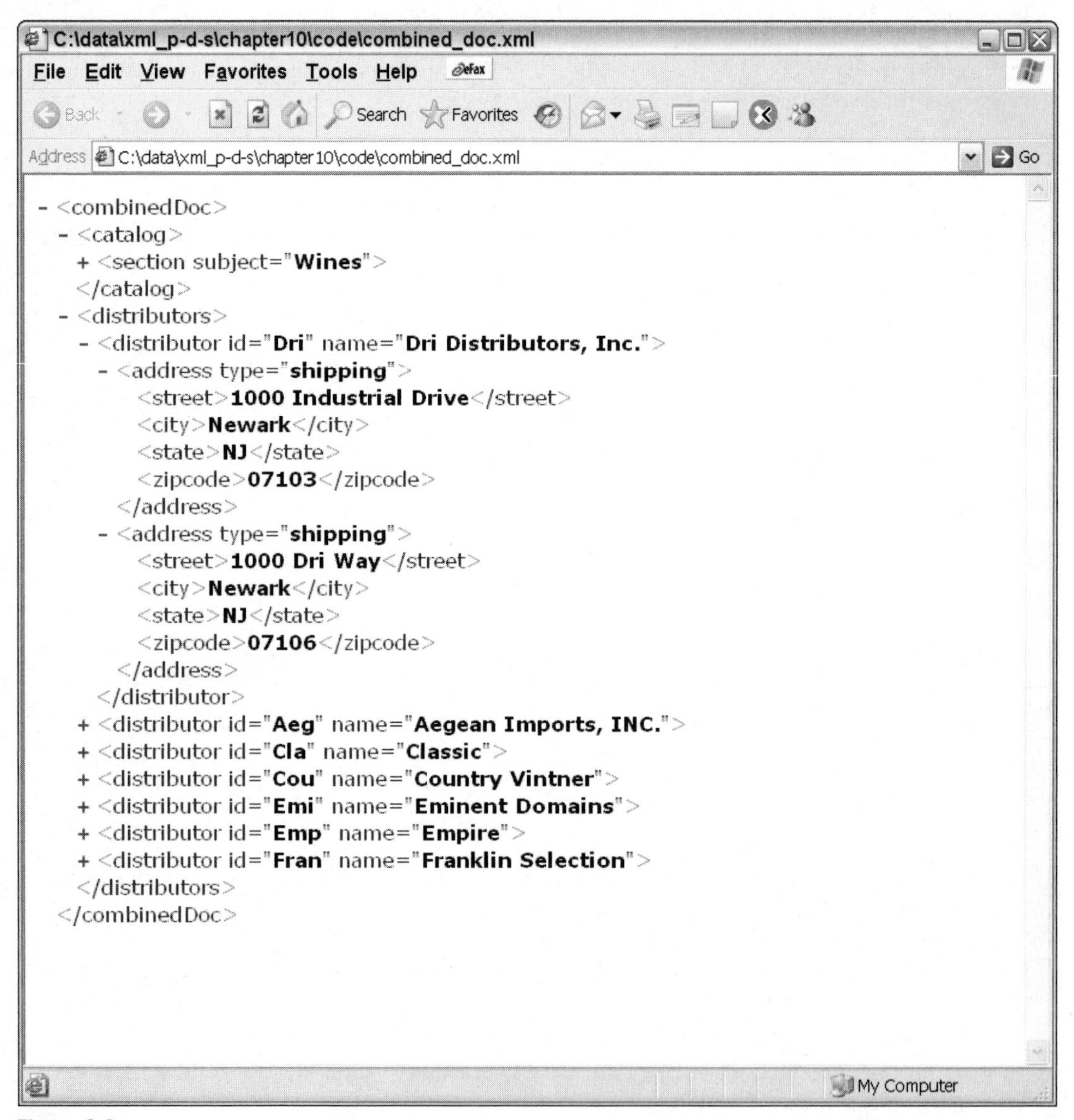

Figure 8-6

The query uses `let` statements, and there isn't a `for` statement as in the previous examples you've seen so far. The `for` statement establishes that a loop iterates over a sequence of nodes; the `let` statement simply assigns a sequence of nodes to a variable. In this example, each variable is assigned a single node — the root nodes of the two documents. But in reality, XQuery expressions always evaluate to sequences of nodes. In this case, those sequences happened to just have a single a single node each. The next query assigns more illustrative sequences to the variables:

```
let $wines := doc("wines.xml")/catalog/section/wine
let $distributors := doc("distributor_addresses.xml")/distributors/distributor
 return
     <combinedDoc>
       {$wines}
    {$distributors}
     </combinedDoc>
```

These examples solve one problem — how to get nodes from different documents merged into a single document. But until now, the queries haven't joined the nodes together in a meaningful way. Consider one of the problems stated at the beginning of the chapter: to do returns, you need the shipping addresses of the distributors by wine. The following query performs the necessary join by using a compound `for` clause and a `where` clause.

```
<results>
 {
  let $wines := doc("wines.xml")//wine
  let $distributors :=
   doc("distributor_addresses.xml")/distributors/distributor
  for $someWine in $wines,
    $someDistributor in $distributors
     where $someWine/distributor = $someDistributor/@id
  return
   <result>
       {<wine>{$someWine/name}</wine>,
        $someDistributor/address[@type = "shipping"]}
   </result>
 }
</results>
```

The result of this query is shown in Figure 8-7.

As you might have noticed earlier, the `distributor_addresses.xml` document has two addresses for each distributor, shipping and office. When returning wine, you are interested in the shipping address. The preceding query expression isolates the shipping address by using an XPath expression. XPath expressions are explored in more detail in the next section.

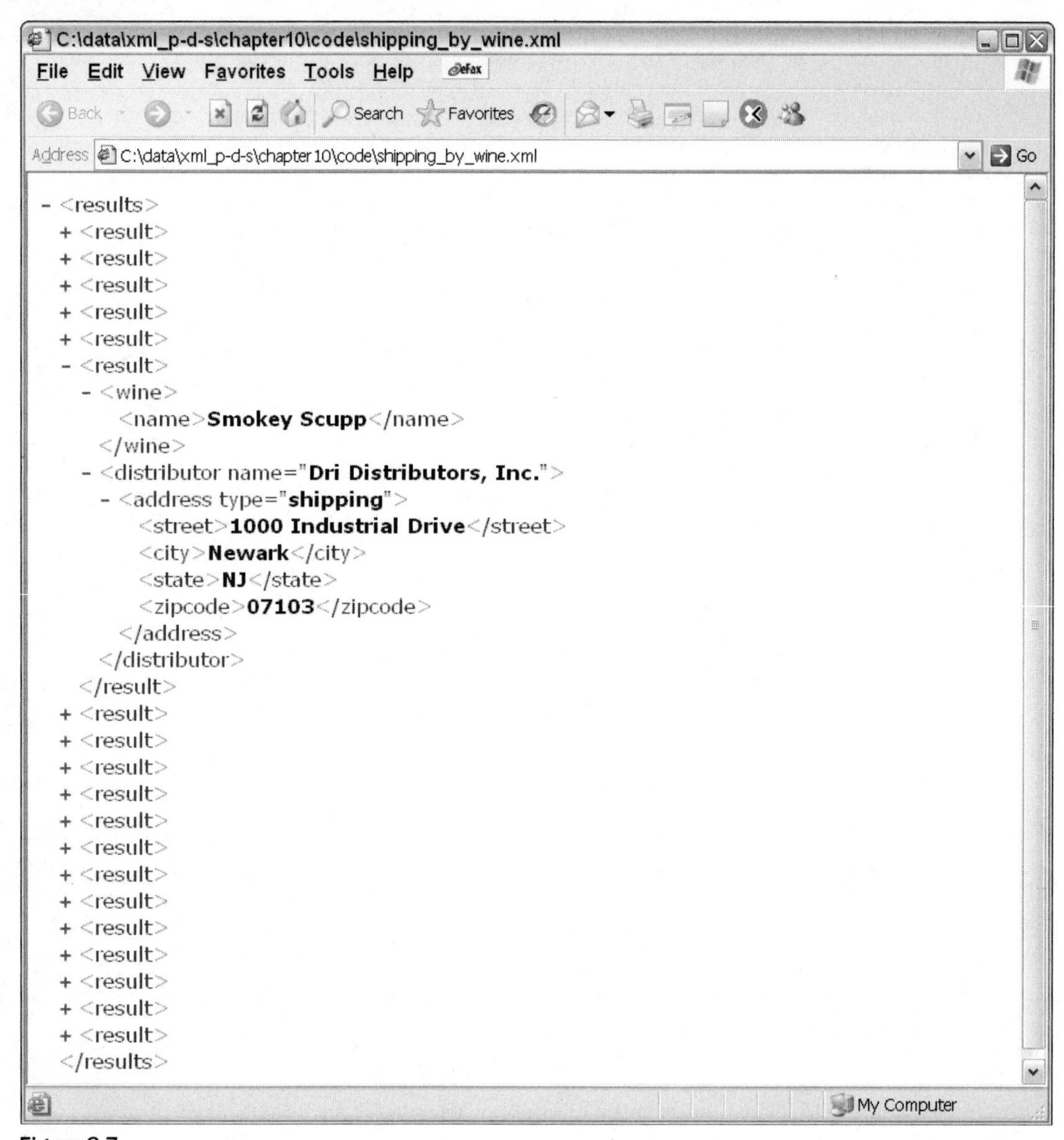

Figure 8-7

XPath Expressions

XQuery and XSLT both use XPath to navigate the hierarchy of an XML document and locate nodes. You've seen Xpath used throughout the XSLT chapters. XPath is especially important for querying a document because it is the key to describing the content you are looking for. This section explores the important concepts of XPath so that you can use it successfully in your XQuery work. Consider one of the XPath expressions used in the previous example:

```
doc("distributor_addresses")/distributors/distributor/address[@type = "shipping"]
```

An XPath expression consists of a primary location path in the form of an axis, a node test, and a predicate. In the preceding example, the axis is the default child axis, the node test is `/distributors/distributo/address`, and the predicate, enclosed in square brackets, is `@type= "shipping"`. The axis identifies a set of nodes that may be included in the result, while the node test and predicate narrow the sequence of nodes.

You dealt with axes in high school math classes — the y axis goes up the page and the x axis goes across the page. To find the coordinate (x=4, y=3), you start at the origin and travel four steps over to the right and then three steps up. Axes in path expressions are similar, except that you use them to locate nodes in the hierarchy. A subtle yet important difference is that each node doesn't fall on each axis as defined by XPath, while every point in your graph has an x coordinate and a y coordinate. For instance, there is an axis that includes attributes of an element. Remembering that attributes and elements are both types of nodes, you can see that there are many nodes (elements) that don't belong on any attribute axis.

The XQuery specification requires five important axes:

- `child` — Includes the immediate children of a particular node. Can be abbreviated as `/` (one forward slash).
- `descendant` — Includes the children of a node, the children's children, the children's children's children, and so on, recursively down the hierarchy.
- `self` — Includes one and only one node — the node being processed. Can be abbreviated as `.` (a period).
- `descendant-or-self` — Includes the current node as well as all descendants. Can be abbreviated as `//` (two forward slashes).
- `attribute` — Includes the attributes of a particular node. Can be abbreviated as `@` (an "at" sign).

In addition, several other axes are defined by XPath and are optionally available. The maker of your XQuery implementation decides whether to include them, and using them could affect the portability of your XQuery code. These optional axes are:

- `parent` — Includes the immediate parent. Can be abbreviated as `..` (two periods).
- `ancestor` — Includes the immediate parent, parent's parent, parent's parent's parent, and so forth, recursively up the tree.
- `ancestor-or-self` — Includes the ancestors and the self-node.
- `following` — Includes all nodes that follow a node in document order.
- `following-sibling` — Includes all nodes that follow a node in document order and share the same parent.
- `preceding` — Includes all nodes that precede a sibling in document order.
- `preceding-sibling` — Includes all nodes that precede a sibling in document order and share the same parent.

The most common axes — `child`, `descendant`, `self`, `descendant-or-self`, and `attribute` — have abbreviations, but all of the axes can be specified with the syntax:

```
axis::node-test
```

For instance, these two expressions are equivalent:

```
$someWine/child::name
$someWine/name
```

The predicates in an XPath expression are used to limit the nodes that would be returned without them. Consider the earlier example that returned all of the wines. You can use a predicate in the path expression to limit the results to only those wines that are of the Cabernet Sauvignon varietal.

```
$someWine/catalog/section/wine[varietal = "Cabernet Sauvignon"]
```

Path expressions are a powerful part of XQuery, as they are in XSLT. If you are used to the path expressions in XSLT, you are well on your way to being successful with them in XQuery.

FLWOR Expressions

As with XSLT, XPath provides a powerful mechanism for locating information in the document hierarchy. XPath is one of the cornerstones of XQuery. FLWOR expressions are another.

FLWOR stands for a number of keywords that are used in conjunction to perform complex queries and precise restructuring of nodes. The syntax and components of the FLWOR expressions are introduced in this section, and then you'll see them in action in the subsequent sections. The keywords that make up the FLWOR acronym are:

- `for` — The `for` clause sets up a loop that is executed one time for each member of a sequence. It is analogous to the `for` clauses in procedural and object-oriented languages but is more closely comparable with the `for-each` clause of XSLT. While the `for` clauses in languages like C/C++, Pascal, and Java are really just arithmetic counters, the `for` clause in XQuery defines the sequence to be processed and defines a variable to be used for the processing.
- `let` — The `let` clause enables you to define variables.
- `where` — The `where` clause, like the `where` clause in SQL, enables you to filter values to be processed.
- `order by` — The `order by` clause, like the `order by` clause in SQL, sorts results.
- `return` — The `return` clause returns the result of the overall FLWOR expression.

Not all of these clauses are required for a FLWOR expression. The `return` clause is always required, and a FLWOR expression must have, at a minimum, one `for` clause or one `let` clause. The `where` and `order by` clauses are always optional.

To best learn FLWOR expressions, you need to build some more, which you'll do later in the section. Now take a look at XQuery structure and operators.

XQuery Structure

In the previous examples, the focus was on the query expressions themselves. But an XQuery query actually consists of two parts — the prolog and the body. So far, you've examined queries that have a body but don't have a prolog. As you've seen, this is acceptable in many circumstances. But the prolog provides some important functionality that is necessary in some situations.

The prolog is at the top of the XQuery query. In the prolog, you can:

- Import XML schemas that influence how the query expression will behave.
- Declare a namespace that is used in the XML output of the query.
- Import libraries of XQuery functions so that you can reuse existing code rather than writing all of the XQuery from scratch.
- Define global variables that can be used anywhere in the XQuery expression.
- Define functions that can be used in the main query expression and that reduce the amount of code repetition in your query expression.

Several of the topics covered in the next section require a prolog. As you work through the examples, you'll see how the prolog is used for the situations just listed. Here's an example of a basic prolog that defines a namespace and a variable:

```
declare namespace xml_pds = "http://xmlbook.agilemarkup.com";
declare variable $region as xs:string external;
```

In this case, the namespace definition changes the results of the query output. The variable declaration gives an external calling environment, such as a Java program, a way to control what this XQuery does. For instance, a Java program that invokes an XQuery with the preceding prolog can give the XQuery a specific region, and the query expression would return only items specific to that region.

Operators

Any programming language has operators—special characters or strings that are used to operate on expressions. XQuery is no exception, and you've already seen quite a few of its operators in the code examples. Before enumerating the various operators, it's important to cover some general aspects of operators in XQuery and review some terminology.

Operators operate on *operands*. For instance, in the expression:

```
$b + 3
```

The operator is the + sign and the operands are `$b` and `3`. If this expression can be evaluated, the result will be 3 plus the numeric value of the variable `$b`. Evaluation isn't guaranteed—what if `$b` has been set to a string, such as "Burgundy"? In that case, the operator can't do its job.

XQuery has to deal with more subtle cases with all of its operators. What if the value of `$b` is the element `<NumberElement>6</NumberElement>`? An element isn't a number, but in this case XQuery doesn't have to work that hard to interpret `$b` as meaning `6` and returning the response `9`. In fact, XQuery does exactly that through a process called atomization. *Atomization* examines a node and attempts to find an atomic value, which is defined by one of the atomic types—that is, `xs:integer`, `xs:string`, and so forth. In the case:

```
<NumberElement>6</NumberElement> + 3
```

the atomic value of `NumberElement` is 6. For the element:

```
<NumberElement num="7"/>
```

and the expression:

```
//NumberElement/@num + 5
```

The left operand is 7 because the value of the attribute num of the element NumberElement is 7. Atomization doesn't always succeed, though. For instance, atomization won't succeed on this NumberElement:

```
<NumberElement><ChildNumber>4</ChildNumber></NumberElement>
```

Atomization applies to the various classes of XQuery operators:

- Arithmetic
- Comparison
- Document order
- Sequence

Arithmetic Operators

Following are descriptions of the arithmetic operators, which are the simplest and the least surprising:

Arithmetic Operator	Description
+	Adds two numbers
-	Subtracts one number from another
*	Multiplies two numbers
div	Divides two numbers. Dividing two integers may result in a noninteger (that is, 3 div 2 = 1.5).
Idiv	Divides two numbers and returns an integer. The result is rounded toward zero to the nearest integer

Comparison Operators

The comparison operators enable you to do comparisons between two operands. The equality operator (=) is used extensively in the examples, and the less than (<) operator was used to find cheap wines. But XQuery has some challenges that most programming languages don't, and to meet these challenges it actually has two classes of comparison operators: value comparison operators and general comparison operators.

The general comparison operators look most similar to those in programming languages such as Java, C#, and C/C++, but they behave most differently. General comparison operators compare the two operands as sequences; value comparison operators assume that both operands are atomic values and perform a comparison that is more typical of other programming languages. To compare the difference between the two different types of operators, consider the two general comparison operators, = (equal) and != (not equal), and their corresponding value comparison operators, eq and ne. For example:

```
<results>
  {
    let $a := (1)
    let $b := (2)

    return
     <result>
      {$a = $b},
      {$a eq $b},
      {$a != $b},
      {$a ne $b}
    </result>
  }
</results>
```

The variables `$a` and `$b` are sequences by definition — the result of an expression is a sequence. But `$a` and `$b` readily atomize to atomic values — 1 and 2, respectively. The result of this query is:

```
<results>
  <result>
      general equals: false,
      value equals: false,
      general not equals: true,
      value not equals: true
   </result>
</results>
```

As with any case where both operands are atomic, the `general` and `value` comparison operators return the same value.

Where the `value` and the `general` comparisons operators differ is when they compare sequences. First, this query won't run at all:

```
<results>
  {

    let $c := (1,2,3)
    let $d := (3,4,5)
    return
     <result>
      value equals: {$c eq $d},
      value not equals: {$c ne $d}
    </result>
  }
</results>
```

The `value` comparison operators only work if the operands can be atomized to atomic values. You can't do that with sequences that contain more than one atomic value. When comparing sequences you can only use the general comparison operators, as shown here:

```
<results>
  {
    let $c := (1,2,3)
```

```
        let $d := (3,4,5)
        return
         <result>
          general equals: {$c = $d},
          general not equals: {$c != $d}
        </result>
    }
</results>
```

What do you expect the result to be? There's a good chance you aren't expecting this:

```
<results>
  <result>
      general equals: true,
      general not equals: true
  </result>
</results>
```

Huh? How can two variables be both equal and not equal? Before explaining, here's another case to deepen the mystery:

```
<results>
  {

    let $a := 1
    let $b := (2)

    let $c := (1,2,3)
    let $d := (1,2,3)
    return
     <result>
      general equals: {$c = $d},
      general not equals: {$c != $d}
    </result>
  }
</results>
```

What do you think the result will be? It is:

```
<results>
  <result>
      general equals: true,
      general not equals: true
  </result>
</results>
```

Again, the two operands are both equal and not equal. What's going on?

The way the general comparison operators work is to evaluate every atomic value in the left operand against every atomic value in the right operand. As soon as any of these comparisons return true, the expression returns true. The first example, `(1,2,3) = (3,4,5)`, returns true because 3 equals 3. `(1,2,3) != (3,4,5)` returns true because 1 doesn't equal 3. In the second example `(1,2,3) = (1,2,3)` returns true because 1 equals 1, and `(1,2,3) != (1,2,3)` returns true because 1 doesn't equal 2.

The following table describes all of the comparison operators.

Comparison Operator	Type	Description
`=`	General	Any value in the sequence on the left equals any value in the sequence on the right.
`!=`	General	Any value in the sequence on the left does not equal any value in the sequence on the right.
`<`	General	Any value in the sequence on the left is less than any value in the sequence on the right.
`<=`	General	Any value in the sequence on the left is less than or equal to any value in the sequence on the right.
`>`	General	Any value in the sequence on the left is greater than any value in the sequence on the right.
`>=`	General	Any value in the sequence on the left is greater than or equal to any value in the sequence on the right.
`eq`	Value	Atomic value on the left equals the atomic value on the right.
`ne`	Value	Atomic value on the left is not equal to the atomic value on the right.
`lt`	Value	Atomic value on the left is less than the atomic value on the right.
`le`	Value	Atomic value on the left is less than or equal to the atomic value on the right.
`gt`	Value	Atomic value on the left is greater than the atomic value on the right.
`ge`	Value	Atomic value on the left is greater than or equal to the atomic value on the right.

The preceding discussion probably puts you on edge about the general comparison operators, and indeed they have some nuances that are best left to the expert user. But remember, the general comparison operators only become "interesting" when one of the operands is a sequence. For basic queries such as comparing a wine's price to some particular number, the general comparison operators act just like the value comparison operators. If you only want the more traditional behavior that the value comparison operators embody, you can avoid the general comparison operators entirely and always use the value comparison operators.

Document Order and Sequence Operators

XQuery has two document order operators, << and >>. They compare the document order of two different nodes. Assuming that `FirstElement` precedes `SecondElement` in an XML document, the following expressions both return true:

```
//FirstElement << //SecondElement
//SecondElement >> //FirstElement
```

The final set of operators are sequence operators — `union`, `intersect`, and `except`. The union operator combines the two sequences and returns the unique nodes. The intersect operator returns each node that is shared across the two sequences. The except operator returns all of the nodes in the first sequence that aren't in the second sequence.

Here's a query that shows the `union` operator at work, joining two sequences together:

```
let $a := (<nodeA/>)
let $b := (<nodeB/>)
return
 $a union $b
```

This query returns:

```
<nodeA/>
<nodeB/>
```

The next query uses the `intersect` operator to return only the nodes that the two sequences have in common:

```
let $a := (<nodeA/>)
let $b := ($a,<nodeB/>)

return
  $a intersect $b
```

The query returns:

```
<nodeA/>
```

And here's an example of a query using the `except` operator:

```
let $a := (<nodeA/>)
let $b := ($a,<nodeB/>)
return
 $b except $a
```

It returns the following:

```
<nodeB/>
```

Complex Queries

With an understanding of FLWOR expressions, XPath, and operators, you are ready to start putting them to work. The examples in this section introduce aspects of XQuery that you haven't seen before.

First, consider the following query, which presents a list of wines of a certain vintage, ordered by price:

```
<wines>
  {
  for $wine at $index in doc("wines.xml")/catalog/section/wine
   let $price := $wine/price/us
   let $vintage := $wine/vintage
   where $vintage > 2000
   order by $price descending
   return
    <wine index = "{$index}">
        {$wine/@*}
      {$wine/*}
        </wine>
  }
 </wines>
```

This query uses a `for` clause to set up a loop over the wine elements in `wines.xml`. But notice one addition to the clause — `at $index`. The `$index` variable yields the position in the sequence that is being processed. In this case, the index becomes an attribute of the returned `wine` element.

The `let` clauses establish variables that are used later in the query. The `where` clause filters the `wine` elements. It eliminates any wines with a vintage of 2000 or earlier. The next clause specifies the order in which the wine eliminates should be passed to the return clause. In this case, the wines are ordered most expensive first.

The `return` clause creates and returns a new `wine` element with the new `index` element. The first expression includes all of the attributes from the original wine element, and the second expression includes all of the child elements. You could also name each attribute and child element, but then the query is harder to maintain — what if more child elements or attributes are added in the future, or if some are removed?

The results of this query are shown in Figure 8-8.

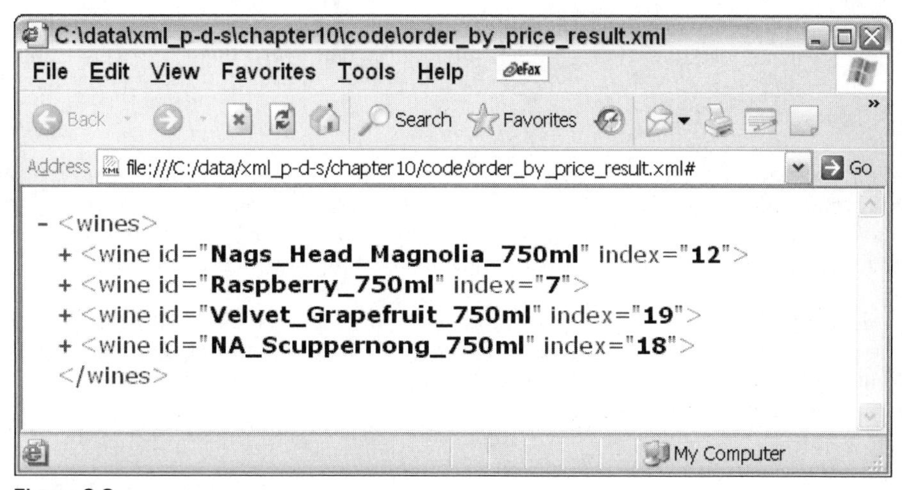

Figure 8-8

Notice that the `index` attributes show the position in the original `wines.xml`. If you want to get the positions of the wines in terms of their price, you need to loop over a sequence that has already been narrowed. The following query shows how you can do this by first assigning the sequence ordered by price to a variable, `$wineList`. Then, a `for` clause iterates over `$wineList` and a second return clause returns a new `wine` element that includes a new attribute called `priceIndex`. The return clause also uses an `if/then/else` clause so that only the top three wines are returned.

```
<wines>
  {
  let $wineList := (
  for $wine at $index in doc("wines.xml")/catalog/section/wine
   let $price := $wine/price/us
   let $vintage := $wine/vintage
   where $vintage > 2000
   order by $price descending
   return
    <wine index = "{$index}">
        {$wine/@*}
     {$wine/*}
       </wine>
  )
   return
      for $filteredWine at $priceIndex in $wineList
      return
       if ($priceIndex <= 3) then
       <wine priceIndex = "{$priceIndex}" >
         {$filteredWine/@*}
         {$filteredWine/*}
       </wine>
       else
        ''

  }
 </wines>
```

The result of this query is shown in Figure 8-9. You might wonder why there is an `else` clause in the query. XQuery requires that every `if` have an `else`. In this case, the `else` returns a null character, which has no significance to XML.

The next query rearranges the entire `wines.xml` document into a new document that represents the geography of the wines in the catalog. In `wines.xml`, the country and region of the winery are listed as part of the `winery` element. The challenge in rearranging `wines.xml` is to pull country and region from the bottom of the `wines.xml` hierarchy and make them the top of the new hierarchy.

There are a couple of new techniques and features of XQuery that are used to accomplish this inversion. First, the `distinct-values` function is used to get the list of both countries and regions. Because the same country and region are listed multiple times, you need a way to eliminate the duplicates. The first part of the query shows how it's done:

```
    <countries>
     {
for $country in distinct-values(doc("wines.xml")/catalog/section/winery/country)
 return
 <country name="{$country}">
```

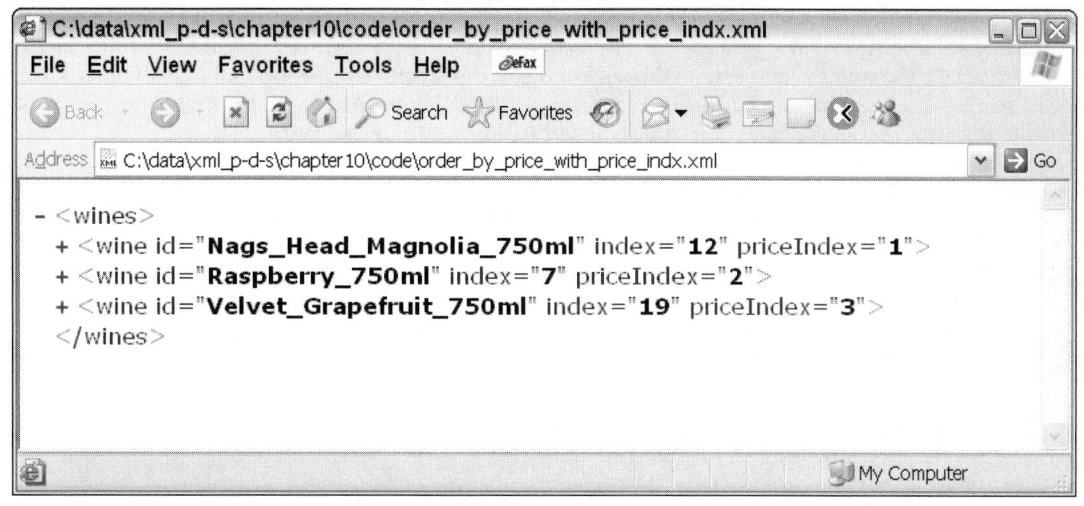

Figure 8-9

This establishes the top of the new hierarchy. The second part of the query creates the next level for regions. The region level presents an interesting problem because you don't know explicitly what regions belong to what countries. Instead, you have to figure this out by looking across all winery elements and seeing which regions appear with the country that is currently being processed.

To do this, you use the `some` and `satisfies` clauses. These clauses narrow the list of wineries to only those that are in the country and the region that are currently being processed. The country being processed is determined by the `for` loop in the first part of the query, and the region is the determined in the `for` loop in the second. The region `for` loop is nested inside the country `for` loop. Here's the second part of the query:

```
{
 for $region in distinct-values(doc("wines.xml")/catalog/section/winery/region)
 let $wineries := doc("wines.xml")/catalog/section/winery
   where
   some $winery in $wineries
   satisfies ($winery/country = $country and $winery/region = $region)
  return
   <region name="{$region}">
```

The next loop builds the winery level of the tree. The `where` clause eliminates wineries that aren't in the current region.

```
{ for $aWinery in doc("wines.xml")/catalog/section/winery
             let $aWineryRegion := $aWinery/region
             where $aWineryRegion = $region
            return
               <winery name="{$aWinery/@name}">
                { for $wine in doc("wines.xml")/catalog/section/wine
                  where $wine/winery = $aWinery/@id
                  return
                   <wine>
```

The final level of the hierarchy is for the wines. One of the child elements of the `wine` element in `wines.xml` is `winery`. Because `winery` is the parent element in the new document, it is redundant to also have a child element pointing to the winery. Thus, the second expression in the following code eliminates the `winery` element while keeping all of the other elements. As before, the first expression pulls in all of the attributes of the original `wine` element into the new `wine` element.

```
                        {$wine/@*}
                        {$wine/*[name() != "winery"]}

                      </wine>
                   }
                 </winery>
             }
           </region>
       }
     </country>
  }
</countries>
```

XQuery and XML Schema Types

As you learned earlier in the book, XML schemas play an important role in providing structure to XML documents. Because XQuery is in the business of creating new XML documents, it is no surprise that XQuery is integrated with XML schemas, as well as DTDs. In fact, XQuery uses XML schemas to give more structure to the XQuery language itself. It does this by using XML Schema as a type system.

A type system, or typing, is an important concept for any kind of programming language. Type systems can provide detection of simple mismatches that otherwise could prove difficult to discover. For instance, a type system can give a language a way to differentiate between numbers and strings. Here's an example:

```
<xml_pds:wines>
  {
  for $wine at $index in doc("wines.xml")/catalog/section/wine
   let $price := $wine/price/us
   where $wine/name > 10
   order by $price descending
   return
     <wine priceRank = "{$index}">
      {$wine/*}
     </wine>
  }
 </xml_pds:wines>
```

In this case, the programmer has made a mistake. A wine name can't be compared numerically to 10. Using typing, you can catch this error at the earliest possible point—before you even begin executing the query. In XQuery, the type checking that catches an error like this is called static typing.

XQuery uses XML Schema to define its simple atomic types and can also use them to define more complex types and to better understand and process input documents. For instance, the expression

```
xs:double($price)
```

casts the value to type `xs:integer`. Casting means that a data value should be treated as a particular type. If the value can't be treated as a particular type, then an error occurs. Consider the following expressions:

```
"14.31"
"12-20-2005"
"fourteen"
"2005-13-46"
```

In the first two cases, the values can be treated as type `xs:decimal` and `xs:date`, respectively, and casting will succeed. In the latter two cases, the same casts would fail. Casting works because some types are more restrictive than others. `"2005-13-46"` is a valid `xs:string` type, but it doesn't represent a valid `xs:date` type. "fourteen" is the word for 14, but in this context it is `xs:string` and not `xs:decimal`.

XQuery raises errors when it encounters simple casting problems like the ones just described. But the timing of when those errors are reported is significant. Do you like to hear bad news as soon as possible or only at the last possible moment? If you are running a query that is doomed to fail, you would probably want to know it as soon as possible. For particularly long-running queries, you might not find out about the problems until the next morning, by which time people may already be expecting answers. It'd be nicer to know the afternoon before that a query isn't going to work so that you can spend the extra few minutes fixing it, rather than wasting days troubleshooting it as you run it again and again.

You want static typing, which takes into account the schema of the XML inputs and reports many simple errors immediately. The following example shows how to reference the wines schema in the prolog so that many errors can be caught statically. If you don't import the schema, the type errors will be found only as the query runs.

```
import schema default element namespace "" at "wines.xsd";
default validation strict
```

The examples so far have been limited to the simple built-in types. In fact, XQuery is integrated with both simple and complex XML Schema types. You can also apply XQuery for types that are composites of the simple types.

XQuery has a couple of operators that support operations related to casting: `instance of`, `typeswitch`, and `treat as`. `instance of` enables you to write code that can check the instance of a particular type before you attempt a cast that could result in an error. Here's an example:

```
where inventorycount instance of xs:integer and inventorycount > 200
```

This would be handy if `inventorycount` sometimes contains "sold out" instead of a number.

The `typeswitch` operator also lets you to vary behavior based on the instance of a data value. Similar to the `case` statement found in many languages, it enables you to define sets of clauses, where only one clause executes based on the type of data. `typeswitch` provides a more convenient way to create code that can also be written using the `instance of` operator; instead of writing several `instance of` clauses, you can write one simpler `typeswitch` clause. `treat as` expressions are similar to the casting expressions discussed earlier — they check to see if a value is of a certain type. But while casting actually changes the value to a value of the particular type, `treat as` doesn't.

Functions

XQuery supports functions that encapsulate expressions and can take parameters. XQuery provides many built-in functions and also enables users to write their own functions, in which they can take advantage of XML Schema typing.

XQuery has a large number of built-in functions that give your queries a lot of power. They include standard numeric functions such as `round`, `floor`, and `ceiling`; standard string functions such `substring`, `upper-case`, `lower-case`, `string-length`, and so on; regular expression pattern-matching functions; and a full suite of date functions.

User-defined functions offer a couple of advantages. First, they give you a way to encapsulate and reuse your queries. Then, instead of having to type in a complicated XQuery, you can just invoke the function. Second, functions enable you to take advantage of the type system discussed earlier.The following code provides an example of a user-defined function. The function uses the inputs of the elements to build a simple element with `id` and `price` as attributes. It is called from the `return` function.

```
declare function local:wine_price($wine as element()) as element()
{
 <wine id="{$wine/@id}" price="{$wine/price/us/text()}"/>
};
```

```
<wines>
  {for $wine
        in doc("wines.xml")//wine
   return local:wine_price($wine)
  }
</wines>
```

The next function returns all of the wines of a certain varietal less than a certain price. It makes use of the type system by using XML Schema types for the inputs. It also returns a sequence of elements as denoted by `as element()*`.

```
declare function local:varietalsLessThanPrice($varietal as xs:string, $price ⮐
as xs:integer) as element()*
{

 for $wine in doc("wines.xml")//wine
  where  $wine/varietal = $varietal and $price >  $wine/price/us
  return
 <wine id="{$wine/@id}" price="{$wine/price/us}"/>

};
```

Here's an XQuery that shows how this function can be called:

```
<wines varietal="Cabernet Sauvignon" lessThan="100">
    {local:varietalsLessThanPrice("Cabernet Sauvignon",100)}
</wines>
```

You can greatly simplify top-level queries by using functions, especially when you use multiple functions together and use them in conjunction with one another. By building libraries of functions and adding to your libraries as you encounter new challenges, you can significantly reduce the amount of code you write and have to maintain.

Solution

You've learned the XQuery basics and how to solve the problems introduced earlier in the chapter. Along the way, hopefully you got a feel for how to use XQuery to attack other merging and querying problems.

With the various queries developed, the last task is to integrate them into your systems. So far, the queries have existed on paper. Regardless of how you execute them, they should work as long as the source XML files are properly available. But how you execute them is a key question that can't be skimmed over. There are a couple of possible scenarios that fit the queries that have been developed. Of course, any query can be executed in any of the different contexts, but if you try to run a query that might take minutes or hours to complete, no one will be pleased if you try to run it from a web application where a hundreds of users are expecting a response in less than five seconds. The character of the query is important when you consider how it should be executed.

As you saw earlier, the easiest way to execute an XQuery is through some kind of desktop tool such as Stylus Studio (see Figure 8-10). You enter the query in the top pane, execute it by clicking the green Preview Result arrow, and view the results in the bottom pane. You can browse the results in different ways: in a tree view, as a web document, or as text XML. You can save the results of the query to a text file after it is completed, and you can also save the query itself as a text file that can be loaded and used anytime you need.

Using a tool like Stylus Studio can be a great fit for queries that you need to run only once or not very often. For instance, the query that creates the geographical hierarchy is a complex query that will take a long time to complete on a large catalog, but the result will only change when new items are added to the catalog. If the catalog doesn't change very often, then when it does change you load the query from file, execute it, and then save the result as the new geographical hierarchy.

Still, it's more common for queries of all types to be executed from inside application code rather than in a tool like Stylus Studio. For instance, SQL also has tools that enable you to type in queries into a GUI, execute them, see the results, and save them, and although experts use such tools to formulate queries, most of the world's SQL queries are executed from inside applications such as desktop applications or web applications that use SQL queries to do the dirty work while presenting a pleasant, intuitive interface to the user. Alternatively, the queries might be enclosed in an application that is executed as a batch job by a scheduler.

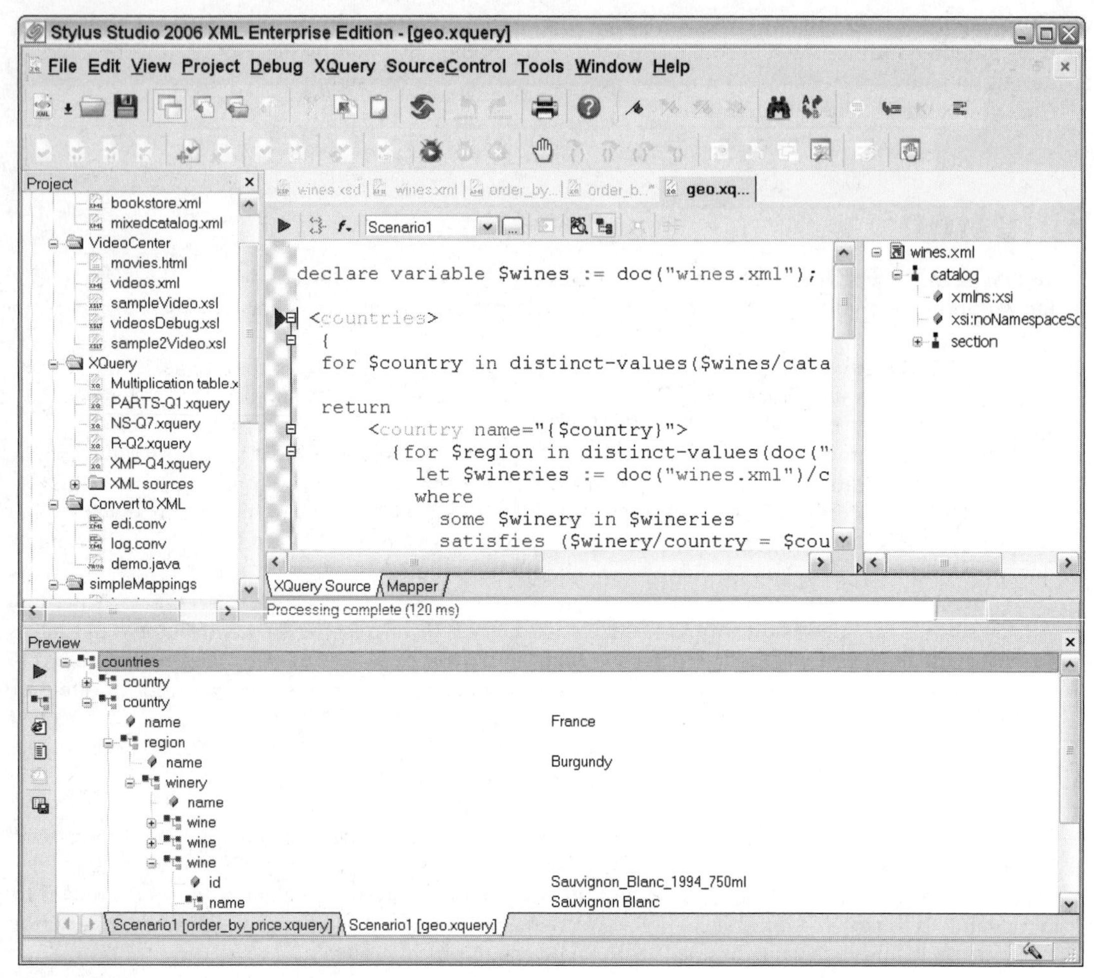

Figure 8-10

XQuery queries, like SQL queries, are also most often found in applications of some sort. For instance, if the catalog is updated every night, you could have a scheduled job run afterward to recreate the geographical document. By the time everyone showed up for work, both the catalog and the geographical hierarchy could be finished. This architecture is shown in Figure 8-11.

Employees might use web or desktop applications to query the catalog. For example, you might have an internal web application that gives the user the capability to query the catalog based on vintage, varietal, and price. It isn't reasonable to teach everyone in the organization XQuery and expect them to be successful entering the queries by hand so the web application makes the query easy for the business user. As shown in Figure 8-12, the user interacts with a form, and the app runs the query. The result can then be handed to a stylesheet that renders the XML into XHTML.

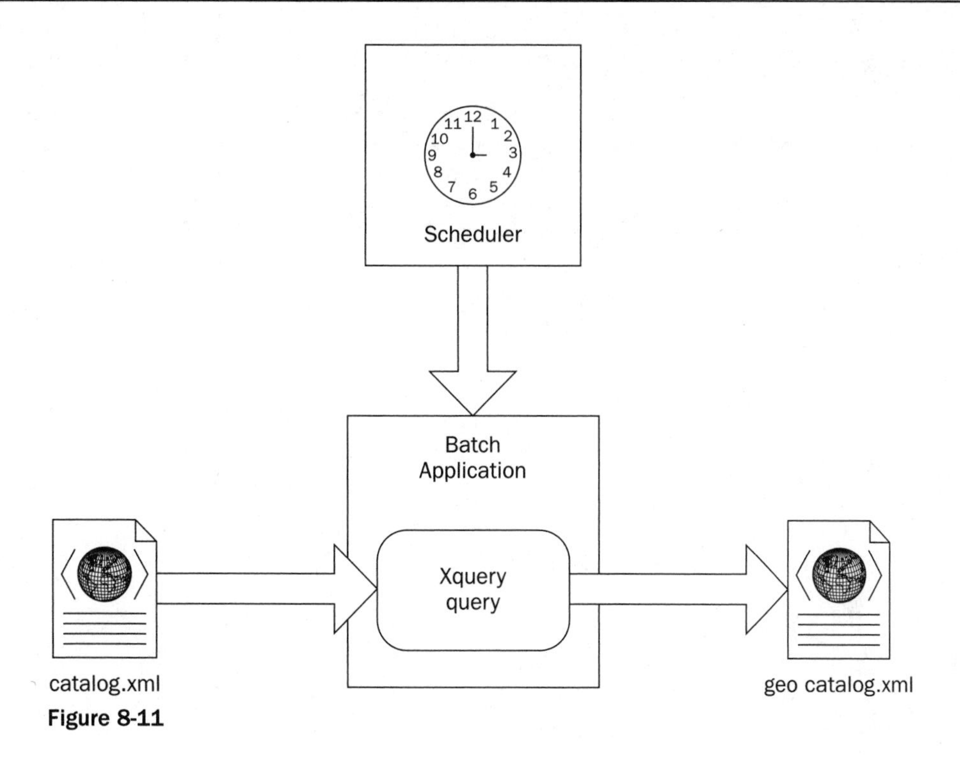

Figure 8-11

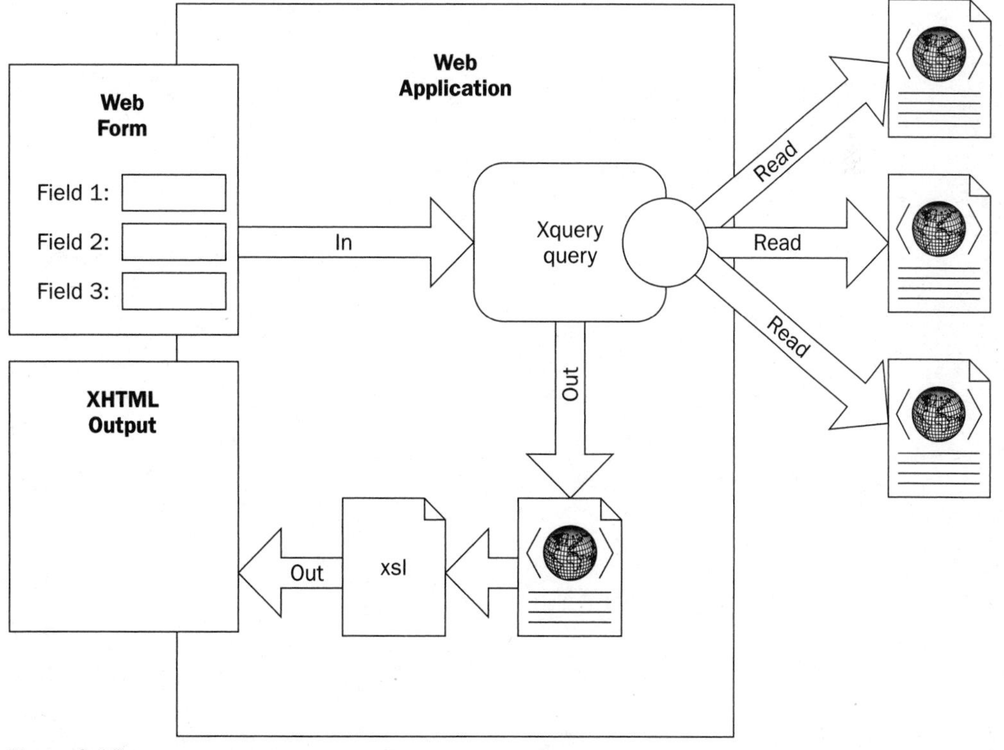

Figure 8-12

Summary

A lot of the success of a web application like this lies in the queries. Granted, it takes a lot of web programming skill to get the application put together. But no amount of skill makes up for queries that take too long to run. There are always certain steps you can take to make queries run faster. A logical first step is to get faster hardware, which can go a long way toward achieving this. You can also improve the format of the source data so that it is easier to query, and you can optimize the queries. The software that executes the queries is part of the story, also, and this is a piece that hasn't been examined so far in this chapter. The next chapter, which covers XML and databases, delves into that topic.

9

Integrating XML with the Rest of Your Data

Few enterprises have all of their data as XML documents, and there aren't many cases where it would be wise for all of an enterprise's data to be XML. Typically, an enterprise has a minimum of one relational database such as Oracle, DB2, or Microsoft SQL Server — and at the very least has data stored in a table format with tools such as Excel and Access. Inevitably, data that is stored in different ways have to be brought together.

This chapter focuses on the integration of XML with relational data and relational databases. You'll see how to create XML documents from data stored in a relational database, and how XQuery can be used to query relational data together with XML documents. You'll also explore the database choices for XML and learn how traditional relational databases have been enhanced for XML.

Problem

The projects for this chapter cover XML integration with relational data in a few different ways:

- Your organization is using XSLT stylesheets for rendering content, and you want to be able to use stylesheets to render data that is stored in the relational database of your inventory system. Because XSLT needs its source data to be XML, you need a way to create XML from your relational data.
- Using XQuery, you want to be able to run queries that return only wines that are in stock, but the inventory data is in the relational database. You need to make the inventory data accessible to your XQuery queries.
- Your inventory system has a tool that uses SQL to read the relational data from the inventory data base. You have some wine data stored in XML that you want to surface to the inventory system tool. You need a way to include XML data in a SQL query that returns a traditional relational result.

These projects assume that you have an inventory system that stores its data in relational databases.

Design

All of this chapter's projects speak to the need for convergence between the relational and XML worlds. If you have been around information technology for any length of time, you might be wondering if this is really a case of "winner take all" where one way of doing things essentially kills the competition—think VHS VCRs versus Beta VCRs, in which, for various reasons, VHS VCRs came to completely dominate the VCR market. Might XML take over or might it just be an upstart that the relational world crushes over time?

While you certainly see relational database vendors adding more and better XML features all the time and becoming tightly integrated with XML, the underlying XML and relational models themselves are distinct and have very different sweetspots. There is certainly a lot of overlap between the two, and sometimes the decision between using XML or a SQL database isn't straightforward. Luckily, the convergence of the XML and relational worlds makes these decisions less risky, if not necessarily easier.

Creating XML from Relational Data with SQL/XML

When relational data is returned from a database via a SQL (Structured Query Language) query, it is typically returned in a tabular format. Although that format is the most natural way to work with SQL results, it may be out of place in an XML environment. For instance, if your organization starts to rely heavily on XSLT for presentation of data, then the tabular results of SQL won't fit in well with your environment. You either need to have separate, parallel tools and skills to deal with relational data, or you need a way to bridge the gap.

SQL/XML is such a bridge. It is a standard set of SQL functions that generate XML output—in other words, it formats relational data as XML. A database such as Oracle that implements SQL/XML provides the SQL/XML functions for use in queries. Using SQL/XML, you can establish the flow shown in Figure 9-1. First, the SQL/XML query queries the relational database and returns the result as XML. Then, any XML tool, such as XSLT, XQuery, or the like, can be used on the XML data. In the diagram, the intermediate XML is used in conjunction with an XSLT stylesheet to create output XML such as XHTML. You can use this pattern to create XML from your relational data.

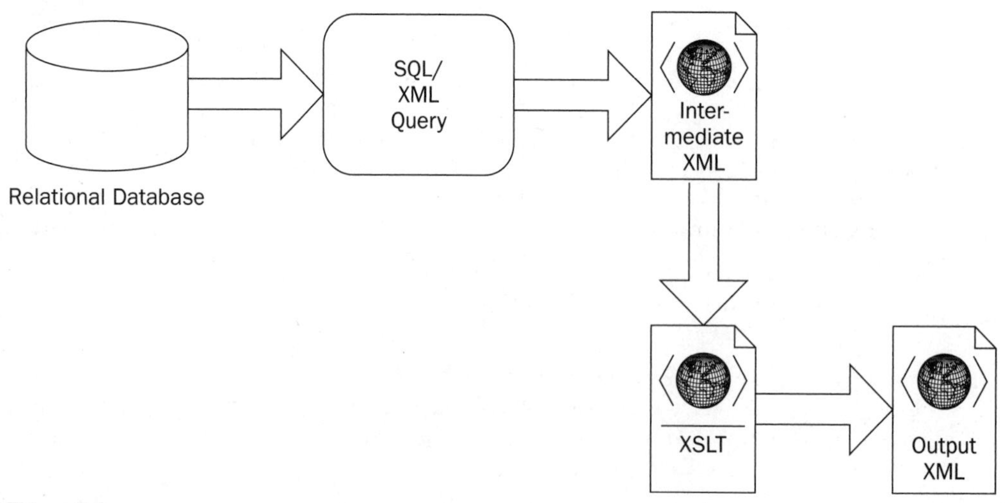

Figure 9-1

Relational Data and XML Conversions: Not a Two-Way Street

You may be wondering if there is a way to bridge the relational and XML gap the other way, rendering XML in a tabular form so that SQL tools can manipulate the XML data. Although there are tools that will extract parts of XML for use with relational data, there aren't methods for converting complete, arbitrary XML documents into relational tables. As touched on in the last chapter, the table structure is more rigid than XML, so it's hard to move from XML to relational. A table structure can always be easily represented as XML. But while some XML documents can be rendered readily as relational tables because they have a flat, uniform structure, you may need many tables with complex relationships between them to represent an XML document of moderate complexity. As you'll see later in this chapter, many databases use their own complex, proprietary methodologies to arbitrarily break XML documents across tables when they store XML. From an ease-of-use standpoint, it is better to form a bridge between relational data and XML by converting relational data to XML.

If you've used SQL to any extent, you've probably encountered functions in the `SELECT` clause of a SQL statement. In the following SQL statement, the `lower()` function is used to lowercase the employee name:

```
SELECT lower(ename)
   FROM emp
   WHERE emp.deptno = 10;
```

There are many types of SQL functions, including mathematical, string manipulation, aggregation, date, and conversion. They vary from one database vendor to another, but all relational databases provide such functions. You can think of SQL/XML as another category of functions that are standardized.

Of all the SQL/XML functions, the simplest is `xmlelement()`. It creates an element based on an inputted field, and can take other SQL/XML functions as parameters so that child nodes can be created. The following SQL shows a simple example that creates a list of elements from the emp table, which is part of the demo data that ships with Oracle databases. (It contains data about employees, such as name, salary, bonus, manager, and department number. The department number references department information in another table named dept.) In the following query, `ename` returns the last name in all caps for each employee in department 10.

```
SELECT xmlelement("EmployeeName",ename)
   FROM emp
   WHERE emp.deptno = 10;
```

The query returns the following results — three rows, each with a single XML element representing the last name for each employee in department 10:

```
<EmployeeName>CLARK</EmployeeName>
<EmployeeName>KING</EmployeeName>
<EmployeeName>MILLER</EmployeeName>

3 rows selected.
```

Typically, SQL returns data in a tabular form. The XML is returned because of the SQL/XML function. In the following examples, the key to generating the XML is the SQL/XML functions such as `xmlelement()`.

The first thing you probably notice about the result is that it isn't XML. Instead, you have a series of XML elements that aren't tied together under a root element. The "3 rows selected" output is included to show that the output is split over three separate rows, which means that any processing application would have additional trouble recognizing them as a coherent entity.

This initial foray into SQL/XML is a reminder of the core underlying problems of bridging relational and XML data. The preceding SQL statement is perfectly legal from both a SQL standpoint and a SQL/XML statement—but it fails to produce well-formed XML. In truth, there are certainly situations where that statement is both practical and valuable, and SQL/XML would be a lesser standard if it weren't allowed. But it's telling that a low-level example doesn't meet the core requirement—creating an XML document from SQL.

Not that it is particularly difficult to create an XML document from SQL. While SQL's natural habitat is tabular and is at its best when returning tables, it is also capable of returning hierarchies by using nested subqueries inside of queries. Because XML is a hierarchical format, these nested queries are the key to bridging the gap.

In the preceding example, the XML elements were spread across three rows. The first step is to get all of the XML elements on to a single row. You accomplish this with `xmlagg()`, an aggregation function—it aggregates other XML elements. Here is the code:

```
SELECT xmlagg(xmlelement("EmployeeName",ename))
   FROM emp
   WHERE emp.deptno = 10;
```

The result of running this statement is:

```
<EmployeeName>CLARK</EmployeeName>
<EmployeeName>KING</EmployeeName>
<EmployeeName>MILLER</EmployeeName>

1 row selected.
```

The next step is to get the elements underneath a parent element by using a subquery. The following query does the job:

```
SELECT xmlelement("DeptEmployees",
   (SELECT xmlagg(xmlelement("EmployeeName",ename))
    FROM emp e
    WHERE e.deptno = d.deptno)
  )
 FROM dept d
 WHERE d.deptno = 10;
```

Here's the output.

```
<DeptEmployees>
  <EmployeeName>CLARK</EmployeeName>
  <EmployeeName>KING</EmployeeName>
```

```
  <EmployeeName>MILLER</EmployeeName>
</DeptEmployees>
```

In spite of not having `xmlagg()` in the outer `SELECT` clause, this query returns a well-formed XML document on a single row. The outer query returns only one row naturally because there is only one department with the department number 10. However, the `xmlagg()` function is required for the subquery because of how SQL handles nested queries. Regardless of SQL/XML, this statement requires that the subquery return a single row. Although the `xmlagg()` function doesn't seem to be doing much work, removing it will cause errors.

So far, the XML document has only elements. You can also create attributes in the result XML. The following code adds the department number as an attribute to the top-level element. The `xmlattributes()` function creates the attribute by setting the value `deptno` from the query to an attribute named `departmentId`:

```
SELECT xmlelement("DeptEmployees",
   xmlattributes(deptno AS "departmentId"),
  (SELECT xmlagg(xmlelement("EmployeeName",ename))
   FROM emp e
   WHERE e.deptno = d.deptno)
  )
 FROM dept d
 WHERE d.deptno = 10;
```

The result of the query is:

```
<DeptEmployees departmentId="10">
  <EmployeeName>CLARK</EmployeeName>
  <EmployeeName>KING</EmployeeName>
  <EmployeeName>MILLER</EmployeeName>
</DeptEmployees>
```

What if you want a list of employees from all departments, broken down by department? For this, the `xmlagg()` function comes back into play because the outer query returns more than one row. The following query returns employees for all departments, with a root element of `Employees`:

```
SELECT xmlelement("Employees",xmlagg(xmlelement("DeptEmployees",
   xmlattributes(deptno AS "departmentId"),
  (SELECT xmlagg(xmlelement("EmployeeName",ename))
   FROM emp e
   WHERE e.deptno = d.deptno)
  )))
 FROM dept d;
```

Here's the result:

```
<Employees>
  <DeptEmployees departmentId="10">
    <EmployeeName>CLARK</EmployeeName>
    <EmployeeName>KING</EmployeeName>
    <EmployeeName>MILLER</EmployeeName>
  </DeptEmployees>
  <DeptEmployees departmentId="20">
```

```
      <EmployeeName>SMITH</EmployeeName>
      <EmployeeName>JONES</EmployeeName>
      <EmployeeName>SCOTT</EmployeeName>
      <EmployeeName>ADAMS</EmployeeName>
      <EmployeeName>FORD</EmployeeName>
    </DeptEmployees>
    <DeptEmployees departmentId="30">
      <EmployeeName>ALLEN</EmployeeName>
      <EmployeeName>WARD</EmployeeName>
      <EmployeeName>MARTIN</EmployeeName>
      <EmployeeName>BLAKE</EmployeeName>
      <EmployeeName>TURNER</EmployeeName>
      <EmployeeName>JAMES</EmployeeName>
    </DeptEmployees>
    <DeptEmployees departmentId="40"/>
  </Employees>
```

So far, the result XML has been flat, where the hierarchy only has a couple of levels, as opposed to deep, where the hierarchy has several levels. A flat result is typical of XML created from relational data. Relational data is flat by nature, and it is easier to write SQL/XML queries that return flat XML. But SQL/XML enables you to generate complex XML documents. One function that makes producing XML less difficult is the `xmlforest()` function, which is used in the following code. Like the other SQL/XML functions, `xmlforest()` creates XML from relational data. It returns several distinct XML element "trees" that do not share a common parent. It enables you to quickly create XML tags for several columns. To keep the result document short, this example query returns only employees for department 10.

```
SELECT xmlelement("Employees",xmlagg(xmlelement("DeptEmployees",
   xmlattributes(deptno AS "departmentId"),
  (SELECT xmlagg(xmlelement("Employee",
      xmlattributes(empno AS "employeeId"),
      xmlforest(e.ename AS "Name",
                e.job AS "Job",
                e.sal AS "Salary")))
   FROM emp e
   WHERE e.deptno = d.deptno)
  )))
 FROM dept d
 WHERE d.deptno = 10;
```

The result of this query is:

```
<Employees>
  <DeptEmployees departmentId="10">
    <Employee employeeId="7782">
      <Name>CLARK</Name>
      <Job>MANAGER</Job>
      <Salary>2450</Salary>
    </Employee>
    <Employee employeeId="7839">
      <Name>KING</Name>
      <Job>PRESIDENT</Job>
      <Salary>5000</Salary>
```

```
    </Employee>
    <Employee employeeId="7934">
      <Name>MILLER</Name>
      <Job>CLERK</Job>
      <Salary>1300</Salary>
    </Employee>
  </DeptEmployees>
</Employees>
```

At this point, you've learned several of the key functions in SQL/XML, and in the process you've learned a large amount of the SQL/XML specification. There are several other functions that you might use in building XML from relational data by creating the other types of XML nodes. The preceding examples showed you how to create the two most common types of nodes — elements and attributes — with the `xmlelement()` and `xmlattributes()`, respectively. You can also create comments with `xmlcomment()` and processing instructions with `xmlpi()`.

The last function to discuss is `xmlparse()`. It is often the case that XML is stored in a column of the database as raw text. Later in the chapter, you'll hear an argument that this isn't necessarily the best solution, but the strategy has its place and is something you might encounter. The `xmlparse()` function enables you to read the raw text, parse it as XML, and then use it in combination with the other functions and with SQL/XML in general. If SQL/XML bridges relational data to XML, then `xmlparse()` is a secondary bridge that takes XML as raw text to SQL/XML.

Let's say that you have a table, `performance_review`, which is where the employees' performance reviews are stored. The table has two columns, empno and review, and the performance review is stored as XML in the review column. You want to build a SQL/XML query that joins the two tables and pulls the employee name, job, and performance review together. The following query accomplishes this:

```
SELECT xmlelement("EmployeeReview",
         xmlelement("Name",ename),
         xmlelement("Job",job),
         xmlparse(performance_review.review))
  FROM emp, performance_review
  WHERE emp.empno = performance_review.empno
        AND emp.empno = 7782;
```

The `xmlelement()` functions create XML elements from relational data, just like they've been doing throughout the examples in this section. The `xmlparse()` function, on the other hand, works on a string that is already an XML element. If the string, `performance_review.review`, is already XML, then why is the `xmlparse()` function necessary? It's essential to use `xmlparse()` so that the resulting value can be used as an argument with the other SQL/XML functions. In this case, it's passed as an argument to `xmlelement()`, but you may also need to use `xmlparse()` in conjunction with other SQL/XML functions.

XQuery and Relational Data

Once you've bridged the gap between relational data and XML by converting your relational data to XML, you can use XQuery to join the XML document produced by SQL/XML with native XML documents. By using SQL/XML to generate an intermediate, temporary XML document, you can join your relational data with your XML data in one XQuery query. Figure 9-2 illustrates this pattern.

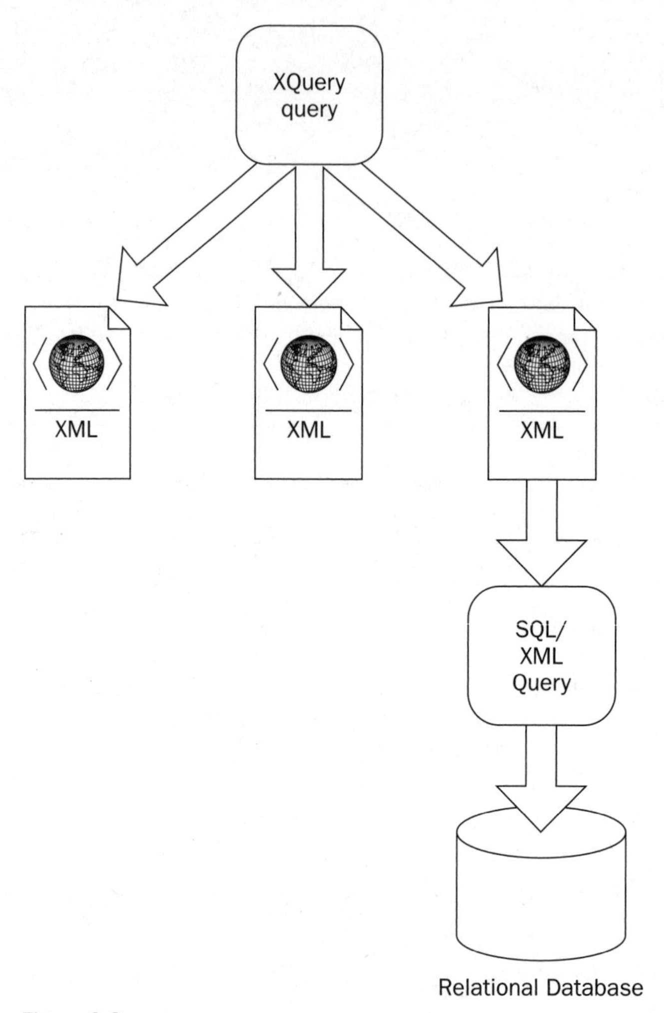

Figure 9-2

Because SQL/XML returns XML, nothing about XQuery changes — it's the same XML querying language that you learned in the previous chapter. What's new is how to integrate the SQL/XML query with your XQuery query. You have two options:

- Use SQL/XML to generate a static document, and then simply include the generated XML document in your query as you would any other document.
- Execute the SQL/XML query dynamically as part of the XQuery query.

In both cases, the syntax and mechanics of your XQuery are the same. You just have to choose whether you want an intermediate document that may not be completely up to date, or the very latest data from the relational database at the risk of a less-performant XQuery query.

In the latter case, the environment in which you execute your XQuery needs to provide a way to execute the SQL/XML query as part of the XQuery. Different XQuery environments handle dynamic SQL/XML execution in different ways. You should consult your XQuery tool's or library's documentation to see how your SQL/XML is integrated with your XQuery environment. As an example, Stylus Studio is discussed here.

Stylus Studio enables you to use the `collection` function to link to a SQL/XML query, which is typical. `collection` is an input function like the `document` function. It differs from `document` in that its result doesn't have to be a well-formed XML document. Instead, the result can be a forest — a collection of XML elements that don't share a common parent. Of course, the `collection` function can also return a single XML document — this would be analogous to a forest with only one tree. Remember from earlier examples that SQL/XML can legally return a forest of XML elements rather than a single XML document. Tools like Stylus Studio use the `collection` function as the gateway to SQL/XML.

Consider the following XQuery, which uses the `collection` input function to get the data from the source called `emp_table`:

```
<result>
  {
    for $i in collection("emp_table")/*
    return
    $i
  }
</result>
```

When executed in Stylus Studio, `emp_table` can resolve to a SQL/XML query as a data source. Before the query can work, you need to define a collection called `emp_table`. Figure 9-3 shows the `emp_table` collection listed as a defined collection in the Scenario Properties. In this case, the `emp_table` is tied to a SQL/XML table in the file called `emp_table_sqlxml.rdbxml`.

Scenario Properties
Existing scenarios:
Scenario1
Add | Clone | Delete | Rename
General | Processor | Parameter Values | Profiling Options | Validation
Inputs
Main input (optional):
Defined collections:

Name	URL
emp_table	db:///emp_table_sqlxml.rdbxml

Output URL (optional):
Use relative paths
Preview result in an external application
OK | Cancel

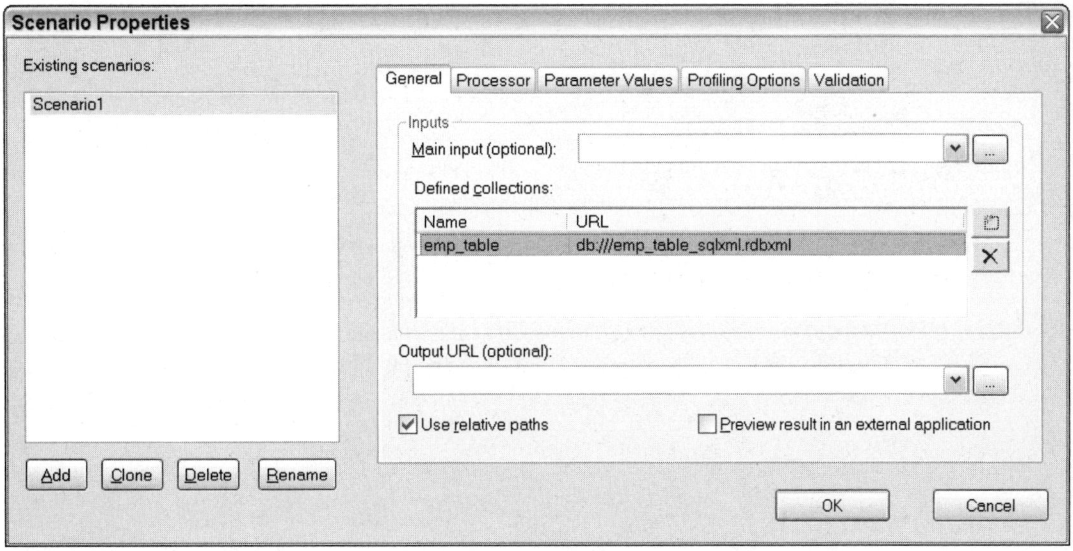

Figure 9-3

The SQL/XML query contained in this file is shown in Figure 9-4. It's a very simple SQL query that doesn't use any of the SQL/XML functions discussed previously. Instead, this example is meant to demonstrate how even straight SQL can be integrated with XQuery. The results of running the SQL query are shown in the bottom pane of the screen shot. They are formatted as XML in a default, generic manner, even though none of the SQL/XML functions were used.

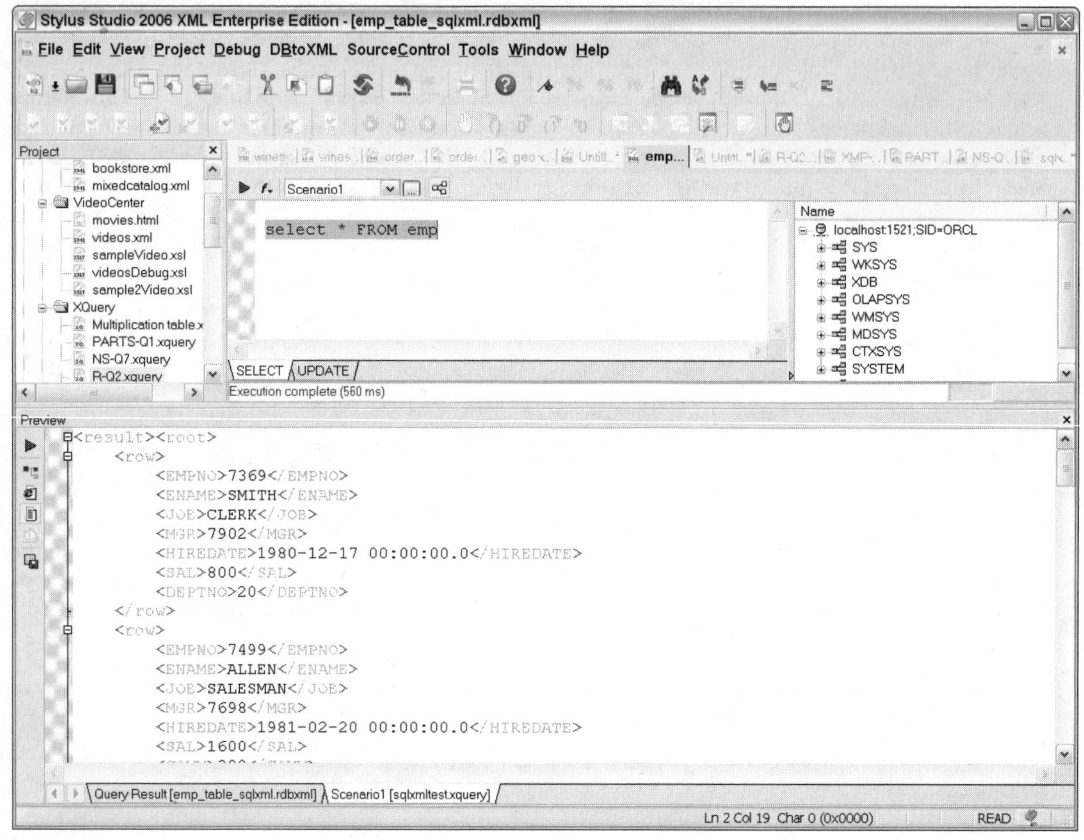

Figure 9-4

The result of executing the XQuery is shown in Figure 9-5. Because of its simplicity, the only change is that the SQL/XML result is wrapped under the root `<result>` element defined by the XQuery.

With the SQL/XML integrated, you are free to use all of the XQuery mechanics you learned in the last chapter. The following query is a little more exciting than the previous one; it filters the nodes based on salary. As you learned in Chapter 8, you can join the SQL/XML result with XML documents simply by using nested `for` clauses, compound `for` clauses, or `let` in conjunction with either of the input functions `document()` or `collection()`.

```
<result>
  {
    for $i in collection("emp_table")/root/row
```

```
        where $i/SAL > 800
           return
          $i
      }
    </result>
```

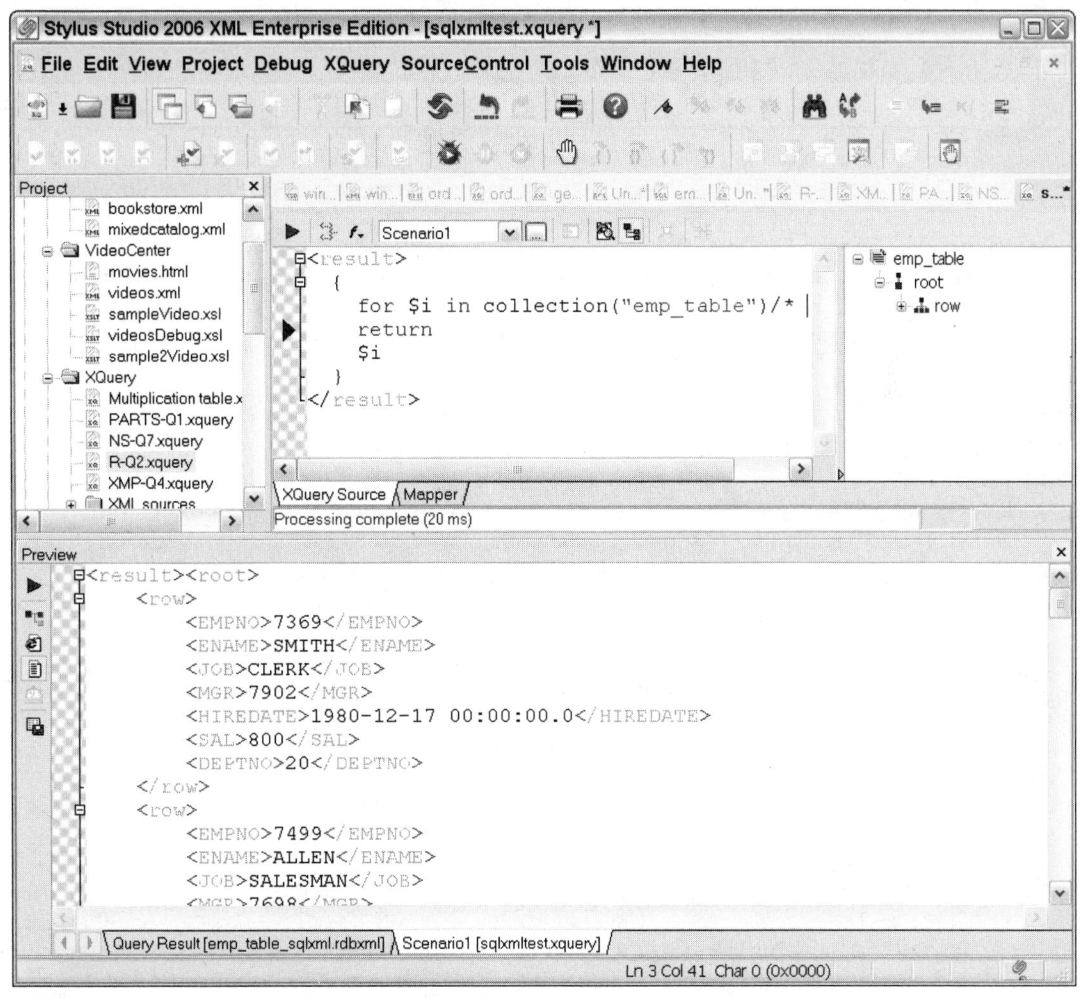

Figure 9-5

In this query, the value for `$i` is set to each row element of the XML document returned by the emp_table SQL/XML query. Indirectly through the temporary, intermediate XML document created by the emp_table SQL/XML query, this XQuery is really just working on the underlying relational data.

Understanding Native XML and XML-Enhanced Relational Databases

How do you align your relational and XML data from a storage perspective? So far, this book has assumed that your XML is stored as files. This doesn't have to be the case. You can store XML in a database for a variety of reasons — you want queries to run faster, you want to take advantage of database backup and recovery tools, certain applications require database storage, and so on. Further, you can store XML in different types of databases.

Before looking at the database choices, make sure that you understand the difference between an XML *document* and what is commonly referred to as an XML *file*. XML is often stored as a file. If you want your XML, you go to some file such as `my.xml` and open it. But an XML document is really a logical concept and XML doesn't have to be stored as a file. Consider the results of an XQuery query or an XSLT transformation. The result is an XML document, but there is no underlying XML file associated with it. The reason that the distinction is important for this discussion is that databases don't have to store your XML documents as files. Not only do they not have to, but in many cases it is likely that they won't because it isn't efficient.

Keeping the distinction between XML documents and XML files in mind, you are ready to consider the two primary types of databases that you might use in conjunction with XML — native XML databases and XML-enhanced relational databases. Native XML databases are specifically engineered with XML in mind, while XML-enhanced relational databases come from the prominent relational database vendors, such as Oracle, IBM and Microsoft, and give you ways to store your XML right alongside your relational databases. The XML-enhanced relational databases are more like one-stop shopping, while the native XML databases are more like specialty shopping. The XML-enhanced relational databases also give you expanded mechanisms for querying relational databases and XML at the same time, which is discussed in the next section.

You hand your XML documents to either type of database, and it stores them for you. It also indexes the XML documents so that queries are easier, and it has querying mechanisms for retrieving the XML documents. How the database stores the XML varies. For instance, some native XML databases actually have relational databases on the back end that they use for storing index information. Some XML-enhanced relational databases use a file storage approach, while others break up an XML document across many relational tables, an approach that's called "shredding."

Your choice of database will probably be influenced largely by two factors: the fit for your particular situation and price. The price factor is easy to understand, especially if your organization has already chosen a relational database. For instance, if you already have a large Oracle footprint, then even if a native XML database may be the best fit for you, you may find that the overall cost determines that you choose the XML-enhanced features of Oracle instead.

When considering what is best for your situation, look at the underlying storage mechanisms as well as the available query mechanisms. The advantage of having a database is that it frees you from having to be concerned with the underlying dynamics of storage. Some database architectures are going to be better for some scenarios than others — for instance, if your data is mostly document-oriented XML, a native XML database may be a better choice, but if you have mostly relational data with a small percentage of XML, than an XML-enhanced relational database may be a better fit. Also, your operations may change — maybe today you are mostly relational, but two years from now you'll be mostly XML. The underlying storage architecture is an important strategic concern, but it shouldn't be a day-to-day tactical concern.

Another storage issue is whether the database has the capability to "round trip" an XML document — can the database return the exact same XML document that it was given in the first place, including the identical white-space characters? This is important when the XML document in question is some kind of contract, and you want to achieve nonrepudiation: neither party can deny that the contract was agreed upon. Some databases, especially XML-enhanced relational databases, slightly modify the document at the time of storage without violating the rules of XML. For instance, they may not keep extraneous white space. But these slight modifications can be enough to violate nonrepudiation, which could cause disagreements as well as interfere with digital verification tools. If you use XML documents as contracts and want to store them in your database, you may need to make nonrepudiation a requirement of the database that you pick.

Both native XML and XML-enhanced relational databases tend to make XQuery available as the querying mechanism. You might also find other XML querying languages, such as Quilt, and you'll need to decide whether you want to move away from XQuery, which is more standardized. XML-enhanced relational databases still use SQL as the primary querying mechanism and provide XQuery and XPath as extensions for querying XML. Such a SQL statement can return a mix of relational and XML data in a tabular format, where one or more columns contains XML results. The XML-specific extensions to SQL are covered in the next section.

SQL with XML Extensions

In a relational database with XML extensions, you use SQL to add XML to the database and to query XML from the database. The SQL is extended so that you can use XML-focused query languages, such as XPath and XQuery, embedded in your SQL statements. Figure 9-6 illustrates the basic architecture: a relational table, where the first three columns are typical columns with simple SQL types. The last column, however, is typed to store XML documents. It isn't just a character string column that happens to store XML, which would present the problems discussed in the last chapter. Instead, the last column is a special type created specifically for XML; it leverages all of the structure and benefits of XML. Different relational databases with XML extensions implement their XML datatypes differently, but all rely on the same basic premise that XML can and should be stored in a table as an XML-specific type.

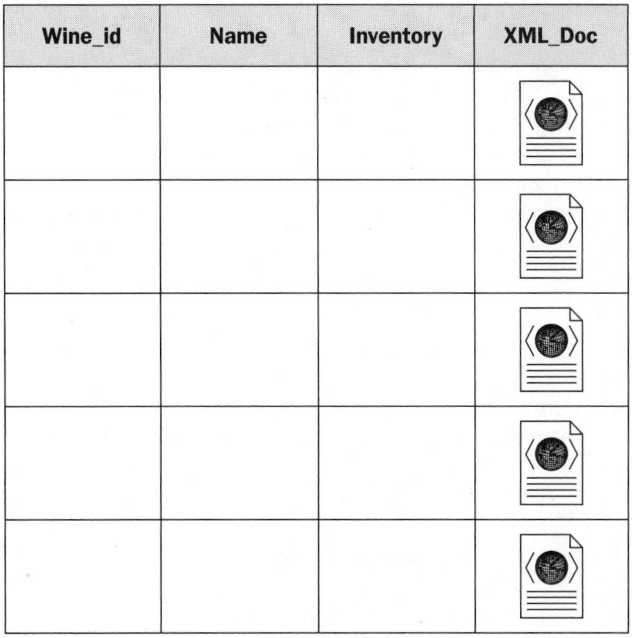

Wine_id	Name	Inventory	XML_Doc

Figure 9-6

Compare this picture to Figure 9-2 in the earlier discussion about XML and SQL/XML. In that case, XQuery was the top-level language and SQL played a supporting role with the help of SQL/XML. In this case, SQL is on top. Through SQL extensions, XPath and XQuery can play supporting roles by querying XML as part of the overall SQL query.

When XML was first emerging on the scene, it was typical to store XML as text. Because XML documents tend to be larger than the simple string types of a relational database, they are often stored as Character Large Objects (CLOBs), which, depending on the database, enable you to store megabytes, if not gigabytes, of data in a single field. You might store an entire XML document as text in the fields of a column, where each row might contain one or more XML documents.

In that simple architecture, the XML text was simply returned as text to a calling application with the expectation that the calling application would know what to do with it. Although the structure of XML gives you a great deal of information about the data, and searching languages such as XPath enable you to leverage that information, the relational database itself couldn't leverage the power of XML from inside SQL. This meant that if you only wanted rows where the XML in that row met certain criteria specified by XPath, your application would have to pull all of the rows back, apply the XPath to the XML of each row, and then throw away the rows that didn't meet the criteria.

Obviously, this was a pain for the application, and a big opportunity for the relational database vendors. By becoming more XML-aware, they could make performing these types of queries easier and also create databases that were a more inviting place to store XML. The approach that different vendors have used is to define a column type specifically for XML. Oracle, for instance, refers to this type as XMLType, and this convention is used in this discussion. This is a type just like the number type or date type, except you can use XML specific functionality related to XML.

Assuming that the database is Oracle, the XML_Doc column is of type XMLType and contains an XML document for each row in the table. In this case, the XML document is the `wine` element that you've seen earlier. Using standard SQL without XML extensions, you are limited to searching the XML as simple text. With XML extensions, you can take advantage of the XML structure of the stored XML stored in the XML_Doc column from inside a SQL query.

XMLType solves the problem of XML and relational integration in one way—you can combine the power of SQL with the power of XPath. You may be required to break up an existing XML document so that each row in the relational database has XML that only relates to that row. In some cases this might be practical, even preferable, but in other cases it might not be. Instead, what you may need is for the XML to remain separate from the relational database tables. This requirement drives an architecture in which you have two different parallel databases—one relational (with XML enhancements) and one a pure XML database.

In the parallel architecture, you can intermingle SQL with XQuery in the same query. The output of the query may be traditional relational data or XML. Inside the query itself, you have several different options. You can:

- Do straight SQL, using SQL/XML to return XML if necessary
- Combine SQL with XPath and the XMLType as discussed previously, and return either relational or XML
- Do straight XQuery and return XML
- Combine XQuery with SQL and return relational output

The details of implementing these different patterns are database vendor–specific and won't be examined further. What you will find is that the traditional relational database vendors are looking to be a one-stop shop for both relational and XML data. Sometimes the combination works well, and at other times it seems clumsy. But because the XML and relational worlds are going to continue to coexist, a relational database with XML extensions can be a way for your relational and XML data to complement one another.

Solution

The beginning of the chapter listed three different problems that arise from the need to integrate XML and relational data. This section tackles those projects in the context of your winery — generating XML from relational data with SQL/XML, including relational data in XQuery queries, and including XML in SQL queries with XML extensions to SQL.

Generating XML from Relational Data

To set up this project, imagine that your winery has an inventory system that stores its data in a relational database. You need to format the data in the relational tables as XML so that you can use it with XSLT stylesheets.

The first step is to understand the data in the relational database. The inventory data in the database is in two tables, item_inventory and item_inventory_total, along with a lookup table for item_inventory that points to a table with information about warehouses. In the item_inventory_total table, the item_id column stores the wine ID, the warehouse_id stores the id for a particular warehouse, and the quantity column stores the quantity of the wine at a particular warehouse. Figure 9-7 illustrates the database setup.

To get the inventory total for a particular wine, you use a SQL statement like the following:

```
SELECT wine_id, inventory_qty
FROM item_inventory_total;
```

This query returns the results in the typical tabular form. Now, you want to create SQL/XML queries based on this query so that you can create XML documents. The following code creates an XML document that reports the inventory total for each wine:

```
SELECT xmlelement("WineInventory",xmlagg(
               xmlelement("Wine",
                xmlelement("Id",item_id),
                xmlelement("Quantity",inventory_qty)
                )))
FROM item_inventory_total;
```

A wine element is created for each wine in the table. The `xmlagg` function aggregates all of the wine elements together under one top-level `WineInventory` element. Following is an abbreviated result of this query:

```
<WineInventory>
   <Wine>
      <Id>Sauvignon_Blanc_1994_750ml</Id>
      <Quantity> 40 </Quantity>
   </Wine>
. . .
</WineInventory>
```

Item_id	Inventory_qty

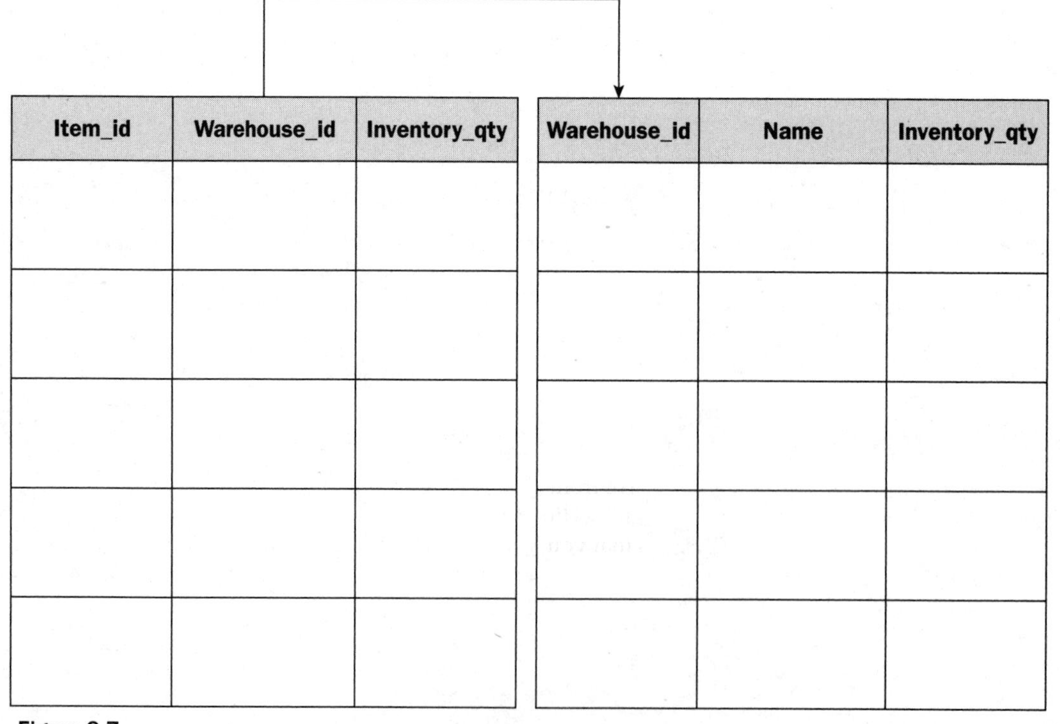

Item_id	Warehouse_id	Inventory_qty

Warehouse_id	Name	Inventory_qty

Figure 9-7

The next SQL/XML query creates an XML document that breaks down inventory by warehouse. It uses a different underlying table, item_inventory, which holds inventory for each wine by each warehouse.

```
SELECT
   xmlelement("WineInventoryByWarehouse",
    xmlagg(
     xmlelement("WineByWarehouse",
      xmlelement("Id",item_inventory.item_id),
      xmlelement("Warehouse",warehouse_info.warehouse_name),
      xmlelement("Quantity",item_inventory.inventory_qty)
     )
    )
   )
FROM item_inventory, warehouse_info
WHERE item_inventory.warehouse_id = warehouse_info.warehouse_id;
```

This returns elements in a format like this:

```
<WineInventoryByWarehouse>
  <WineByWarehouse>
    <Id>Cabernet_Sauvignon_1992_750ml</Id>
    <Warehouse>North</Warehouse>
    <Quantity>10</Quantity>
  </WineByWarehouse>
  <WineByWarehouse>
    <Id>Cabernet_Sauvignon_1992_750ml</Id>
    <Warehouse>East</Warehouse>
    <Quantity>8</Quantity>
  </WineByWarehouse>
  <WineByWarehouse>
    <Id>Cabernet_Sauvignon_1992_750ml</Id>
    <Warehouse>South</Warehouse>
    <Quantity>6</Quantity>
  </WineByWarehouse>
  <WineByWarehouse>
    <Id>Cabernet_Sauvignon_1992_750ml</Id>
    <Warehouse>West</Warehouse>
    <Quantity>4</Quantity>
  </WineByWarehouse>
 . . .
```

Including Relational Data in XQuery Queries

In the previous section, you created XML from the relational data in the inventory system's tables using SQL/XML. As discussed in the "Design" section earlier in the chapter, SQL/XML queries can be used to created intermediate XML documents that you can then use with your XQueries. You'll recognize the following query from the last chapter. It returns all of the wines of a particular varietal — in this case, Cabernet Sauvignon.

```
<wines>
     {
      for $wine
```

```
          in doc("wines.xml")//wine
          where $wine/varietal = "Cabernet Sauvignon"
        return
          $wine
      }
</wines>
```

Now, you want to include the total quantity in inventory of each wine returned by the query. You can already get the data from the relational system with the SQL/XML query in the previous section. You just need to join the XML generated from the relational inventory tables to the `wines.xml` query. Assuming that you have defined a collection named `WineInventoryTotals` that invokes the SQL/XML query to the inventory system, the following query should handle it:

```
    <WineInventory>
      {
       for $wine
in doc("wines.xml")//wine
       let $wineInventoryInfo :=
  collection("WineInventoryTotals")/WineInventory/wine[id=$wine/@id]
       where $wine/varietal = "Cabernet Sauvignon"
       return
<Wine>
    {$wine/@id}
 {$wine/name}
{$wineInventoryInfo/quantity}
</Wine>
        }
     </WineInventory>
```

As you can imagine, there are many possible queries that join data from a relational system to XML. The trick is to first render the relational data as SQL/XML and then execute the SQL/XML as part of the XQuery query.

Including XML in SQL Queries

When you included relational data in an XML document using XQuery, you needed to transform relational to XML. There are also plenty of reasons that you might want to go the other way — transforming XML data and using it alongside relational data in a SQL query because you need to feed an application that natively consumes relational data.

To perform this task, assume that you are using a relational database with XML enhancements. For this example, Oracle is used. Imagine that you have a table schema like the one shown in Figure 9-8. The first table stores information about wine orders. Following a normalized database design style, the second is a lookup table that consists of the wine ID and an XMLType column that stores the `wine` element for each wine. The `wine` elements are just like the ones that you are already familiar with from `wines.xml`.

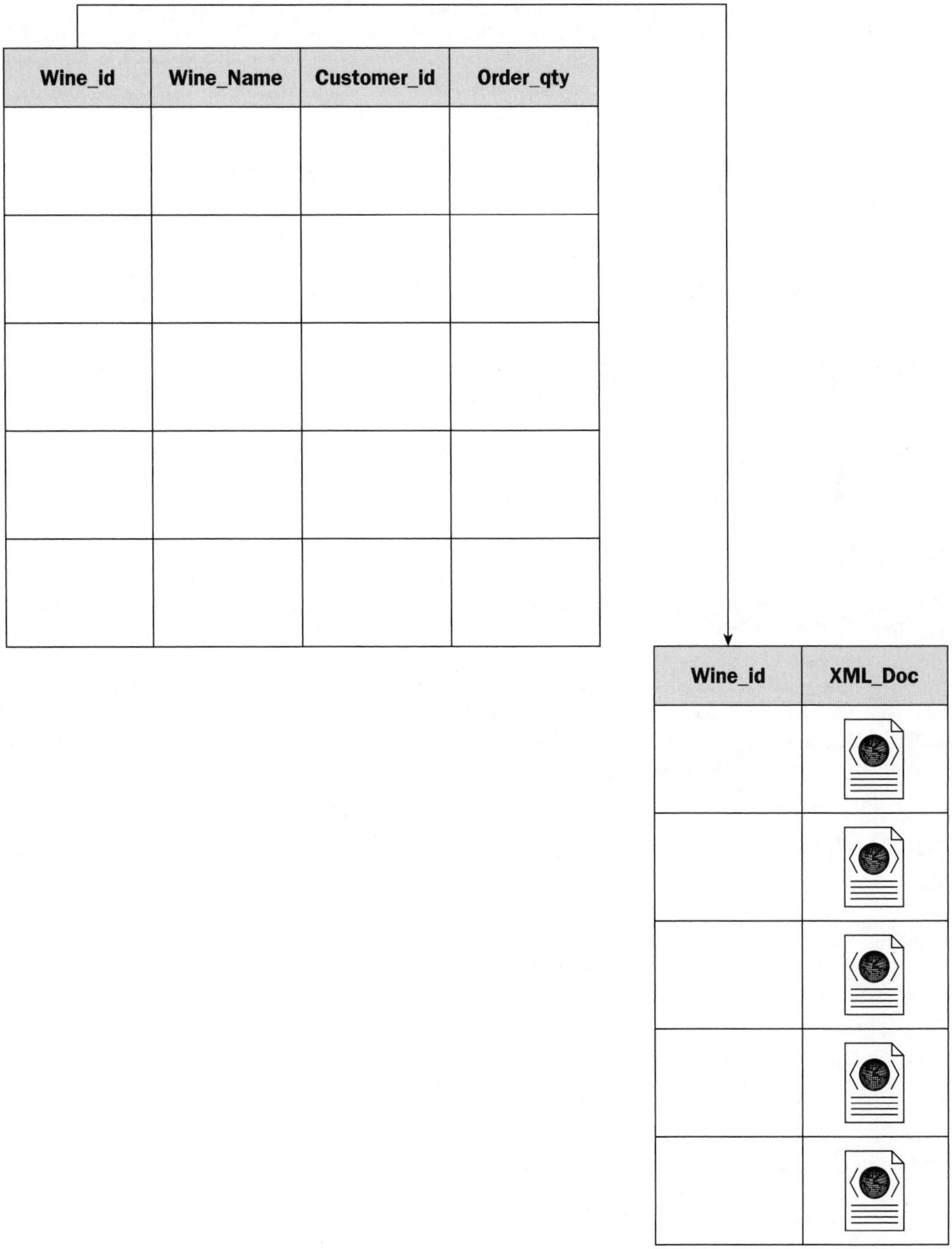

Wine_id	Wine_Name	Customer_id	Order_qty

Wine_id	XML_Doc

Figure 9-8

You want to include the description from the `wine` element with the other order information as normal relational data, but you don't want to return XML because the calling application is a SQL application that only deals with relational data. Using the `extractValue()` function, an XML extension that Oracle provides, you can perform this with the following query:

```
SELECT wine_order.wine_id,
       wine_order.wine_name,
       wine_order.customer_id,
       wine_order.order_qty,
       extractValue(wine_xml.wine_elem, '/wine/description') AS wine_description
FROM   wine_order, wine_xml
WHERE wine_order.wine_id = wine_xml.wine_id;
```

This query returns its results in a tabular form, where data from XML is transformed into relational data. A query like this solves the inverse of the problems considered for much of this chapter, where the concern was transforming relational data to XML. But just as you may need relational data merged into XML for ultimate use with XML-based processes and tools, you may need XML data to be merged into relational output for ultimate use with relational database-based processes and tools.

Summary

As you begin to consider how to integrate XML with the rest of your enterprise's data, you are sure to run into relational databases. Relational databases are a worthy, important part of most organizations' data strategies, and it is important to understand not only how XML and relational data complement each other but also how to get XML and relational data working together. This chapter showed you how to create XML from relational data using SQL/XML and then how to use XQuery in conjunction with SQL/XML to query relational and XML data together. You also saw how to grab XML data for use in relational queries and different storage options using native XML databases and XML-enhanced relational databases.

While this chapter focused on bridging two different universes — XML and relational — the next chapter looks at bridging gaps within the XML universe. The gaps are between different standardized XML schemas, which are increasingly becoming the basis for XML solutions spanning entire industries. Sometimes you need to bridge different XML schemas, and the next chapter shows you how.

10

Transforming Business Documents

Companies were quick to embrace the World Wide Web as a valuable tool for doing business. The company web site is the key tool for establishing an identity in cyberspace and for providing valuable information on demand to customers and casual surfers. The online catalog is used extensively as a strategic tool for presenting their products and services to millions of prospective customers anywhere in the world and providing detailed information for closing the sales loop.

The technologies backing the online strategies evolved quickly to satisfy the demand for a richer set of tools to create more dynamic and functional web sites. XML technologies matured in lockstep with those demands, filling the technology gap. XML satisfies the need for a universal set of tools that can be used in many different facets of online business strategies.

Not all XML documents need to be displayed on the web. In this chapter, you explore transformations of XML documents from one language to another. You also examine XSLT and XPath in detail, specifically from the point of view of transformations between XML languages.

Problem

Companies use different formats to represent their business data and documents. As XML technologies matured, some companies moved quickly to adopt XML as a standardized way to represent business documents. Because XML is extensible, each company created its own markups to represent its business data. This strategy allows an organization to tightly control its data and document schemas.

More often than not, an organization has to work with the data from several other organizations in its business operations. A company may also need to convert the XML content of another organization into a suitable form for use in its XML application. Widespread adoption of XML has resulted in many companies and organizations creating an XML language for their own industry or business.

This momentum helped make XML the de facto representation for business documents, but it also had some drawbacks. The absence of universal standards for marking up business documents in any given industry created a large set of XML-based languages that often represent the same business domain. Consistent representation and markup enables the creation of better business applications that can share data with other applications and can be easily integrated with other applications.

Chapters 13 and 14 look at the next generation of business applications and show how XML enables the integration of business processes.

This chapter's project tackles the data representation challenges by focusing on two of the most common business documents: the catalog and the purchase order (PO).

Converting XML Catalogs

Daddy-O Wine Distributors, Inc. is a new wine distributor catering to wineries that have complementary offerings. The two wineries in this example, Mad Melvin Inc. and Crazy Susan Inc., have entered into a strategic partnership to provide their customers a combined offering. Daddy-O Wine Distributors has to create an online catalog representing the products of both wineries that will benefit the combined customer base of both wineries. Each winery maintains its business systems and documents and only exposes business information needed to make the partnership a success, while carefully protecting all other information.

After the fanfare of any business announcement, the systems analysts have to get to work designing and implementing a strategy to use disparate data and documents from each partner. Some analysts argue that the catalog invariably is the most challenging document to convert or merge. A catalog marks up a product or a set of products based on the company's internal classifications and product designations. If there are no industry-wide standards for that particular product, there is a plethora of markups available to describe the same product — one from each manufacturer.

In Chapter 1, you created the `wines.xml` document to represent the products from the Mad Melvin's winery in beautiful North Carolina. In this chapter, you'll use an abbreviated version of Melvin's product catalog called `melvin.xml`, and you'll `create` another small catalog for the products of — Crazy Sue's Winery in California — and call it `susan.xml`.

To remove extraneous noise from the discussion, assume both catalogs contain well-formed and valid XML. There are a limited number of wine elements in each catalog to simplify the output XML and make it easier to read.

Here's a segment from Melvin's catalog (`melvin.xml`) showing a couple wine elements:

```
<catalog>
   <section subject="Wines">
     <distributor id="DaddyO" name="Daddy-O Wine Distributor, Inc."
        region="North Carolina"/>
      <winery id="Melvin">
         <name>Mad Melvin's Muscadine Wines</name>
         <region>North Carolina</region>
         <country>United States</country>
      </winery>
      <wine id="Smoky_Scupp_750ml">
         <name>Smoky Scupp</name>
```

```
        <varietal>Scupp</varietal>
        <vintage>1992</vintage>
        <winery>Melvin</winery>
        <distributor>DaddyO</distributor>
        <bottlesize>750ml</bottlesize>
        <description>
          A dry red muscadine with hints of oak. A delicious wine
          produced from a unique mix of Carlos and Magnolia Scuppernong grapes.
          Blackberry aromas lead to fat, smoky flavors and long spicy finish.
        </description>
      </wine>
      <wine id="Carolina_Blue_750ml">
        <name>Carolina Blue</name>
        <varietal>Other</varietal>
        <vintage>1992</vintage>
        <winery>Melvin</winery>
        <distributor>DaddyO</distributor>
        <bottlesize>750ml</bottlesize>
        <description>
          Medium-bodied with lively oak aftertones. Great with red meat dishes,
          pizza, and even mac-and-cheese.
        </description>
      </wine>

      ...(other wine elements deleted for brevity)
    </section>
</catalog>
```

The <catalog> element marks up the entire document as a wine catalog for use by Mad Melvin's applications and its business partners. It shows that Daddy-O Wine Distributor, Inc. markets Mad Melvin's products in North Carolina, USA, as identified by the <distributor>, <region>, and <winery> elements. Daddy-O also provides complementary products such as cheeses and gift baskets, and the <section> element is used to define the type of products offered in the catalog.

The <wine> elements mark up the individual wines produced by Mad Melvin, Inc., and each has a unique id attribute. The child elements provide some redundant information on the winery and the distributor as well as details of the individual wines such as the <name>, <varietal>, <vintage>, <bottlesize>, and <description>.

Following is a section of Susan's catalog (susan.xml).

```
<wine-catalog>
  <distributor id="DaddyO" name="Daddy-O Wine Distributor, Inc."
      region="North Carolina"/>
  <winery id="Susan" name="Crazy Susan, Inc." region="North Carolina"
      country="United States"/>
  <wine code="A120569" name="Catawba Fantasy" appellation="South Carolina">
    <properties>
      <color>red</color>
      <alcohol-content>12.5</alcohol-content>
    </properties>
    <price>12.25</price>
    <size>750ml</size>
    <year>2001</year>
```

```
      <comment>
        A sweet red table wine.
      </comment>
    </wine>
    <wine code="B199056" name="Chardonnay Special" appellation="Virginia">
      <properties>
        <color>white</color>
        <alcohol-content>11.5</alcohol-content>
      </properties>
      <price>19.95</price>
      <size>750ml</size>
      <year>2003</year>
      <comment>
        A lean crisp wine with a hint of the fruitiness of lemons, apples, and pears
      </comment>
    </wine>

    ....(other wine elements deleted for brevity)
  </wine-catalog>
```

The `<wine-catalog>` element marks up Crazy Susan's wine catalog. Susan's winery offers only wines—no complementary products such as cheeses, meats, or gift baskets. The `<wine>` element has attributes such as the unique identification `code` in Susan's inventory system. The attribute `appellation` is a fancy word used in the wine industry to describe a region. The `<properties>` child element of the `wine` element provides details of the characteristics of each wine such as the `<color>` and `<alcohol-content>`. The other children of the wine element are `<price>`, `<size>`, `<year>`, and `<comment>`.

A casual examination of the two catalogs highlights the challenge of merging the data from the two. While each provides all the basic information to describe a wine, the markup tags are very different. The catalogs cannot be combined directly, and the systems analysts have to make some decisions and choices on how to proceed before merging the two catalogs.

Converting Other Business Documents

The purchase order (PO) is the most common document transmitted between companies in the B2B (business-to-business) model. A company issues a purchase order to another company from which it wants to buy goods and services. It is a legal document that allows buyers to communicate their intentions to sellers, and the sellers are protected by having the documentation of a formal declaration of intent to buy their goods or services.

This chapter's project focuses attention on electronic purchase orders, although the design and solutions can also be used to determine the electronic data formats generated by systems that are used to manually enter the data from paper purchase orders.

A winery can issue a purchase order for raw materials and supplies that it needs from other vendors. For example, the winery may need yeast for fermentation, oak barrels for aging, chemical cleaners, and industrial utensils for the production process. A winery can also receive a purchase requisition from a distributor or a specialty products manufacturer for the wines it produces.

The following is a list of items that are typically found on a purchase order:

- PO number
- PO date
- Seller ID
- Buyer ID
- Delivery request date
- Shipping address
- Billing address
- Requested terms
- List of products with quantities and prices.
- Notes and special instructions

The winery business systems will be required to read and interpret these pieces of data from an electronic purchase order. While you'll concentrate on purchase orders that are in XML format, note that electronic documents in other formats could be converted to XML after suitable preprocessing.

The winery business systems can generate purchase requisitions in the same format that will be sent to its vendors. The following code shows the XML markup of a purchase order that the business systems can generate or consume:

```
<purchase-order>
  <po-number>DO-126534</po-number>
  <po-date>01-15-2006</po-date>
  <seller id="198754">
    Freds Wholesale Oak Barrels, Inc.
  </seller>
  <buyer id="876543">
    Mad Melvin Inc.
  </buyer>
  <delivery-date>01-30-2006</delivery-date>
  <ship-to>
    <name>Mad Melvin Inc.</name>
    <street>One Factory Drive</street>
    <city-state-zip>Smallville, NC, 26543</city-state-zip>
    <country>USA</country>
  </ship-to>
  <bill-to>
    <name>Mad Melvin Inc.</name>
    <street>World HQ, One Wine Way</street>
    <city-state-zip>Smallville, NC 27564</city-state-zip>
    <country>USA</country>
  </bill-to>
  <payment-terms>NET 30</payment-terms>
  <products>
    <product>
      <name>#31 Oak Barrel</name>
      <quantity>5</quantity>
      <price>$150.00</price>
```

```
    </product>
    <product>
      <name>#18 Oak Barrel</name>
      <quantity>2</quantity>
      <price>$250.00</price>
    </product>
    <product>
      <name>#92 Oak Barrel</name>
      <quantity>1</quantity>
      <price>$1,250.00</price>
    </product>
  </products>
  <instructions>
    <instruction>
      Please include packing list with goods delivered.
    </instruction>
    <instruction>
      Invoices submitted to Accounts Payable without a
      Purchase Order number referenced will be returned
      to the supplier unpaid by the Accounts Payable department.
    </instruction>
  </instructions>
</purchase-order>
```

The purchase order from Mad Melvin Inc. captures all of the significant information to be transmitted to the supplier to make the purchase of the oak barrels. The supplier's order entry system will accept the document and extract all critical information needed to fulfill Mad Melvin's order.

Fred's Wholesale Oak Barrels, Inc. uses state-of-the-art supply chain management software written by its in-house IT staff. The internal business and IT standards have determined that the PO being submitted to the order entry system should be in the following format:

```
<po>
  <number>DO-126534</number>
  <date>01-15-2006</date>
  <seller id="198754" name="Freds Wholesale Oak Barrels, Inc."/>
  <buyer id="876543" name="Mad Melvin Inc."/>
  <requested-by>01-30-2006</requested-by >
  <terms>NET 30</terms>
  <ship-to>
    <line>Mad Melvin Inc.</line>
    <line>One Factory Drive</line>
    <line>Smallville, NC, 26543</line>
    <line>USA</line>
  </ship-to>
  <bill-to>
    <line>Mad Melvin Inc.</line>
    <line>World HQ </line>
    <line>One Wine Way </line>
    <line>Smallville, NC, 26543</line>
    <line>USA</line>
  </bill-to>
  <items>
    <item>
```

```
      <name>#31 Oak Barrel</name>
      <quantity>5</quantity>
      <price>$150.00</price>
    </item>
    <item>
      <name>#18 Oak Barrel</name>
      <quantity>2</quantity>
      <price>$250.00</price>
    </item>
    <item>
      <name>#92 Oak Barrel</name>
      <quantity>1</quantity>
      <price>$1,250.00</price>
    </item>
  </items>
  <notes>
    <note>
      Please include packing list with goods delivered.
    </note>
    <note>
      Invoices submitted to Accounts Payable without a
      Purchase Order number referenced will be returned
      to the supplier unpaid by the Accounts Payable department.
    </note>
  </notes>
</po>
```

The format of the purchase order for Fred's Oak Barrel Inc. is not radically different from Mad Melvin's PO. It contains all the essential information for a complete purchase order but marked up differently. However, the order entry system at Fred's Oak Barrel needs the data in the format shown above (Fred's PO format) to be able to read and interpret the purchase order data coming from Mad Melvin.

Here's a look at a purchase order coming from Daddy-O Wine Distributor, Inc. to Mad Melvin for some of its wines.

```
<purchase-requisition>
  <po-number>A126534</po-number>
  <po-date>01-19-2006</po-date>
  <seller>
    <id>876543</id>
    <name>Mad Melvin Inc.</name>
  </seller>
  <buyer>
    <id>902090</id>
    <name>Daddy-O Wine Distributor Inc.</name>
  </buyer>
  <delivery-date>02-15-2006</delivery-date>
  <ship-to>
    <name>Daddy-O Wine Distributor Inc.</name>
    <address1>Two Daddy Way</address1>
    <address1>Daddyville, NC 26567, USA</address1>
  </ship-to>
  <bill-to>
    <name>Daddy-O Wine Distributor Inc.</name>
```

```
        <address1>Two Daddy Way</address1>
        <address1>Daddyville, NC 26567, USA</address1>
      </bill-to>
      <payment-terms>NET 30</payment-terms>
      <wines>
        <wine>
          <name>N.C. Burgundy</name>
          <quantity>10 cases</quantity>
        </wine>
        <wine>
          <name>Velvet Grapefruit</name>
          <quantity>20 cases</quantity>
        </wine>
        <wine>
          <name>Nags Head Scuppernong</name>
          <quantity>15 cases</quantity>
        </wine>
      </wines>
      <instructions>
        <instruction>
          Please include packing list with goods delivered.
        </instruction>
        <instruction>
          Wholesale discount prices per case negotiated with sales representative
          should appear on invoice.
        </instruction>
      </instructions>
    </purchase-requisition>
```

Daddy-O's business systems generate purchase requisitions instead of purchase orders. A closer examination reveals that the purchase requisition contains all the critical information needed by Mad Melvin's order entry system. However, the elements are marked up differently, and some translation is needed to interpret the tags and their meaning with respect to Mad Melvin's business data definitions.

In the next section you examine the different ways in which these documents can be consumed and explore the strategies for transforming documents between XML languages.

Design

Again, although this book's problems focus on business documents, the designs and solution are applicable to XML documents in any domain.

> **The web page `xml.coverpages.org/xmlApplications.html` has a list of XML applications and industry initiatives that provides a window into some of the ongoing efforts to create XML language standards.**

This section explores three approaches to solving the problems presented earlier:

- Applying custom software solutions
- Creating common languages
- Using industry standards

There are some advantages and disadvantages to each of these.

Custom Software Solutions

A company can create a custom application or framework extension to work with each XML language used by its vendors and partners. This allows the company to have very tight control over what data is extracted from the XML documents and entered into the business database. The software utilizes any of the commercial or open source SAX (Simple API for XML) or DOM (Document Object Model) parsers available in the market.

The application can validate the XML documents against a published schema. However, for complex documents, a schema may not validate all constraints on data elements or attributes contained within. So, the custom software module must have custom business rules and a module to provide additional validation of the data.

This approach works well if there are a small number of partners and vendors, and they don't change frequently. The approach can get very expensive if there is constant change in partners and vendors or if they change their XML languages often.

Common Languages

A company interested in creating profitable partnerships with its suppliers and vendors will invest in resources and strategies for integrating their business data and systems. The partners could collaborate and create standardized schemas for the common business documents that they share with each other.

Creating a new XML language may sound like an easy task, but in reality it is difficult, time-consuming, and challenging. It becomes even more complicated if there are many stakeholders involved. In addition to the cost of creating the schema, there is the cost of building the software or adaptors for the business applications to consume the documents created using the new languages.

The advantage of this approach is that the business partners concur on the schema and agree that it will not change too frequently. As new business partnerships are forged, the schema can be shared as the standard for creating business documents. The disadvantage is that the process is lengthy and expensive.

There is a strong possibility that someone else in the industry has already created an XML language for the domain.

Industry Standards

There are several organizations that have been working to create standardized XML languages for business documents, and there are many XML business languages in use. In this section, you get a brief look at two representative organizations — RosettaNet and OASIS — and the standards they present and a selection of the XML business languages. Use your favorite web search engine with the keywords *XML languages for business documents*, and you'll find many good links to explore the ongoing efforts and standards in this arena.

RosettaNet

RosettaNet (www.rosettanet.org) is a standards organization that has support from companies around the globe. It has been leading the effort to create an environment conducive to electronic commerce and collaboration across the world. Approximately 500 companies in many different countries have adopted the standards designed to create a global supply chain.

RosettaNet is also trying to create simple collaborative processes by moving toward merging with other popular standards prevalent in the industry. Companies that have not standardized their B2B activities face challenges arising from the use of different terminology. RosettaNet standards include the definitions of business processes used between trading partners and a directory of process definitions for easy reference. The *RosettaNet Business Dictionary* (RNBD) provides a list of properties used to define business activities. The *RosettaNet Technical Dictionary* (RNTD) provides the properties for defining the products and services that a company offers. The standards also provide the specification of an implementation framework for core messages and business activity triggers and schema requirements that trading partners have to meet to participate in the network.

Details of each of the standards are beyond the scope of this book; you can visit the RosettaNet web site for the latest information on them.

OASIS (Organization for the Advancement of Structured Information Standards)

OASIS (www.oasis-open.org) is an international consortium that is creating and promoting new e-business standards. The organization also actively tries to merge with other leading standards. OASIS has more than 5,000 registered participants from 600 organizations in 100 countries. These numbers are constantly growing as more organizations try to reach out to global suppliers and consumers.

OASIS supports three popular portals on e-business, XML, and Web Services:

Name	URL	Description
XML.org	www.xml.org	Provides a common forum for users and designers of XML standards to discuss their ideas and to promote open standards.
EbXML.org	www.ebxml.org	Provides the specifications for companies of all sizes around the world to do business with each other over the Internet. The specifications include business messages, protocols for trading relationships, common dictionaries, and business process registries.
Cover Pages	xml.coverpages.org	Edited by Robin Cover, this site is developing into a comprehensive collection of XML vocabularies, schemas, and standards.

Business XML Standards

As you're aware, there are too many XML languages for business to cover in this book, so let's just look at three of the contemporary standards:

- **ebXML** — The vision of ebXML (Electronic Business using Extensible Markup Language) is to create a global networked marketplace where companies trade with each other by exchanging XML messages. It has a collection of specifications for supporting an electronic business framework. You can find details at `www.ebxml.org`.
- **xCBL** — The XML Common Business Library (xCBL) is a library of XML components that support business-to-business electronic commerce. For more information on xCBL, check its web site, `www.xcbl.org`.
- **UBL** — Developed by the OASIS Technical Committee (`www.oasis-open.org`), Universal Business Language (UBL) is a library of standard XML documents for business (`http://docs.oasis-open.org/ubl/cd-UBL-1.0`).

So, what are the implementation strategies for working with business documents represented in different XML languages?

Solution

The key to consuming documents in different XML languages is to be able to modify the markup in one document to reflect all the content accurately in another XML language using a different markup. There are several ways to achieve this, although you'll examine these three:

- Custom applications
- Transformation sheets
- Dynamic pipelines

Custom Applications

A custom application uses a parser to consume the data in an XML document. When the data is within the application's memory, rules can be applied to transform the content and the location of the data nodes in the hierarchy. Each type of parser handles this process differently, as you'll learn. When the set of transformations is complete, the results can be written out in a new XML document.

The DOM parser reads in the XML data and creates a tree of nodes in memory. The initial structure of the tree corresponds to the hierarchy of XML elements in the document. The DOM API allows the application to work on sections of the tree and modify sections of the tree structure. After all the steps in the transformation are complete, the result tree can be consumed by another application module or written out as a new XML document.

The SAX parser reads in XML data as events when nodes are encountered during the parsing process. SAX allows the application to perform tasks within the functions that are triggered by these events. The functions can be used to transform the data within these elements and create a new XML document at the end of the transformations.

Transformation Sheets

Chapter 5 introduced XSLT and XPath for presenting XML content in a web browser. The process of applying a stylesheet to an XML document consists of transforming the XML into another XML language, which is suitable for consumption in a viewer such as a web browser. XHTML is an XML language used to display the transformed XML content. A stylesheet is written in XSL, which itself is an XML language.

Another application of XSL is to transform XML documents. We will use the same set of XSLT elements introduced in earlier chapters and a few new ones to navigate the source document tree and apply templates to create the output document. You will recall that a stylesheet will have an `xsl:stylesheet` element in the document. In previous chapters, we only focused on the presentation aspect of the stylesheet. To highlight the fact that we are transforming to another XML language but not for presentation purposes, we will use the `xsl:transform` element in the XSL sheets and call them transform sheets instead of stylesheets. Please note, `xsl:transform` is just a synonym for `xsl:stylesheet` and a transform sheet is nothing but an XSL stylesheet.

Transforming Catalogs

Daddy-O Wine Distributors, Inc. may have its own XML language for catalogs, but to keep the discussion simple, let's assume that it has a long-standing partnership with Mad Melvin, whose systems analysts helped Daddy-O create the catalog application based on Mad Melvin's XML catalog (`melvin.xml`). Now that Daddy-O has entered into a new partnership with Crazy Susan as a result of their business relationship, it will try to preserve its investment in the existing applications and find a way to transform Susan's catalog (`susan.xml`) into the same catalog language used by Melvin.

The systems analysts at Daddy-O will create a transform sheet created in XSL to navigate Susan's XML catalog and transform each node into the corresponding node in Melvin's catalog. The result of this effort is the transform sheet `susan2melvin.xsl`. Just as in earlier chapters, you'll use the Saxon utility to apply the transform sheets to the XML catalogs. Here's the command to create the output catalog:

```
saxon -jar saxon8.jar susan.xml susan2melvin.xsl > susan2melvin.xml
```

Let's examine the transform sheet in chunks to highlight significant actions that will be performed during the transformation. The `xsl:transform` element has two attributes — `xmlns:xsl` — which define the namespace for the XSL document (`http://www.w3.org/1999/XSL/Transform`). and the `version` number of XSLT:

```
<xsl:transform version="2.0" xmlns:xsl="http://www.w3.org/1999/XSL/Transform">
  <xsl:output method="xml" />

  <xsl:template match="/">
        <xsl:apply-templates/>
  </xsl:template>

  <xsl:template match="/wine-catalog">
    <catalog>
      <section subject="Wines">
        <xsl:apply-templates/>
      </section>
    </catalog>
```

```
    </xsl:template>

    <xsl:template match="distributor">
      <xsl:copy-of select="."/>
    </xsl:template>
```

The root (/) template has nothing significant and is provided only as a default starting point for the transformation process. The `wine-catalog` node in `susan.xml` has to create the `catalog` element and the nested `section` element, which encapsulate all `wine` nodes in `melvin.xml`. The `distributor` nodes have identical names and attributes in both catalogs, so they can be copied over using the `xsl:copy-of` element. The `select` expression (`"."`) evaluates to the current node (`distributor`).

The `winery` element in Susan's catalog has all the details of the winery as attributes to the winery element:

```
    <xsl:template match="winery">
      <xsl:element name="winery">
          <xsl:attribute name="id">
            <xsl:value-of select="@id" />
          </xsl:attribute>
          <xsl:element name="name">
            <xsl:value-of select="@name" />
          </xsl:element>

          <xsl:element name="region">
            <xsl:value-of select="@region" />
          </xsl:element>

          <xsl:element name="country">
            <xsl:value-of select="@country" />
          </xsl:element>
      </xsl:element>
    </xsl:template>
```

Except for the `id` attribute, Melvin's catalog has the rest of the details as nested elements. XPath expressions will extract the attributes and write them out as element names. `xsl:element` creates a new `element` node and names it using the attribute `name`.

The `xsl:attribute` element, which has a `name` attribute for naming the new attribute (`id`), writes the `id` attribute from Susan's catalog to the `id` attribute of the new winery node. The value of the attribute `id` in the `winery` node will be the value of the attribute `id` from the current `winery` node in Susan's catalog. It's extracted using the `xsl:value-of` element in which the value of `select` is an XPath expression that evaluates to the `id` attribute (`@id`) of the current node.

Similarly, you use `xsl:element` and `xsl:value-of` elements to create a region and country nodes within the winery node. The values of the `select` attributes are XPath expressions that extract the region and country attributes of the current node in Susan's catalog.

To transform the `wine` nodes in Susan's catalog to the corresponding nodes in Melvin's catalog, you use `xsl:element` to create the a `wine` node for each `wine` node in Susan's catalog. The attribute of the new `wine` node is named `id`, although its value is that of the `code` attribute. An XPath expression in the `select` of the `xsl:value-of` element handles that.

```
    <xsl:template match="wine">
      <xsl:element name="wine">
        <xsl:attribute name="id"><xsl:value-of select="@code" /></xsl:attribute>

      <xsl:element name="name">
            <xsl:value-of select="@name" />
      </xsl:element>

      <xsl:element name="varietal">
            <xsl:value-of select="@name" />
      </xsl:element>

      <xsl:element name="vintage">
            <xsl:value-of select="year" />
      </xsl:element>

      <xsl:element name="winery">
        <xsl:value-of select="../winery/@id" />
      </xsl:element>

      <xsl:element name="distributor">
            <xsl:value-of select="../distributor/@id" />
      </xsl:element>

      <xsl:element name="bottlesize">
        <xsl:value-of select="size" />
      </xsl:element>

      <xsl:element name="description">
            <xsl:value-of select="comment" />
      </xsl:element>

      </xsl:element>
    </xsl:template>

  </xsl:transform>
```

Next, you have to create a name element within the new wine node; its content will be the value of the name attribute from the current wine node. The systems analyst may set a business rule that all nodes being created should have some data and never be empty. In this example Susan's catalog does not contain any information about the varietal of the wine product. However, in most cases the name of a wine reflects the varietal of the wine. So, this transformation project reuses the name of the wine as the content for the varietal element to meet the rule that none of the nodes can be empty after a transformation.

The vintage node in melvin.xml corresponds to the year node in susan.xml, so an xsl:element is created, and the xsl:value-of element copies the contents from the year element over to the new vintage node. The same steps are repeated for the bottlesize element, whose value will be the contents of the size node, and the description element, whose value will be the comment node.

Melvin's catalog has the names of the winery and distributor as child elements of every wine node. This information is not available in the wine nodes of Susan's catalog, but it is available as id attributes of the distributor and winery nodes elsewhere in the document. The xsl:value-of element can be used to extract those pieces of data from the other nodes. The `select` attribute will contain an XPath expression that can navigate up the tree from the current node to the respective nodes and extract the information from the attributes of those nodes as seen in the following code:

```
<xsl:value-of select="../winery/@id" />
<xsl:value-of select="../distributor/@id" />
```

The following code shows the output (`susan2melvin.xml`) of the transformation on Susan's catalog.

```
<catalog>
  <section subject="Wines">
    <distributor id="DaddyO" name="Daddy-O Wine Distributor, Inc."
        region="North Carolina"/>
    <winery id="Susan">
      <name>Crazy Susan, Inc.</name>
      <region>North Carolina</region>
      <country>United States</country>
    </winery>
    <wine id="A120569">
      <name>Catawba Fantasy</name>
      <varietal>Catawba Fantasy</varietal>
      <vintage>2001</vintage>
      <winery>Susan</winery>
      <distributor>DaddyO</distributor>
      <bottlesize>750ml</bottlesize>
      <description>A sweet red table wine</description>
    </wine>
    <wine id="C209010">
      <name>Petit Verdot Delight</name>
      <varietal>Petit Verdot Delight</varietal>
      <vintage>1999</vintage>
      <winery>Susan</winery>
      <distributor>DaddyO</distributor>
      <bottlesize>750ml</bottlesize>
      <description>A spicy concentrated tannic wine rich in color.</description>
    </wine>
    <wine id="B199056">
      <name>Chardonay Special</name>
      <varietal>Chardonay Special</varietal>
      <vintage>2003</vintage>
      <winery>Susan</winery>
      <distributor>DaddyO</distributor>
      <bottlesize>750ml</bottlesize>
      <description>A lean crisp wine with a hint of the fruitiness of lemons,
      apples and pears</description>
    </wine>
  </section>
</catalog>
```

Compare this output to Melvin's catalog. Note that you have successfully transformed Susan's catalog into the XML language used to represent Melvin's catalog. Because the two catalogs are now in the same XML language, Daddy-O can now merge the two documents to create a unified catalog to be served up to the distributor's customers.

Chapter 8 provides an in-depth study of how to merge multiple XML documents.

You could just as easily transform Melvin's catalog to the language used by Susan's catalog. That's left as an exercise for you, to try out your new knowledge and skills in transforming XML catalogs.

Transforming the Purchase Order

Early in the chapter you saw a purchase order issued by Mad Melvin, Inc. to Fred's Wholesale Oak Barrels, Inc. ordering several barrels for its wine production operation. Since they use different XML languages to represent the same business document, one of them will have to transform the other's document before it can be used.

For this project, assume that Fred's IT department has created a transform sheet to transform Mad Melvin's purchase order. Check out the transform sheet (`melvin-po2fred-po.xsl`). Here's the beginning of it:

```
<xsl:transform version="2.0" xmlns:xsl="http://www.w3.org/1999/XSL/Transform">

   <xsl:output method="xml" />

   <xsl:template match="/">
          <xsl:apply-templates/>
   </xsl:template>
```

As in the previous example, the root template provides an anchor for the transformation at the start of the operation.

The `purchase-order` template is interesting because it explicitly lists all the other templates:

```
   <xsl:template match="/purchase-order">
     <po>
       <xsl:apply-templates select="po-number"/>
       <xsl:apply-templates select="po-date"/>
       <xsl:apply-templates select="seller"/>
       <xsl:apply-templates select="buyer"/>
       <xsl:apply-templates select="delivery-date"/>
       <xsl:apply-templates select="payment-terms"/>
       <xsl:apply-templates select="ship-to"/>
       <xsl:apply-templates select="bill-to"/>
       <xsl:apply-templates select="products"/>
       <xsl:apply-templates select="instructions"/>

     </po>
   </xsl:template>
```

Looking closely at Melvin's and Fred's purchase orders, you can see that the `payment-terms` node does not occur at the same place in the list order in the two documents. If you used the `xsl:apply-templates` element in the `purchase-order` node, the `payment-terms` node would be out of order in the resulting document. This may or may not create a problem in the target application that consumes this data, but because it's better to err on the side of caution, Fred's systems analysts forced the order of selection in the `purchase-order` template. This guarantees that the output document will have the nodes in the correct order.

The `po-number` template creates the new node (`number`) and uses the `xsl:value-of` element with an XPath expression in the `select` clause to extract the content of the current node (`po-number`) and write it to the new node (`number`). The `po-date` node is transformed in a similar manner to create the `date` node:

```
<xsl:template match="po-number">
  <number>
    <xsl:value-of select="." />
  </number>
</xsl:template>

<xsl:template match="po-date">
  <date>
    <xsl:value-of select="." />
  </date>
</xsl:template>
```

In the template for the `seller` node, the new node is created with an `xsl:element`, and an attribute named `id` is creat[illegible]g the `xsl:attribute` element. The value of the attribute is extracted using an XP[illegible] which is the value of the attribute named `id` of the current node. The template [illegible]entical to the seller node:


```
atch="seller">
name="seller">
ute name="id">
-of select="@id" />
ute>

e name="name">
of select="." />
te>

="buyer">
="buyer">
ame="id">
 select="@id" />

ibute name="name">
      <xsl:value-of select="." />
    </xsl:attribute>
  </xsl:element>
</xsl:template>
```

The transformations of the `delivery-date` and `payment-terms` nodes rely on the `xsl:value-of` element and the XPath expression that extracts the contents of the current nodes:

```
<xsl:template match="delivery-date">
  <requested-by>
    <xsl:value-of select="." />
  </requested-by>
</xsl:template>

<xsl:template match="payment-terms">
  <terms>
    <xsl:value-of select="." />
  </terms>
</xsl:template>
```

When the transformation engine hits the template for the `ship-to` node, it will create a top-level element named `ship-to` and four child elements, all named `line`. Each `line` node in the `ship-to` address will get the contents of the respective elements `name`, `street`, `city-state-zip`, and `country`:

```
<xsl:template match="ship-to">
  <xsl:element name="ship-to">
    <xsl:element name="line">
      <xsl:value-of select="name" />
    </xsl:element>
    <xsl:element name="line">
      <xsl:value-of select="street" />
    </xsl:element>
    <xsl:element name="line">
      <xsl:value-of select="city-state-zip" />
    </xsl:element>
    <xsl:element name="line">
      <xsl:value-of select="country" />
    </xsl:element>
  </xsl:element>
</xsl:template>
```

This example demonstrates that while you have very little control over the target XML language definitions or the XML document you are consuming, XSLT and XPath give you the flexibility to consume and create any type of nodes and attributes.

The `bill-to` template is identical to the `ship-to` template:

```
<xsl:template match="bill-to">
  <xsl:element name="bill-to">
    <xsl:element name="line">
      <xsl:value-of select="name" />
    </xsl:element>
    <xsl:element name="line">
      <xsl:value-of select="street" />
    </xsl:element>
    <xsl:element name="line">
      <xsl:value-of select="city-state-zip" />
    </xsl:element>
    <xsl:element name="line">
      <xsl:value-of select="country" />
    </xsl:element>
  </xsl:element>
</xsl:template>
```

The `products` node is made up of one or more `product` nodes. The `product` node is, in turn, described by the child elements `name`, `quantity`, and `price`. Because the source tree and the destination tree have the same names for the children, you can use the `xsl:copy-of` element. The attribute `select` is an XPath expression that will evaluate to the name of the child node that you want to transform (i.e., copy over):

```
<xsl:template match="products">
  <items>
    <xsl:apply-templates select="product"/>
  </items>
```

```
    </xsl:template>

    <xsl:template match="product">
      <item>
        <xsl:copy-of select="name"/>
        <xsl:copy-of select="quantity"/>
        <xsl:copy-of select="price"/>
      </item>
    </xsl:template>
```

Finally, the `instructions` node is made up of one or more `instruction` nodes. It will be transformed to the `items` node, and an `instruction` node will be transformed to an `item` node. The `xsl:value-of` element will extract the contents of the node and write it out to the new node:

```
    <xsl:template match="instructions">
      <notes>
        <xsl:apply-templates select="instruction"/>
      </notes>
    </xsl:template>

    <xsl:template match="instruction">
      <note>
        <xsl:value-of select="." />
      </note>
    </xsl:template>

  </xsl:transform>
```

This transformation creates an output document that is identical to Fred's purchase order presented earlier in the chapter. The final output is included in the code bundle on the companion web site for the book. Run the samples and verify for yourself that this is in fact the case.

In the B2B model, Melvin could receive a purchase order from a distributor. In that case, Melvin would transform the incoming document to the XML language for consumption by its business systems. You are encouraged to practice the concepts presented in this chapter, and transform the `daddyo-po.xml` to the Melvin XML Language and compare it to the `melvin-po.xml`. Sample solutions are included in the code bundle for each of these examples.

XML Pipelines

No discussion of XML transformations is complete without discussing XML pipelines. Transforming XML within an application using DOM and SAX can occur during runtime, and once the data is in the application, further transformations can be done on the internal representation of the data tree. The transformed data can be written out as a new XML document. The transformation rules are hard-coded within the application and cannot be changed during runtime.

XSL transform sheets offer some flexibility in selecting different transformation steps. Transform sheets for each scenario are created beforehand, and the application can select a different transformation based on some rules defined in different stages of the process. In most applications, the XML data has to go through one or more transformation stages before it is ready for delivery to the final stage, which may be presentation in a viewer or input to an external application. The transformed document from each stage has to be written out before it can be consumed by the next stage. The drawback with this approach is that the transformation steps have to be predefined and the selection of stages is static.

The XML pipeline takes the model of transformation in stages to the next level. An XML pipeline is created by connecting one or more XML processing stages to get the desired output. This concept is similar to the pipelines that work on bytes in the Unix operating system. In an XML pipeline SAX events are used to transfer data between stages. Figure 10-1 illustrates the abstract concept of chaining stages for pipeline transformations.

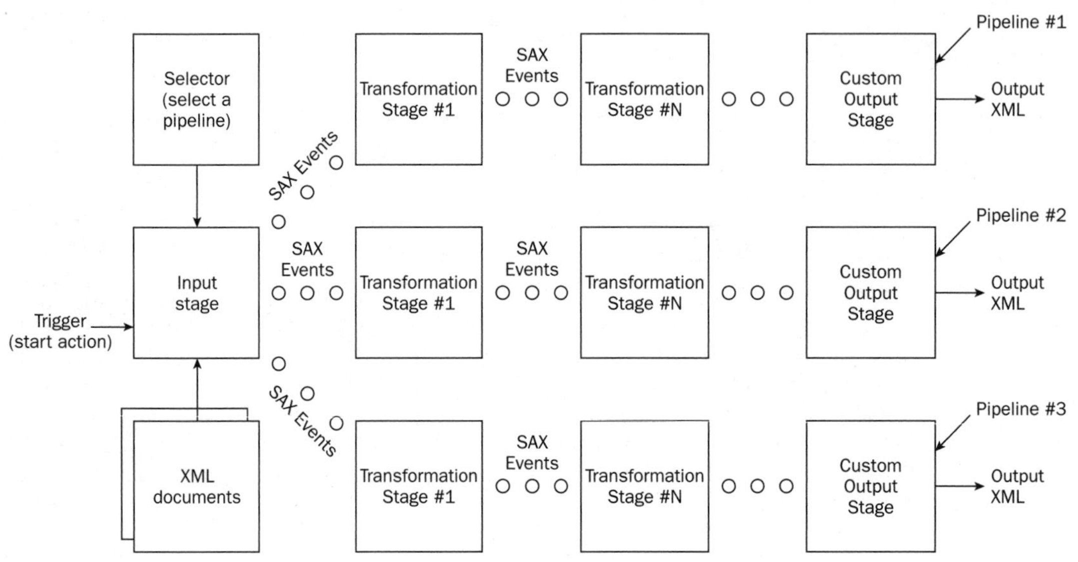

Figure 10-1

The figure shows three pipelines. Each has one or more transformation components or stages (numbered 1..N). The universal input stage is where the XML documents are consumed. The selection of a specific pipeline is dynamic and can be done during runtime in response to a trigger sent by an external application. The input trigger is used to start the processing of the documents, and some kind of selector is used to choose one of the pipelines to process the SAX events generated by the input stage. The selector could be a keyword that comes in with the input trigger. For example, the selector in the case of a web application is the unique URI (Uniform Resource Identifier) or URL (Uniform Resource Locator), which can serve as both the trigger and the selector. The SAX events make their way down the pipeline going through each transformation stage, until they reach the custom output stage for that pipeline where they are consumed and the output XML document is created.

As stated earlier an XML pipeline consists of many connected stages. The first stage consumes an XML document and produces the SAX events, which are then passed down the line. Subsequent stages transform these events using transform sheets. The SAX events can pass through multiple transformation stages before they are finally ready for consumption. The results of the transformations can be written out to a document or sent to an optional final stage that prepares the SAX events for consumption in some other application, such as a visual presenter like a browser or a Braille reader, or a special adapter to a business application or database.

Each XML processing stage is implemented as a component in a particular programming language. The components are grouped broadly based on the functions they perform: consume, transform, or produce. A special configuration is used to assemble the stages or components and ready the pipeline to accept transformation jobs. The controller works with this configuration to manage the triggers, selectors, and the operation of the pipelines. Here's a list of technologies and standards available for creation of XML pipelines:

- W3C XML Pipeline Definition Language
- W3C XML Pipeline Language (XPL)
- Apache Cocoon
- smallx XML Pipelines
- Serving XML

A brief description of each follows.

W3C XML Pipeline Definition Language

Version 1.0 of the W3C XML Pipeline Definition Language is a submission to the W3C to define the syntax and features of a language for defining XML pipelines. The key features are the description of processes that work on XML resources as input and outputs of the pipeline. These are defined in a document that is used by a pipeline controller to dynamically choose the stages of processing to get the desired result.

Although little new work has been done on the standards definition, both Sun Microsystems, Inc. and Oracle Corporation have created implementations of the controller and include it with some of their software products.

The World Wide Web Consortium (W3C) is a body that works on creating standards and specifications as well as software and tools for interoperability between technologies. Its web site is `www.w3.org`.

W3C XML Pipeline Language (XPL)

The W3C XML Pipeline Language (XPL) Version 1.0 is a draft submitted by Orbeon, Inc. (`www.orbeon.com`). It has an open source implementation of the XPL called the Orbeon PresentationServer.

You can use XPL to define operations on XML resources in stages. XML processors are self-contained components that define individual operations such as producing, consuming, and transforming XML Information Sets. XPL supports operations such as loops, branching, change of control, and runtime error processing. XPL attempts to set the stage for creating reusable business components for processing XML resources.

Apache Cocoon

Apache Cocoon is a web development framework sometimes characterized as an XML publishing framework or more loosely as a content management system. One of the goals is to promote the concept of separation of concerns for web development. It has a rich set of components and supports creation of component pipelines using a centralized configuration mechanism called the sitemap.

The Apache Software Foundation (`www.apache.org`) creates and supports open source software projects.

smallx XML Pipelines

Smallx is an open source project that's creating a set of tools to process XML Information Sets using pipelines and streaming of documents. The project description pages say that one advantage of streaming is the capability to process large XML Information Sets without consuming lots of memory. It can also process local XML documents as files that have not been streamed.

Serving XML

Serving XML is yet another open source project for creating an XML-based language that has constructs for defining XML pipelines. It also has an extensible application framework that can perform dynamic transformation of XML documents.

Pipeline Implementations

Implementation of XML pipelines differs for each of the technologies discussed, and providing an example of each would require a detailed description of each system itself. To keep the discussion focused on transformation strategies, let's explore the controller of Apache Cocoon, which is representative of the overall concept of XML pipeline implementation and does not require a comprehensive explanation of the installation and configuration of the Cocoon application itself. The Apache Cocoon support site provides excellent documentation and examples on how to implement a complete project.

The Controller

In Apache Cocoon, the controller is implemented as an XML configuration file called the *sitemap*. Here's a typical sitemap:

```
<map:sitemap xmlns:map="http://apache.org/cocoon/sitemap/1.0">
  <map:components/>
  <map:views/>
  <map:resources/>
  <map:action-sets/>
  <map:pipelines/>
</map:sitemap>
```

The code provides an high-level overview of the format of the sitemap. The `map` element defines a sitemap and has an attribute that defines the namespace `xmlns:map` (`http://apache.org/cocoon/sitemap/1.0`). The elements `components`, `views`, `resources`, `action-sets`, and `pipelines` are used to define and assemble components that will create the XML pipelines needed to execute the functions of the application. This discussion focuses only on the `components` and `pipelines` elements. The rest of the elements in the `map` are specific to other application functions and in-depth coverage is beyond the scope of this chapter.

```
<map:components>
  <map:generators/>
  <map:transformers/>
  <map:serializers/>
```

```
    <map:selectors/>
    <map:matchers/>
    ...{other elements deleted for brevity}
    <map:pipelines/>
  </map:components>
```

Apache Cocoon, provides a rich set of components that enables the creation of complex applications. Remember, consuming, transforming, and producing of XML documents are three major functions of an XML pipeline.

Consume, Transform, and Produce XML Documents

A `generator` component is the input stage of a Cocoon pipeline. It is used to consume an XML document and creates SAX events that are sent down the pipeline for further processing in other stages. The `generators` element defines all generators the application can use. The following code shows specific examples of generators provided by Cocoon:

```
<map:generators default="file">
  <map:generator name="file" src="org.apache.cocoon.generation.FileGenerator"/>
  <map:generator name="dir" src="myproject.SomeCustomeDirectoryGenerator"/>
</map:generators>
```

The `transformers` tag defines all the transformers to be used by the application to work on the SAX events flowing through the pipeline. A `transformer` transforms a SAX event to another SAX event. The following code shows two transformers defined in the `transformers` tag:

```
<map:transformers default="xslt">
  <map:transformer name="xslt"
      src="org.apache.cocoon.transformation.TraxTransformer">
    <use-request-parameters>false</use-request-parameters>
    <use-browser-capabilities-db>false</use-browser-capabilities-db>
    ...{other elements deleted for brevity}
  </map:transformer>

  <map:transformer name="xinclude"
      src="org.apache.cocoon.transformation.XIncludeTransformer"/>
</map:transformers>
```

The XSLT `transformer` component does basic XSL transformations. In the pipeline tag, you will see how this one is used for performing transformations using a transform sheet. The code also shows some additional child elements of the XSLT `transformer` that define the default behavior of the component in the pipeline.

The second `transformer` is a component for including and merging SAX events from other XML documents. There are several other transformers for performing specific transformations and a complete list can be obtained from the Apache Cocoon web site.

`serializers` produce an output XML document after all transformations are complete. The following code shows the definition of two serializers: `html` and `wap`. These produce XML output for web browsers and wireless device browsers, respectively. To keep the focus on XML pipeline transformations, let's skip the details of serializers.

```
<map:serializers default="html">
  <map:serializer name="html" mime-type="text/html"
        src="org.apache.cocoon.serialization.HTMLSerializer">
    ...{other elements deleted for brevity}
  </map:serializer>

  <map:serializer name="wap" mime-type="text/vnd.wap.wml"
        src="org.apache.cocoon.serialization.XMLSerializer">
    ...{other elements deleted for brevity}
  </map:serializer>

</map:serializers>
```

`selectors` are used for conditional branching within a pipeline. Here's the format for defining selectors (the names of the specific selectors shown — *dataload* and *auth* — have no special significance and are provided only to illustrate the process):

```
<map:selectors default="browser">
  <map:selector name="dataload"
    src="org.apache.cocoon.selection.MachineLoadSelector"/>

  <map:selector name="auth"
    src="org.apache.cocoon.selection.AuthenticationSelector"/>
  </map:selector>

</map:selection>
```

`matchers` are used for pattern matching. Cocoon provides a few custom `matchers` , two of which are shown in the following code:

```
<map:matchers default="wildcard">
  <map:matcher name="wildcard"
        src="org.apache.cocoon.matching.WildcardURIMatcher">
    ...{other elements deleted for brevity}
  </map:matcher>

  <map:matcher name="regexp"
        src="org.apache.cocoon.matching.RegexpURIMatcher">
    ...{other elements deleted for brevity}
  </map:matcher>
</map:matchers>
```

Pipelining of SAX Events

The `pipelines` element defines all the `pipeline` paths defined for the application. A pipeline consists of one generator, one or more transformers, and possibly one serializer. A pipeline can also define custom error handling. The pipeline uses `matchers` and `selectors` to define the specific paths for processing an XML document.

```
<map:pipelines>
  <map:pipeline>
    <map:match pattern="trigger">
      <map:generate src="data.xml"/>
```

```
        <map:transform type="xinclude"/>
        <map:transform type="xslt" src="transform/data2result.xsl"/>

        <map:handle-errors>
          <map:select type="exception">
            <map:when test="processing">...</map:when>
            <map:when test="sax">...</map:when>
            <map:when test="application">...</map:when>
          </map:select>
        </map:handle-errors>

        <map:serialize/>
    </map:pipeline>

    <map:pipeline pattern="preprocess">
      ...{other elements deleted for brevity}
    </map:pipeline>

    <map:pipeline pattern="filterdata">
      ...{other elements deleted for brevity}
    </map:pipeline>

  </map:pipelines>
```

The `pipelines` tag defines three alternate paths of processing within the application. Each `pipeline` can be identified by the attribute named `pattern.` , so this code defines three pipelines, named `trigger`, `preprocess`, and `filterdata`. The `pattern` name is used to select the processing path in the application. You can see the details of the `trigger` pipeline in the preceding code.

The `generate` tag uses the default file generator to read in the XML document (`data.xml`). The SAX events that are generated are sent down the pipeline to the first transformation stage. The `xinclude` transformer includes any XML document data that may be needed if the `data.xml` has any `<xi:include >` elements as shown here:

```
<data xmlns:xi="http://www.w3.org/2001/XInclude">
  <name>Fred</name>
  <bio>
    <summary>Fred is an accomplished wine maker</summary>
    <xi:include href="include.xml"/>
  </bio>
</data>
```

The XML data to be included is in the file `include.xml`:

```
<experience>
  <school>Wine Making Institute of California</school>
</experience>
```

The result of this transformation is that the elements from the `include.xml` file are merged in the `data.xml` SAX elements and sent down the pipeline. If the `data.xml` document has no `xi:include` elements, the SAX events are passed through to the next stage.

The XSLT transformation stage applies the transform sheet (`data2result.xsl`) to the SAX events flowing through the stage. There can be many more transformation stages defined in this pipeline. After all the transformations are completed, the SAX events are sent to the final stage where they are serialized out to an XML document or prepared for use by an external application.

The other pipelines also have one generator, one or more transformers, and zero or one serializer. The controller uses the pattern name to activate the appropriate pipeline. There may also be a custom error-handling mechanism, as was displayed in the `trigger` pipeline. XML pipelines are powerful and can be used to create very complex business integration applications.

The other pipeline technologies have similar constructs to define and control the pipeline. Explore XML pipelines further by visiting the sites listed.

Summary

In this chapter, you tackled the problem of having many different XML languages or vocabularies for representing documents of the same type and in the same domain, and undertook the challenges of converting documents between XML languages. Although the chapter focused on just the business perspective, the discussions apply to XML documents in any language.

In the design section, you explored three ways of approaching the solution to the problem of converting XML documents:

- Custom software solutions, which are designed for specific XML languages for specific customers and suppliers. This solution is inflexible and can be expensive.
- Creating common languages by working with business partners to derive shared XML formats and definitions for typical business documents. This process requires support from all partners and can be time-consuming and expensive.
- Using industry standards. There are many organizations that create and maintain various standards, and that usually provide implementation and tools for the standards. This was deemed the best solution for this chapter's project.

In the solution section, you examined three approaches to solving the document conversion problems:

- Using custom applications that enable you to tightly control the data that's consumed from XML documents. They use the DOM and SAX parser.
- Employing transformation sheets, which are XSL stylesheets. XSLT and XPath are used to transform the XML documents.
- Creating dynamic pipelines that connect individual XML processing components, using some binding mechanism or configuration file. SAX events are a major part of this solution.

11

Consuming Data with Web Services and Syndication

In the seventeenth century, John Donne wrote, "No man is an island." This certainly applies to organizations as well, especially with the pervasiveness, of networking in the twenty-first century. Organizations must be capable of integrating with data from other sources and are also obligated to provide data so that applications in other organizations can make use of it. Web services, which is based on XML, provides a modern mechanism for sharing data in this manner. Syndication — the aggregation of content from various sources so that it can be provided through a web site — uses a web services–like model and is also discussed here. This chapter looks at web services and syndication from the standpoint of consuming data from other sources. The next chapter shows you how to provide your web services to the world.

Problem

There is any number of reasons that you might need your organization's applications to connect with the applications of other organizations. This chapter examines the following as examples of the kind of problems that can be solved with web services and syndication:

- On your home page, you want to display a list of links to recent articles that have been published by a popular wine magazine.
- After a customer has purchased a bottle of wine, you want to present him with a list of related products, such as books about the type of wine he's chosen and a link to Amazon so that the customer can purchase them.
- When your inventory system determines that there is too much stock of a certain wine, you want to automatically post listings on eBay.
- A distributor has created its own web service, and you want to integrate with it to streamline operations.

Design

In a world without pervasive networking, the problems presented here would have to be solved by physically transferring the data from one computer to another. In a world dominated by the Internet, though, the network is expected to play a role in such data transfers. The network can often transfer data from a remote computer so seamlessly that the data seems to part of a local data store.

Although the Internet and the abundance of bandwidth make flawless data integration possible, they don't necessarily make it probable. You can think of the Internet and the World Wide Web (WWW) as being like a new phone line connecting two countries where the people speak different languages — people from the different countries would be able to call one another, but they wouldn't be able to communicate.

Web services is a collection of standards and techniques that works to overcome such interoperability problems between different applications. Web services is deeply integrated with XML and derives a lot of its prowess from XML's capability to broker data between different contexts. This chapter and the next propose web services as a solution to the problems of accessing data and functionality across the network. The discussion includes syndication and RSS, which is a web services–type of approach to the problem of relaying web content across the web to other applications. For instance, CNN.com as well as blogs can publish new content as RSS feeds so that other applications, including web sites, can combine and render the new content in their own way.

This chapter focuses on the consumption of data using the web services model, and the next chapter discusses how you can provide data and functionality to the world by creating a web services provider.

What Does RSS Stand For?

When you see a technical term in all caps like RSS, it's usually an acronym. Sometimes, though, a term that starts out as an acronym later becomes just a technical term with the same letters and is always written in all caps, but no longer stands for anything. Company names also sometimes become "de-acronymized" — for instance, software vendor SAS's name used to stand for Statistical Analysis Software, but as the company grew and diversified the name was changed to just SAS, without standing for anything.

With RSS, the acronym-only is wrought with even more drama. As you'll learn, RSS has a disjoint history, with different groups writing different standards all called RSS and all addressing the same basic problems with the same basic mechanics. Over time, RSS has alternatively stood for Really Simple Syndication, RDF Site Summary, and Rich Site Summary — or nothing at all. All of these terms give you some idea as to what RSS does, and it would be nice to just say that one is what RSS stands for, but hopefully you'll come to understand the hesitation in saying that it stands for any one thing.

Understanding Web Services

To make the most of web services, it's important to understand the underlying standards. You can think of web services as bridging several technologies: networking and programming across the network; data and how to use XML as a transport and definition of your data; and the specifics of some particular domain that pertains to the data you are using with web services.

Web Services and the World Wide Web

The problems that web services tackles aren't particularly new, and web services isn't the first technology that has attempted to take them on. There are other standards such as CORBA (Common Object Request Broker Architecture) and RPC (remote procedure calls) programming that could deal with the problems that were introduced at the beginning of this chapter. But web services brings a unique slant on the solutions because of its origins in the technologies of the World Wide Web. Thus, a good way to begin with web services is to understand it in the context of the web.

The World Wide Web is pervasive today, so it can be difficult to imagine a world where it didn't exist, yet it has only been around since 1989 and has only been truly "world wide" since the mid-1990s. With its meteoritic rise in popularity, you'd think that there must have been some basic breakthrough that made it possible — maybe some triumph in network switching or processor speed. But in truth, the underlying technologies and standards, such as TCP/IP had been around for several years. The real break through of the World Wide Web was an approach that focused on simplicity, open standards, and interoperability. This heritage is shared with web services.

The web is implemented with two main standards: HTTP and HTML. HyperText Transfer Protocol (HTTP) is a simple protocol that works on a request-response paradigm, while HyperText Markup Language (HTML) is returned in response to a request. An HTTP transaction begins when your browser issues a request and ends when a response is received from the server. The basic model is shown in Figure 11-1.

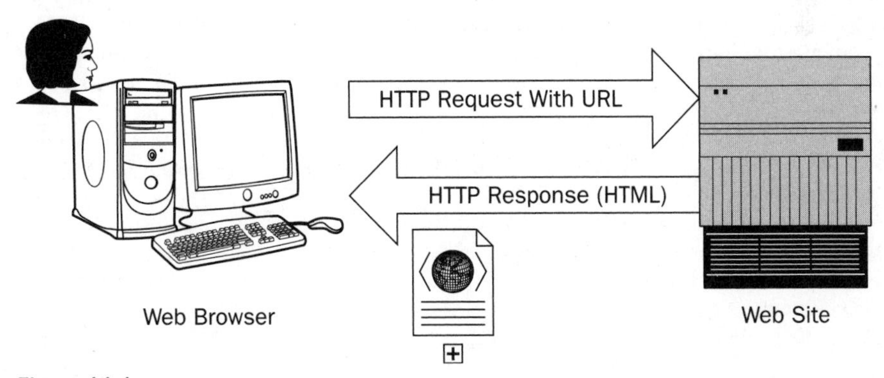

Figure 11-1

In many cases, all the web server does is grab an HTML document and return it across the wire. But if the web only consisted of static content, it wouldn't be as interesting as it actually is. You wouldn't have e-commerce, online stock trading and banking, eBay, Google, or any of multitudes of web applications. A web application is simply a computer program that is used to generate the HTTP response. Web applications fit neatly into the picture, augmenting the basic HTTP/HTML paradigm without making the core architecture more complicated, as shown in Figure 11-2.

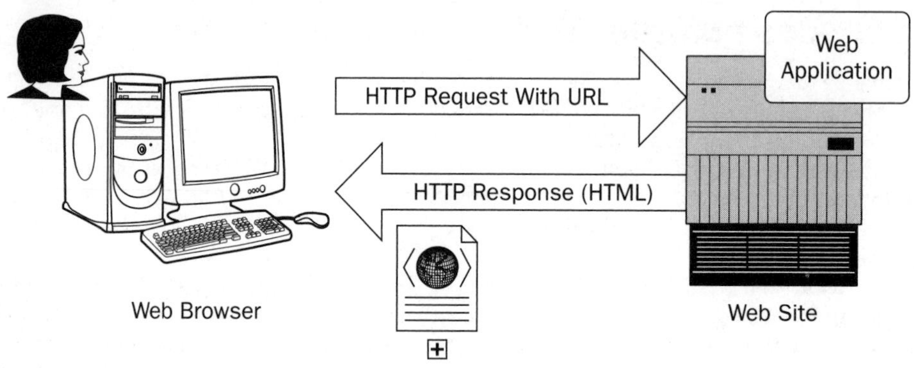

Figure 11-2

The World Wide Web functions to serve content to a browser, and the browser is meant to present it to a human reader. In fact, if you look at HTML itself, it is optimized for presenting information to a human reader — think of the bold tag, for instance. But a lot of times you would like a computer application to read the data coming off the web instead of looking at in a web browser.

Web services change the paradigm, as shown in Figure 11-3. Instead of using HTML, which is really meant for formatting information for display to humans, XML is the format for the response. Because requests can be more complicated than is typical in the web world, XML might also be used to augment the requests. HTTP is still the transport vehicle so that it is easy for web services to be compatible with typical network topologies. The provider (shown on the right) can be wired into an application that produces the response. In fact, web services providers are much more likely to be tied to a back-end application than a traditional WWW server. Most importantly, the web browser (on the left) is replaced by a web services consumer. The web services consumer is tied to an application that formulates the request and processes the response. No humans are directly involved in the web services HTTP transaction.

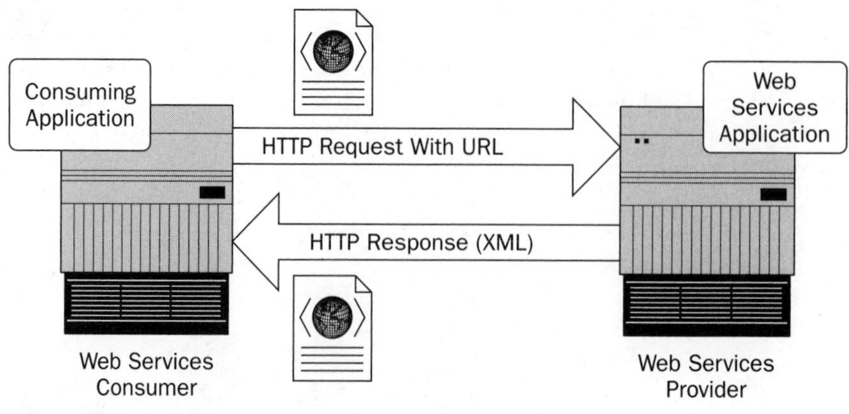

Figure 11-3

This is the basic model of web services. In this chapter, you explore three different architectures underneath the web services model:

- **RSS** — Not considered web services, but functionally similar. RSS mainly deals with the problem of moving web content such as articles, news stories, and blog postings to applications that can render and display them in their own way.
- **REST (Representational State Transfer) web services** — A "webbish" that says the way to solve the web services problem is to look at how the web has been successful and mimic its fundamentals.
- **SOAP (Simple Object Access Protocol) web services** — The SOAP approach is rooted in the tradition of distributed computing that predates the web and sees web services as a distributed computing problem that must be solved using the web infrastructure.

REST and SOAP web services significantly overlap each other in what they can provide but are really two different paradigms.

RSS

Web services are broadly defined as a machine-to-machine interaction. One of the simplest and most common types of machine-to-machine interactions on the web today is syndication, or feeds, and the driving family of standards for syndication is RSS.

What RSS does, generally called syndication, can be considered a subset of web services. Syndication enables you to grab content from web sites that provide feeds and have some type of application process them. Figure 11-4 shows two example uses of RSS.

At the top of the diagram, a desktop application aggregates the content from several web sites. Many sites provide content as RSS feeds, including such well-known sites as CNN.com, Reuters.com, and BBC.com. Instead of having to visit all of your favorite sites each day by manually pointing your web browser at them, you can have an aggregator gather them all on your desktop for you. The aggregator can sit inside popular web browsers as well as popular email readers such as Outlook.

In the second case, a module on your web site consumes the RSS feeds. Your web site watches for new content on the other sites and creates a link as well as a title and short description that can be displayed on your web site. You can, for example, aggregate current articles about wines that appear on other web sites and display links to them on the winery web site.

RSS isn't a single standard. There are a few different standards that share the same name, but are really distinct standards. Of the different standards, RSS 1.x and RSS 2.x are the most important. Most client software and client libraries know how to consume both standards, so on the client side you don't have to be too concerned about the differences. But when you are providing content you have some decisions to make. The different standards and their pros and cons are discussed in the next chapter.

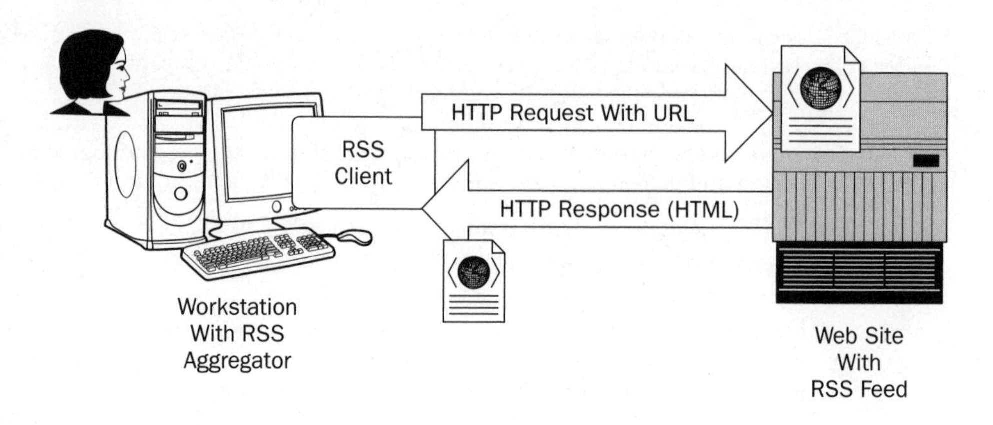

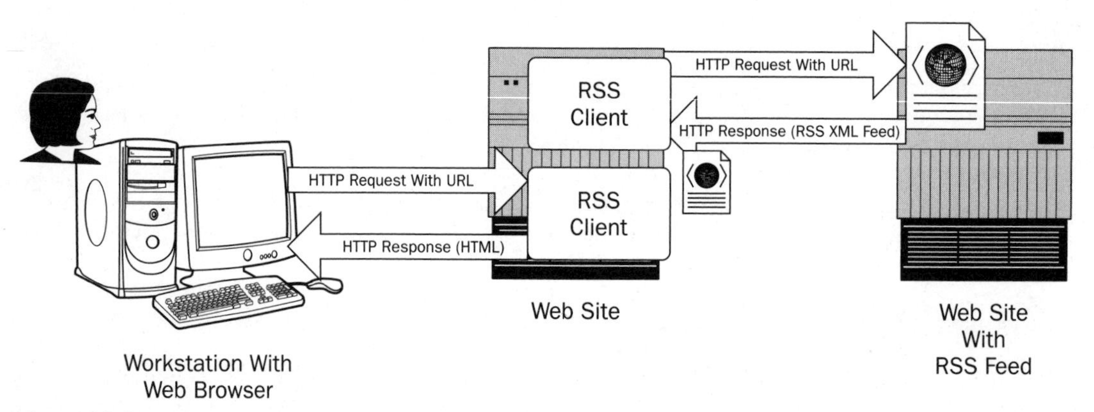

Figure 11-4

This second case is more complicated because it involves web programming, but it also provides a nice enhancement to your site and value to your users. There are RSS client libraries available for most programming languages that are popular for web development, such as Java, C#, Python, Perl, and the like. The basic architecture for implementing site-side RSS aggregation is further discussed in the "Solution" section of this chapter.

REST Web Services

If Representational State Transfer sounds very academic, there is a reason: it was coined in the Ph.D. dissertation of Dr. Roy Fielding to describe an architectural style of networked systems. In his words:

Representational State Transfer is intended to evoke an image of how a well-designed web application behaves: a network of web pages (a virtual state-machine), where the user progresses through an application by selecting links (state transitions), resulting in the next page (representing the next state of the application) being transferred to the user and rendered for their use.

If you have taken some computer science classes, you might recognize the terms "virtual state machine" or "state transitions." You might also get the sense that Dr. Fielding is trying to translate the proven mechanisms of the web into the language and formalisms of computer science.

What does this all have to do with web services and applications talking to applications over the web? REST lays out the architecture style of the web. Its technology advocates say that web services should follow the architecture style that the web has defined and that has proved successful.

At the ground level, this means that the architectural style of your web site used by humans and doing traditional web stuff — like serving dynamic web pages and having the user fill out forms — should be the same architectural style that your web services uses. For something to be a REST web service, it has to make this claim. SOAP web services might be able to make this claim, but it might not and probably won't — it just isn't a core tenet of the SOAP school of thought.

From the standpoint of a web services consumer, this means that your application is going to behave much like a human at a web browser behaves. When you want a resource, the application is going to send a URI out on the network to fetch it, just as a human enters a URI into the address field of a web browser. The application will get the resource back, most likely formatted as XML, while the human would get HTML back. The human would read the HTML page, click on links, and so on. The application would parse the XML and analyze it, and might also possibly do the equivalent of clicking on links. Just as auxiliary network components, such as proxy servers and content caches, might help out the human and the web browser, the same components can come into play to help the web services consumer.

The next chapter returns to the REST discussion when creating REST web services is discussed. Between now and then, you'll see how Amazon's very popular REST web service interface works in the "Solution" section of this chapter.

SOAP Web Services Standards

SOAP web services are based on the RPC approach to distributed computing. The model is established on the idea of passing input objects to a service and then returning one or more objects as a result. SOAP can be used independently, but it is strongly associated with two other standards, Web Services Description Language (WSDL) and Universal Description, Discovery and Integration (UDDI), and is usually used in conjunction with at least WSDL. These standards together form the "find, bind, and execute" paradigm of SOAP web services, which defines the execution model from discovery of a service through the execution.

For example, the consumer (requestor) first goes to UDDI to find an appropriate web services. If the consumer needs to process a money transfer, for instance, it goes to UDDI to find the best services, perhaps choosing the one that offers the lowest commission. Next, the requestor must bind to the web services, which means it must figure out which protocol is used, where the service resides, and the inputs and outputs required. This information is gleaned from the WSDL file. The last step is to use SOAP for the actual communication. The requestor agent sends a SOAP request with the appropriate inputs and receives a response with the expected outputs.

Of these three standards, SOAP and WSDL are much more prevalent and important, and are the focus of the more detailed sections that follow. UDDI sometimes plays an important role, but isn't on equal footing with the other two. The original vision for UDDI was that all web services would be registered with UDDI, which would act as Yellow Pages for web services consumers. But it is a big leap to say that a piece of software can be trusted to pick a new business partner and figure out how to work with the new partner correctly. Going to the Yellow Pages, finding the best repair service, and getting it to your house might seem like a simple exercise to you and me, but it requires a lot of intuitive decision making. Just as computers have a hard time with innately human tasks such as facial recognition, computers would struggle with calling a plumber.

In reality, you don't forge new business relationships programmatically. In most cases, UDDI isn't necessary because the consumer isn't choosing between services or trying to locate a service. It already knows where the service is and is implicitly bound to the particular provider. Also, a lot of web services aren't meant to be truly public. Registering private web services in a public UDDI might even invite security problems.

However, UDDI is useful in some ways and shouldn't be neglected. First, you can run your own UDDI registries that can only be seen inside your enterprise or among selected organizations and nodes on the Internet. Second, you can use UDDI to provide functionality similar to other lookup services such as Lightweight Directory Access Protocol (LDAP), Domain Name Service (DNS), and Java Naming Directory Interface (JNDI). If requestors go to UDDI to locate a service, it's easier to move both the WSDL resource and the web services around. If the web services moves from one address to another, the requestor will pick up the scent when it visits UDDI and then go to the new location seamlessly. If, instead, the web services requestor expects web services to be at a certain location and doesn't have UDDI available to perform a lookup, moving a service could become problematic. Still, it should be noted that you can be quite successful with web services without ever using UDDI.

You should have a high-level view of how the different standards relate to one another. The rest of this section examines each of the standards in enough depth so that you understand them at an architectural level.

XML and SOAP Web Services

The relationship between XML and SOAP web services can be classified into two parts:

- XML defines the core web services specifications — SOAP, WSDL, and UDDI.
- XML is used to interchange data between requestors and providers.

You can think of XML as playing both an outer role and an inner role. On the outside, XML is used to define how the web services infrastructure works. On the inside, XML is used to describe the payload that web services moves across the network.

To a web services developer, the second is more important. The fact that the SOAP, WSDL, and UDDI are defined using XML is interesting, but one could imagine non-XML formats that accomplish the same purpose with little impact to how people design and develop web services. A web service developer usually deals with the core standards indirectly through APIs, which hide how the standards are implemented.

SOAP

SOAP describes the way that data is exchanged between different web applications by defining:

- A structure for SOAP messages
- Message Exchange Patterns for how SOAP messages are exchanged between applications
- How SOAP can be sent over HTTP
- A type system for encoding data in SOAP messages

This section examines the structure of SOAP messages and how SOAP works with HTTP. Message Exchange Patterns (MEPs) are interesting if you like networking. A MEP defines the request-response paradigm that is typical of the web as well as one-way communication. MEPs are important to SOAP and web services, but a more detailed discussion isn't necessary for this chapter. The type system defined in SOAP also won't be covered in depth in this chapter because it has been the cause of interoperability problems; it will be addressed in the next chapter.

A SOAP message is an XML document that follows the rules of the SOAP schema. It can have attachments, such as images, that reside outside of the XML document but arrive at the receiver as part of the same communication. Here's a high-level view of a SOAP message:

```
<?xml version="1.0" encoding="UTF-8"?>
<env:Envelope
   xmlns:env="http://schemas.xmlsoap.org/soap/envelope/"
   encodingStyle ="">
 <env:Header>
   <!--  Headers -->
 </env:Header>
 <env:Body>
   <!-- Body -->
 </env:Body>
</env:Envelope>
```

`Envelope` is the root element for SOAP messages. The specification requires that a SOAP envelope reference the namespace name `"http://schemas.xmlsoap.org/soap/envelope/"`. SOAP uses the namespace reference for version control. If a SOAP processor doesn't find a reference to the specified namespace, it assumes that it is dealing with an incompatible version.

Any SOAP element can also have the optional `encodingStyle` attribute, which is used to signify that data in the contained elements follows a certain style. For instance, you can use it to signify that a message is encoded per the rules in section 5 of the specification. You can use the `encodingStyle` attribute with any element. In the preceding example, the attribute signifies that no encoding style is specified. You can use the null string to nullify an encoding style that has been set by a higher element. SOAP doesn't specify a default encoding style.

`Body` is the most important element. It is always required. The `Body` element contains XML that the receiving application is expected to understand and use, while the `Header` element contains metadata about how the message should be processed. For simple web services that you design yourself, it's likely that you will just use the `Body` element and not use the `Header` element. However, the `Header` element plays an important role in the overall architecture of SOAP web services. You'll see the `Header` element come into play if:

- Your web services uses higher-level specifications that are based on SOAP, including ones that cover web services security and transactions.
- You take advantage of a SOAP concept called *intermediaries*, where one or more intermediary modules process a message before it reaches its ultimate receiver.

The first situation — where higher-level specifications come into play — is the more common case. One of the strengths of SOAP web services is that there have been many, many specifications written on top of the SOAP and WSDL specifications. Two examples of such specifications are WS-Security and

WS-Transaction. WS-Security describes how to make web services secure by specifying how to provide for authentication and authorization, among other things. WS-Transaction defines how to aggregate several discrete web services into atomic transactions. The goals of both of these specifications are achieved by declaring uses for the `Header` element. If any higher-level specification instead tried to define a use for the `Body` element, it would most certainly run into trouble at some point because it would interfere with how a service wants to pass its data around. While the `Body` element is reserved for the specific business for a particular web service, the `Header` element is available so that any web service can fit into one or more higher-level frameworks.

The SOAP specification defines two attributes that can be used in conjunction with headers: `actor` and `mustUnderstand`. These attributes enable the concept of intermediaries. An *intermediary* is an application that isn't the end receiver but is performing some processing of a message in advance of the message. The `actor` attribute is used by an intermediary to determine whether the intermediary should handle a `Header`. If the `mustUnderstand` attribute is set to `true`, the intermediary must generate an error if it wasn't able to understand the `Header`.

In addition to `Header` and `Body`, the SOAP specification also defines the `Fault` element. `Fault` is used to communicate that some error has occurred. While your web services consumer might not ever have to deal with a `Header` element, it needs to be prepared to deal with a `Fault` element. There can be only one `Fault` element, and it must be an immediate child of the `Body` element. Here's an example of a message that contains a `Fault`:

```
<?xml version="1.0" encoding="UTF-8"?>
<env:Envelope
   xmlns:env="http://schemas.xmlsoap.org/soap/envelope/"
   encodingStyle ="">
 <env:Header>
   <!--  Headers -->
 </env:Header>
 <env:Body>
  <env:Fault>
   <faultcode>env:Server</faultcode>
   <faultstring>The server produced an internal error</faultstring>
   <faultactor>
    http://www.ibiblio.org/mdthomas/dummyService
   </faultactor>
   <detail>
     <!--More detailed information, such as a Java error message -->
   </detail>
  </env:Fault>
 </env:Body>
</env:Envelope>
```

In this case, the `Fault` message is communicating that some error occurred in the provider and the provider had no choice but to stop processing and return the `Fault`.

The SOAP specification defines the following faultcodes — you can't make up your own; you must use the codes described in the following table.

Faultcode	Description
Client	The client sent a request that can't be handled by the application. For example, it didn't include some data that is required. The client shouldn't send the same message again.
Server	The server has internal problems. For instance, the database is down. The client may be able to send the same message later, and the server may be able to successfully process it at that time.
VersionMismatch	The request wasn't the appropriate version. Specifically, the request didn't reference the http://schemas.xmlsoap.org/soap/envelope/ namespace.
MustUnderstand	An intermediary couldn't comprehend a header that it was required to understand.

The following table summarizes the SOAP schema by describing its message parts.

Name	Type	Required	Description
Envelope	element	Yes	Top-level element of the SOAP message document.
Header	element	No	Mechanism for storing metadata about how the message should be processed.
actor	attribute	No	Used by intermediaries to determine if they should process the header to which the attribute belongs.
mustUnderstand	attribute	No	If set to true, the intended intermediary should return an error if it doesn't understand the header.
Body	element	Yes	The payload of the message. The Body contains information that the receiving application is expected to process.
Fault	element	Yes, if an error occurred	The top-level element that defines information about the error.
faultcode	element	Yes, if an error occurred	The type of error that occurred.
faultstring	element	Yes, if an error occurred	A short description of the error.
faultactor	element	No	The actor that caused the error. (An actor is an intermediary or the end recipient of the request.)
faultdetail	element	No	Detailed information about the error.

As you can see, the SOAP schema itself is quite simple and short. You can also visit `http://schemas.xmlsoap.org/soap/envelope` to examine the complete schema.

SOAP doesn't stipulate how messages must be transported. However, the specification does define a binding between SOAP and HTTP. The following HTTP request shows a simplified SOAP request over HTTP. The unhighlighted lines signify parts of the HTTP request that have been omitted to keep the example brief. This SOAP message has both the SOAP envelope discussed earlier and an attachment:

```
POST /insuranceClaims HTTP/1.1SOAPAction: ""
Other HTTP headers

--MIME_boundary
Content-Type: text/xml; charset=UTF-8
Content-Transfer-Encoding: 8bit
Content-ID: <claim061400a.xml@claiming-it.com>

<?xml version='1.0' ?>
SOAP Envelope

--MIME_boundary
Content-Type: image/tiff
Content-Transfer-Encoding: base64
Content-ID: <claim-411AF.tiff@ins-company.com>

...Base64 encoded TIFF image...
--MIME_boundary
```

There are a couple of things to notice about this request:

- The HTTP method is `POST`, which is how a web form is submitted to a web server. (The `GET` method, on the other hand, is used when you type a URI into the browser's address field or click on a typical hyperlink.)
- There is an HTTP header called `SOAPAction`. SOAP requires a `SOAPAction` header in a SOAP-over-HTTP request so that a server knows that the request is SOAP.
- The `Content-Type` is set to `text/xml` for the SOAP `Envelope` as required by the SOAP specification. The `Content-Type` is also set for the attachment, which is `image/tiff`.

When the server receives the request, it returns a response. The response is simply a SOAP message—an XML document compliant with the SOAP schema—and possibly one or more attachments.

WSDL

When you program in a language like Java or C#, you make lots of calls to subroutines. These languages call the subroutines *methods* (other languages may call them functions or procedures). Before you can call the subroutine, you have to know a few things about it: its name, the inputs that you should pass to it, and the outputs it will pass back. To work with a web service, you have to know all those things, as well as other information such as the network address of the service and the protocol that should be used to access it. You must know all of this information before you invoke the service, and you find it out by looking at the WSDL.

Although you should be able to figure out a WSDL document, humans aren't its primary audience. Generally, a tool reads a WSDL document and generates stub code that a web services consumer can use. Let's explore the core WSDL concepts and see how they fit into the overall picture.

WSDL Concepts

WSDL describes a service, which implies that it has to be capable of defining a method or subroutine call generically, without being tied to any particular programming language. In addition, WSDL must define a network address for an operation, the protocol used, and the message exchange pattern (request-response or one way). It accomplishes all of these goals without being bound to either SOAP or HTTP. Although you usually see WSDL and SOAP used together, WSDL is designed to be independent of SOAP.

To understand how WSDL accomplishes all of these goals, you need to be aware of the WSDL terminology, described in the following table, and then see how the concepts fit together.

Name	Description
Operation	A particular action supported by a service.
Message	Typed data that is acting as either an input to an operation (`IN`), output of an operation (`OUT`) or both (`INOUT`).
Type	A data type that is typically defined with XSD. A message is an instance of a type.
Port Type	A collection of one or more operations.
Binding	Binds a particular port type to a protocol and data format.
Port	A network endpoint defined by a network address and a binding.
Service	A collection of ports.

WSDL Example

The following code shows a highly simplified WSDL file. It illustrates the structure at a high level and doesn't contain any of the actual definitions that a real WSDL file would have to have to be useful.

```
<definitions>
  <types>
   <!-- definition of types -->
  </types>
  <message>
   <!-- definition of a message -->
  </message>
  <portType>
   <!-- definition of a port -->
  </portType>
  <binding>
   <!-- definition of a binding -->
  </binding>
  <service>
   <!-- definition of a service -->
  </service>
</definitions>
```

The next several sections look at each high-level element of WSDL and describe the function that it performs and provide an example.

portType Element

The best place to begin an examination of WSDL is the `portType` element, which is comparable to a Java interface. The `portType` is a collection of different operations. The two shown here create and fetch a purchase order:

```
<portType name="PurchaseOrderWebService">

 <operation name="getPurchaseOrderById">
  <input message="tns:InvoiceWebService_getPurchaseOrderById" />
  <output message="tns:InvoiceWebService_getPurchaseOrderIdResponse" />
 </operation>

 <operation name="createPurchaseOrder ">
  <input message="tns:InvoiceWebService_createPurchaseOrder " />
  <output message="tns:InvoiceWebService_createPurchaseOrderIdResponse" />
 </operation>

</portType>
```

This port type defines a single operation, although you could certainly have more than one in a port type. This operation has one input message and one output message. You can have more than one input message and more than one output message. An in/out message is signified by naming it in both an input and output element.

message Element

The port type defines operations that, in turn, declare their messages. The `messages` associated with `getPurchaseOrderById` are:

```
<message name="InvoiceWebService_getPurchaseOrderById">
 <part name="parameters" element="ns:getPurchaseOrderById" />
</message>
<message name="InvoiceWebService_getPurchaseOrderByIdResponse">
 <part name="result" element="ns:getPurchaseOrderByIdResponse" />
</message>
```

WSDL requires a `message name` to be unique for the entire WSDL document. The `part` element is a way to compose and aggregate complex messages and is tied to a type. In these examples, the `element` attribute is used, signifying that the type is represented by an XSD element. Alternatively, the `type` attribute can be used to reference an XSD simple or complex type.

types Element

The `types` element contains the type definitions for the WSDL document. Typically, the types are defined by using XSD. The invoice web service types, `getPurchaseOrderById` and `getPurchaseOrderByIdResponse`, are defined using XSD. Both are included in the following schema element:

```
<types>
 <schema xmlns="http://www.w3.org/2001/XMLSchema" xmlns:tns=↩
"http://www.ibiblio.org/mdthomas/po/types" xmlns:soap11-enc="http://↩
schemas.xmlsoap.org/soap/encoding/" xmlns:xsi="http://www.w3.org/2001/↩
XMLSchema-instance" xmlns:wsdl="http://schemas.xmlsoap.org/wsdl/"
targetNamespace="http://www.ibiblio.org/mdthomas/po/types">
  <import namespace="http://schemas.xmlsoap.org/soap/encoding/" />

  </schema>
 </types>
```

binding Element

The `binding` element binds a port type to a protocol and data format. Usually, the port type is bound to SOAP. Here's a `binding` element that defines a binding for the operation `getInvoiceById`:

```
<binding name="PurchaseOrderWebServiceBinding" type="tns:PurchaseOrderWebService">
 <operation name="getPurchaseOrderById">
  <input>
   <soap:body use="literal" />
  </input>
  <output>
   <soap:body use="literal" />
  </output>
  <soap:operation soapAction="" />
 </operation>
 <soap:binding transport="http://schemas.xmlsoap.org/soap/http"
             style="document" />
</binding>
```

A binding can include more than one operation. The `use` attribute of the `soap:body` elements define that `soap:body` should be interpreted literally instead of using SOAP section 5 encoding. The types will be checked using XSD.

The `soap:binding` element implies that SOAP is the protocol used for transmission and specifies that the message will be transported over HTTP. It also declares that the document style of transmission is used.

Through the `soap:binding` element's `style` attribute and the `soap:body` element's `use` attribute, this binding declares that the document/literal style is used to encode data. The document/literal style is the most interoperable binding style because the major environments, including Java and .NET, agree on how messages should be exchanged using that style.

service Element

The `service` element adds a very important piece of information — the network address:

```
<service name="PurchaseOrderWebService">
 <port name="PurchaseOrderWebServicePort"
       binding="tns:PurchaseOrderWebServiceBinding">
  <soap:address xmlns:wsdl="http://schemas.xmlsoap.org/wsdl/"
location="http://localhost:8080/po/invoice" />
 </port>
</service>
```

The network address of the web services is specified by the `location` attribute for a particular port. Declare the port by specifying a name and referencing the binding. The only requirement of the port name is that it be unique to the WSDL document.

Solution

Now that you know how web services and syndication work, you probably have some idea about how to apply them to the problems introduced at the beginning of the chapter. Let's implement the solutions to those challenges.

Integrating an RSS Feed

The first problem is to consume an RSS feed from a wine magazine and display links to recent wine articles as part of the winery's home page. The RSS feed needs to be consumed by a web application that drives the web site. Usually in cases like this, someone has already picked a programming language for developing the web application, and it's best to stick with that.

If you are beginning development of a web application from scratch to provide this functionality, consider several factors when picking a programming language, such as the skill set of your organization, corporate standards, whether you have .NET or Java aspirations, and so on. While some programming languages may be a better fit for RSS than others, it is only one of a lot of factors that you should consider, and most likely not the most important one. Fortunately, the popular web application development languages have some kind of interface available to RSS. You might have to download and install a library, but you'll be able to integrate RSS into your app without having to write code to parse RSS directly.

Let's assume that the programming language of choice for your site is Java. An easy way of integrating the RSS feed is to use the RSS Utilities tag library in conjunction with Java Server Pages (JSPs). They give you a way to embed functionality into an HTML page, much as PHP and Microsoft's Active Server Pages (ASPs) do. First, you establish the feed with the following tag:

```
<rss:feedurl="http://xmlbook.agilemarkup.com/fake_wine_mag/rssFeed.xml"
     feedId="wine_mag"/>
```

This creates a feed that is read from a particular URL and gives it an ID of `wine_mag`. When you want to get content from the feed, you reference the `wine_mag` ID.

Then, there are several tags available to access content. The following code displays the channel title and image on the web page, as well as a link that points back to the channel's home page.

```
<p>
  <rss:channelImage feedId="wine_mag"/>
  <rss:channelTitle feedId="wine_mag"/>
  <rss:channelLink feedId="wine_mag" asLink="true"/>
<p>
```

Here's the code that displays the first five items of the channel in a bulleted list:

```
<ul>
  <rss:forEachItem feedId="wine_mag" startIndex="0" endIndex="4">
   <li>
   <rss:itemDescription feedId="wine_mag"/>
  </li>
  <br/>
 </rss:forEachItem>
</ul>
```

Your web application isn't doing any processing of the articles. You certainly might want to — maybe you only want to show articles about wines that your winery specializes in. As long as the feed provides enough auxiliary information about the items, you can perform such analysis. However, it wouldn't be good programming practice to do such analysis in the JSP page. Instead, do it inside your Java code. You can access the exact same RSS feed from your Java classes with the code:

```
RssParser parser = RssParserFactory.createDefault();
URL rssURL = new URL("http://xmlbook.agilemarkup.com/fake_wine_mag/rssFeed.xml");
Rss rssObject = parser.parse(rssURL);
```

This code shows how to aggregate content from an RSS feed with JSP and Java. Other languages integrate with RSS in much the same way. You can also perform more complicated aggregations from multiple sources by simply attaching to more RSS feed URIs. After hooking to the feeds, creating interesting aggregators becomes mostly an exercise in web development.

Consuming the Amazon Web Service from a Web Application

The next problem is to integrate the winery web site with Amazon by referring your web site visitors to products that they may find useful. This not only makes your web site a more interesting place to visit, but it can also serve as a foundation for a business relationship between your winery and Amazon.

The first step in developing the functionality is to sign up with Amazon and review the agreements thoroughly from a business perspective. Amazon and any other organization providing publicly available web services have specific motivations for their agreements. They want their services used in certain ways and see dangers to their businesses otherwise. Just as you wouldn't want someone to misuse a service that you provide, you need to make sure you understand what any web service provider expects and disallows.

For this project, you need to use Amazon e-commerce web services. It provides product data as well as e-commerce functionality. You just want to look up some products that may be interesting to your web site visitors and direct them to Amazon for purchase. At some later time, you may want to be more elaborate and enable your users to actually purchase items from Amazon through your site. But for now, the integration with Amazon is similar to the RSS feed integration discussed earlier — the user will see a list of items that he can link to.

The next step is to pick the programming language that you will use, which should be the one you prefer for your web application development. Then decide whether to use the SOAP web services interface or the REST web services interface. You will probably find it easier to develop your query with REST, but SOAP can be easier to integrate into object-oriented systems.

For this project, let's use the REST approach. This means that you will construct a URL that acts as the query, and in response you'll get an XML document. You want to look at books that have to do with the type of wine that is selected. For instance, if a user chooses a Cabernet Sauvignon, then you want to display books related to Cabernet Sauvignon. You also want the top books in the list to be those that have received the best reviews. Simply entering the following URL into your browser returns an XML document with what you want.

```
http://webservices.amazon.com/onca/xml?Service=AWSECommerceService&AWSAccessKeyId=
Your_Access_Key_Id_Here&Operation=ItemSearch&SearchIndex=Books&Keywords=cabernet%20
sauvignon&ResponseGroup=Medium&reviewrank=high&
```

Replace `Your_Access_Key_Id_Here` with the developer key that you received from Amazon when you registered. You'll get the XML shown in Figure 11-5.

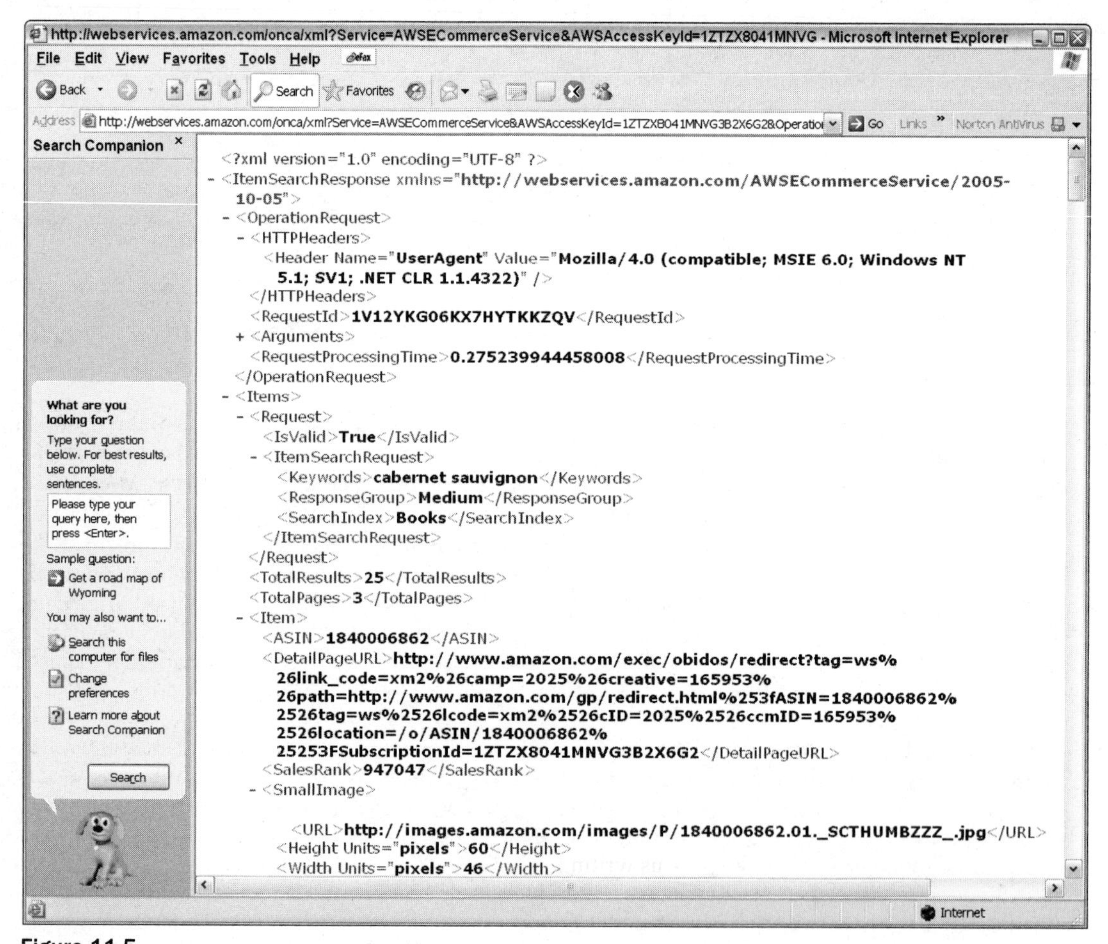

Figure 11-5

That URL is pretty long, and if you aren't familiar with web development you may have some trouble digesting it. It contains a series of key-value pairs that act as parameters. All of the parameters are contained in the query string — the part of the URL that follows the question mark. An ampersand (&) separates each key-value pair. The equals sign (=) delineates the key and value themselves, so you read the parameters of the URL like this:

```
Service=AWSECommerceService
AWSAccessKeyId=Your_Access_Key_Id_Here
Operation=ItemSearch
SearchIndex=Books
Keywords=Cabernet Sauvignon
ResponseGroup=Medium
reviewrank=high
```

This particular query is using the service named `AWSECommerceService` to do the operation `ItemSearch`. The `SearchIndex` used for the operation is books, which keeps other types of merchandise out of the results. The keywords passed to the query are `Cabernet Sauvignon`. The `ResponseGroup` parameter specifies how much information will be returned. The `reviewrank` parameter is a sorting parameter that specifies that the most highly reviewed books will be returned first in the list.

At this point, you have a working query. In your web application, you just need to plug in the particular type of wine where `Cabernet Sauvignon` is now. The more complicated task is to process the returned XML. One possibility is to use an XML parser, such as Xerces, using a language like Java. Then you can do as much analysis as you want and even issue additional queries for more information. For your project, applying an XSLT stylesheet can also work well. The Amazon web services actually supports this — just pass the parameter `Style` the URL to your stylesheet and the web services will return the result with the stylesheet already applied.

To ensure greater control, you might want to keep the XSLT processing closer to home and process the results with your own XSLT processor. In this simple architecture, the processed result is pushed into the page that is returned to the user. There are a couple of problems with this plan that arise when your site gets busy. First, a remote call over to Amazon is issued every time the page is accessed. This can slow down the performance for the user. Second, Amazon can throttle your accesses to its server. At the time of this writing, it allows only one call per application per IP address per second. On a busy site, you might have several accesses per second and they would have to be queued up.

To get around this problem, you need to explore some kind of caching strategy. For example, you don't really need to issue a new search every time someone picks Cabernet Sauvignon or Merlot. Instead, you could issue one query each for Cabernet Sauvignon and Merlot every day and keep the results on your server somewhere. Then, instead of having as many calls to Amazon as you have visits to the page in a 24-hour period, you would only have as many calls to Amazon as you have types of wines.

If you go this way, you have to be careful that your data doesn't get stale. This isn't only in your interest but also in Amazon's. At the time of this writing, Amazon had specific requirements about caching certain types of data, such as pricing data, because they don't want the prices that you are presenting to your users to be out of step with the actual prices. If you are displaying such data, having old data isn't just annoying to your users — it can also be a violation of your service agreement with Amazon.

Integrating an eBay Web Service with an Inventory System

EBay also offers a web services interface that allows software applications a variety of ways to integrate with it at a functional level. In this project, you want to list excess wines on eBay in the hope of selling them. The web services consumer needs to be integrated with your inventory system.

The most complicated piece of the puzzle is determining the business rules for when a wine should be automatically listed on eBay. Your rules can be either simple or complex — they could just post any wine with more than a certain quantity in inventory, or they could use complex algorithms that track sales over time and only post slow-moving wines. The business rules themselves are outside of the scope of this exercise because they are basically the domain of a business expert and an application developer. Assume that the business rules correctly determine when a wine should be listed on eBay.

For now, the focus is on the web services consumer and how it ties the inventory system with eBay. A lot of the equation depends on the inventory system and how it allows integration. Assume that it allows you to plug in your own Java code that runs once a day.

As with the Amazon web services, you need to register with eBay and decide whether you want to use REST or SOAP web services. This time, let's use SOAP. With eBay, you can get the eBay SDK for Java as well as other languages, which simplifies the process of building a web services consumer because you don't have to be concerned with any of the underlying communications, SOAP, WSDL, and so on. Following is the Java code you need to create a listing for a wine on eBay using the eBay SDK for Java. First, you establish the context of your call and set the account information:

```
ApiContext ctx = new ApiContext();
      ApiCredential credential = ctx.getApiCredential();
      ApiAccount ac = credential.getApiAccount();
      eBayAccount ec = credential.geteBayAccount();
      ac.setDeveloper(developerId);
      ac.setApplication(appId);
      ac.setCertificate(appCertificate);
      ec.setUsername(userId);
      ec.setPassword(userPassword);
      ctx.setApiServerUrl(soapServerURL);
```

Next, you establish the wine that you want to list on eBay. The various variables, such as `wineTitle`, `qty` and `startPrice`, would be derived from the inventory system by the business rules for posting excess wines to eBay:

```
ItemType item = new ItemType();
      item.setCurrency(CurrencyCodeType.USD);
      item.setCountry(CountryCodeType.US);
      item.setPaymentMethods(new BuyerPaymentMethodCodeType[]
{BuyerPaymentMethodCodeType.PaymentSeeDescription} );
      item.setRegionID("0");
      item.setListingDuration(ListingDurationCodeType.Days_3);

      item.setTitle(wineTitle);
      item.setDescription(wineDescription);
      item.setLocation(wineLocation);
```

```
item.setQuantity(qty);
item.setStartPrice(new AmountType(startPrice));

CategoryType categoryType = new CategoryType();
cat.setCategoryID(catId);
item.setPrimaryCategory(categoryType);
```

The last step is to post the item and record the fees that the listing generated:

```
AddItemCall addItemCall = new AddItemCall(ctx);
FeesType fees = addItemCall.addItem(item);
```

The fees that eBay charged your account can be found be examining the `fees` object returned by the `addItem` call.

Consuming Partner Web Service

The last problem calls for integration with a distributor's web service. While Amazon, eBay, and other top web sites are very sophisticated with their web services and give users lots of choices about how to build their services, you can't expect such accommodation from every web services provider. In the case of the distributor's web services, for example, it's likely that it only provide the WSDL file that describes the web services. From that WSDL, you have to create the web services consumer.

Luckily, there are lots of tools to help you do this. Ideally, you want the task of developing the web services consumer to be easy for your application developer. eBay makes it very easy by providing an SDK. Although the wine distributor probably hasn't gone to the trouble of developing multiple SDKs for different programming languages as eBay has, it is simple to create the root client-side files, called *stubs*. Most popular web application development languages give you tools that automatically generate code simply by examining the WSDL file. Java, for instance, uses a tool called `wscompile`, while C# uses a tool called `wsdl.exe`. With these tools in mind, the path for creating a web services that integrates with your partner is:

1. Locate the WSDL file.
2. Point the language-specific code generation tool, such as `wscompile` or `wsdl.exe`, at the WSDL file and generate the stubs.
3. Develop the application using the generated stubs — no XML or SOAP parsing required.

Summary

Web services and syndication have two distinct sides — consumption and provision. In many cases, you either consume or provide. This chapter focused on the consumer side of web services and syndication. In addition to learning the basics of RSS, REST web services, and SOAP web services, you saw how consumers are built and can be used to achieve your business objectives. The next chapter looks at the other side, where you'll see how the winery can extend its reach by providing web services and RSS feeds.

12

Providing Web Services

You've just explored how you can consume web services and RSS feeds. This chapter turns to the other side of web services — how to provide your own.

Problem

Imagine that you want your winery to provide its own web service. You want to allow partners to query your catalog with their own applications. The partner applications will formulate queries, pass them to your service, and then process the result.

Surveying the potential audience, you want to leverage the large library of web services standards and proposals that revolve around SOAP and WSDL. You want to build on those standards so that your web service can benefit from the growth of the SOAP/WSDL style.

Design

The first step in designing your web service is to consider the architecture alternatives. In the last chapter, you saw three technologies that can be broadly classified as services architectures: RSS, REST-style web services, and SOAP/WSDL web services. Each has its own adherents and pros and cons regarding specific problems. Although this particular project is going to be addressed by SOAP/WSDL, it's important to understand how services are constructed with the other standards.

You may have heard of Service-Oriented Architecture (SOA), which is broad set of ideas on rules about how any services architecture should be built. Its lessons are especially relevant if you're building complex systems that use SOAP and WSDL to their fullest, but they also provide insight into building simple RSS channels. Before you examine SOA, though, let's review the services architectures and take a look at SOAP/WSDL interoperability. Interoperability is a key goal of all of web services, but it's proved illusive when the industry is also trying to standardize fairly low-level behavior. Basically, the standards aren't watertight, and there are some traps and gotchas to avoid so that your services can be as interoperable as possible.

RSS Feeds

Part of creating an RSS feed is understanding all of the different versions of RSS. When you are just consuming RSS, you can lean on your client library or software to navigate the different versions for you. But when you are providing a feed, you have to make a choice. The different versions of RSS are covered after the basics of providing RSS feeds are discussed.

Providing RSS Feeds

In the RSS example from the last chapter, the URL for the channel was straightforward:

```
http://xmlbook.agilemarkup.com/fake_wine_mag/rssFeed.xml
```

Basically, creating an RSS channel is simply creating an XML file and putting it on a web server. If the content doesn't change often, it is reasonable that you maintain the channel by occasionally editing the RSS XML file. If the content on your site is more active, though, you want an automated way to update the RSS file so that you have one less thing to do. At the very least, you want a way to validate your RSS XML file so that you can be sure that it will work with the consumers of your channel.

Web publishing tools such as Dreamweaver have extensions that allow easy publishing of RSS channels. Other tools, some free, aid in creating and validating the RSS feeds. As you saw in earlier chapters, you can also create RSS XML documents by querying a database, from XML documents, or through XSLT transformations. In essence, you distribute an unchanging URL to your subscribers, and then change the underlying RSS XML document on the server as often as you want and in any way that you want.

What hasn't been discussed yet is the format of the underlying RSS XML document. The next section tackles the underlying format but also tells the story of a "standard" that fragmented into different branches. As you'll see, there isn't one answer to the question "What is the RSS format?"

Understanding Different RSS Dialects

RSS has been very successful, but has also been a cautionary tale about what can happen when a standard lacks strong sponsorship and becomes fractured. There have been nine RSS specifications written, none of which is totally compatible with any of the others. The RSS specifications all have version numbers, ranging from RSS 0.9 to RSS 3. But these aren't versions in the typical sense. You would expect that an RSS 0.9 document would be a valid RSS 2.0 document or RSS 1.0 document. This isn't the case. RSS doesn't even stand for the same thing across all of the different versions — as mentioned in the last chapter, it alternatively stands for Rich Site Summary, RDF Site Summary, Really Simple Syndication, or nothing at all. Adding to the confusion, there is a post-RSS standard called Atom that attempts to unify the various RSS versions, but because the usage of the more popular versions is entrenched, it is effectively just another standard with the same target.

The problem is that the standard branched just as it was getting popular and two different parallel efforts emerged. Fortunately, the two main dialects are similar enough on a functionality basis that most RSS clients can handle either. This means that you when you choose one of the main dialects over another, you aren't choosing to exclude a large portion of your target audience. For example, choosing your RSS version isn't the same kind of decision as choosing whether or not to develop a desktop application for windows, which effectively eliminates Macintosh and Unix users from your potential audience.

The two main families of RSS versions are RSS 2.0 and RSS 1.0. The RSS 1 family includes RSS 1.0 and RSS 1.1 and is related to, but not fully backward-compatible with RSS 0.9.0. The RSS 2 family is related to RSS 0.9.1, 0.9.2 through 0.9.4, RSS 2.0, and RSS 2.0.1. The RSS 2 family is simpler and more popular. The following code is an example of the RSS 2.0 (or RSS 2.0.1) version:

```
<?xml version="1.0"?>
<rss version="2.0">
 <channel>
  <title>Pining For Wine Magazine</title>
  <link>http://xmlbook.agilemarkup.com/fake_wine_mag/</link>
  <description>The magazine for people who pine for wine</description>
  <language>en-us</language>
  <pubDate>Tue, 10 Dec 2005 07:32:11 GMT</pubDate>
  <lastBuildDate>Tue, 10 Dec 2005 09:41:01 GMT</lastBuildDate>
  <managingEditor>fakewinemag@agilemarkup.com</managingEditor>
  <webMaster>fakewinemag@agilemarkup.com</webMaster>

  <item>
   <title>The Beleagured Merlot</title>
   <link>
     http://xmlbook.agilemarkup.com/fake_wine_mag/articles/merlot.html
   </link>
   <description>
    Ever since the movie Sideways, Merlot sales have dropped. That's too bad -- and
just plain wrong.
   </description>
   <pubDate>Tue, 03 Jun 2003 09:39:21 GMT</pubDate>
   <guid> http://xmlbook.agilemarkup.com/fake_wine_mag/articles/home#item510</guid>
  </item>

 </rss>
</channel>
```

Here's how you'd render the same feed as RSS 1.1:

```
<rdf:RDF
  xmlns:rdf="http://www.w3.org/1999/02/22-rdf-syntax-ns#"
  xmlns="http://purl.org/rss/1.0/"
  xmlns:dc="http://purl.org/dc/elements/1.1/">
  <channel rdf:about=" http://xmlbook.agilemarkup.com/fake_wine_mag/rdf-about/"/>
    <title>Pining For Wine Magazine</title>
    <link>http://xmlbook.agilemarkup.com/fake_wine_mag/</link>
    <description>The magazine for people who pine for wine</description>
    <language>en-us</language>
  </channel>

    <items>
     <rdf:Seq>
      <rdf:li
rdf:resource="http://xmlbook.agilemarkup.com/fake_wine_mag/articles/merlot.html"/>
     </rdf:Seq>
    </items>
```

```
    </channel>
    <item
  rdf:about="http://xmlbook.agilemarkup.com/fake_wine_mag/articles/merlot.html">
     <title>The Beleagured Merlot</title>
     <description>
       Ever sense the movie Sideways, Merlot sales have dropped. That's too bad --
  and just plain wrong.
     </description>
     <link>http://xmlbook.agilemarkup.com/fake_wine_mag/articles/merlot.html </link>
     <dc:creator>Michael Thomas </dc:creator>
     <dc:date>2005-12-10</dc:date>
    </item>
  </rdf:RDF>
```

The RSS 1 family is based on Resource Description Framework (RDF). RDF is used for defining and interchanging metadata about resources. Its purpose is to classify different resources on the web so that it is easier to locate relevant information. The expectation is that the content providers annotate their content with RDF tags at the time of creation and modification. The RSS 1.1 feed is a good example of what RDF is intended for. The document uses RSS 1 namespaces so that the elements and attributes belong to RDF. The RSS feed is really RDF metadata about the underlying articles. The RSS 2 feed could also be called metadata, but it is not tied to the larger RDF schema.

Both RSS 1 and RSS 2 have their pros and cons, and unfortunately your first step is choosing one. Unless you are already using RDF in your organization or want to be integrated with RDF, the simplicity of RSS 2 probably makes it a better choice. The best option is to use a tool to generate your RSS feed, or at the very least use a validator to check it after you have created it.

Creating REST-Style Services

REST is an architectural style, not a standard. While compliance with SOAP and WSDL is judged by comparing the messages and documents against a detailed specification, a REST web service is more a way of thinking. REST models application-to-application service calls around the way the web works already, while SOAP/WSDL use the web as a way to perform remote procedure calls. If the following are true for your service, it should classify as REST:

- Your service is fundamentally built around the concept of resources rather than the concept of remote procedure calls as SOAP/WSDL is. For instance, a REST-style web service fetches, modifies, creates, and deletes resources, while a SOAP/WSDL web service exposes remote procedure calls that may (or may not) act upon resources in the same way.
- The resources that a service returns are identified and fetched using a URI. Fetching a resource should be side-effect-free.
- Your services application is prepared for mechanisms such as proxy servers, caches, and security mechanisms that may live between the provider and the end consumer.
- Your resources reference other resources using URI hyperlinks, just as HTML documents do.

Here's a very simple REST web service that you can easily create—you just need a web server and the wines catalog XML document from earlier chapters. Put `wines.xml` on the web server, and then you can provide the "service" of providing the catalog to other applications. For instance, the consumer application can point at this URI:

```
http://xmlbook.agilemarkup.com/wine_store/xmlbook/catalog/wines.xml
```

When the application accesses that URI, it retrieves the entire wines catalog, at which point the application can process it. Don't worry that you are missing something because it seems simple and works just the same way that the traditional, user-targeted web handles resources. It's the point of REST to be simple and to work exactly as successful web sites do. A REST-style web service could also provide access to a single wine with a URI like this:

```
http://xmlbook.agilemarkup.com/wine_store/xmlbook/catalog?wine_id=Smokey_Scupp_750m
l
```

In this case, the web server would route the request to a web application that would query the main catalog and return only an element about this particular wine. As long as the application code handles this URI only as a request for a resource, your application code can get the resource any way it wants. For instance, it could parse the XML using Java or C#, it could use XQuery, or it could transform the `wines.xml` with a stylesheet so that only the one particular wine is returned.

The purpose of many web services is to allow the consumer to perform some action on the server. For instance, a web service can allow the consumer application to make a purchase. The REST approach dictates that in reality you are creating a new resource, a purchase order. Part of creating the new purchase order resource is that the purchase is processed — a charge is made against the customer's account or credit card, an item is taken out of inventory, the accounting system is updated, instructions are sent to pack and ship the item, and so on. The response to the purchase request would be a URI that points to the purchase order. As the purchase proceeds, the consumer can check the purchase order to see what state the purchase is in — for example, whether it has shipped.

The REST approach is simple and closely mirrors the workings of the traditional web. It is successful even though it is often overshadowed by SOAP/WSDL. For instance, Amazon, which offers both a REST interface and a SOAP/WSDL interface, has reported that the REST interface is more popular.

REST is also much more tied to XML. A lot of SOAP/WSDL development tools are created to ignore the XML underneath, yet in REST, XML is front and center because the consumers deal with XML directly. This can be a pro and a con at the same time, as you'll see in the next section.

In comparison with SOAP/WSDL, REST suffers most significantly in platform support. For example, both J2EE (Java 2 Platform, Enterprise Edition) and .NET (Microsoft's web services strategy) have embraced SOAP/WSDL. You can certainly put together REST-style web services on the J2EE and .NET platforms, but they've made it much easier to put together SOAP/WSDL web services. This has lead to a polarization in the web services universe — REST is the resource-oriented, or document-oriented approach, and SOAP/WSDL is the remote procedure call (RPC) approach. Certainly there is a need for both approaches, and both have their strong suits and ragged edges. As you work through the SOAP/WSDL section, you'll get a better feel for how to choose one over the other.

SOAP/WSDL Web Services

While REST extends the basic model of the web, SOAP and WSDL really represent the RPC tradition. The RPC model predates the web and is really the root of distributed computing. RPCs solve the problem of one machine invoking functionality on another machine. With the advent of object-oriented languages, RPC architectures such as CORBA add objects to the mix — objects are passed as part of the RPC and objects are returned.

To discuss a purchase in a REST architecture, for example, you have to think of it in terms of creation and modification of resources. Yet it's more intuitive to think of a purchase as a procedure — you take some inputs such as product ID, quantity, account number, shipping address, and so on; the procedure executes, and results are returned. In a SOAP web service, the inputs are contained in the body of a SOAP message and the results are returned in the body of a SOAP message. WSDL describes the inputs that should be provided to the procedure and the outputs that are to be returned.

But while a purchase models better on the SOAP/WSDL paradigm than on REST, the same isn't true for simply fetching a resource. REST is very straightforward on this point — you just address it with a URI. The SOAP/WSDL approach isn't as clear-cut. To perform the exact same act using SOAP, the consumer creates a SOAP message that contains the wine ID in its body according to the format specified in the accompanying WSDL. On the server, the web app must return the result inside a SOAP message — even if the result is XML — and the consumer must process the SOAP message to retrieve the result.

In spite of the complexity of the simple operation of fetching a resource, SOAP/WSDL has the advantage of being tightly integrated with popular object-oriented languages. As you'll see when you develop the solution later in this chapter, SOAP/WSDL web services can be seamlessly integrated with application code in both the consumer and provider applications. While REST is an unstandardized style, the SOAP and WSDL specifications are detailed enough that this kind of integration is possible and means that application developers don't have to be skilled in handling the underlying XML directly.

In addition to enabling tighter integration with object-oriented languages, the structure of SOAP also allows other specifications to extend web services via the `Header` element. While the REST XML response can be any XML schema, the SOAP response has to follow the SOAP schema, which specifies the `Header` element and the `Body` element. The `Body` element can contain XML of any schema, so you can think of it as being equivalent to the entire REST response. While SOAP is content plus an optional header, REST is all content. Because of the `Header` element, other specifications can define higher level behavior that is completely independent of the content that is transferred in the `Body` element. Two examples of standards that define their mechanics via the `Header` element are WS-Security and WS-Transaction, which were introduced in Chapter 11.

All of the different services architectures discussed so far can benefit from a SOA, which is discussed next.

Service-Oriented Architecture

In a lot of people's minds, Service-Oriented Architecture (SOA) is tightly correlated with web services. SOA often comes up in conversations about web services, and it is good to know SOA basics. But you should know that SOA isn't part of web services and wasn't invented for web services. SOA is a general paradigm that serves web services well and serves other distributed systems well, too. In the next few pages, you'll look at SOA basics, compare SOA to other models such as object-oriented programming, and apply SOA to web services.

The Place of SOA

SOA is complementary to object-oriented programming and component-based programming. SOA doesn't suggest that you forget all of the great principles of development such as reusability, encapsulation, abstraction, and polymorphism; it reinforces them. It defines how to merge the ideologies of object-oriented programming and good distributed systems development.

Procedures, objects, components, and services are the cornerstone entities of procedural programming, object-oriented programming, component-based development, and SOA, respectively. The procedure was the first attempt at achieving reusability and encapsulation, but the scope of a good procedure is relatively small. Objects combine data and procedures and give a better way to represent the problem domain, yet a typical system tends to have lots of objects and it can be difficult to pull a single object out and either reuse it somewhere else or replace it. Component-based development attempts to address that problem by grouping objects into a more maintainable entity. For instance, you can write a component that knows how to graph data, and you can use that component in several different applications.

A service is closest to a component. You can think about a service as a network-ready component or as an encapsulation of several components. SOA is a direct descendent of object-oriented programming and component-based development. What SOA brings to the party are the principles of good distributed computing across the network. OOP can guide you when you are developing an application that runs entirely on one machine. SOA advises you when your functionality crosses machines and when you expose that functionality to the network.

SOA Vocabulary

The primary entity of SOA is a service, which is A set of functionality available over the network. At any given point of time, it has a network address. Service in SOA is synonymous with "web service."

Other key entities are defined in the following table, which includes the equivalent web services terms:

SOA Term	Definition	Web Services Term
Service provider	The organization or entity that is providing a service.	Web service provider
Service consumer	The organization or entity that is using the service.	Web service consumer
Message	Inputs and outputs to a service.	SOAP message
Service contract	The description of how a service consumer and service provider should interact. WSDL describes the service contract.	WSDL (in association with W3C Schema Language)
Service registry	A directory where you can find services.	UDDI

The various definitions align closely with the web services vocabulary you've already learned. These are the SOA definitions that are most applicable to web services. There are other SOA concepts such as service leases and service proxies that are important parts of SOA but aren't necessarily relevant to basic web services.

SOA Criteria

SOA defines the following criteria regarding how providers and consumers should interact with each other:

- Services provide an interface to the network.
- Service providers and consumers are loosely coupled. They don't expose implementation details to each other.

- Interoperability is important.
- The interfaces are coarse-grained.
- A consumer can bind to a provider dynamically at runtime.
- The location of a service provider can change while remaining available to consumers.

First and foremost, a service's entry point is over the network. This differentiates a service from an object or a component that only exposes its interface to other entities within the same application. If you are familiar with application programming interfaces (APIs), then you are familiar with the concept of having a library of objects and method calls that give an application access to needed functionality. You use an API by just making a call to a method in the API, after ensuring the API is available to your application. But the API executable code has to live on the same machine as the application. A service, on the other hand, is called across the network. The executable code for the service can live on any machine accessible over the network. If the application can access the Internet, the service can live virtually anywhere in the world.

The consumer and the provider need to be loosely coupled. If they are too dependent on each other, then changes in one necessitate changes to the other. When multiple consumers are involved, changes could cascade to all of them, too. The less that consumers and providers know about the other's implementation details, the better.

Closely tied to loose-coupling is interoperability. When a service provider is interoperable, it means that its service consumers can be written in any language and deployed on any operating system. Web services satisfies this principle because the interchange of data is done via XML, which is independent of any language or operating system. In contrast, there are distributed computing architectures that pass data over the network in a native format specific to a particular programming language. Transferring data in a native format can be more efficient than using XML, but it comes at the cost of not playing well with others — the providers and consumers need to be written in the same language. If your service provider has a narrow, well-defined audience that happens to exclusively use the language in question, this isn't a problem, but even then the language dependence constrains the scope that the service could otherwise achieve.

The next principle is one of granularity, in which the options are coarse-grained or fine-grained. A good service is coarse-grained, meaning that each call does a lot of work; in a fine-grained service, many calls are required to do the same amount of work. The reason you want a coarse-grained interface is that calls across the network are expensive, and a good services architecture minimizes them. Consider a service that returns customer orders in which a consumer is interested. A coarse-grained approach would return all of the interesting customer orders with a single call; a fine-grained approach might return a list of customer IDs with one call and then require the consumer to make another call for each interesting customer order. If there are 100 customer orders of interest, the coarse-grained approach requires only 1 call while the fine-grained approach requires 101 calls. If each call takes a second to complete, the fine-grained approach could easily take a minute and a half longer to complete than the coarse-grained approach.

Although you should strive for your services to be coarse-grained, you can go overboard. For example, a very coarsely grained service would have one call that returned all of the data that the consumer is authorized to see, but it would likely be impractical for the consumer to process the data all at once and costly to send all of the data across the network. You want the level of granularity that satisfies the specific needs of your service. The goal is to minimize calls across the network. To accomplish this, you need to understand not only the set of operations that your consumers require but also how they are used.

The next concept means that you don't have to hard-code your consumer to only work with a particular provider when you develop it. Instead, you want your consumers to be able to dynamically bind to a provider at runtime. For some web services, this isn't an issue — the consumer is hard-coded to work with a particular provider. But if you want to choose between different available web services, you need to be able to select and bind to a specific web service at runtime. For example, imagine that all wine distributors provide the same web services that tells you about their current offerings. If you develop a consumer for one distributor, you probably are interested in getting data from different wine distributors at different times. It doesn't make sense to have a different consumer for each wine distributor because they all provide the same web services defined with the same WSDL. Instead, you want the consumer to be able to choose from among all of the different wine distributors at runtime.

Service Location and Discovery

The last of the criteria concerns the location of a particular service provider and how a provider can be relocated without becoming unavailable to its consumers. This is analogous to how Domain Name Service (DNS) works — a particular host has an IP address, such as 123.201.40.22, as well as a DNS name, such as `my.server.ibiblio.org`. But the IP address may need to change, or you may need to redirect the user to one of several available IP addresses when the server is under load. As long as the users arrive at your machine by binding to the DNS name, DNS can take care of getting them to the right IP address automatically.

Good services should have the same kind of pattern in which a consumer first inquires about the location of a service through some kind of registry and then attaches to a service only after the registry responds. By having the registry act as a traffic cop, you can move and load balance the service as necessary. WSDL provides the first level of indirection — it hides the underlying URI and protocol of web services. UDDI provides a separate level of indirection by holding the location of the WSDL for a particular web services and allowing a consumer to choose between different available versions of a web services.

Service Modularity

The last tenets of SOA apply to the modularity of services:

- Services are self-contained.
- Services are modular and can be aggregated to form higher-level services.

The coarse-grained nature of services is important to remember in considering the modularity of services.

When creating services, think in terms of providing one-stop shopping for the consumers. A consumer should be able to get a lot done with as few calls as possible. It's also important to remember that there are costs associated with locating and binding to a service, so it's helpful if a single service exposes as much functionality as possible. At the same time, the concept of reusability still applies — going to the trouble of writing a service is more worthwhile if you are able to use it somewhere else at a later date as part of a solution to a another, larger problem. But in typical procedural or object-oriented programming, the desire for reusability would lead you to write in a more finely grained style — smaller building blocks give you more flexibility. Unfortunately, there is tension between the concepts of modularity and granularity, and good services have to balance these goals. It's impossible to suggest how to approach every situation, but there are advantages to addressing granularity first. If a service isn't performing in the first place, it probably won't ever see the opportunity of being aggregated with other services.

Interoperability

If you are looking for one purpose that drives web services, it's interoperability. Web services make it easy for systems to talk to systems. They aren't the fastest distributed computing systems, and they can be cumbersome. But if you want the best guarantee that your software will interoperate with someone else's software over a network, then you need to use web services.

The good news is that the IT industry is highly aware of the interoperability challenges facing web services. The Web Services Interoperability Organization (`www.ws-i.org`) exists to "Promote consistent and reliable interoperability recommendations among Web services implementations across platforms, applications, and programming languages." The organization includes IBM, Microsoft, Sun, and BEA as well as many others.

WS-I is contributing to web services interoperability in a couple of different ways. Perhaps more importantly, it's defining profiles that declare what web services standards should be used and how they should be used. The most important profile that WS-I publishes is the Basic Profile. The Basic Profile looks across all of the SOAP web services specifications and declares rules that should be followed to ensure that your services are as interoperable as possible. The WS-I Basic Profile can't absolutely guarantee interoperability for a web services provider, but it can help you avoid many common pitfalls.

The WS-I is also providing tools and test suites that ensure interoperability. These tools are tied to the Basic Profile. Instead of having to dig through the Basic Profile spec, you can just use the WS-I tools to test compliance.

Solution

The problem for this chapter is to provide a web services interface to the wine catalog so that partners can query the catalog with their own applications. As with any solution, there are some decisions to be made. First you decide whether to provide a REST-style web service or a WSDL/SOAP web service. As discussed earlier, the WSDL/SOAP direction is better suited if you want to comply with various emerging web services standards. At the same time, REST is certainly a valid alternative and can be easy to implement from both the provider's standpoint as well as the consumer's standpoint.

To build a web service with WSDL and SOAP, you need:

- ❑ A WSDL document that describes the service, and includes XML schema definitions.
- ❑ A web application module that receives SOAP requests, processes them, and returns SOAP messages to the consumer.

Creating the WSDL by hand can be cumbersome and prone to error. Likewise, processing incoming SOAP messages and creating outgoing SOAP messages can become a development nightmare that distracts from the key business problems at hand. Just as there are automated tools to help build consumers, there are development tools to help build providers. Because SOAP and WSDL are generally accessed over HTTP, a web services provider is a type of web application. But while most web applications receive simple HTTP requests and send back HTML, a web services provider has to receive and process SOAP and then create and send a SOAP response. In between receiving and responding to SOAP, you address the actual business problem that is the reason the web service exists.

As a developer, you would probably rather focus on the business problem that needs to be solved rather than the details of marshaling and unmarshaling SOAP messages. The development tools enable you to do that because they take care of translating SOAP into objects appropriate to your development language. At the end of the day, you not only get to focus on the business problem instead of the gory details of SOAP processing, but you can't even tell the difference between code that is doing the work of a web services and standard application code.

Both Java and .NET platforms have tools that help you create web services, and both follow essentially the same flow:

1. Define the methods that you want to expose as web services, implement them, and declare that they should be exposed as web services.
2. Use the tools to create the web application part of the provider that receives requests, transforms objects to and from SOAP messages, and sends responses.
3. Deploy the web services provider as a web application on the application server.
4. In .NET languages, such as C# and ASP.NET, you declare that a method should be exposed as a web services by including the WebMethod aspect prior to the method itself:

```
public class PurchaseOrderWebService {


    [WebMethod]
    public PurchaseOrderResponse SubmitPurchaseOrder(PurchaseOrder po) {
      //implementation
    }

    [WebMethod]
    public PurchaseOrder GetPurchaseOrderById(String id) {
      //implementation
    }

}
```

Then, you deploy the implementation classes along with a `.asmx` file that references it to the virtual directory of your .NET server. When the .NET server sees the `WebMethod` declarations, it takes care of the rest of the mechanics of dealing with the SOAP messages. The implementation of these two methods is regular C# code. The only way to tell the difference between the web services code and regular application code is the `WebMethod` declaration.

With Java, you define a remote interface for the methods that you want to expose, as shown here:

```
public interface PurchaseOrderWebService extends Remote {

  public PurchaseOrderResult submitPurchase(PurchaseOrder po)
    throws RemoteException;

  public PurchaseOrder getPurchaseOrderById(String id)
    throws RemoteException;

}
```

The implementation of the methods is in a class that implements the interface, such as `PurchaseOrder WebServiceImpl`.

From here, Java takes a code generation approach. You use the `wscompile` tool to create the WSDL file as well as code for the web application piece of the web services provider. The generated code includes servlets and other classes that handle processing SOAP messages and transforming them into Java objects. You then use `wsdeploy` to deploy your application code as well as the generated code to the application server.

In the earlier discussions, you started with application code and then defined the WSDL from there. If you are able to dictate the web services definition, this is probably the quickest way to get a web services up and running. But you don't always get to choose the WSDL. For instance, you may be trying to implement web services defined by some industry group. The industry group has already defined the WSDL, and there are already consumers written that work with the WSDL. In that case, you need to start with the WSDL rather than your application code. Both .NET and Java support generating application code from an existing WSDL document. If you already have application code you want to use for the web services, you can still use it, although you'll have to graft the generated code to your existing application code.

In this section, you've learned the basics of how to use development tools to create web services providers. There is nothing to prevent you from developing web services providers entirely by hand — you can write the WSDL from scratch and then write all of the code that processes and creates the raw SOAP messages. Of course, using the development tools to help has the obvious advantage of dramatically reducing the amount of code that you have to write and maintain. There is also a more subtle advantage when it comes to interoperability. When you use development tools, the burden of creating interoperable WSDL and SOAP falls to the development tools. The tools aren't infallible, but they contain a lot of knowledge about web services interoperability and can keep you from having to become a web services interoperability expert yourself.

Summary

This chapter focused on providing web services and RSS channels, which require you to develop some expertise in web application development and distributed computing. In the case of RSS, you have to choose between the various RSS flavors. With web services, it's important to understand the principles of SOA as a way to build good distributed systems. With an understanding of SOA, you can develop good services applications using either SOAP or REST web services. REST is a simpler architectural design that is closer to both XML and the spirit of the web, but SOAP web services are closer to the RPC model underlying a great deal of distributed application development. Because SOAP web services are closely related to the leading application development languages, the solutions section showed you how you can create web services with development tools.

At the heart of services is the need to integrate different software components, and what you've seen in this chapter and the preceding one is how different standards that use XML can accomplish integration. The next chapter moves from the tactical focus of these chapters to the more strategic challenge of integrating different XML catalogs. Thus far, the challenge has been to develop a catalog and use it to solve your business problems. For the next chapter, you have to consider that other catalogs can be introduced into your organization and that you need to get the new catalogs to play nicely with ones that you've developed.

13

Combining Catalogs

This chapter is the first of two that will look at the strategic applications of XML technology for business. It examines the issues involved in combining catalogs and explores the technologies and strategies for combining data and documents. This chapter is especially useful for business analysts and architects who need to understand the high-level technical issues to be taken into account when designing a solution for combining data and documents. The technical details and coding techniques have been covered in previous chapters and are referenced to reinforce the concepts for the benefit of the developers and programmers.

Problem

During the life of a business, the company can be sold to another company or can choose to buy other companies to achieve some specific business goal. As part of the merger or acquisition deal, the new company gets all the tangible assets, some of the great employees, and all the intellectual capital and data of the acquired company.

A company also can decide to increase its competitive advantage by creating strategic partnerships with its vendors and suppliers. To do so successfully, the company may have to modify its data to be compatible with that of its partners or it may have to specify standards that partners have to comply with to make their data useful to the company.

There are many obstacles to making such deals, but once the agreements are inked, the real challenges begin: the organizations have to start working together. Acquisitions have always proven to place heavy demands on the time and resources of IT organizations. They are usually given a very short turnaround time to resolve issues of disparate systems, networks, applications, and data.

Some companies choose to cope with the integration by hiring more staff to perform manual data transfer tasks between applications. While this may be effective for small amounts of data, it can prove inefficient and costly in the long run. There are also the problems and costs of errors arising from the use of a manual process. Postponing the inevitable integration projects may not bring the business to a standstill, but the organizations' data and technology have to be shared, merged, or combined for the partnership or business acquisition to be successful.

Each organization may have a catalog application that creates and maintains product information for use by the customer or by other business systems. The data that drives the catalog application may already be defined in XML or may be available in a relational database. The problem can be summarized as follows: How do you combine, merge, or otherwise include data and documents from multiple sources? For the discussion in this chapter, the problem can be split into two parts:

- How do you combine catalog data stored in relational databases?
- How do you combine catalogs already represented in XML languages?

Let's evaluate the underlying issues of each of these questions.

Combining Structured Relational Data

Many companies have invested a lot of time and resources in creating and maintaining sophisticated database applications that drive their business applications. The database schema is well defined, and all internal applications are streamlined to work with this schema. The companies often choose an enterprise-wide database strategy and a small set of database and application products to achieve a greater level of integration of applications and business processes.

Although database application vendors state that their products comply with all the standards, data representation still varies between databases. Unquestionably, it is a challenge to merge data from heterogeneous database repositories. Over the past few years, processes called ETL (Extract, Transform, and Load) have been refined to help companies with multiple databases merge data from various sources into a universal data repository. The repository may be used for ongoing business operations or to drive a data warehouse application.

The ETL process is a feasible solution for merging data only when the data from the sources is not changing in time. There are specific business uses for such static repositories specifically in strategic marketing departments or businesses that specialize in market analysis.

ETL

ETL (Extract, Transform, and Load) describes the processes that are used by companies to combine data from multiple sources whose data may not be compatible. The data is extracted from each source using any standard SQL (structured query language) data extraction tools or specialized applications that read in the data, reformat it based on rules, and then load the transformed data into the target data repository.

The ETL process is used in the creation of data warehouses. Remember, though, that data warehouses are static repositories and are used by strategic marketing organizations for historical performance analysis, business intelligence, decision support systems, and report generation. The integrated repository you create for this chapter's project is dynamic data and will be the operational database for the merged business applications and systems. The data in the new repository represents the merged data from all sources and can be used to create XML documents as described in Chapter 8.

Data used in day-to-day business operations changes rapidly, and it is impossible to continuously execute an ETL process merging data from live business databases. In a business merger or acquisition, though, companies often create a snapshot of their merged business data using an ETL process and then use the new repository for ongoing business operations. In such cases, once the transformation and loading is completed, the new database is used to drive the business applications and new data is dynamically added to the merged repository. Very often the company determines that the ETL process is too costly and time-consuming. In those cases, companies may choose to integrate structured data at the business application layer.

Combining XML Documents

Many organizations have embraced XML as the de facto standard for representing internal data and documents. Over the past several years, as the technology matured, organizations moved from generic XML representations to the creation of sophisticated XML language standards (schemas). They've defined their own custom tags and namespaces to model their data and communicate that representation to the external world.

Companies within an industry or a sector have continued to create their own standards for defining data and documents within their vertical markets. Many companies have taken the initiative to work with other companies within their sector to standardize the schemas and create robust business applications based on these schemas. However, not every company has taken the trouble to comply with standards, and this gives rise to several problems when trying to combine data between organizations.

There need to be some rules that govern the creation of the documents for them to be used by multiple business applications across the enterprise as well as outside it. Without these rules, another user or application could change the structure of the XML document. There also needs to be a mechanism that enforces the rules automatically, thereby preventing changes to the structure of the document and guaranteeing the structure of the data in the document.

Let's look at how you might design a solution for combining and merging catalog data, and also survey the techniques for guaranteeing the validity of sources of that data.

Design

So, a company may have data stored in a relational database or as XML documents. The data and documents may be static and unchanging over time or they may be dynamic, changing in real time as the business operates — making the task of combining and merging the data a moving target for the IT and business folks.

To get a handle on the problem, the business has to make a strategic decision on the design approach to working with the data from multiple sources. For this discussion, there are two terms to consider: the *big bang approach*, which is analogous to the scientific big bang theory about the origin of the universe, and the *wave approach*, which is similar to the waves in the ocean.

An integration project's business requirements may force the technology architects to have one big effort to integrate all technology processes, data, and documents before any new application development proceeds. That'd be the big bang. If a company chooses to integrate the data, documents, and processes in stages, it'd be using the wave approach. As you can see, the two terms are symbolic of how integration projects proceed.

The next section expand son these definitions and explores their implemented in practice.

Merging XML Data: Big Bang versus Wave Approach

When companies are acquired or merged, one of the business entities ceases to operate and all of the assets are taken over by the other business entity that continues to operate. In those cases, all assets, product inventories, and data of the acquired entity are static and unchanging and have to be merged into the assets, inventories, and data of the operating company. When companies partner with others, they do not own all the data but have to use whatever data is made available by their partners.

One-Shot Integration

The operating company has to initiate an integration project to perform the tasks of evaluating the data and making any necessary conversions to match the format and structure of its own data. In the big bang approach, changes to a given repository of data and documents are frozen. During the one-shot integration phase, the business continues to operate using copies of the repositories. The data needed for the combined repository has to be completely integrated before it can be used.

The integration is generally conducted at the level of the structured data in relational databases or at level of the XML data and documents. Regardless, it is a one-time project that could take a long time as all the assets and data are assimilated into the new systems and repositories. The data integration effort invariably occurs as part of a business process reengineering effort across the company.

The business does not stop operating during the integration project. Integration is commonly done on systems running parallel to those supporting the current business operations. Once the integration project is completed, the new system is used for the business operations and the old systems are termed legacy and eventually phased out and turned off. The end result of the project is data — either structured relational or XML — integrated and available for the operating business entities applications.

Staggered Integration

There is no massive one-time integration project and the business repositories do not have to be frozen to create the merged repositories in the wave approach. If the data is static, integration is staggered and occurs slowly over time. If the data is dynamic and changing in real time, it can be combined while the business system is running and by accessing the distributed data repositories.

A growing business constantly seeks to increase its market share by creating new partnerships and merging with or acquiring other companies. Thus, the integration of assets and data can be an ongoing process. The big bang approach — the one-shot integration strategy — does not work well in these companies because the business or partnerships are working together in real time to serve their customers. This means the business data is constantly changing and there will never be a point in time when the data can be declared frozen. In these situations, the company may choose a staggered process for combining business data.

As new data becomes available from partners or acquisitions, the company starts modifying the static data available or applying filters to transform the dynamic data so that it becomes compatible with the current active business applications. (Later in this chapter you look at additional details of the process and technologies that are used to modify data and those that are used for applying filters to transform data.)

To bring data from new business partners into your running applications, you need to create a framework that can be extended to access the new repositories. This is usually done using preconfigured data access points or service access points. The running business applications can be configured to accept the new data when it becomes available from these access points, thereby combining or merging data from multiple sources dynamically in real time.

Guaranteeing the Content from Each Source

Before you start merging, combining, or including data from a new source, you need to verify that the it is clean, valid, and compatible with the data from all sources. This holds true for structured relational data as well as XML data. Let's take a look at the design issues involved in verifying data of any format from all sources.

Validating Data from Relational Databases

A good feature of relational data is that the structure (schema) is fixed and does not change dynamically. Thus any XML application always knows the structure of the relational data with which it's working and can always expect to find the data in that format.

Chapter 8 demonstrated techniques to create XML documents using structured data from a relational database.

Database vendors use different data representation standards to store data. They also use different naming conventions to define data in schemas. Nevertheless, the set of data types — integers, floating point numbers, strings, Boolean, and so on — that can be modeled is not that large and most applications work with it.

For example, one winery describes a bottle of wine or the vintage using a specific set of attributes, while other wineries choose other sets of attributes. If the industry has not come up with a standardized set of attributes for its products, there will be as many different ways of representing the product as there are companies in that industry. If the applications are working with only one database engine, there is really no big issue because the application vendors will have mapped the application data representations with those of the database engine.

During the data integration effort, data analysts study the structure of the dataset from each repository and create validation criteria for the data models. Some of the well-designed source data repositories may have validation rules in place, while others may not. To maintain the integrity of the data in the merged repository, the database designers can create primary or foreign keys and place unique constraints on the columns in the database schema.

Problems do arise when trying to merge data from heterogeneous databases. If there is a failure as a result of a constraint violation during the data merge process, for example, the database analyst has to manually intervene and make necessary corrections before proceeding. This is not so much an issue in the wave approach, and you'll examine why this is the case in the next section. In the big bang approach, the data from all sources have to be merged into one big repository, which is then used as the universal repository by all business applications. The process can be time-consuming, but if done correctly, the quality and integrity of the final merged data can be guaranteed.

Validating XML Documents

To successfully support B2B (business-to-business) processes and electronic commerce, the company needs to guarantee the content of the XML documents it creates and uses for its operations. It is easy for someone to take an XML document and modify the structure to suit his specific needs. However, to work with a particular company's processes or applications, business partners should not be allowed to change the structure of the XML documents the company creates during the life of the application to guarantee the integrity of the data.

Because XML documents can be extended or modified as needed, the business document can undergo revisions and version upgrades from time to time. However, the current version of the business applications should continue to work with the particular version of an XML document that it was created for even if there are modified or newer versions of the document published by the document's owner. These newer versions could be created for use with a newer version of the application or for a future upgrade of the business process. To create and share XML documents effectively and guarantee the integrity of information contained, the documents must comply with some rules and standards with respect to the data they are modeling or encapsulating. Validation is how you guarantee the structure, markup, and element types of an XML document. XML schemas are one technique for validating an XML document.

XML Schema Languages

An XML Schema language defines the constraints on interpretation of an XML document's content. Validation is the process of testing if the XML instance document conforms to the rules set forth in the schema language. An XML Schema language can be viewed as a transformation that takes an XML document and produces a validation report.

There are several XML Schema languages available to validate an XML document, and new techniques are constantly being proposed in professional circles. The schema languages fall into categories or *families*, including:

- Document Type Definitions (DTD)
- W3C XML Schema
- RELAX NG

The following sections provide a brief overview of each family of validation languages.

You'll find detailed discussion and code samples of XML Schema languages in Chapters 2 and 3.

Document Type Definition (DTD)

A DTD is a set of rules that define what makes the given XML document valid. An application's XML parser validates the XML document against the rules specified in the DTD. The advantage of a DTD is that it is simple and easy to use; the disadvantage is that its language and structure are not XML. DTDs are not extensible and have limited capabilities. Some users find the DTD syntax to be confusing and difficult to understand. Additionally, they do not support namespaces, data types, or inheritance.

A DTD defines all the elements in an XML document. The rules specify the type of each element and identify both required and optional elements. A DTD specifies the number of times that a repeating element can occur in the document. If elements are nested, the order in which the nesting occurs is specified in the DTD.

The key point to remember is that a DTD is defined for a particular instance or set of related instances of documents and only validates those instances.

W3C XML Schema

An XML schema uses an XML format to define the rules governing the validation of instances of XML documents. You can use it to define the types of the data used in an XML document and to associate the elements of the XML document with namespaces. These are some of advantages of using XML Schema:

- You don't have to learn a new syntax to create these validation documents.
- They provide support for all the data types used in programming languages.
- They support user-defined data types.
- They are extensible.
- They are reusable.
- They support namespaces.

One of the drawbacks of the XML Schema is that it does not allow the definition of internal, external parsed or unparsed entities. You also cannot define notations in XML Schema.

Each company provides its own XML schema to validate its XML documents. A validating parser enforces the rules contained in the XML schema against the XML documents.

RELAX NG

RELAX NG, yet another XML Schema language, is based on RELAX (Regular Language description for XML) and TREX (Tree Regular Expressions for XML). The schema defines XML documents that match defined patterns of structure and content for the documents. The RELAX NG schema is written in XML syntax and supports namespaces.

The home page for RELAX NG is at `www.relaxng.org`, and you can find additional information on the XML Cover Pages web site at `http://xml.coverpages.org/relax-ng.html`.

Choosing Merge Points

All the stakeholders in a business integration effort — the business managers, business analysts, IT managers, IT architects and designers, IT developers, IT operations personnel, and IT maintenance engineers — have a vested interest in seeing the combined applications deliver the best performance and the most accurate results possible. To successfully merge and combine business operations, the merge points of the business partners or acquisitions have to be carefully chosen. A merge point is any point where the two business partners can integrate their data, applications, services, or business processes. There is no magic formula for choosing the merge points, and the final decision is made based on ease of integration, how long the project will take, and how costly it will be.

Now let's look at the most common design strategies for integrating businesses:

- Merging at the data layer
- Merging at the software application layer
- Merging at the service layer
- Merging at the business process layer

Merging at the Data Layer

The big bang (one-shot) integration strategy works only with static data sources, where the data from several data sources are frozen and merged to create a new repository that includes the data from each source.

If the solution is to merge at the data layer, a lot of work has to go into identifying the data from the sources and evaluating the quality of it before it can be combined. Validation rules in the database schema will guarantee data integrity of the new repository.

You examine the tools that are used for the data merging strategy in the "Solution" section of this chapter.

Merging at the Software Application Layer

There are several situations in which you cannot merge data at the data level. For example, some legacy systems use proprietary data formats for which there are no drivers available that interface with the newer applications like Java and C#. Companies have several thousand lines of legacy code that have used custom interfaces to extract the data for use in their legacy applications. In these cases, it's often easier to create an API (application programming interface) at the application level to share the proprietary legacy data that lies behind the application.

In the wave approach, described earlier in the chapter, dynamic data from business partners could not be frozen in time to allow for a big bang integration strategy. The applications for each business partner's systems are already interfacing with their own data repositories. For a host of reasons, including security and confidentiality, business partners don't always give open access to their private databases to each other. They do, however, create custom applications to expose the subset of their data needed to make the partnership successful — each partner defines and publishes an API that the others in the partnership can use for cross-application communication.

A custom application can then be written to combine the data from each API to the business systems and combine the results based on a set of predefined business rules. The result dataset can be made available to an application that will create an XML document.

In the case of data that is already in XML format, an application can be written to parse and validate each XML data source against a schema. After validation, the elements of the XML documents can be read in and combined to create a new document that integrates the relevant data from each source.

Merging at the Service Layer

There are many problems associated with combining business data at the application level. The running applications need access to the data, systems, and networks of the partners. This is not just a logistical nightmare for the IT operations manager; it also gives the IT security department sleepless nights. The entire murky world of firewalls, application gateways, routers, access control, and permissions gets proportionately more complicated when integration has to happen across business enterprises.

A trend that caught on in the mid- to late 1990s was to create applications that offered services to other applications at a published service endpoint. An application makes its data and other resources available to users and other applications on the network. This is called Service-Oriented Architecture (SOA). A mandatory requirement is connectivity and uptime for this strategy to work.

There are many technologies and standards for SOA; however, the one that has gained popularity over the last couple years is web services. Web services provides standardized ways to publish service end-points over well-known ports for access by any other application that uses the same standards. Many intranet applications can leverage web services or a host of other SOA strategies to integrate and combine data, documents, information, and processes.

The falling costs of setting up network access to the Internet has made it feasible for companies of all sizes to deploy the infrastructure that supports SOA and web services for public access.

Chapters 11 and 12 provide in-depth explanations of producing and using web services.

Merging at the Business Process Layer

Over the past few years, there has been a demand for a different method of integrating and combining businesses because it isn't always convenient or accurate to integrate all businesses at the data, application, or service level. To automate and optimize the function of businesses with their partners, it becomes necessary to merge and integrate companies at a higher level.

Chapter 14 explores the issues involved in integrating intercompany and intracompany processes using XML-based technologies.

Sol

n of the strategies discussed in this chapter. The following sections

n good strategy when the data from all sources is frozen in
luated and validated to verify that it can be integrated into a
cess the data from multiple sources and integrate them in

e. ations for each of the three stages of the ETL process. The
m. ransform, and load processes can be automated or run
tha e of the ETL process creates a temporary data repository
data xt stage. SQL applications can read and transform the
done is a time-consuming process, and if the data verification is

If merg ining data is an ongoing need within a company, it may be best to use one of the commer tools available. The leading database vendors such as IBM, Microsoft, and Oracle all offer ETL tools. The technologies are established on the standards for data extraction based on JDBC (Java Database Connectivity), Microsoft Open Database Connectivity, or custom applications for SQL extraction.

Third-party vendors also offer software ETL tools. Listing all of them and discussing their individual features is out of the scope of this chapter, but a search on the Internet will provide an exhaustive list of these vendors and tools.

Application Integration

Combining information by integrating data at the application layer is easier said than done. Business applications can be written in many different software languages, each of which has its own standards for representing data at the application level, its own naming conventions for parameters, and its own mechanisms for invoking functions within the applications.

A code review analysis of the custom-developed software assets of most companies will highlight the challenges of integrating applications written in the same programming language. The complexity of integrating across programming languages is an order of magnitude greater. Using application connectors can solve the problem.

The Power of Application Connectors

To ease the burden and problems of integrating data at the application level, vendors have come out with connectors for specific applications. There are also frameworks available for creating custom connectors between business applications from various vendors. Vendors of database drivers publish a well-known API that an application can use to access database resources. Connectors are analogous to database drivers in that they use a published API that allows applications to connect to each other and use each other's resources.

.NET and ASP applications can be integrated using connectors provided by Microsoft. Third-party vendors also provide connectors for specific business applications running within the .NET Framework. These are sometimes called COM connectors because they use the Microsoft Component Object Model architecture.

Enterprise Java applications can be developed using the J2EE Connector Architecture (JCA) of the J2EE (Java Enterprise Edition) framework. Java applications can use the standardized API that addresses the problems of connectivity between enterprise application servers.

A detailed discussion of COM, JCA, or the connector architecture frameworks is beyond the scope of this book, and a list of specific products is not provided. A search on the Internet brings up several good resources that provide the most current information and can guide you in your selection of the appropriate technologies to fit your needs.

Application Integration Strategies

Based on the requirements for an integration project, the IT architects and software designers decide on the best strategy for implementation. This includes decisions about commercial off-the-shelf (COTS) products, application servers, and hardware and software to meet the technology needs.

They also must determine whether to develop a custom application or buy a commercial application. The final decision depends on the results of a comparative evaluation of the requirements against the features of the commercial applications available.

Custom Applications

More often than not, IT architects and designers decide that commercial business applications do not meet all the unique needs of their business operations. Creating custom business applications for integrating is expensive and time-consuming. The decision is never an easy one for the stakeholders to make.

The availability of connectors to interface with different applications has made it easier to create applications that integrate with other applications. Occasionally, there may be no connectors available for legacy applications. In that case, the application integration effort will include creating custom connectors to those applications.

If the company chooses custom application development for integration, care should be taken in developing the integration points by creating standardized APIs. These help in software maintenance and future enhancement projects. If the project is a one-shot integration effort, the rollout of the application into production signifies a successful integration effort. If the company anticipates a staggered integration of applications, standardized APIs make the process a lot easier.

Enterprise Resource Planning

The goals of Enterprise Resource Planning (ERP) are to create one business application system that integrates all business units, applications, and business functions across the enterprise. At a high level, ERP systems seek to eliminate the data islands that were created to serve specific business functions in companies.

For example a company may have dedicated applications for finance and accounting, sales and marketing, human resources, manufacturing, and logistics. In many companies, the data that back those systems sit in isolation and cannot be shared with other applications that need the data. Some companies duplicate the data and save it on systems that need it. This keeps operations running, but it creates the problem of maintaining data integrity across the enterprise.

The ERP system is an integrated software solution that a business purchases and deploys. ERP systems have individual modules for each business function. The entire business system shares a data repository. The application modules comply with open API standards and can invoke functions on each other. This allows the applications to integrate and share information at the application level. When a company migrates to an ERP solution, the islands of data can be integrated using the big bang approach using the ETL processes. All new data generated with the running ERP system will reside in the new repository. The challenge of using an ERP solution arises when legacy data cannot be easily converted. In this case, the ERP system will have to depend on application connectors to integrate with the legacy applications at the application layer.

ERP is an expensive and time-consuming strategy for integrating applications. A few companies have achieved success in deploying commercial ERP systems and several others have effectively created their own custom ERP solutions. A discussion of specific ERP solutions is beyond the scope of this book. You can find several good resources on the Internet that describe the technologies available.

Enterprise Application Integration

Most companies have invested a lot of capital in business systems and applications, and, of course, what was once contemporary (new) is now classified as legacy (old). However, that doesn't mean that the applications and systems and data do not add value and are not critical for the business operations. For either financial or tactical reasons, the company may not want to strip out all of its systems and try to implement one big business system that performs all the functions of the disparate applications.

Enterprise Application Integration (EAI) is defined as the methods, tools, and plans for integrating and coordinating the distributed computing resources in a business. The final goal is to create an integrated view of all business resources and allow them to be used in e-commerce and e-business strategies.

The EAI strategy has been gaining momentum over the past couple years as a feasible approach to integrating heterogeneous enterprise applications. The strategy allows the company to reuse all its legacy resources while providing a migration path for adding newer applications to enable electronic commerce and business over the Internet.

The core approach of EAI is to create or deploy flexible middleware solutions based on message-oriented middleware (MOM) architecture. Application integration may be achieved using asynchronous message queues. EAI draws on the features and strengths of using XML as the data representation standard. There are several commercial and open source EAI solutions available and a search of the Internet provides some excellent resources.

A message queue is a special software application that enables the communication between applications, services, and processes. Data and control is sent between the two parties in the form of messages. In asynchronous messaging, the sender and receiver of the message need not be connected at the same time waiting for the messages. The message queuing mechanism saves the messages until they are consumed. Commercial implementations of message queues are called message-oriented middleware (MOM). IBM, Oracle, Microsoft, and JBoss provide message queue implementations.

Service-Oriented Architecture

When a company implements a service-oriented architecture (SOA) application, the goal is to publish an endpoint (API) for a public service. The published service utilizes resources such as data and applications within the business to benefit their customers and partners.

Application development frameworks such as .NET and J2EE provide the tools needed to create robust SOA solutions. Third-party vendors have used those tools to provide commercial SOA applications.

SOA is not a new concept; it's been implemented in companies for a very long time. The next few sections briefly look at the various technologies available for implementing SOA.

Distributed Component Object Model

The Distributed Component Object Model (DCOM) is Microsoft's solution for extending its Component Object Model (COM). The framework defines the standards for creating a set of published interfaces that allow applications to request DCOM services from each other across the network.

The older ASP development environment leverages DCOM for creating SOA applications.

.NET Remoting

DCOM uses a proprietary protocol and only supports communications between Microsoft applications running on the same server or on servers with the Microsoft operating system in a networked environment. .NET Remoting allows interprocess communications between .NET objects running on machines in a connected network (intranet or Internet). It supports several different communications protocols.

You can find a wealth of information on this topic on the Microsoft Developers Network at `http://msdn.microsoft.com`.

Java Remote Method Invocation (RMI)

Sun Microsystems provides the Java Remote Method Invocation (RMI), an API and toolset for creating custom distributed applications using the Java programming language. In this strategy, the business objects provide services to each other via published interfaces.

There are several third-party applications based on Java RMI that are used to provide SOA services to other applications and users.

Common Object Request Broker Architecture (CORBA)

DCOM and Java RMI are vendor- and programming language–specific and are not suitable for use in a heterogeneous environment. Common Object Request Broker Architecture (CORBA) is an open framework that is independent of the programming language and the systems on which the applications run.

Applications use an Object Request Broker (ORB) and Internet Inter-ORB Protocol (IIOP), a standard protocol, to communicate with each other. The ORB is designed for specific applications and operating systems.

The Object Management Group (OMG) specifies the standards that define the interoperability of applications. CORBA is one of the standards and specifications for middleware architecture.

Some companies have developed their own custom CORBA applications that integrate with other CORBA-based programs. Third-party vendors have created robust enterprise applications based on CORBA. A few of the EAI solutions use CORBA as the middleware architecture for integrating applications across the company.

Web Services

Web services has been gaining in popularity as a SOA solution for both the intranet and the Internet. Companies can easily create and publish web services, which expose business functions for their business partners to integrate with.

Chapters 11 and 12 provide an excellent study of web services strategies, including examples of applications that consume web services and a roadmap for creating and publishing web services.

Content Integration

There is one more layer at which you can integrate, made possible by the popularity of portals and content management systems (CMS). Content can be defined as value-added data and may include graphics, audio, video, text, and images. Portals and CMSs are two different technologies, however, both can be used to integrate and manage content.

Portals are web applications that incorporate many back-end business and content applications to provide services to customers. They offer an integrated view of the businesses resources and services and are useful for the end customer. External applications cannot use the portal interface in its entirety. A web page that aggregates content is the interface to the portal. Other applications can use specific services within the portal.

Portals are made up of components called *portlets* that use XML languages to create content. A web portal is useful for dynamically integrating and aggregating data. XML catalogs can be combined from various back-end sources in real time and presented to the customer in the web portal.

The portal is designed to use the services of distributed applications, other middleware applications, and external services. It not only integrates applications but can also perform the functions of a content management system. CMSs are used to organize content, which is invariably in an XML format. Documents are created and managed within these systems. CMS can also perform the tasks of aggregation and integration of content.

XML content does not have to be integrated using the big bang approach. If the content is available only during runtime, it can be acquired and combined in real time. The following are two features that most CMS should have to combine XML documents dynamically. Cocoon, a project from the Apache Foundation, is an example of a content management system that has leveraged these two features.

Pipeline Architecture

The CMS is made up of discrete stages that work on specific tasks in the processing of an XML document. One stage acquires the document and performs the validation steps. The parsed data is sent to the next stage, which may aggregate the content, integrating structured data from relational data sources. There may be many stages for transforming the XML data before it is sent to the final stage, which prepares the output to be consumed by some target application such as a web browser, cell phone, PDA, or another XML CMS.

Dynamic Transformations

Static transformations are useful for creating output to a predetermined consumer. However, if the consumer application is not known until runtime, the output XML documents cannot be precreated because of the dynamic data.

Dynamic transformations achieved in Cocoon and other CMS applications can help solve this problem. Because the consumer application is not determined until runtime, the transformations are triggered based on the selection when the client application makes a request to the CMS. Within the CMS, one or more of the stages can apply predefined transformations on the XML data as it moves down the pipeline. The final stage transforms the output data to a format suitable for the consumer application.

Summary

This chapter examined the problem of combining and merging data and XML documents. Quality and integrity of the data in each source are the factors that determine the success of the integration efforts. ETL (Extract, Transform, and Load) describes processes as well as a category of tools that help merge relational data from heterogeneous sources.

You explored two strategies for combining data and XML documents: the big bang and wave approaches. And you learned that you can choose to validate an XML document either using a DTD or an XML schema.

IT architects and software designers have four choices for the layer at which to combine data: data, application, service, or business process. Each has advantages and disadvantages.

Everything discussed in this chapter sets the stage for the final chapter in which you investigate the latest trend of combining and integrating companies: integrating at the business process layer.

14

Integrating and Automating Business Processes

Throughout this book, your winery has been used to demonstrate techniques for real-world applications of XML. You've explored methods for merging and searching data in the winery catalog, (which advanced the business case for standardizing the company's data representation using XML) and seen how XML from one system could be transformed into some other XML schema for use by a different business application.

It's clear that access to dynamic data enables a company to create a viable and powerful B2C (business-to-customer) presence on the World Wide Web. The new marketing channel allows the company to increase sales by targeting a new segment of consumers, thus increase revenues and the company's bottom line. You expanded on the business case by using applications to leverage dynamic information provided by external applications using web services, and saw the winery lay the foundations for a B2B strategy by providing timely information and dynamic data to external consumers using web services.

During the life of the winery — and this holds true for any business in any industry or sector — the company executives may decide to increase its market share by merging with or acquiring other companies in the industry. This process is often very tumultuous and costly as business managers and information technology managers struggle to cope with the challenges of merging their processes, applications, and data with those of the newly acquired business entities. You've already explored some strategies to tackle the challenges of merging data between businesses.

To complete a well-rounded study of XML at work, though, you need to look at how XML can be used to integrate and automate business processes between a company and its partners. XML can define business documents and collaborative workflows; enable the synchronization of business functions across business enterprises, heterogeneous systems, and business applications; and serve as the glue to merging the operations and disparate technologies of business partners and vendors.

This chapter examines issues of significance to both business analysts and technical architects, focusing on the critical issues of integrating and automating business processes. There are many good vendor solutions in the market; some of these are proprietary solutions, while others are based on standards. The standards themselves are evolving and many of the vendors have active representation in the standards organizations to help incorporate the best practices in the industry.

This chapter provides an overview of the strategies and best practices for process integration. It doesn't attempt to implement any code to demonstrate concepts for the simple reason that code needs an application server to run in and we want to stay vendor- and standard-neutral. This strategy is not out of a fear of offending any one vendor by omitting it from the list but out of the practical need to keep the discussion focused at a higher level and on the strategic role of XML in process integration.

Problem

Globalization and the global economy have been a mixed blessing to businesses. On one hand, companies have access to wider markets and consumer segments; on the other hand, they now have to face more competitors in the market, some of whom have a local advantage. The companies with that advantage have to stay ahead of the curve by improving their internal business operations and keeping costs low so that they can produce their goods more efficiently and compete more effectively.

Over the past few decades, there has been a lot of research conducted on how a company can achieve success in business. The universal agreement among the experts is that technology is a very powerful factor in enabling businesses to become more efficient. Companies have access to state-of-the-art applications that allow managers to effectively monitor and control their internal operations, which increase operational efficiency and reduce operating costs.

Lack of interconnectivity is a major barrier to companies integrating their systems. For years now, most companies have had a fairly efficient internal network to connect all their systems, applications, and databases, although business partners were forced to deploy very expensive virtual private networks (VPNs) or point-to-point network connections to connect partner systems. Ever since the Internet became available for use by private enterprise and individuals, the connectivity problem has been effectively solved. Network providers are addressing various associated issues such as reliability, performance, and security, and those factors won't prevent a company from using the Internet to work with its partners.

Low-Tech Success

It is important to note that there are many small to medium-sized businesses that have always been very profitable and efficient without relying on high-technology solutions. There are scores of family-owned businesses that rely on the skills and business acumen of a few individuals who are the sole driving force behind the business operations. They have every business trick stored in their head with minimal reliance on business systems. The only applications they rely on are accounting systems for regulatory reporting needs and only because they are forced to do so by their accountants. These managers know how to streamline the production line, purchasing, and their vendor and supplier relationships to maximize profits and achieve business success. They are happy, their businesses are flourishing, and we wish them continued success. There's no need to focus on their operations or conduct a case study on their techniques or speculate about how they can achieve the scale needed to compete and grow in the global economy.

The Value Proposition of Partnerships

A long time ago, merchants and traders realized that they could not execute all aspects of their business on their own and had to learn to work with partners. Each entrepreneur focused on a small niche product or service and learned to work effectively with other entrepreneurs who provided complimentary skills and products. They created rules for working with each other efficiently, thereby ensuring their mutual success.

The wisdom gained from studying successful entrepreneurs through the ages has special significance to the companies that are trying to stay one step ahead of their competition in the current age.

Both global and local companies can achieve greater success by focusing on their core business functions and creating partnerships with their suppliers and consumers. The core functions of all the partners should work together smoothly and efficiently as they together create value for the consumer.

There are, of course, many small and medium-sized businesses that do not spend time or money creating business partnerships with the organizations in their value chain. Some maintain tight control of their sales and distribution strategies by hosting the operations in-house. For some of these companies, the relationships with their suppliers are usually ad hoc, which gives them the flexibility to change their vendors easily and quickly.

For most businesses, however, all evidence points to their becoming more profitable by creating partnerships and working efficiently with their partners. They can also gain a competitive advantage by leveraging technology to achieve their business goals. Partnerships imply a trust relationship between trading partners; a lot of care and planning should go into creating these relationships to guarantee the success of all partners.

Many management philosophies have evolved to address the issues of partnering, and a discussion of these are beyond the scope of this book. A search on the web will bring up some very good references that explore all aspects of business partnerships.

The Challenges of Integrating Data and Systems

Business applications have been the driving force behind the proficient operations of many companies. Most of the best applications were streamlined to effectively deal with a single business operation. Software vendors or in-house IT departments provided efficient applications for specific business operations such as finance, procurement, sales, and manufacturing. Each application invariably created and maintained its own data repository. These applications were referred to as *silo applications*, because they worked in isolation and it was difficult, although not impossible, to access the application from outside the functional department that owned and operated them. It is a huge, costly challenge to get these systems to integrate and work seamlessly with other applications within the organization or with the systems and applications of business partners.

One solution is to integrate at the data layer. This is an even bigger challenge because it isn't always easy to integrate the data formats from each database vendor. In Chapter 9, you saw XML used to effectively solve the problem of merging data formats. An XML schema can be created for integrating with relational data for each data repository. An application has access to the framework and can execute queries on several merged XML documents representing data from different sources.

Business applications evolved to meet the growing demands of a fast-paced global marketplace. Standards like XML for representation of business data and documents have helped spur the evolution of business applications and frameworks. Applications have become more sophisticated, and the analysts and architects have more choices than just data integration for merging businesses. The next few sections briefly discuss four significant business integration strategies that spurred the evolution of business applications and frameworks:

- Electronic Data Interchange (EDI)
- Enterprise Resource Planning (ERP)
- Enterprise Application Integration (EAI)
- Business Process Integration and Workflow

Electronic Data Interchange

Electronic Data Interchange (EDI) has been around since the late 1960s and is one of the earliest standards for businesses to conduct electronic commerce. It defines a set of business documents using mutually standardized notations. Trading partners are connected using the EDI network and exchange EDI documents via their mailboxes on the network. Very few business applications can use EDI documents directly; specialized applications are needed to bridge between systems. Translator software modules convert the EDI document to the company's format for that particular business document. The translator also converts the company data into the appropriate EDI document, which is delivered to the business partner's mailbox.

Companies have to pay for connecting to the proprietary EDI network, maintaining a mailbox as well as incur a per-document charge for using the network. EDI-enabling a business is very expensive, and only large companies can afford to implement this strategy. Many companies have been successful using this strategy to work with business partners. XML, the Internet, and the World Wide Web are reshaping the direction of EDI and making it more affordable for smaller businesses to use its technologies to work with partners.

Enterprise Resource Planning

Another popular strategy is the use of large Enterprise Resource Planning (ERP) systems that integrate modules for the most common business functions. The modules have to be customized to work with each business's processes.

ERP systems share common data repositories and avoid the problem of data integration. These are a good solution for most large manufacturing and sales organizations, but very few companies can successfully implement the strategy. ERP systems are very expensive, and the outlay for customizing and deploying them in an enterprise is formidable. Small vendors and suppliers cannot justify the expenditure and effort needed to implement an ERP system.

ERP systems help companies take control of their data and systems. XML plays an important role in the standardization of data representations and allows tighter integration between modules. Using XML to represent data also provides an added benefit when business partners want to integrate their ERP systems across the Internet.

Enterprise Application Integration

Enterprise Application Integration (EAI) involves the creation or deployment of a middleware application that integrates other business applications, databases, and legacy systems within an enterprise.

With EAI, the middleware application uses application connectors and asynchronous messaging frameworks to form a bridge between the various applications. EAI depends on message queues in the middleware applications that use messages for passing data and control information between the systems. Using XML to represent the data and control information within a message is critical for integrating disparate business applications and data repositories. This, too, is a costly strategy with a sizeable amount of custom code generation needed to effectively integrate the systems.

The relatively low Internet connectivity costs have made it possible for companies of all sizes to create a B2C presence on the World Wide Web and connect to the B2B arena. However, it has not solved the problem of integration between business partners. Not all partners can afford to deploy the same solutions. Heterogeneous systems, applications, and data are the reality of doing business in this day and age, and no company can dictate what systems their partners must deploy or use. Small vendors and distribution channels may have streamlined systems that are tailored to their operations. Integration can be achieved by creating custom connectors for each partner but this may not be financially feasible for every company. Integration at the data level may not be an option because very few partners will provide open access to their data. Using XML as the standard for data representation and intersystem communications also supports integration with the systems of business partners across the Internet.

A search on the Internet will provide a comprehensive list of the popular ERP and EAI systems on the market. Over the past few years, research has focused on workflows and business processes. The new breeds of technology solutions revolve around integrating businesses at the process or workflow, concepts explored in the following section.

Business Process Integration and Workflow

Dr. Michael Hammer defines a process as:

An organized group of related activities that together create a result of value to the customers.

Dr. Michael Hammer is a management consultant and president of Hammer and Company. He is the author of three books, and coauthor of the bestseller Reengineering the Corporation (Revised and Updated Edition, 2004, Collins; ISBN 0060559535).

That definition highlights some of the characteristics of processes. A process is a group of activities and all activities working together help create value. Activities are related and organized. They are interconnected and performed in sequence. A stream of activities produces the desired outcome, which is a common goal. Activities are aligned around a purpose, and the process results in value to the customers.

A *business process* is a function or set of functions within an organization that helps successfully deliver a product or service to the customer. The customer may be an end consumer in a B2C relationship or another company in a B2B relationship; the latter takes the input and adds additional value for its customers.

Organization structures vary widely across industries, yet they all perform similar business processes, typically:

- Finance
- Human resources
- Logistics
- Procurement
- Quality assurance
- Sales
- Marketing
- Manufacturing
- Engineering

Many other business processes support these core business functions, and the support processes can be set or improved by benchmarking against industry leaders. Effective communication between business partners is critical for the success of the partnership. This includes communication of data, information, and people. An effective integration strategy should include processes and technologies that support all three types of communications.

Workflow is the flow of work between people and the departments within an organization or across organizations. It deals with the routing and approval processes for business documents. A business activity may be triggered by a business document, or a business document may be created to signify the end of an activity. This is why business workflow is routinely associated with business document processing.

Workflow Engines

Workflow engines are information systems that manage and monitor the flow of documents and stages of approval in an organization. They generally:

- Provide the functions to define and track documents in the approval pipeline
- Automate a range of tasks in the approval process and route to the right people at the right time
- Have a mailbox capability that notifies users of pending work

Managers and supervisors can create and route approvals as well as observe the status of an approval at any time. Workflow engines support automation of the approval process but also allow for manual intervention for customized tasks. The finance department of a company has many functions and accounts payable (AP) is the favorite of all vendors because that is how they get paid for their products and services. Within each business function, a company may have a specific process to execute tasks. The check approval process within the AP function of the finance department is one example of a business workflow.

Custom Solutions and Vendor-Based Proprietary Systems

Software vendors created powerful workflow engines for a long time. Earlier on in the chapter we covered the evolution of business systems from the simple accounting software packages to the ERP systems and finally the EAI middleware solutions for integrating business processes. These systems were very successful in integrating internal applications. Some of these solutions were very successful at achieving automation of the internal business processes and workflow. However they could not be integrated with disparate systems and data formats. The proprietary data formats and messaging solutions used to integrate systems within an enterprise do not do very well in integrating across business enterprises.

Business Process Integration

A typical interaction between business partners involves several different business processes within many business functions. For example, order processing, customer management, inventory tracking, shipping, invoice generation, order fulfillment, and accounts payable. Each process may be supported or enabled by one or more business systems. For the smooth functioning of the business, all the processes must work in synchrony with no disruptions.

Critical data from one stage in a particular process may be needed by another stage in an entirely different system. Automatic sharing of the data is preferred because manual data entry is prone to errors. The processes should be integrated so that the work flows between systems and organizations seamlessly. Tighter integration between the systems allows the processes to be automated.

To integrate custom applications, each system has the interactions coded in a sequence corresponding to the steps of the business process. The data generated by that sequence of steps is saved along with the state of the process. The next sequence in another system is invoked and the process continues. The data and state of the previous system is available because the systems use a common repository and there is strict control of the data formats. Complex business functions are long running, so failure in one subfunction requires a rollback to the state in previous stages. Once corrections are made, the process needs to be rerun.

Using software components to model business process is cumbersome. Because subfunctions are hardcoded, it becomes a change and maintenance problem if the business process changes. For example, marketing strategies and pricing may be amended frequently, and tax laws are subject to change often.

Workflow engines have steps that map to the steps of a business process. They also have connectors to the business system driving the processes.

There is another category of software called *rule engines*, which can be used as standalone systems or to drive workflow engines. These text-based rules engines manage business rules and are effective for some processes, but managers often use experience rather than documented business rules to make business decisions. These cannot be modeled in any text-based rule or coded in software components.

Design

You now have a clear picture of the problems facing most organizations as they try to find ways to work together with their business partners. The organization and partners must commit to changing their processes and creating the environment for integration. This means building a trust relationship, overcoming cultural obstacles, and changing their organizational structures. Once the commitment is made, the organizations can follow standard roadmaps to create and implement new processes.

Business Process Reengineering

To stay competitive, organizations constantly strive to improve their processes. The continuous improvement model is used to get a detailed understanding of the current process while generating metrics that describe the effectiveness of the process. As a result, you can identify areas for improvement, make iterative changes, rerun the process, gather new metrics, and continue the improvement cycle.

Another way to change process is to use the Business Process Reengineering (BPR) approach. If an organization does not have the time to make incremental changes, it may choose to make rapid, often dramatic changes to its processes. BPR assumes that the current process is broken and can be discarded, and the organization can start out fresh defining a new process. The organization defines a scope and objectives for the reengineering, benchmarks other organizations that excel in the same process, and creates an ideal "to-be" process (how the process will work after reengineering) for the organization. Analyzing the gap between the current and ideal structures leads to a plan to transition the organization to the new state. The plan includes changes to the organization structure, removing cultural obstacles, educating employees on the new culture, retiring legacy systems and applications, deploying state-of-the-art systems, and training employees on the new systems. The final step is implementing the plan.

An organization can choose which approach to follow based on its current state. For example, some businesses jumped on the Internet bandwagon immediately, modifying processes and deploying the technology to support some level of e-commerce. They subsequently floundered because of a lack of clear direction in the industry and lack of standards based tools. These organizations can employ the techniques of continuous improvement to gradually move them toward true business process integration.

Some companies held back and did not jump of the Internet wagon. These organizations must make drastic changes in their processes to integrate their workflows with their supply chains. BPR can help those companies made rapid changes.

Business Process Management (BPM) are the activities that a business manager performs, including monitoring and optimizing business processes or adapting them to new business needs. BPM is also a synonym for the set of tools that support business managers' activities. A clear understanding of the business manager is essential to changing or streamlining business processes.

Patterns for Business Process Integration

Patterns are models that are created by observing recurring solutions to known problems in the real world. Patterns are widely used in software design and integration. Business integration patterns are similar in that they have evolved from standard solutions for integration problems. These can be used as templates for creating solutions for certain business integration scenarios.

Here are three common business integration patterns:

- **Application to application** — Defines the interaction between the systems of two trading partners in a supply chain.
- **Data exchange** — Requires a common data format to be defined. XML is the logical choice for a universal data format.
- **B2B process integration** — Uses XML-based messages to manage processes. This pattern is shaping the standards and protocols that define business transactions.

A detailed discussion of all the business integration patterns is beyond the scope of this book. A search on the web turns up several very good references that can help increase your understanding of using patterns in the redesign of your business processes.

Leveraging Technology for Process Integration

XML has been thrust into the forefront for data representation in application integration scenarios because it can hide the actual data representation used by each system. XML is also used to represent business documents and even the EDI standard has changed to use XML representations of its document formats. XML enables SOA (Service-Oriented Architecture), which is a collection of services. Systems interact using service calls and communication is achieved by passing messages.

As discussed in Chapter 12, web services are software systems that support communications between systems using messages. SOAP (the protocol for communications), WSDL (the interface definition), and UDDI (a directory protocol) are all based on XML.

The next generation of software solutions needs to support the definition and execution of collaborative workflows and business transactions that can cross the organization's data, network, system, and application boundaries and integrate disparate applications across enterprises.

Business Process Management Systems (BPMS)

Business managers need to constantly monitor business operations and optimize processes or change them to meet new business needs. These tasks are called *business process management*, and the category of software tools and systems that help a manager perform these tasks is called business process management systems (BPMS).

BPMS build on the functions of workflow systems and allow for direct execution of processes. They do not fall under the category of rules-based engines and do not need text-based rules to be defined. They do not need custom software modules to be developed for each task. Commercial BPMS software focuses on graphical process model development rather than text-based business rules.

Business process modeling is done in a graphical user interface (GUI). BPMS incorporates process modeling software with graphical views for modeling business processes. Business rules are auto-generated from the GUI icons in the model.

All BPMS support three basic process functions:

- Definition
- Execution
- Monitoring

BPMS eliminate the need for costly and long software development cycles. They allow for the direct execution of business processes and use services in applications or send messages to humans to perform nonautomated tasks.

The GUI enables managers to monitor the execution in real time and access metrics to analyze the performance of a process that is running so that they can tweak the process or make complete changes as the need arises.

XML Standards for BPMS

There are various standards and protocols to be used in process and workflow integration. Following is a brief description of the major ones:

- **Business Process Modeling Notation (BPMN)**—Enables managers, analysts, and technical architects to describe business processes using a universal scheme. It is the bridge between defining the business models and the execution of the models. It also can also be used to generate execution modules from the diagram notations.
- **Web Services Business Process Execution Language (WS-BPEL)**—Describes business processes and uses web services (SOAP/XML) for message passing.
- **XML Process Definition Language (XPDL)**—A standard proposed by the Workflow Management Coalition (WfMC), a nonprofit organization dedicated to creating standards for workflow products to interoperate.
- **Web Services-Choreography Definition Language (WS-CDL)**—Creates a framework to define collaborations between peers as well as message passing for execution of processes. Based on XML.
- **XML/EDI**—Creates XML formats for defining standard EDI (Electronic Data Interchange) documents.
- **BizTalk**—BizTalk is the name given to the collective set of tools, framework, and server that are at the heart of Microsoft's business integration strategy. BizTalk uses XML to enable communications and integration of applications and has widespread backing from companies and vendors all over the world.
- **RosettaNet**—A nonprofit consortium of companies that have banded together to define standards for the management of the supply chain and distribution processes and efficient techniques for collaborative commerce among organizations of various sizes.

Most commercial vendors support one or more of these standards and protocols, and this allows applications on different systems to be easily integrated as long as XML is used as the format for data representation and message passing. There is a lot of rapid change taking place in the area of standards and protocols. There is also a lot of merging and consolidation of standards. Newer proposals will supersede some of the names on this list, and a detailed discussion of each is beyond the scope of this chapter. You can find the most current information on each of the standards and protocols on the web.

Solution

How can business process and workflow integration help the streamline the operations of the winery? Let's examine the winery's operations and discuss how integration and automation can help the business to more efficient and profitable.

Remember, the winery solution cannot be a one-size-fits-all answer, so it may not be relevant to other organizations or industries.

The Winery Operations

Figure 14-1 shows a high-level flow chart of the wine production process. The size of a winemaking business can vary from a small home-based operation to a large winery, but they all follow some basic steps in the manufacturing process.

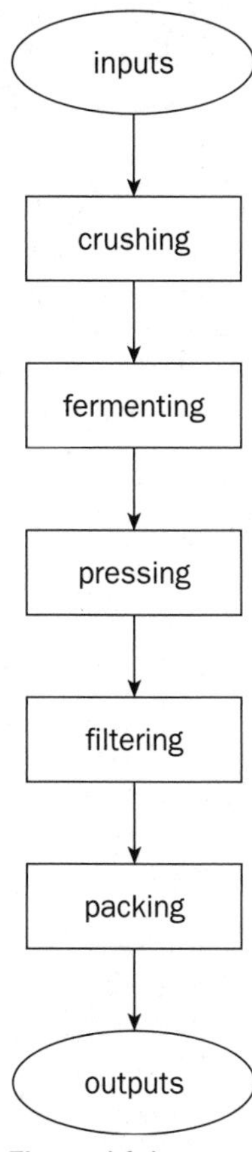

Figure 14-1

Good-quality grapes are the most essential input to the wine production process. Some winemakers may start with grape juice but most of the wineries control the quality of the finished product by starting with the fruit. Not all winemakers grow their own grapes; their production begins with the purchase of the fruit from vendors. Several wineries maintain tighter control on the finished product by owning the growing process. (The study of vine cultivation is called viticulture, a very complicated process that will not be part of this discussion.) Those wineries control their own vineyards, carefully select premium quality vines, and maintain strict controls on the cultivation of the grapes. The growing process becomes an integral part of the manufacturing process.

For this chapter's project, begin your study at the point the grapes arrive at the winery. Vinification is the process of converting the fruit to wine. There are minor variations in the process for the production of white, red, sparkling, and fortified wines, but all you need to do here is focus on the basic steps, which are common to all winemakers.

Oenology (enology in the United States) is the study of wine and winemaking. The name is derived from the Greek *oenos* (wine) and *-logos* (one who deals with).

The process starts with the setup stage in which all equipment is cleaned, pretreated, and sanitized with special chemicals. Ripe grapes from the vineyard are transported to the winery where they are cleaned, destemmed, and crushed. The output of this step is called must, which is pumped into fermentation tanks where yeast culture is added to start the fermentation process in which the sugars in the juice are converted to alcohol. After fermentation the mixture is sent to a wine press where the juice is separated from the residue and unused yeast. The wine is then transferred to storage tanks or oak barrels for aging. The length of the aging process varies for different varieties of wine. Filtration is an optional step in the process where sediment is removed form the juice before the bottling of the finished product.

Basically, the inputs required for the production process include:

- Grapes
- Chemicals to sanitize the equipment
- Special varieties of yeast cultures for the fermentation
- Oak barrels for aging
- Special filters for filtration
- Packaging materials

Oak barrels are critical elements in the production process with a limited life span and have to be changed frequently. They are not considered fixed equipment and have been included as inputs to the process like any of the materials essential to keep the production process running smoothly.

The Supply Chain

Wine production is a seasonal activity and is not driven by customer orders. To be successful, the winery has to listen to customer needs, and adjust the selection and production of certain varieties of wines accordingly. The production process itself begins and ends on a predetermined schedule and is not affected by customer demands. The duration of the production process is fixed and cannot be altered without affecting the quality of the product.

Procurement

The production process begins a long time before the end of the harvest season and is often a year-round process. The winemaker keeps tabs on weather and soil conditions, and makes a best guess at how the harvest will affect the next production cycle in terms of quantity. The master winemaker begins selecting the quality of the fruit and deciding the type of product it will go into as part of the production planning process. Before production starts, the winery has to ensure that all equipment is working and that there are adequate stocks of raw materials, supplies, and equipment for each stage of production process.

In a nonautomated business, the production staff is responsible for keeping track of the materials and supplies needed for a production run. If any of the essential materials are in short supply, the staff contacts the procurement department, which initiates the manual process of buying the supplies. After choosing a vendor and negotiating the quantity and price, a purchase order is generated and sent to the vendor. The vendor receives the purchase order and hopefully till has adequate stock to fill the request. The product is shipped, and the winery updates its supply inventory to indicate the new materials. The supplier also creates an invoice and sends it to the winery finance department, which starts the check approval process, after which the winery pays the supplier for the materials sent.

The manual procurement process is labor intensive, prone to human error, and very time-consuming. After studying the processes of all partners and implementing suitable process reengineering, you determine that the winery can create better business relationships with its suppliers and vendors. As part of the partnership, all partners (winery, suppliers, and vendors) can choose to deploy technologies that allow their business systems and processes to be integrated. By tightly integrating and automating the supply chain, all partners can become more efficient and see marked improvements in their processes, resulting in cost savings and increased profitability to all the participants.

Here is a possible scenario for the automated procurement process:

1. The winery's materials tracking system detects a shortage of a particular essential input for the production process.
2. The materials system sends an XML message to the integrated procurement system indicating a need for a specific quantity of that item.
3. The procurement system accepts the request and sends an XML message that queries the sales catalog system.
4. The supplier's system extracts the pricing information and sends an XML message back to the procurement system.

   The procurement system can make similar queries to all of its preferred vendors and, after all reply messages have been received, make a selection based on the best price.
5. The winery's procurement system creates an XML purchase order document and sends it to the chosen vendor's XML-based order entry system.
6. The vendor extracts and validates critical information such as the price quoted in the request and availability of the quantity in its inventory system, before entering the request into the order fulfillment system.
7. The vendor sends an XML message acknowledging receipt of the purchase order.
8. The vendor's order fulfillment system automatically decrements the level of the inventory system, and fulfillment operations prepare the product for delivery and submit a shipping request to the transportation system.
9. When the winery receives and signs for the shipment, a message is sent to the vendor's order fulfillment system acknowledging receipt of the product.
10. The vendor's system generates an invoice and sends it in an XML message to the winery's procurement system.

This completes the full cycle of a procurement process.

Production

For most wineries, the production process requires manual intervention, and data about the stages have to be manually recorded and logged into production-tracking software applications. Some wineries have taken advantage of state-of-the-art technology to automate and control all stages of the production process using electronic equipment and computers. Production data, signals, and triggers from each of the automated stages can be viewed and controlled. The manufacturing modules of the business systems use XML to represent the state of the system and communicate using XML messages to other business systems. Depending on the size of the winery, the cost of deploying a web-enabled intelligent manufacturing system may or may not be justified.

Reducing production costs is one way to increase the profitability of a company. Just-in-time delivery of raw materials and finished inventories can help to improve the efficiency of the production process. The data from automated production systems lets the business managers monitor the state of the production process at any given time.

Automated production processes are supported by just-in-time delivery mechanisms. There is always a huge cost of storing raw materials and finished products. Automation leads to shorter setup time for producing batches of products, lower inventories, less waste of raw materials, and faster delivery to the distributors. If there is a problem in the production line, it is discovered earlier and corrective action can be taken to prevent a complete loss of the batch.

Furthermore, if the automated production management systems are integrated into the other business process management systems, the signals and triggers from the automated production process can be used to drive the supply chain. Figure 14-2 shows the winery supply chain, including postproduction buyers and consumers.

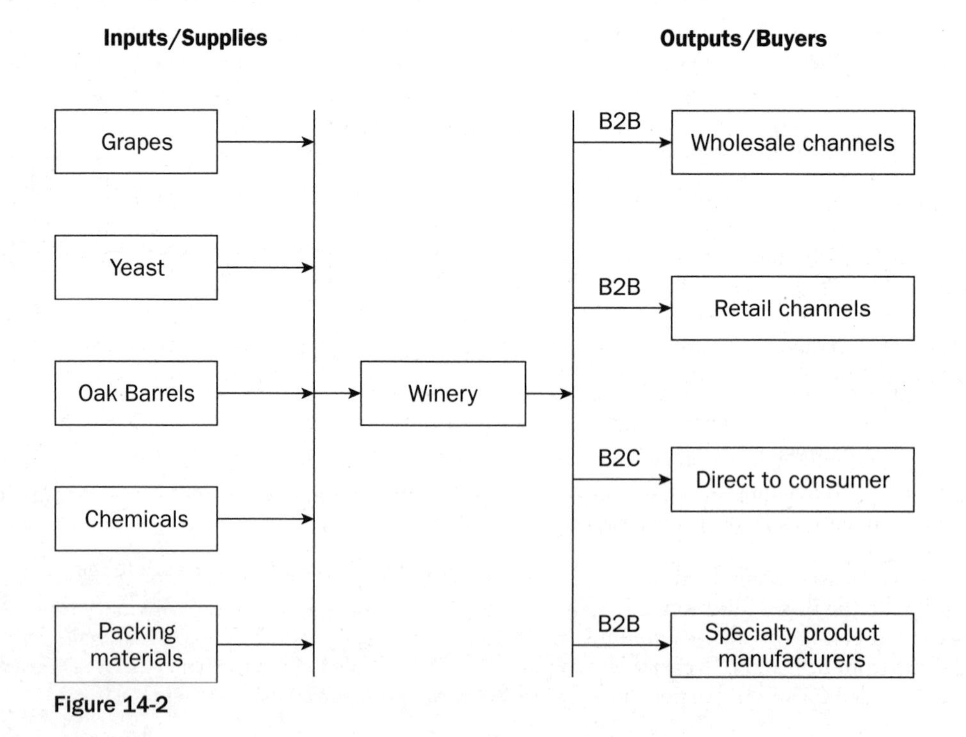

Figure 14-2

For example, when raw materials for a particular stage are low, an automated request can be sent to the procurement process to order more and have it delivered just when it is needed. At the end of the production process the packaged goods can be picked up on time for delivery to the distributors. The logistics and transportation systems are informed by the production systems, and suitable arrangements are made to deliver the product to the distribution channel.

Sales and Distribution

After some length of time in the production pipeline, the wine is available as output. The production data at the end of the process feeds into the inventory system. The sales systems have a real-time view of the levels of inventory. The sales and marketing managers can make quick decisions about prices and the catalogs are updated automatically with the new data.

In the B2C channel, the winery markets directly to the end consumer. The buyer can log on to the e-commerce-enabled web site and make purchases. The e-commerce web site is integrated into the other business systems. After conducting research on the types and history of a particular wine, the buyer can check on the availability and prices before placing the order. The order entry system is integrated with the order fulfillment system and the finance systems with a merchant banking system to accept credit card payments. This completes the sales loop for the B2C process.

Wholesalers and retailers can also be integrated into the winery B2B business model. The distributor's systems can query the winery catalog and automatically extract pricing and inventory levels. The distributor's procurement system initiates XML messages to the winery catalog and inventory system and can automatically enter orders received by to the winery order fulfillment systems. An invoice message is sent to the distributors at the end of the procurement process.

A winery could also sell in bulk to manufacturers of specialty wine products. The winery then becomes a vendor in that manufacturer's supply chain. The same XML-enabled business systems can be used to integrate with the specialty manufacturer's XML-enabled business system as long as one or both have an XML enabled workflow engine to drive and automate the integrated business processes.

Integrating Internal Processes

The winery may choose to integrate the production process with other business processes. In the previous section, you saw how the winery could play the role of a supplier to its B2B customers. Integrating and automating the catalog systems with the inventory and sales systems will enable those customers to integrate their processes with the winery's.

Integrating the logistics processes allows the winery to monitor and maintain tight control of transportation and warehousing. Automating and optimizing these processes can help reduce operating costs of the winery.

By integrating the finance systems, the winery managers can monitor the financial health of the business in real time — they won't have to wait for month end closing to figure out what the net sales were and how much revenue was generated from operations.

The invoice messages sent by the suppliers can be validated against stored data and then automatically submitted to the finance systems accounts payable (AP) process for payment. The winery sends a message to their bank to credit the amount of the invoice to the supplier's bank account directly. Similarly payments from B2C and B2B customers can automatically be credited to the winery bank account, eliminating the need for writing paper checks which, in turn, reduces the costs of doing business.

The Benefits of Integration and Automation

What's described in the preceding sections are not imaginary scenarios. The technology to create collaborative workflows powered by standards-based XML messaging systems are available in the currently available in the market and are being actively used by businesses to automate and activate their processes.

As discussed earlier, an XML-based workflow engine that integrates with the other XML-driven business systems enables the tight coupling and integration between the winery systems and those of business partners. Collaborative workflows are defined, and passing XML messages between the systems drives the workflow.

Business communications benefit tremendously from integration and automation. Labor-intensive tasks of data entry and transferring between systems are minimized or eliminated. The costs of business communications are greatly reduced. Figure 14-3 shows one way to integrate the winery business processes. The business process management system is at the core of the integration.

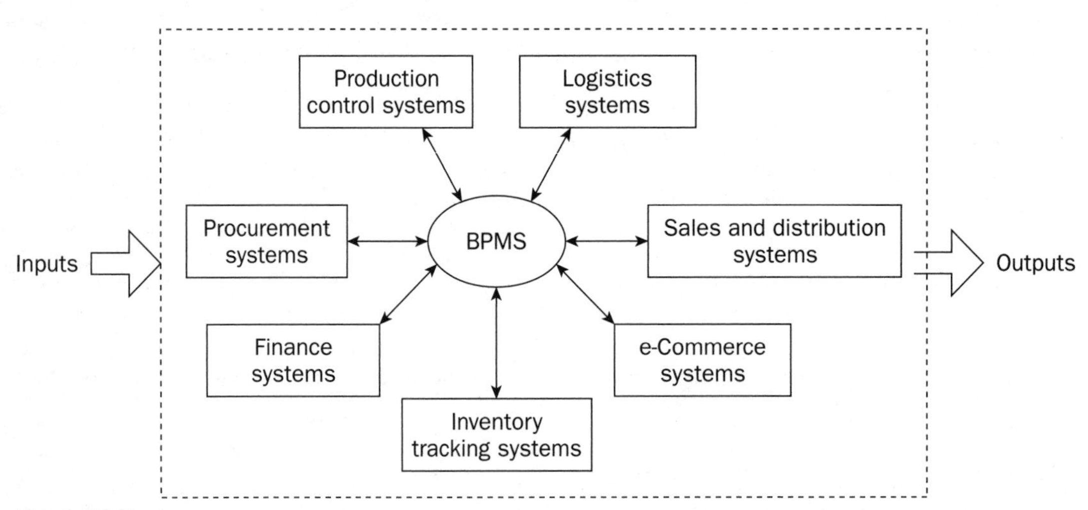

Figure 14-3

The Business Process Management Systems provides managers with instantaneous graphical overviews of the state of all aspects of the business, such as the production process, inventory, sales, and finances. The processes can be monitored and optimized to reduce waste and operating costs. All of the BPMS leverage the power of XML for data representation, triggers, and control within the BPMS as well as external systems under their control.

Vendors realize benefit, too, by saving on business communications. They can turn inventory around quicker, reducing warehousing costs. They get paid faster and, therefore, can give better payment terms and prices for partners whose systems are integrated and automated.

There is constant change occurring in the field of business process management systems, and vendors are consolidating their offerings as newer standards and protocols are adopted. A search on the Internet provides the names of the latest BPMS and their features. The following is a nonexhaustive list of commercial and open source business process management systems available in the market:

- **Oracle BPEL Process Manager**—Oracle Corporation (`www.oracle.com`)
- **BEA Weblogic**—EA (`www.bea.com`)
- **IBM Websphere**—IBM (`www.ibm.com`)
- **Intalio BPMS**—Intalio (`www.intalio.com`)
- **Project Agila**—Apache Software Foundation (`http://incubator.apache.org/projects/agila`)
- **JBPM**—JBoss (`www.jboss.com/products/jbpm`)

Summary

Integrating systems and processes with business partners' isn't always simple. Organization culture, trust relationships, and technology are some of the significant issues that can prevent companies from forming effective partnerships. Yet there are profitable results from successful partnering.

XML-enabled business systems and workflow engines make it easy to integrate systems and processes, especially when using XML for business documents or passing messages between the systems. BPMSs are the new breed of applications that are driven by XML and enable integration with other business systems and automation of process workflows.

This chapter illustrated how your winery could benefit from the new XML-enabled integrated and automated processes. You examined the procurement, production, sales, and distribution processes as well as how integration with other business processes such as finance would work.

So, here we are, at the end of our journey together. We chose the wine industry as the focus of our discussions to provide an interesting and fun way of exploring XML and looking at a relatively uncomplicated manufacturing operation.

XML offers a flexible and powerful means to represent data, integrate systems, applications, and processes. It drives all of the latest technologies that support and enable business integration. A company can streamline its business processes and create tighter integration with its partners by using systems enabled by XML. This results in higher productivity, less waste of time and resources, and ultimately helps make the company more profitable.

A

Tools

As we, the authors, considered the book, a conscious decision was made to avoid relying too heavily upon any particular authoring application or development environment. The choice was motivated by a desire to focus on the markup, rather than the tools. Also, some environments are designed with the motivation that users shouldn't ever see XML markup. If you've made the decision to ask questions and committed to find the answers, that kind of user interface design heuristic can be more of a hindrance than a help. Tools are often aimed at just one of a number of professional disciplines and could make the material unintentionally favor one viewpoint above another. It just didn't seem right for a book that has as one of its aims to get people started using XML. We wanted you to see the markup.

The strategy of using generalized markup is a risk-mitigating factor, avoiding toolchain lock-in. Being able to see and manipulate the markup directly without having to go through a special API is priceless. Still, XML-aware tools are an important force multiplier, and we regularly use a number of tools. This appendix lists several of the tools we've used during the writing of the book, even if they weren't a visible part of the projects or discussion. The presence of a product in this list is not meant as an endorsement of any kind, any more than the absence of a product should indicate any kind of disapproval.

XSLT Engines

Saxon

Saxon-B (8.6.1), an open source XSLT, XPath, and XQuery processor, was used for many of the XSLT transformations. Saxon was written by Michael Kay, currently of Saxonica. Saxonica also commercially licenses Saxon in the form of Saxon-SA, which adds a Schema processor and schema-aware features to its XSLT 2.0, XPath 2.0, and XQuery 1.0 capabilities.

Saxon-B is available for free download from `http://saxon.sourceforge.net`. Saxon-SA can be purchased from `http://saxonica.com`. Because Saxon is written in Java, you'll also need Java to execute the processor. The J2SE 5.0 version of Java can be downloaded from `http://java.sun.com/j2se/1.5.0/download.jsp`.

Saxon-B can be used as a Java library and includes a command-line interface. The 8.6.1 Saxon-B command-line interface provides several options, shown here in the output from invoking the tool with no arguments:

```
java -jar saxonb-8.6.1\saxon8.jar

Saxon 8.6.1 from Saxonica
Usage: java net.sf.saxon.Transform [options] source-doc style-doc {param=value}.
..
Options:
  -a                Use xml-stylesheet PI, not style-doc argument
  -c                Indicates that style-doc is a compiled stylesheet
  -cr classname     Use specified collection URI resolver class
  -ds               Use standard tree data structure
  -dt               Use tinytree data structure (default)
  -im modename      Start transformation in specified mode
  -it template      Start transformation by calling named template
  -l                Retain line numbers in source document tree
  -o filename       Send output to named file or directory
  -m classname      Use specified Emitter class for xsl:message output
  -novw             Suppress warning when running with an XSLT 1.0 stylesheet
  -r classname      Use specified URIResolver class
  -p                Recognize Saxon file extensions and query parameters
  -sall             Strip all whitespace text nodes
  -signorable       Strip ignorable whitespace text nodes (default)
  -snone            Strip no whitespace text nodes
  -t                Display version and timing information
  -T                Set standard TraceListener
  -TJ               Trace calls to external Java functions
  -TL classname     Set a specific TraceListener
  -u                Names are URLs not filenames
  -v                Validate source documents using DTD
  -w0               Recover silently from recoverable errors
  -w1               Report recoverable errors and continue (default)
  -w2               Treat recoverable errors as fatal
  -x classname      Use specified SAX parser for source file
  -y classname      Use specified SAX parser for stylesheet
  -1.1              Allow XML 1.1 documents
  -?                Display this message
  param=value       Set stylesheet string parameter
  +param=file       Set stylesheet document parameter
  !option=value     Set serialization option
```

For convenience under Microsoft platforms, a batch file can be written to set common options. For instance, the `saxon.bat` file used in some of the chapters consists of the following lines:

```
@echo off
java -jar "%~d0%~p0saxon8.jar" -w0 %1 %2 %3 %4 %5 %6 %7 %8 %9
```

%d0%~p0 is a way to access the path of the current batch file. When the batch file is placed into the saxon-b.8.6.1 directory, the script knows to find the saxon8.jar file without having to set CLASSPATHs explicitly.

While Saxon-B is an XSLT 2.0 processor, it is quite capable of running XSLT 1.0 stylesheets.

Xalan

Xalan is another well-known open source XSLT processor, associated with the Apache project. Xalan was sometimes used as a comparison-other. Unlike Saxon, Xalan implements the XSLT 1.0 and XPath 1.0 Recommendations rather than the 2.0 versions', and does not implement XQuery. Xalan is also associated with the Apache XML parser Xerces, although it can be configured to use another parser. (Saxon relies on the parser provided in the Java platform or a parser that you specify.)

Xalan is available in a Java version called Xalan-J, which can be downloaded from http://xml.apache.org/xalan-j/downloads.html. The version used during the writing of the book was Xalan-J 2.7.0. As with Saxon, you need Java to run Xalan-J.

The command line for Xalan is quite extensive, as shown by the help message:

```
java org.apache.xalan.xslt.Process
Xalan-J command line Process class options:

                        -Common Options-

   [-XSLTC (use XSLTC for transformation)]
   [-IN inputXMLURL]
   [-XSL XSLTransformationURL]
   [-OUT outputFileName]
   [-E (Do not expand entity refs)]
   [-EDUMP {optional filename} (Do stackdump on error.)]
   [-XML (Use XML formatter and add XML header.)]
   [-TEXT (Use simple Text formatter.)]
   [-HTML (Use HTML formatter.)]
   [-PARAM name expression (Set a stylesheet parameter)]
   [-MEDIA mediaType (use media attribute to find stylesheet associated
    with a document.)]
   [-FLAVOR flavorName (Explicitly use s2s=SAX or d2d=DOM to do transform.)]
   [-DIAG (Print overall milliseconds transform took.)]
   [-URIRESOLVER full class name (URIResolver to be used to resolve URIs)]
   [-ENTITYRESOLVER full class name (EntityResolver to be used to
    resolve entities)]
   [-CONTENTHANDLER full class name (ContentHandler to be used to
    serialize output)]
   [-SECURE (set the secure processing feature to true.)]
   [-QC (Quiet Pattern Conflicts Warnings)]
   [-TT (Trace the templates as they are being called.)]
   [-TG (Trace each generation event.)]
   [-TS (Trace each selection event.)]
   [-TTC (Trace the template children as they are being processed.)]
   [-TCLASS (TraceListener class for trace extensions.)]
```

```
    [-L use line numbers for source document]
    [-INCREMENTAL (request incremental DTM construction by setting
     http://xml.apache.org/xalan/features/incremental true.)]
    [-NOOPTIMIMIZE (request no stylesheet optimization processing by setting
     http://xml.apache.org/xalan/features/optimize false.)]
    [-RL recursionlimit (assert numeric limit on stylesheet recursion depth.)]
    [-XO [transletName] (assign the name to the generated translet)]
    [-XD destinationDirectory (specify a destination directory for translet)]
    [-XJ jarfile (packages translet classes into a jar file of name <jarfile>)]
    [-XP package (specifies a package name prefix for all generated translet
     classes)]
    [-XN (enables template inlining)]
    [-XX (turns on additional debugging message output)]
    [-XT (use translet to transform if possible)]
```

Following the same batch file approach, a `xalan.bat` can be made that makes the interface look similar to the `saxon.bat` invocation, at least for simple transforms:

```
@echo off
set CP=%~d0%~p0
set CLASSPATH=%CP%\xalan.jar;%CP%\serializer.jar;%CP%\xml-
apis.jar;%CP%\xercesImpl.jar
java org.apache.xalan.xslt.Process -IN %1 -XSL %2
```

XSL-FO Processors

FOP

As noted in the chapters, FOP was used for most of the examples. It is another open source tool under the umbrella of the Apache XML project. The FOP used in the materials was version 0.91 beta. At the time the book was written, the beta represented a major leap forward in functionality of FOP.

Like Saxon and Xalan, FOP is Java based and you need Java to run it (see the link in the earlier Saxon section). FOP can be downloaded for free from `http://xmlgraphics.apache.org/fop/download.html`.

Like Saxon and Xalan, FOP can be used as a library for adding FO capabilities to Java applications. FOP also comes with its own command-line client and Windows batch script. The help output follows.

```
fop-0.91beta\fop

USAGE
Fop [options] [-fo|-xml] infile [-xsl file] [-awt|-pdf|-mif|-rtf|-tiff|
  -png|-pcl|-ps|-txt|-at|-print] <outfile>
 [OPTIONS]
  -d             debug mode
  -x             dump configuration settings
  -q             quiet mode
  -c cfg.xml     use additional configuration file cfg.xml
  -l lang        the language to use for user information
  -r             relaxed/less strict validation (where available)
```

```
  -dpi xxx        target resolution in dots per inch (dpi) where xxx is
a number
  -s              for area tree XML, down to block areas only
  -v              to show FOP version being used

  -o [password]   PDF file will be encrypted with option owner password
  -u [password]   PDF file will be encrypted with option user password
  -noprint        PDF file will be encrypted without printing permission
  -nocopy         PDF file will be encrypted without copy content permission
  -noedit         PDF file will be encrypted without edit content permission
  -noannotations  PDF file will be encrypted without edit annotation permission

 [INPUT]
  infile            xsl:fo input file (the same as the next)
  -fo  infile       xsl:fo input file
  -xml infile       xml input file, must be used together with -xsl
  -xsl stylesheet   xslt stylesheet

  -param name value <value> to use for parameter <name> in xslt stylesheet
                    (repeat '-param name value' for each parameter)

 [OUTPUT]
  outfile           input will be rendered as pdf file into outfile
  -pdf outfile      input will be rendered as pdf file (outfile req'd)
  -awt              input will be displayed on screen
  -mif outfile      input will be rendered as mif file (outfile req'd)
  -rtf outfile      input will be rendered as rtf file (outfile req'd)
  -tiff outfile     input will be rendered as tiff file (outfile req'd)
  -png outfile      input will be rendered as png file (outfile req'd)
  -pcl outfile      input will be rendered as pcl file (outfile req'd)
  -ps outfile       input will be rendered as PostScript file (outfile req'd)
  -txt outfile      input will be rendered as text file (outfile req'd)
  -svg outfile      input will be rendered as an svg slides file (outfile
req'd)

  -at outfile       representation of area tree as XML (outfile req'd)
  -print            input file will be rendered and sent to the printer
                    see options with "-print help"
  -out mime outfile input will be rendered using the given MIME type
                    (outfile req'd) Example: "-out application/pdf D:\out.pdf"
                    (Tip: "-out list" prints the list of supported MIME types)

  -foout outfile    input will only be XSL transformed. The intermediate
                    XSL-FO file is saved and no rendering is performed.
                    (Only available if you use -xml and -xsl parameters)

 [Examples]
  Fop foo.fo foo.pdf
  Fop -fo foo.fo -pdf foo.pdf (does the same as the previous line)
  Fop -xml foo.xml -xsl foo.xsl -pdf foo.pdf
  Fop -xml foo.xml -xsl foo.xsl -foout foo.fo
  Fop foo.fo -mif foo.mif
  Fop foo.fo -rtf foo.rtf
  Fop foo.fo -print or Fop -print foo.fo
  Fop foo.fo -awt
```

XED

RenderX's XEP FO processor was used, like Xalan, as a comparison other when developing the FO examples. Version 4.5 was available at the time the book was written. XEP is a commercial product. Licenses, including evaluations, can be obtained at `http://renderx.com/tools/xep.html`.

XSL Formatter

Antenna House produces XSL Formatter, a popular commercial product that boasts a high level of conformance to the XSL 1.0 Recommendation. Its site is also a good source of examples. More information can be obtained from `http://antennahouse.com`.

(Neither the XSL Formatter nor the XED product were used directly in the examples.)

Browsers

Mozilla/Firefox

Firefox is built from the ground up as an XML-aware browser. Even its graphical user interface is specified in an XML format, and Firefox directly implements both XML and XHTML browsing capabilities. Firefox was used to compare and contrast the browser examples, which were designed to display on a minimally conformant (IE6) HTML browser.

Firefox is an open source project, available from `http://mozilla.com`.

Internet Explorer 6

Most of the browser examples in the earlier chapters were checked for legibility on IE6. The reason for this is simply the lowest common denominator effect. In comparison with the other browser, IE6 has limited direct support for XML.

Editors and IDEs

oXygen XML

oXygen XML is a well-balanced mix of features, price, and performance. Versions 6 and 7 were used during the authoring, although they were not referenced in the book directly. Aside from the development environment capabilities like the XPath toolbar and Schema editing, oXygen comes with support for several XSLT processors. Some of the Saxon and FOP testing were performed by configuring the oXygen interface to use the respective processors as external tools.

oXygen is a commercial product, available from SyncRO Soft Ltd. More information on licensing and purchasing is available from `http://oxygenxml.com`.

Trang

Trang is a tool to convert between different schema languages for XML. The schema languages supported include Relax NG (both XML and compact syntaxes), XML 1.0 DTDs, and W3C XML Schema. Trang can also be used to infer an initial schema from one or more XML sample input documents, and it's used to add schema conversion features to commercial tools such as the oXygen XML editor.

Trang is an open source tool available from `http://thaiopensource.com/relaxng/trang.html`.

Turbo XML

One of the authors used Turbo XML, a commercial Java tool available from TIBCO. Turbo XML is an integrated development environment for working with XML, and includes many features for Schema creation and manipulation. Turbo XML is available at `http://tibco.com/software/business_integration/turboxml.jsp`.

Turbo XML has the capability to open a DTD or schema. Then, it will save your structure (elements and attributes) as several flavors of DTD or schema, providing for an easy though basic conversion from one to the other.

This is also a good tool for checking a DTD for errors, which author Kay Ethier does for DTDs created using FrameMaker. FrameMaker does not have a DTD-checking tool.

XMLSpy

Altova XMLSpy is a viewing and editing tool that provides for editing and creation of XML files. It has multiple editing views so that you can choose the view that works best for you. XMLSpy also provides editing and validation tools for working with DTDs and schemas. More information on XMLSpy and related tools are on the Altova web site: `http://altova.com`.

Stylus Studio

Data Direct's Stylus Studio includes XML development tools, along with tools for working with XQuery, schemas, XSLT, and even web services. Several editions of Stylus Studio are available. For more information, visit the Data Direct web site for this product: `http://stylusstudio.com`.

XMetaL

XMetaL is another tool for editing and authoring XML documents. There is also an XMetaL Reviewer tool that allows annotation of XML documents. More information on XMetaL may be found on the Blast Radius web site: `www.blastradius.com`.

Graphic Editors

GIMP

GIMP (the GNU Image Manipulation Program) isn't really an XML tool, but it is a great image-editing program. One of the authors used GIMP to make and adjust screen captures, as well as to throw together quick sketches for artwork. GIMP is an open-source tool available from `http://gimp.org`.

Inkscape

The Inkscape editor is an XML tool, more specifically an SVG editor. It is a vector art drawing tool. Inkscape was used by one of the authors as an alternative to hand sketching artwork. While the final artwork is not totally representative of this tool, it was a handy way of making the concept art.

Commercial tools in this category include Corel Draw and Adobe Illustrator. While the 0.43 version used was not entirely stable nor as feature rich as the commercial applications, it provided more than enough functionality to make it a productive sketching environment. Inkscape is an open source tool available from `http://inkscape.org`.

Additional Reading

Although there are many books available on the subject of XML and XML-related technologies, this appendix offers only a short list of books, either written by or recommended by the authors of this book.

XML Topics

- *Oracle XSQL* — By Michael D. Thomas, 448 pages, Wiley, 2003, ISBN: 0-471-27120-9. Even if you are not working with XSQL (the combination of XML and SQL), you may find this book useful for the XSLT tutorial buried in the middle. This tutorial covers the XSLT building blocks in a logical and easy-to-follow fashion.
- *Cocoon 2 Programming: Web Publishing with XML and Java* — By Bill Brogden, Conrad D'Cruz, Mark Gaither, 352 pages, Sybex; 2002, ISBN: 0782141315.
- *XML and FrameMaker* (paperback) — By Kay Ethier, 416 pages, 2004, ISBN: 1-590-59276-X.
- *XML Schema Essentials* — By R. Allen Wyke, Andrew Watt, 400 pages, Wiley, 2002, ISBN: 0-471-41259-7.
- *Beginning XML, 3rd Edition* — By David Hunter, Andrew Watt, Jeff Rafter, Jon Duckett, Danny Ayers, Nicholas Chase, Joe Fawcett, Tom Gaven, Bill Patterson. 1027 pages, Wiley, 2004, ISBN: 0-7645-7077-3.
- *XML in Theory and Practice* — By Chris Bates, 482 pages, Wiley, 2003, ISBN: 0-470-84344-6.
- *XML Design Handbook* — By Scott Bonneau, Tammy Kohl, Jeni Tennison, Jon Duckett, and Kevin Williams. 310 pages, Wrox, 2003, ISBN: 1-86100-768-X.
- *Web Design with XML* — By Manfred Knobloch, Matthias Kopp, 240 pages, Wiley, 2003, ISBN: 0-470-84718-2.
- RELAX NG — By Eric van der Vlist, 304 pages, O'Reilly, 2003, ISBN: 0-596-00241-4. Provides a great tutorial and reference for RELAX NG, a schema language for XML that's a simple and coherent alternative to the W3C Schema Recommendation.

XSLT Topics

- *Mastering XSLT*—By Chuck White, 905 pages, Wiley, 2002, ISBN: 0-782-14094-7.
- *Learn SVG*—By Jon Frost, Stefan Goessner, and Michel Hirtzler, (revisited by Robert DiBlasi and Tobias Reif), 519 pages, 2003, LearnSVG.com, ISBN: 0-9741773-0-X. As an XML format for two-dimensional graphics, SVG can be used for text and graphical composition and complements XSL-FO. This is a very good reference for SVG. The book is also available for downloading in PDF format at `www.learnsvg.com`.
- *XSLT*—By Doug Tidwell, 478 pages, O'Reilly, 2001, ISBN: 0-596-00053-7. Includes some good examples of how to transform XML into SVG, XHTML, and many other formats. The example files are provided via the Internet.
- *Beginning XSLT 2.0: From Novice to Professional* (paperback)—Jeni Tennison, 824 pages, Apress, 2005, ISBN: 1590593243.
- *XSLT 2.0 Programmer's Reference*—By Michael H. Kay, 960 pages, Wrox, 2004, ISBN: 0-764-56909-0.
- *XPath 2.0 Programmer's Reference*—By Michael H. Kay, 552 pages, Wrox, 2004, ISBN: 0-764-56910-4.

Miscellaneous Business Topics

There are several newer books on business process and partnerships, but this book had an ambitious goal of bridging between business concepts and technology design in two chapters. The business books are referenced to explain two very old concepts: partnerships and process. These concepts are still relevant today when creating new business integration strategies and are meant to support the concepts covered in the chapters.

- *A Comparative Evolution of Business Partnerships: The Islamic World and Europe, With Specific Reference to the Ottoman Archives* (*Ottoman Empire and Its Heritage*, Vol. 8) (Hardcover)—Murat Cizakca, 232 pages, Brill Academic Publishers, 1996, ISBN 9004106014.
- *Reengineering the Corporation: A Manifesto for Business Revolution* (Paperback)—by Michael Hammer and James Champy, 256 pages, HarperBusiness, Reprint Edition, 1994, ISBN: 088730687X.

Online Resources

There are so many resources available online that it is sometimes difficult to know where to begin. Some sites are updated more frequently or checked for accuracy more often than others. The authors have pulled together a list of resources believed to be of good quality:

- `www.w3schools.com` — This site includes a variety of tutorials on such topics as XML, XHTML, and other XML-related technologies. It's a good first stop on your search for XML information.
- `xml.coverpages.org/xmlApplications.html` — Provides an overview of the ongoing efforts to create XML language standards.
- `www.dpawson.co.uk/xsl/xslfaq.html` — There are several FAQ sites for XML and related technologies. Dave Pawson gleaned hundreds of issues from XSL list discussions and organized them by topic.
- `www.w3.org` — The main site of the World Wide Web Consortium (W3C). Many standards, including XML, can be researched on this site.
- `www.xml.org` — This site provides information on XML and related standards. It's overseen by OASIS, a standards agency known also for the `www.oasis-open.org` web site.
- `www.xml.com` — An O'Reilly web site with information on XML.
- `www.xml.gov` — This government web site provides information on events of interest to government XML users. It also offers some tutorial information.
- `en.wikipedia.org/wiki/XML` — This wiki site allows users to read entries that have been posted or edited by other users, with the option of editing or adding to the site.
- `www-128.ibm.com/developerworks` — Managed by IBM, the DeveloperWorks web site is well known for its informative tutorials and articles. IBM provides visitors with loads of information by sharing lessons learned from its own experiences.

- `www.zvon.org`—A reference site, with several tutorials but even more transformed versions of the many XML-related specifications. A multilingual educational site created with XML technologies, it is supported by Systinet Corp.
- `www.ebxml.org`—Provides the specifications for companies of all sizes around the world to do business with each other over the Internet. The specifications include business messages, protocols for trading relationships, common dictionaries, and business process registries.
- `www.xcbl.org`—Provides details on the library of business components for business-to-business electronic commerce called xCBL (XML Common Business Library).
- `www.oasis-open.org`—OASIS (Organization for the Advancement of Structured Information Standards) is an international consortium that develops e-business standards.
- `docs.oasis-open.org/ubl/cd-UBL-1.0`—UBL (Universal Business Language) is a library of standard XML documents for business developed by the OASIS Technical Committee.
- `www.w3.org/Submission/xpl`—W3C XML Pipeline Language (XPL)—XML Pipeline Language (XPL) Version 1.0 is a draft, that was submitted by a Orbeon, Inc. (`www.orbeon.com`) that has an open source implementation of the XPL called the Orbeon PresentationServer.
- `www.apache.org`—The Apache Software Foundation creates and supports open source software projects. The main web page provides a complete list of all projects.
- `http://cocoon.apache.org` —Apache Cocoon is an XML-based web development framework.

Glossary

Apache Cocoon An open source XML publishing system developed under the banner of the Apache Software Foundation.

Attribute Metadata on an XML tag that provides additional information.

BizTalk An XML-based framework from the Microsoft Corporation that enables communications and integration of business applications.

BPMN Business Process Modeling Notation.

BPMS Business process management systems.

BPR Business process reengineering.

CDATA Character DATA, which is not interpreted or parsed.

CMS Content management system.

COM Component Object Model.

Comment Characters included between the comment delimiters `<!--` and `-->` that are not considered part of the document's character content.

CORBA Common Object Request Broker Architecture.

DCOM Distributed Component Object Model.

Declaration If present, this is the first line within an XML file, which essentially lets parsers, tools, and readers know that the file contains XML.

DOM Document Object Model.

DTD Document type definition; a file that contains element and attribute definitions.

ebXML Electronic Business using Extensible Markup Language.

Elements The structural units represented by the starting and ending tags that make up XML files.

Encoding The manner in which the abstract characters of a coded character set, such as Unicode, are converted into an integer code representation suitable for storage, transmission, and manipulation.

Entity An item that can be included in an XML document by referring to it by a representative name.

ETL Extract, Transform, and Load.

FO Formating Objects.

Markup Logical delimiters of a document, consisting of start tags, end tags, empty element tags, entity references, character references, comments, CDATA section delimiters, document type declarations, processing instructions, XML declarations, text declarations, and white space outside of the document element.

Parameter Entity A distinct type of entity that is used to modify the structures of a DTD.

PCDATA Parsed Character Data, which is parsed and uses XML syntax.

Pipeline A chain of application components that allows processing data in stages.

Processing Instruction Markup used to convey information directly to an application, without being part of the document's character data.

Prologue The optional XML declaration, document type declaration, and any comments, processing instructions, or spaces that occur at the very beginning of an XML document.

RMI Remote Method Invocation.

RosettaNet An organization that defines standards for business processes such as supply chain and distribution management.

SAX Simple API for XML.

SGML Standard Generalized Markup Language, somewhat related to XML and HTML.

SOA Service-Oriented Architecture.

SOAP Simple Object Access Protocol.

Tag The markup delimiters, element name, and (for a start tag) the attributes, demarcating the start and end of an element instance within a document. In XML an element is expressed either as a paired start tag and end tag, or as a single empty element tag. Contrast with "element," which encompasses the entire logical structure.

UBL Universal Business Language.

Valid A well-formed XML document, which has an associated document type declaration and which complies with the constraints expressed therein.

Well-Formed A markup document that matches the XML "document" production, and the other well-formedness constraints of the XML Recommendation.

WS-BPEL Web Services Business Process Execution Language.

WS-CDL Web Services-Choreography Definition Language.

xCBL XML Common Business Library.

XML Extensible Markup Language.

XML Document A data object consisting of explicit markup for declarations, elements, comments, entity references, and processing instructions. By definition, at a minimum an XML document must be well formed.

XPath A concise expression language used for addressing parts of an XML document.

XPDL XML Process Definition Language.

XPL XML Pipeline Language.

XQuery XQuery enables you to query XML much the same way that you use SQL to access databases.

XSL Extensible Stylesheet Language, also sometimes called XSL-FO (Formatting Objects), a language for specifying formatting semantics.

XSLT Extensible Stylesheet Language Transformations, or XSLT.

Index

Index

SYMBOLS

A

B

D

E

F

G

H

I

J

K

L

M

N

O

P

T

U

V

W

X

Y